THE MACARTHUR NEW TESTAMENT COMMENTARY

EPHESIANS

John MacArthur, Jr.

MOODY PRESS/CHICAGO

Unless noted otherwise, all Scripture quotations in this book are from *The New American Standard Bible,* © 1960, 1962, 1963, 1968, 1971, 1972, 1973, 1975, and 1977 by The Lockman Foundation, and are used by permission.

Library of Congress Cataloging-in-Publication Data

MacArthur, John F.
  Ephesians.

  (The MacArthur New Testament commentary)
  1. Bible. N.T. Ephesians—Commentaries.
I. Title.   II. Series: MacArthur, John F. MacArthur
New Testament commentary.
BS2695.3.M27   1986   227'.5077   86-5336
ISBN 0-8024-2358-2

4 5 6 7 8 Printing/AK/Year 93 92 91 90 89 88

Printed in the United States of America

Contents

Preface

It continues to be a rewarding divine communion for me to preach expositionally through the New Testament. My goal is always to have deep fellowship with the Lord in the understanding of His Word, and out of that experience to explain to His people what a passage means. In the words of Nehemiah 8:8, I strive "to give the sense" of it so they may truly hear God speak and, in so doing, may respond to Him.

Obviously, God's people need to understand Him, which demands knowing His Word of truth (2 Tim. 2:15) and allowing that Word to dwell in us richly (Col. 3:16). The dominant thrust of my ministry, therefore, is to help make God's living Word alive to His people. It is a refreshing adventure.

This New Testament commentary series reflects this objective of explaining and applying Scripture. Some commentaries are primarily linguistic, others are mostly theological, and some are mainly homiletical. This one is basically explanatory, or expository. It is not linguistically technical, but deals with linguistics when this seems helpful to proper interpretation. It is not theologically expansive, but focuses on the major doctrines in each text and on how they relate to the whole of Scripture. It is not primarily homiletical, though each unit of thought is generally treated as one chapter, with a clear outline and logical flow of thought. Most truths are illustrated and applied with other Scripture. After establishing the context of a passage, I have tried to follow closely the writer's development and reasoning.

My prayer is that each reader will fully understand what the Holy Spirit is saying through this part of His Word, so that His revelation may lodge in the minds of believers and bring greater obedience and faithfulness—to the glory of our great God.

Introduction

Several years ago the *Los Angeles Times* reported the story of an elderly man and wife who were found dead in their apartment. Autopsies revealed that both had died of severe malnutrition, although investigators found a total of $40,000 stored in paper bags in a closet.

For many years Hetty Green was called America's greatest miser. When she died in 1916, she left an estate valued at $100 million, an especially vast fortune for that day. But she was so miserly that she ate cold oatmeal in order to save the expense of heating the water. When her son had a severe leg injury, she took so long trying to find a free clinic to treat him that his leg had to be amputated because of advanced infection. It has been said that she hastened her own death by bringing on a fit of apoplexy while arguing the merits of skim milk because it was cheaper than whole milk.

The book of Ephesians is written to Christians who might be prone to treat their spiritual resources much like that miserly couple and Hetty Green treated their financial resources. Such believers are in danger of suffering from spiritual malnutrition, because they do not take advantage of the great storehouse of spiritual nourishment and resources that is at their disposal.

Ephesians has been given such titles as the believer's bank, the Christian's checkbook, and the treasure house of the Bible. This beautiful letter tells Christians of their great riches, inheritances, and fullnesses in Jesus Christ and in His church.

It tells them what they possess and how they can claim and enjoy their possessions.

During the great depression of the 1930s, many banks would allow their customers to withdraw no more than 10 percent of their accounts during a given period of time, because the banks did not have enough reserves to cover all deposits.

But God's heavenly bank has no such limitations or restrictions. No Christian, therefore, has reason to be spiritually deprived, undernourished, or impoverished. In fact, he has no reason not to be completely healthy and immeasurably rich in the things of God. The Lord's heavenly resources are more than adequate to cover all our past debts, all our present liabilities, and all our future needs—and still not reduce the heavenly assets. That is the marvel of God's gracious provision for His children.

In this epistle Paul speaks of "the riches of His [God's] grace" (1:7), "the unfathomable riches of Christ" (3:8), and "the riches of His glory" (3:16). He calls the believer to "attain to the unity of the faith, and of the knowledge of the Son of God, to a mature man, to the measure of the stature which belongs to the fulness of Christ" (4:13), to "be filled with the Spirit" (5:18), and to "be filled up to all the fulness of God" (3:19).

In this book the word *riches* is used five times; *grace* twelve times; *glory* eight times; *fulness, filled up,* or *fills* six times; and the key phrase *in Christ* (or *in Him*) fifteen times. Christ is the source, the sphere, and the guarantee of every spiritual blessing and of all spiritual riches, and those who are in Him have access to all that He is and has.

In our union with Jesus Christ, God makes us "fellow heirs with Christ" (Rom. 8:17) and to be of "one spirit with Him" (1 Cor. 6:17). When we are "in Christ," He is not ashamed to call us brothers (Heb. 2:11) and will share with us all that He possesses, "an inheritance which is imperishable and undefiled and will not fade away, reserved in heaven" for us (1 Pet. 1:4).

Our riches are based on Christ's grace (1:2, 6-7; 2:7), His peace (1:2), His will (1:5), His kind intention (1:9), His purpose (1:9, 11), His glory (1:12, 14), His calling (1:18), His inheritance (1:18), His power (1:19), His love (2:4), His workmanship (2:10), His Spirit (3:16), His gifts (4:11), His sacrifice (5:2), His strength (6:10), and His armor (6:11, 13).

THE MYSTERY OF THE CHURCH

Also because we are in Christ, we are in His Body, the church. Ephesians focuses on the basic doctrine of the church—what it is and how believers function within it. This truth about the church was revealed to Paul by God as a mystery (3:3). As Paul explains, "When you read you can understand my insight into the mystery of Christ, which in other generations was not made known to the sons of men, as it has now been revealed to His holy apostles and prophets in the Spirit" (vv. 4-5).

This mystery, which had been hidden even from Israel, God's chosen people, is "that the Gentiles are fellow heirs and fellow members of the body, and fellow partakers of the promise in Christ Jesus through the gospel" (v. 6). In Christ, Jew and Gentile alike would henceforth be one in His Body, the church.

God's disclosure of His truth may be divided into three categories. In the first category are the truths He reveals to no one, "the secret things [that] belong to the Lord our God" (Deut. 29:29). His limitless truth is far beyond man's finite mind to fathom or comprehend. In His wisdom and sovereignty God has chosen not to disclose certain truths to any man at any time.

In the second category are those truths God has chosen to reveal to special people throughout history. All men can know something of God's nature, "because that which is known about God is evident within them; for God made it evident to them. For since the creation of the world His invisible attributes, His eternal power and divine nature, have been clearly seen, being understood through what has been made" (Rom. 1:19-20). But the deeper and fuller truths of His nature and will are unknown and incomprehensible to unbelievers.

The special people to whom God reveals His will and plan are not an elite group of seers or prophets but are believers. The revelation He has given through His prophets and apostles is for all of His people, for every person who belongs to Him by faith. "The secret of the Lord is for those who fear Him, and He will make them know His covenant" (Ps. 25:14). The Lord "is intimate with the upright" (Prov. 3:32). "Surely the Lord God does nothing unless He reveals His secret counsel to His servants the prophets" (Amos 3:7). Those who received revelation directly from the Lord made it known to the people.

In the third category are those truths that God kept secret for a period of time but finally disclosed to His people in the New Testament. Here God gives new truth for a new age, truth about which even the godliest of Old Testament saints were unaware. These new truths are the mysteries *(mustēria)*, the once-hidden but now revealed truths God gives in His New Covenant.

That is the category of truth Paul reveals to such a great extent in Ephesians—especially in the truth about the church of Jesus Christ, which God eternally designed to include both Jew and Gentile. Knowledge of that mystery is one of the great riches that only believers of this present age possess.

Matthew told us that Jesus did not speak to the multitudes "without a parable, so that what was spoken through the prophet might be fulfilled, saying, 'I will open My mouth in parables; I will utter things hidden since the foundation of the world'" (Matt. 13:34-35). When Jesus' disciples asked why He spoke in parables, He explained, "To you it has been granted to know the mysteries of the kingdom of heaven, but to them it has not been granted" (Matt. 13:11; cf. 11:25). Paul echoes the same truth in 1 Corinthians: "A natural man does not accept the things of the Spirit of God; for they are foolishness to him, and he cannot understand them, because they are spiritually appraised" (2:14). Believers and unbelievers can hear or read the same truths from God's Word, yet be affected in completely different ways. What is clear and meaningful to the believer is incomprehensible nonsense to the unbeliever.

The "mysteries of the kingdom of heaven" refer to the truths revealed in the present form of God's kingdom. The Old Testament speaks much of God's kingdom and of His rule over it. The coming Messiah was shown as a ruling Messiah, the great Anointed One whose eternal reign was prophesied even in the book of Genesis. As he pronounced blessings on his sons, Jacob said to Judah, "The scepter shall not depart from Judah, nor the ruler's staff from between his feet, until Shiloh comes, and to him shall be the obedience of the peoples" (Gen. 49:10).

Both John the Baptist and Jesus began their ministries by proclaiming, "Repent, for the kingdom of heaven is at hand" (Matt. 3:2; 4:17). Jesus was born a King, acknowledged by the magi to be a King, feared by Herod as a rival King, and even questioned by Pilate about His kingship. Jesus offered His kingdom to Israel if she would accept Him as her King. But because Israel rejected Him, she forfeited the kingdom, and for Israel it was postponed. Because the Jews declared, "We do not want this man to reign over us" (Luke 19:14), that Man would not reign over them. Consequently, He has delayed establishing His earthly kingdom until Israel is saved and He comes again to reign on earth for a thousand years (Rev. 20:4).

Meanwhile the King is absent from earth. Yet, from heaven Christ now rules His earthly kingdom. Whereas He will rule the entire world externally during the Millennium, He now rules internally, in the lives of those who belong to Him. The present form of the kingdom is the sphere of salvation by grace through faith. He is King over those who have confessed Him as sovereign Lord. The blessings that will be externally dispensed during the Millennium are now internally dispensed to believers. Just as Christ will be outwardly enthroned in Jerusalem during the Millennium, He now is inwardly enthroned in the hearts of His saints. As in the future kingdom He will dispense grace, so He does even now to those who trust in Him. As He then will bring external peace to the whole world, He now brings internal peace in the lives of believers. As He will then bestow joy and happiness externally, He now internally bestows those blessings upon His own people.

Of this interim, internal kingdom the Old Testament saints knew nothing. It is a parenthesis in the divine outworking of redemption, which until the New Testament was a secret. The kingdom of which the Old Testament speaks, and which will be fully manifested in the Millennium, now exists in a kind of a preliminary and partial fulfillment. As Peter explained in his Pentecost sermon, the remarkable events that had just taken place in Jerusalem (Acts 2:1-13) were a preview of that which the prophet Joel prophesied of the millennial kingdom: "'And it shall be in the last days,' God says, 'that I will pour forth of My Spirit upon all mankind'" (v. 17; cf. Joel 2:28).

Within the central mystery of the kingdom are other revealed mysteries (see Matt. 13:11). One is the mystery of the indwelling Christ, "the mystery which has been hidden from the past ages and generations; but has now been manifested to His saints, to whom God willed to make known what is the riches of the glory of this mystery among the Gentiles, which is Christ in you, the hope of glory" (Col. 1:26-27). Other mysteries are that of God in flesh, the incarnation of the Son of

God, a truth not fully revealed in the Old Testament (Col. 2:2-3); the mystery of Israel's unbelief and rejection of the Messiah (Rom. 11:25); the mystery of iniquity (2 Thess. 2:7); the mystery of Babylon—the terrible, vile, economic and religious system of the end times (Rev. 17); the mystery of the unity of believers (Eph. 3:3-6); the mystery of the church as Christ's bride (Eph. 5:24-32); and the mystery of the rapture (1 Cor. 15:51-52). The mystery age will be completed when Christ returns in glory (Rev. 10:7).

THE CHURCH AS CHRIST'S BODY

The rich doctrine of the church as Christ's Body is a metaphor that shows the church not as an organization but as a living organism made up of many interrelated and mutually dependent parts. Christ is the head of that Body, and the Holy Spirit is, as it were, its lifeblood.

The New Testament uses many metaphors for the church that the Old Testament uses of Israel. They are both called a bride, or wife (Hos. 1:2; cf. Jer. 3:20; Rev. 21:2), a family household (Ps. 107:41; Jer. 31:1; Eph. 2); a flock (Isa. 40:11; cf. Ps. 23; Luke 12:32; Acts 20:28-29), and a vineyard or vine branches (Isa. 5:1-7; John 15:5). But the Old Testament never speaks of Israel as God's body. That is a distinct and formerly unrevealed figure for God's people in the New Covenant. Christ's church is His present reincarnated Body on earth.

It is only this outward incarnation of Christ that the world sees. Consequently, the church should be just as whole and full statured as Jesus was when He ministered on earth. Members of the Body of Christ are inextricably united in their Lord, and when one member malfunctions, the whole Body is weakened. When its members disobey the Head, the Body limps and stumbles. Yet when its members faithfully respond to the Head, the church manifests the Lord's beauty, power, and glory.

The Body functions through the use of spiritual gifts and through the responsibilities of fellowship and mutual ministry. When the church is faithful, Christ comes to full stature in His present earthly Body. When the church is not faithful, the world's view of Christ is distorted, the church is weakened, and the Lord is dishonored.

THE AUTHOR

Paul, whose original name was Saul, was of the tribe of Benjamin and probably was named after Israel's first king and her most prominent Benjamite. Saul was well educated in what today are called the humanities, but his most extensive training was in rabbinic studies under the famous Gamaliel (Acts 22:3). He became an outstanding rabbi in his own right and was a member of the Sanhedrin, the ruling Jewish council at Jerusalem. He also became probably the most ardent anti-Christian leader in Judaism (Acts 22:4-5). He passionately hated the followers of Jesus Christ and was on his way to arrest some of them in

Damascus when the Lord miraculously and dramatically stopped him in his tracks and brought him to Himself (Acts 9:1-8).

After spending three years in the desert of Nabataean Arabia, Paul jointly pastored a church in Antioch of Syria with Barnabas, Simeon, Lucius, and Manaen (Acts 13:1). During this earlier ministry Saul came to be known as Paul (Acts 13:9). The new man took on a new name. From Antioch the Holy Spirit sent him out with Barnabas to begin the greatest missionary enterprise in the history of the church. At that point Paul began his work as God's unique apostle to the Gentiles (Acts 9:15; Rom. 11:13).

DATE AND DESTINATION OF THE EPISTLE

Sometime between 60 and 62, Paul wrote this letter from prison in Rome (see 3:1) to the believers whom he had pastored. Because the phrase *who are at Ephesus* is not in many early manuscripts, and because there is no mention of a local situation or individual believer, many scholars think this letter was an encyclical, intended to be circulated among all the churches in Asia Minor (including those in Smyrna, Pergamos, Thyatira, and Sardis, as well as Ephesus). It may be that the letter was sent first to Ephesus and therefore became especially associated with that church.

The first three chapters of Ephesians emphasize doctrine, and the last three chapters emphasize behavior. The first half is theological, and the second half is practical.

The Salutation

1

Paul, an apostle of Christ Jesus by the will of God, to the saints who are at Ephesus, and who are faithful in Christ Jesus: Grace to you and peace from God our Father and the Lord Jesus Christ. (1:1-2)

In his salutation, Paul presents the dual source of his apostolic authority, a dual description of believers, a dual blessing for believers, and the dual source of those blessings.

THE DUAL SOURCE OF AUTHORITY

Paul, an apostle of Christ Jesus by the will of God, (1:1a)

Paul wrote with the authority of an **apostle**. *Apostolos* means "sent one" and in the New Testament is used as an official title of the men God uniquely chose to be the foundation layers of the church and the receivers, teachers, and writers of His final revelation—the New Testament. The apostolic duties were to preach the gospel (1 Cor. 1:17), teach and pray (Acts 6:4), work miracles (2 Cor. 12:12), build up other leaders of the church (Acts 14:23), and write the Word of God (Eph. 1:1; etc.).

Besides the original twelve and Matthias (Acts 1:26), who replaced Judas, Paul was the only other **apostle**, "as it were . . . one untimely born" (1 Cor. 15:8). Yet he was not inferior to the other apostles, having met all the requirements for that office (1 Cor. 9:1).

Paul's credentials were not his academic training or his rabbinical leadership but his being an **apostle of Christ Jesus by the will of God**. Paul did not teach and write by his own authority but by the dual yet totally unified authority of the Son **(Christ Jesus)** and of the Father **(God)**. In stating that truth Paul was not boasting of personal merit or elevating himself above other believers. He well remembered that he had been a blasphemer, a violent persecutor of the church, and an unworthy and ignorant unbeliever; and he still considered himself the foremost of sinners (1 Tim. 1:13, 15). Like every Christian, he was first of all "a bond-servant of Christ Jesus" his Lord (Rom. 1:1). By mentioning his apostleship, Paul simply established his undeserved but divinely-bestowed authority to speak in God's behalf—which he states at the beginning of each of his epistles except Philippians and 1 and 2 Thessalonians.

THE DUAL DESIGNATION OF BELIEVERS

to the saints who are at Ephesus, and who are faithful in Christ Jesus: (1:1b)

From God's side believers are those whom He has made holy, which is the meaning of **saints**. From man's side believers are those who are **faithful**, those who have trusted **in Christ Jesus** as their Lord and Savior.

Every Christian is a saint, because every Christian has been set apart and made holy through the perfect righteousness of Christ that has been placed to his account (Rom. 3:21-22; 1 Cor. 1:30; Phil. 3:9; etc.). When a person acts in faith to receive Christ, God acts in grace to give that person Christ's own righteousness. It is Christ's perfect righteousness—not a person's own character or accomplishments, no matter how great they may seem in men's eyes—that establishes *every* believer as one of God's **saints** through saving faith.

THE DUAL BLESSINGS OF BELIEVERS

Grace to you and peace (1:2a)

This was a common greeting among Christians in the early church. *Charis* **(grace)** is God's great kindness toward those who are undeserving of His favor but who have placed their faith in His Son, Jesus Christ. To greet a Christian brother or sister in this way is much more than a wish for their general well-being. It is also an acknowledgment of the divine grace in which we stand and which has made us mutual members of Christ's Body and of God's divine family.

Grace is the fountain of which **peace** (*eirēnē*) is the stream. Because we have grace from God we have peace *with* God and the peace *of* God, "which sur-passes all comprehension" (Phil. 4:7). **Peace** is the equivalent of the Hebrew *shālôm,* which, in its highest connotation, signifies spiritual prosperity and completeness.

THE DUAL SOURCE OF BLESSING

from God our Father and the Lord Jesus Christ. (1:2*b*)

The dual source of blessing is the same as the dual source of authority— **God our Father and the Lord Jesus Christ.** Those are not separate and distinct sources but two manifestations of the same Source, as indicated by the connective *kai* (**and**), which can indicate equivalence, and here indicates that the **Lord Jesus Christ** is deity just like **God our Father.**

Paul's message throughout this epistle is that believers might understand and experience more fully all of the blessings granted by their heavenly Father and His Son and their Savior, Jesus Christ.

The Body Formed in Eternity Past

2

Blessed be the God and Father of our Lord Jesus Christ, who has blessed us with every spiritual blessing in the heavenly places in Christ, just as He chose us in Him before the foundation of the world, that we should be holy and blameless before Him. In love He predestined us to adoption as sons through Jesus Christ to Himself, according to the kind intention of His will, to the praise of the glory of His grace. (1:3-6a)

In the Greek, verses 3-14 comprise one sentence and encompass the past, present, and future of God's eternal purpose for the church. It is Paul's outline of God's master plan for salvation. In 3-6a we are shown the past aspect, election; in 6b-11 we are shown the present aspect, redemption; and in 12-14 we are shown the future aspect, inheritance. Within God's master plan of salvation is every believer who has or will ever trust in God and be saved. As it is sometimes expressed, history is simply the outworking of "His story," which has already been planned and prewritten in eternity.

This passage can also be divided into three sections, each of which focuses on a different Person of the Trinity. Verses 3-6a center on the Father, verses 6b-12 center on the Son, and verses 13-14 center on the Holy Spirit. Paul takes us to the very throne room of the Godhead to show the greatness and the vastness of the blessings and treasures that belong to those who are in Jesus Christ.

People today are greatly concerned about identity, life purpose, self-worth, and self-acceptance. Consequently there is a plethora of books, articles, seminars, and schemes that attempt to fulfill those longings. But because God and His Word are not considered in most such attempts, the only source for finding the truth is eliminated, and men inevitably are led back to themselves for the answers. In spite of many variations and sometimes complex formulas, the end result is to tell men they are really all right after all and that what identity, worth, and meaning they find in life they must find in and for themselves.

We are told to think of ourselves first and are shown how to get on top by using and manipulating others, by intimidating before being intimidated. We are told how to be successful and how to be number one. We are counseled to find meaning in the heritage of our family and ethnic roots, with the expectation that finding out where we came from will help explain where we are and perhaps where we are headed. But such approaches give only a psychological gloss that helps cover, but does not help remove, the underlying problem of meaning in life.

Others set about trying to establish their worth by works righteousness, some even becoming heavily involved in church work and other Christian activities. They look for praise and commendation, and before long they are entrapped in the same kind of hypocritical religious games that characterized the scribes and Pharisees of Jesus' day. As their self-satisfaction grows their spiritual lives shrivel, because such effort feeds the flesh and cripples the soul.

But every human effort at self-improvement or self-satisfaction—no matter what its religious covering may be—is subject to the law of diminishing returns. Genuine and lasting satisfaction is never achieved, and increased achievement only brings increased desire. More importantly, the guilt and fear that cause the dissatisfaction are suppressed but not alleviated. The longer such superficial games are played, the deeper become the depression, anxiety, and feelings of guilt.

The only way a person can achieve a true sense of self-worth, meaning, and significance is to have a right relationship to his Creator. A person without Christ has no spiritual value, no standing before God, no purpose or meaning in the world. He is like "chaff which the wind drives away" (Ps. 1:4).

A Christian, however, is a child of God and a joint heir with Jesus Christ. If he has no comprehension of those blessings he needs to understand the position he already has in his Savior. To give such Christians the right understanding of their position and possessions is the foundational thrust of Paul's Ephesian letter.

If we belong to Christ, Paul says, we can be sure that God put our name down as part of His church even before the world began. Out of grace and in divine sovereignty, He chose each one of us to belong to Him. It was not because we were more worthy than anyone else or more deserving or meritorious—but simply because God willed to choose us.

Though this is an incomprehensible truth to finite thinking, it is one of the most repeated in Scripture. The record of God's redemptive history is that of His reaching down and drawing to Himself those whom He has chosen to save. In these opening verses of Ephesians Paul gives us a glimpse of eternity past. He lets us eavesdrop as God planned to save us—not only long before we were born but long before the earth was born.

THE ASPECTS OF BLESSING

Blessed be the God and Father of our Lord Jesus Christ, who has blessed us with every spiritual blessing in the heavenly places in Christ, (1:3)

Paul here presents six aspects of the divine blessing he is about to unfold: the blessed One, God; the Blesser, also God; the blessed ones, believers; the blessings, all things spiritual; the blessing location, the heavenly places; and the blessing Agent, Jesus Christ.

THE BLESSED ONE—GOD

Such gracious truth is introduced appropriately by praise to the One who has made such provision: **Blessed be the God and Father of our Lord Jesus Christ.** From *eulogeō* (**blessed**) we get eulogy, a message of praise and commendation, the declaration of a person's goodness. Because no one is truly good but **God** (Matt. 19:17), our supreme eulogy, our supreme praise, is for Him alone.

Goodness is God's nature. **God the Father** not only does good things, He *is* good in a way and to a degree that no human being except His own incarnate Son, **our Lord Jesus Christ,** can be. Consequently from Genesis to Revelation, godly men, recognizing the surpassing and humanly unattainable goodness of God, have proclaimed blessing upon Him. Melchizedek declared, "Blessed be God Most High" (Gen. 14:20). In the last days, "every created thing which is in heaven and on the earth and under the earth and on the sea, and all things in them" will be "heard saying, 'To Him who sits on the throne, and to the Lamb, be blessing and honor and glory and dominion forever and ever'" (Rev. 5:13).

Nothing is more appropriate for God's people than to bless Him for His great goodness. In all things—whether pain, struggle, trials, frustration, opposition, or adversity—we are to praise God, because He is good in the midst of it all. For that we praise and bless Him.

THE BLESSER—GOD

Consistent with His perfection and praiseworthiness, the One who is to be supremely blessed for His goodness is Himself the supreme Blesser who bestows goodness. It is He **who has blessed us with every spiritual blessing.** "Every good thing bestowed and every perfect gift," James reminds us, "is from above, coming down from the Father of lights" (James 1:17). Paul assures us "that God causes all things to work together for good to those who love God, to those who are called according to His purpose" (Rom. 8:28). God blesses because He is the source of all blessing, of every good thing. Goodness can only come from God because there is no source of goodness outside of God.

THE BLESSED ONES—BELIEVERS

The **us** whom God **has blessed** refers to believers, "the saints . . . in Christ Jesus" Paul addresses in verse 1. In His wonderful grace, marvelous providence, and sovereign plan God has chosen to bless **us**. God has eternally ordained that "those who are of faith are blessed" (Gal. 3:9).

When we bless God we speak good of Him. When God blesses us, He communicates good to us. We bless Him with words; He blesses us with deeds. All we can do is to speak well of Him because in ourselves we have nothing good to give, and in Himself He lacks no goodness. But when He blesses us the situation is reversed. He cannot bless us *for* our goodness, because we have none. Rather, He blesses us *with* goodness. Our heavenly Father lavishes us with every goodness, every good gift, every blessing. That is His nature, and that is our need.

THE BLESSINGS—EVERYTHING SPIRITUAL

Our heavenly Father blesses **us with every spiritual blessing**. In the New Testament *pneumatikos* (**spiritual**) is always used in relation to the work of the Holy Spirit. Therefore it does not here refer to immaterial blessings as opposed to material ones but to the divine origin of the blessings—whether they help us in our spirits, our minds, our bodies, our daily living, or however else. **Spiritual** refers to the source, not the extent, of **blessing**.

Many Christians continually ask God for what He has already given. They pray for Him to give them more love, although they should know that "the love of God has been poured out within our hearts through the Holy Spirit who was given to us" (Rom. 5:5). They pray for peace, although Jesus said, "Peace I leave with you; My peace I give to you" (John 14:27). They pray for happiness and joy, although Jesus said, "These things I have spoken to you, that My joy may be in you, and that your joy may be made full" (John 15:11). They ask God for strength, although His Word tells them that they "can do all things through Him who strengthens" them (Phil. 4:13).

God's "divine power has granted to us everything pertaining to life and godliness, through the true knowledge of Him who called us by His own glory and excellence" (2 Pet. 1:3). It is not that God *will* give us but that He has *already* given us "everything pertaining to life and godliness." He **has blessed us** already **with every spiritual blessing**. We are complete "in Him" (Col. 2:10).

Our resources in God are not simply promised; they are possessed. Every Christian has what Paul calls "the provision of the Spirit of Jesus Christ" (Phil. 1:19). God cannot give us more than He has already given us in His Son. There is nothing more to receive. The believer's need, therefore, is not to receive something more but to do something more with what he has.

Our heavenly position and possession are so certain and secure that Paul speaks of God's having already "raised us up with Him, and seated us with Him in the heavenly places, in Christ Jesus" (Eph. 2:6).

THE LOCATION OF BLESSING—THE HEAVENLY PLACES

These abundant, unlimited blessings from God are **in the heavenly places.** More than heaven itself is included. **The heavenly places** (cf. 1:20; 2:6; 3:10) encompass the entire supernatural realm of God, His complete domain, the full extent of His divine operation.

Christians have a paradoxical, two-level existence—a dual citizenship. While we remain on earth we are citizens of earth. But in Christ our primary and infinitely more important citizenship is in heaven (Phil. 3:20). Christ is our Lord and King, and we are citizens of His realm, **the heavenly places.** That is why we are to pursue "things above, where Christ is, seated at the right hand of God" (Col. 3:1).

Because we are members of God's dominion, unlike the "sons of this age" (Luke 16:8), we are able to understand the supernatural things of God, things which the "natural man does not accept" and "cannot understand . . . because they are spiritually appraised" (1 Cor. 2:14).

When an American citizen travels to another country, he is every bit as much an American citizen as when he is in the United States. Whether he is in Africa, the Near East, Europe, Antarctica, or anywhere else outside his homeland, he is still completely an American citizen, with all the rights and privileges that such citizenship holds.

As citizens of God's heavenly dominion, Christians hold all the rights and privileges that citizenship grants, even while they are living in the "foreign" and sometimes hostile land of earth. Our true life is in the supernatural, **the heavenly places.** Our Father is there, our Savior is there, our family and loved ones are there, our name is there, and our eternal dwelling place and throne are there.

But we are presently trapped in the tension between the earthly and the heavenly. Paul reflected that tension when he said, "We are afflicted in every way, but not crushed; perplexed, but not despairing; persecuted, but not forsaken; struck down, but not destroyed . . . as sorrowful yet always rejoicing, as poor yet making many rich, as having nothing yet possessing all things" (2 Cor. 4:8-9; 6:10).

The key to living as a heavenly citizen while living in an unheavenly situation is walking by the Spirit. "Walk by the Spirit," Paul says, "and you will not carry out the desire of the flesh" (Gal. 5:16). When we walk in His power He produces His fruit in us: "love, joy, peace, patience, kindness, goodness, faithfulness, gentleness, self-control" (vv. 22-23). We receive our heavenly blessings by living in the power of God's Holy Spirit.

THE BLESSING AGENT—JESUS CHRIST

Christians possess **every spiritual blessing in the heavenly places** because they are **in Christ.** When we trust in Him as Lord and Savior, we are placed in a marvelous union with Jesus Christ. "The one who joins himself to the Lord is one spirit with Him" (1 Cor. 6:17). Our unity as Christians is more than simply that of common agreement; it is the unity of a commonness of life, the common eternal life of God that pulses through the soul of every believer (cf. Rom. 15:5-7).

All that the Lord has, those in Christ have. "The Spirit Himself bears witness with our spirit that we are children of God, and if children, heirs also, heirs of God and fellow heirs with Christ" (Rom. 8:16-17). Christ's riches are our riches, His resources are our resources, His righteousness is our righteousness, and His power is our power. His position is our position: where He is, we are. His privilege is our privilege: what He is we are. His possession is our possession: what He has, we have. His practice is our practice: what He does, we do.

We are those things and have those things and do those things by the grace of God, which never fails to work His will in those who trust Him (1 Cor. 15:10).

The Elements of the Eternal Forming of the Body

just as He chose us in Him before the foundation of the world, that we should be holy and blameless before Him. In love He predestined us to adoption as sons through Jesus Christ to Himself, according to the kind intention of His will, to the praise of the glory of His grace. (1:4-6a)

These verses reveal the past part of God's eternal plan in forming the church, the Body of Jesus Christ. His plan is shown in seven elements: the method, election; the object, the elect; the time, eternity past; the purpose, holiness; the motive, love; the result, sonship; and the goal, glory.

THE METHOD—ELECTION

The Bible speaks of three kinds of election. One is God's theocratic election of Israel. "You are a holy people to the Lord your God," Moses told Israel in the desert of Sinai; "the Lord your God has chosen you to be a people for His own possession out of all the peoples who are on the face of the earth" (Deut. 7:6).

That election had no bearing on personal salvation. "They are not all Israel who are descended from Israel," Paul explains; "neither are they all children because they are Abraham's descendants" (Rom. 9:6-7). Racial descent from Abraham as father of the Hebrew people did not mean spiritual descent from him as father of the faithful (Rom. 4:11).

A second kind of election is vocational. The Lord called out the tribe of Levi to be His priests, but Levites were not thereby guaranteed salvation. Jesus called twelve men to be apostles but only eleven of them to salvation. After Paul came to Christ because of God's election to salvation, God then chose him in another way to be His special apostle to the Gentiles (Acts 9:15; Rom. 1:5).

The third kind of election is salvational, the kind of which Paul is speaking in our present text. "No one can come to Me," Jesus said, "unless the Father who sent Me draws him" (John 6:44). *Helkuō* (**draws**) carries the idea of an irresistible force and was used in ancient Greek literature of a desperately hungry man being drawn to food and of demonic forces being drawn to animals when they were not able to possess men.

Salvage yards use giant electromagnets to lift and partially sort scrap metal. When the magnet is turned on, a tremendous magnetic force draws all the ferrous metals that are near it, but has no effect on other metals such as aluminum and brass.

In a similar way, God's elective will irresistibly draws to Himself those whom He has predetermined to love and forgive, while having no effect on those whom He has not.

From all eternity, **before the foundation of the world**, and therefore completely apart from any merit or deserving that any person could have, God **chose us in Him**, "in Christ" (v. 3). By God's sovereign election, those who are saved were placed in eternal union with Christ before creation even took place.

Although man's will is not free in the sense that many people suppose, he does have a will, a will that Scripture clearly recognizes. Apart from God, man's will is captive to sin. But he is nevertheless able to choose God because God has made that choice possible. Jesus said that whoever believes in Him will not perish but have eternal life (John 3:16) and that "everyone who lives and believes in Me shall never die" (11:26). The frequent commands to the unsaved to respond to the Lord (e. g., Josh. 24:15; Isa. 55:1; Matt. 3:1-2; 4:17; 11:28-30; John 5:40; 6:37; 7:37-39; Rev. 22:17) clearly indicate the responsibility of man to exercise his own will.

Yet the Bible is just as clear that no person receives Jesus Christ as Savior who has not been chosen by God (cf. Rom. 8:29; 9:11; 1 Thess. 1:3-4; 1 Pet. 1:2). Jesus gives both truths in one verse in the gospel of John: "All that the Father gives Me shall come to Me, and the one who comes to Me I will certainly not cast out" (John 6:37).

God's sovereign election and man's exercise of responsibility in choosing Jesus Christ seem opposite and irreconcilable truths—and from our limited human perspective they *are* opposite and irreconcilable. That is why so many earnest, well-meaning Christians throughout the history of the church have floundered trying to reconcile them. Since the problem cannot be resolved by our finite minds, the result is always to compromise one truth in favor of the other or to weaken both by trying to take a position somewhere between them.

We should let the antimony remain, believing both truths completely and leaving the harmonizing of them to God.

Eklegō **(chose)** is here in the aorist tense and the middle voice, indicating God's totally independent choice. Because the verb is reflexive it signifies that God not only chose by Himself but for Himself. His primary purpose in electing the church was the praise of His own glory (vv. 6, 12, 14). Believers were chosen for the Lord's glory before they were chosen for their own good. The very reason for calling out believers into the church was that "the manifold wisdom of God might now be made known through the church to the rulers and the authorities in the heavenly places" (3:10).

Israel was God's elect, His "chosen one" (Isa. 45:4; cf. 65:9, 22). But she was told, "The Lord did not set His love on you nor choose you because you were more in number than any of the peoples, for you were the fewest of all peoples, but because the Lord loved you" (Deut. 7:7-8). God chose the Jews simply out of His sovereign love.

God's heavenly angels also are elect (1 Tim. 5:21), chosen by Him to glorify His name and to be His messengers. Christ Himself was elect (1 Pet. 2:6, KJV), and the apostles were elect (John 15:16). By the same sovereign plan and will the church is elect. God "has saved us, and called us with a holy calling, not according to our works, but according to His own purpose and grace which was granted us in Christ Jesus from all eternity" (2 Tim. 1:9). In Acts we are told, "And as many as had been appointed to eternal life believed" (13:48).

Paul said, "For this reason I endure all things for the sake of those who are chosen, that they also may obtain the salvation which is in Christ Jesus and with it eternal glory" (2 Tim. 2:10). His heart's desire was to reach the elect, the ones who were already chosen, in order that they might take hold of the faith already granted them in God's sovereign decree.

Paul gave thanks for the church because it was God's elect. "We should always give thanks to God for you, brethren beloved by the Lord, because God has chosen you from the beginning for salvation through sanctification by the Spirit and faith in the truth" (2 Thess. 2:13).

In his book *Evangelism and the Sovereignty of God,* J. I. Packer observes:

> All Christians believe in divine sovereignty, but some are not aware that they do, and mistakenly imagine and insist that they reject it. What causes this odd state of affairs? The root cause is the same as in most cases of error in the Church—the intruding of rationalistic speculations, the passion for systematic consistency, a reluctance to recognize the existence of mystery and to let God be wiser than men, and a consequent subjecting of Scripture to the supposed demands of human logic. People see the Bible teaches man's responsibility for his actions; they do not see (man, indeed, cannot see) how this is consistent with the sovereign Lordship of God over those actions. They are not content to let the two truths live side by side, as they do in the Scriptures, but jump to the conclusion that, in order to uphold the biblical truth of human responsibility, they are bound to reject the equally biblical and equally true doctrine of divine sovereignty, and to explain away the great number of texts that teach it. The desire to over-simplify the Bible by cutting out the mysteries is natural to our perverse minds, and it is not surprising that even godly men should fall victim to it. Hence this persistent and troublesome dispute. The irony of the situation, however, is that when we ask how the two sides pray, it becomes apparent that those who profess to deny God's sovereignty really believe in it just as strongly as those who affirm it. ([Chicago: Inter-Varsity, 1961], pp. 16-17)

Because we cannot stand the tension of mystery, paradox, or antinomy, we are inclined to adjust what the Bible teaches so that it will fit our own systems of order and consistency. But that presumptuous approach is unfaithful to God's

Word and leads to confused doctrine and weakened living. It should be noted that other essential scriptural doctrines are also apparently paradoxical to our limited capacity. It is antinomous that Scripture itself is the work of human authors, yet the very words of God; that Jesus Christ is fully God and fully man; that salvation is forever, yet saints must remain obedient and persevere to the end; that the Christian's life is lived in total commitment and discipline of self, yet is all of Christ. Such inscrutable truths are an encouragement that the mind of God infinitely surpasses the mind of man and are a great proof of the divine authorship of Scripture. Humans writing a Bible on their own would have attempted to resolve such problems.

It is not that God's sovereign election, or predestination, eliminates man's choice in faith. Divine sovereignty and human response are integral and inseparable parts of salvation—though exactly how they operate together only the infinite mind of God knows.

Nor is it, as many believe and teach, that God simply looks into the future to see which people are going to believe and then elects them to salvation. Taken out of context, Romans 8:29 is often used to support that view. But verse 28 makes it clear that those whom God foresees and predestines to salvation are those whom He has already "called according to His purpose." Any teaching that diminishes the sovereign, electing love of God by giving more credit to men also diminishes God's glory, thus striking a blow at the very purpose of salvation.

We should be satisfied simply to declare with John Chadwick,

> I sought the Lord,
> And afterwards I knew
> He moved my soul to seek Him,
> Seeking me!
> It was not that I found,
> O Saviour true;
> No, I was found by Thee.

THE OBJECT—THE ELECT

The object of election is **us**, not everyone, but only those whom God **chose**, the saints and "faithful in Christ Jesus" (v. 1). Those whom God elects are those whom He has declared holy before the foundation of the world and who have identified with His Son Jesus Christ by faith. Being a Christian is having been chosen by God to be His child and to inherit all things through and with Jesus Christ.

THE TIME—ETERNITY PAST

God elected us **before the foundation of the world**. Before the creation, the Fall, the covenants, or the law, we were sovereignly predestined by God to be His. He designed the church, the Body of His Son, before the world began.

Because in God's plan Christ was crucified for us "before the foundation of the world" (1 Pet. 1:20), we were designated for salvation by that same plan at that same time. It was then that our inheritance in God's kingdom was determined (Matt. 25:34). We belonged to God before time began, and we will be His after time has long run its course. Our names as believers were "written from the foundation of the world in the book of life of the Lamb who has been slain" (Rev. 13:8; cf. 17:8).

THE PURPOSE—HOLINESS

God chose us in order that we might be **holy and blameless.** *Amōmos* **(blameless)** literally means without blemish, or spotless. Because we are chosen **in Him** we are **holy and blameless before Him.** Because Jesus Christ gave Himself for us as "a lamb unblemished and spotless" (1 Pet. 1:19), we have been given His own unblemished and spotless nature. The unworthy have been declared worthy, the unrighteous declared holy. It is Christ's eternal and foreordained plan to "present to Himself the church in all her glory, having no spot or wrinkle or any such thing; but that she should be holy and blameless" (Eph. 5:27).

Obviously Paul is talking about our position and not our practice. We know that in our living we are far from the holy standard and far from being blameless. Yet "in Him," Paul said in another place, we "have been made complete" (Col. 2:10). All that God is, we become in Jesus Christ. That is why salvation is secure. We have Christ's perfect righteousness. Our practice can and does fall short, but our position can never fall short, because it is exactly the same **holy and blameless** position before God that Christ has. We are as secure as our Savior, because we are in Him, waiting for the full redemption and glorious holiness that awaits us in His presence.

And because God declares us and leads us to be **holy and blameless,** we should strive to live lives now that reflect the holiness and blamelessness that are our destiny.

THE MOTIVE—LOVE

God elects those who are saved because of His **love. In love He predestined us to adoption as sons.** Just as He chose Israel to be His special people only because of His love (Deut. 7:8), so He also chose the church, the family of the redeemed.

Biblical *agapē* **love** is not an emotion but a disposition of the heart to seek the welfare and meet the needs of others. "Greater love has no one than this, that one lay down his life for his friends," Jesus said (John 15:13). And that is exactly what Jesus Himself did on behalf of those God has chosen to be saved. In the ultimate divine act of **love,** God determined before the foundation of the earth that He would give His only Son to save us. "God, being rich in mercy, because of His great love with which He loved us, even when we were dead in our transgressions, made us alive together with Christ" (Eph. 2:4-5). He loved us, and will eternally continue to love us, **according to the kind intention of His will.**

THE RESULT—SONSHIP

The result of God's election is our **adoption as sons.** In Christ we become subjects of His kingdom, and because He is our Lord we are His servants. He even calls us friends because, He says, "All things that I have heard from My Father I have made known to you" (John 15:15). But in His great love He makes us more than citizens and servants, and even more than friends. He makes us children. God lovingly draws redeemed sinners into the intimacy of His own family.

When we become Christians we become children of God. "For you have not received a spirit of slavery leading to fear," Paul says, "but you have received a spirit of adoption as sons by which we cry out, 'Abba! Father!'" (Rom. 8:15). *Abba* was an Aramaic word of endearment somewhat equivalent to Daddy or Papa.

To be saved is to have the very life of God in our souls, His own Spirit enlivening our spirits. Human parents can adopt children and come to love them every bit as much as they love their natural children. They can give an adopted child complete equality in the family life, resources, and inheritance. But no human parent can impart his own distinct nature to an adopted child. Yet that is what God miraculously does to every person whom He has elected and who has trusted in Christ. He makes them sons just like His divine Son. Christians not only have all of the Son's riches and blessings but all of the Son's nature.

THE GOAL—GLORY

Why did God do all of that for us? Why did He want us to be His sons? We are saved and made sons **to the praise of the glory of His grace.** Above all else, He elects and saves us for His own **glory.** When Jesus said, "Do not be afraid, little flock, for your Father has chosen gladly to give you the kingdom" (Luke 12:32), He was affirming the delight of God in putting His glory on display. As Paul further explained, "God is at work in [us] . . . for His good pleasure" (Phil. 2:13).

The apostle Paul interceded for the Thessalonians, praying "that our God may count you worthy of your calling . . . in order that the name of our Lord Jesus may be glorified in you, and you in Him" (2 Thess. 1:11-12).

Even the beasts of the field will glorify the Lord, Isaiah tells us (43:20), and the heavens tell of the glory of God (Ps. 19:1). The only rebels in the universe are fallen angels and fallen man. Everything else glorifies its Creator. The fallen angels have already been eternally removed from God's presence, and those fallen men who will not be saved by Jesus Christ will join those angels in that eternal separation.

God chose and preordained the Body before the foundation of the world in order that no human being could boast or take glory for himself, but that all the **glory** might be His. Salvation is not partly of God and partly of man, but entirely of

God. To guarantee that, every provision and every detail of salvation was accomplished before any human being was ever born or before a planet was formed on which he could be born.

The ultimate reason for everything that exists is **the glory of His grace.** That is why, as God's children, Christians should do everything they do—even such mundane things as eating and drinking—to the glory of God (1 Cor. 10:31).

Redemption Through His Blood

3

which He freely bestowed on us in the Beloved. In Him we have redemption through His blood, the forgiveness of our trespasses, according to the riches of His grace, which He lavished upon us. In all wisdom and insight He made known to us the mystery of His will, according to His kind intention which He purposed in Him with a view to an administration suitable to the fulness of the times, that is, the summing up of all things in Christ, things in the heavens and things upon the earth. (1:6*b*-10)

Some years ago trading stamps were popular. For each dollar amount purchased a given number of trading stamps was given as a bonus. When sufficient stamps were saved up, they were taken to a redemption center and exchanged for merchandise.

Redemption is one of the central themes of Scripture and of the book of Ephesians, but it carries much more than the idea simply of exchanging one thing for another of equal value.

THE MEANING OF REDEMPTION

Redemption comes from one of six terms taken from the field of law and used in the New Testament in relation to salvation. *Dikaioō* and related terms referred to legal acquittal of a charge and are used theologically to speak of a sinner's being vindicated, justified, and declared righteous before God (see, for example, Rom. 3:4; 4:25; 5:18; 1 Tim. 3:16). *Aphiēmi* basically means to send away and was used to indicate the legal repayment or cancellation of a debt or the granting of a pardon. It is used in Scripture to refer to God's forgiveness of sin (see Matt. 9:2; Rom. 4:7; Eph. 1:7; 4:32; etc.). *Huiothesia* referred to the legal process of adopting a child and is used by Paul to represent the believer's adoption into God's family (see Rom. 8:15; Gal. 4:5; Eph. 1:5). *Katallassō* meant to legally reconcile two disputing parties in court and in the New Testament is used of a believer's reconciliation with God through Jesus Christ (Rom. 5:10; 2 Cor. 5:18-20).

Two Greek legal terms are related to redemption. *Agorazō,* and the related *exagorazō,* refer to buying or purchasing. The source of the terms is *agora,* which means marketplace, and the root idea of the derived verbs and nouns referred to buying and trading in the marketplace. In the New Testament they are used to denote spiritual purchase or redemption (see Gal. 3:13; Rev. 5:9; 14:3-4; etc.).

The other term for redemption, *lutroō* (along with its related forms), meant to release from captivity. It carried an even stronger meaning than *agorazō* and is behind the noun rendered here as **redemption**. This word was used to refer to paying a ransom in order to release a person from bondage, especially that of slavery.

During New Testament times the Roman Empire had as many as six million slaves, and the buying and selling of them was a major business. If a person wanted to free a loved one or friend who was a slave, he would buy that slave for himself and then grant him freedom, testifying to the deliverance by a written certificate. *Lutroō* was used to designate the freeing of a slave in that way.

That is precisely the idea carried in the New Testament use of the term to represent Christ's atoning sacrifice on the cross. He paid the redemption price to buy for Himself fallen mankind and to set them free from their sin.

Every human being born since the Fall has come into the world enslaved to sin, under total bondage to a nature that is corrupt, evil, and separated from its Creator. No person is spiritually free. No human being is free of sin or free of its consequences, the ultimate consequence, or penalty, for which is death (Rom. 6:23). "The soul who sins will die" (Ezek. 18:4).

Jesus said, "Truly, truly, I say to you, everyone who commits sin is the slave of sin" (John 8:34), and Paul points out that every person has committed sin: "There is none righteous, not even one" (Rom. 3:10; cf. Ps. 14:1). In the same letter the apostle says that we are all "sold into bondage to sin" (7:14) and that, in fact, the whole of creation is enslaved to the corruption of sin (8:21).

Sin is man's captor and slave owner, and it demands a price for his release. Death is the price that had to be paid for man's redemption from sin. Biblical redemption therefore refers to the act of God by which He Himself paid as a ransom the price for sin.

In Romans Paul speaks of redemption as "our having been freed from sin" and become "slaves of righteousness" (6:18). In Galatians He describes redemption in saying that Jesus Christ "gave Himself for our sins, that He might deliver us out of this present evil age, according to the will of our God and Father" (1:3-4); that "Christ redeemed us from the curse of the Law, having become a curse for us" (3:13); and that "it was for freedom that Christ set us free; therefore keep standing firm and do not be subject again to a yoke of slavery" (5:1). In Colossians the apostle says that "He delivered us from the domain of darkness, and transferred us to the kingdom of His beloved Son, in whom we have redemption, the forgiveness of sins" (1:13-14).

The writer of Hebrews explains redemption in these words: "Since then the children share in flesh and blood, He Himself [Christ] likewise also partook of the same, that through death He might render powerless him who had the power of death, that is, the devil; and might deliver those who through fear of death were subject to slavery all their lives" (2:14-15).

THE ELEMENTS OF REDEMPTION

which He freely bestowed on us in the Beloved. In Him we have redemption through His blood, the forgiveness of our trespasses, according to the riches of His grace, which He lavished upon us. In all wisdom and insight He made known to us the mystery of His will, according to His kind intention which He purposed in Him with a view to an administration suitable to the fulness of the times, that is, the summing up of all things in Christ, things in the heavens and things upon the earth. (1:6b-10)

In this passage Paul mentions five elements of the **redemption** God offers fallen men through His Son, Jesus Christ: the Redeemer, the redeemed, and the redemption price, results, and reason.

THE REDEEMER

Grace (v. 6a) is the antecedent of **which**. It is God's grace (undeserved love and goodness) that **He freely bestowed on us in the Beloved**, and because we are in **Him we have redemption**. Jesus Christ is our Redeemer from sin, **the Beloved** (the word indicates the One who is in the state of being loved by God) who Himself paid the price for our release from sin and death. Because we now belong to Christ, by faith made one with Him and placed in His Body, we are now acceptable to God.

From the beginning of Jesus' ministry the Father declared Him to be "My beloved Son" (Matt. 3:17). And because we have believed in Him, "He delivered us from the domain of darkness, and transferred us to the kingdom of His beloved Son" (Col. 1:13). Because we are now **in the Beloved**, we, too, are "beloved of God" (Rom. 1:7).

Only Jesus Christ has the inherent right to all the goodness of God. But because we are identified with Him by faith, that goodness is now also our goodness. Because our Savior and Lord is the Beloved of the Father and possesses all the goodness of the Father, we are also the beloved of the Father and possess all His goodness. Jesus said, "He who has My commandments and keeps them, he it is who loves Me; and he who loves Me shall be loved by My Father" (John 14:21).

The Father now loves us as He loves Christ and wants us to have everything that Christ has. That is why Paul could say He "has blessed us with every spiritual blessing in the heavenly places in Christ" (Eph. 1:3). Every Christian is God's beloved child because the Lord Jesus Christ has become our Redeemer.

The Old Testament concept of a kinsman-redeemer set forth three qualifications: he had to be related to the one needing redemption, able to pay the price, and willing to do so. The Lord Jesus perfectly met these requirements.

A poet has expressed the magnificent reality of redemption in the words,

> Near, so very near to God,
> Nearer I could not be;
> For in the person of His Son,
> I'm just as near as He.
>
> Dear, so very dear to God,
> Dearer I could not be;
> For in the person of His Son,
> I'm just as dear as He.

Charitoō (**freely bestowed**) is from *charis* (grace, v. 6a), and therefore Paul is saying that God has graced us with His grace. Christians are those who have been graced by God.

THE REDEEMED

On **us**, "the saints . . . who are faithful in Christ Jesus" (v. 1), the Redeemer has **freely bestowed** His grace. **We** are the ones who have **redemption through His blood.**

In chapter 2 Paul reminds us of what we were like when God so graciously redeemed us. We "were dead in [our] trespasses and sins"; we "walked according to the course of this world, according to the prince of the power of the air"; we "lived in the lusts of our flesh, indulging the desires of the flesh and of the mind, and were by nature children of wrath"; and we were without "hope and without God in the world" (vv. 1-3, 12). In chapter 4 he reminds us that we formerly walked in futility of mind, "darkened in [our] understanding, excluded from the life of God," because of ignorance and hardness of heart (vv. 17-18). Those are the kinds of people (the only kind who exist) that God chose to redeem.

It is of course because men *are* like that that they need redemption. Good men would not need a Redeemer. That is why Christ "gave Himself for us, that He might redeem us from every lawless deed and purify for Himself a people for His own possession, zealous for good deeds" (Titus 2:14).

Until a person realizes his need for redemption, however, he sees no need for a Redeemer. Until he recognizes that he is hopelessly enslaved to sin, he will not seek release from it. But when he does, he will be freed from the curse of sin, placed in Christ's Body, and blessed with His every spiritual blessing.

THE REDEMPTION PRICE

In Him we have redemption through His blood, (7a)

The price of redemption is **His blood**. It cost the **blood** of the Son of God to buy men back from the slave market of sin (cf. Lev. 17:11; Heb. 9:22).

Shedding of blood is a metonym for death, which is the penalty and the price of sin. Christ's own death, by the shedding of **His blood**, was the substitute for our death. That which we deserved and could not save ourselves from, the beloved Savior, though He did not deserve it, took upon Himself. He made payment for what otherwise would have condemned us to death and hell.

The blood of sacrificial animals was continually offered on the altars of the Tabernacle and then the Temple. But that blood was never able, and was never intended, to cleanse the offerers from sin. Those animals were only symbolic, typical substitutes. As the writer of Hebrews explains, "It is impossible for the blood of bulls and goats to take away sins" (Heb. 10:4). But in the shedding of **His blood**, "we have been sanctified through the offering of the body of Jesus Christ once for all" (10:10). He "gave Himself up for us, an offering and a sacrifice to God as a fragrant aroma" (Eph. 5:2). The Savior Himself said that His blood was "poured out for many for forgiveness of sins" (Matt. 26:28). As the writer of Hebrews explains, Christ's sacrifice was "not through the blood of goats and calves, but through His own blood, He entered the holy place once for all, having obtained eternal redemption. For if the blood of goats and bulls and the ashes of a heifer sprinkling those who have been defiled, sanctify for the cleansing of the flesh, how much more will the blood of Christ, who through the eternal Spirit offered Himself without blemish to God, cleanse your conscience from dead works to serve the living God?" (Heb. 9:12-14).

We "were not redeemed with perishable things like silver or gold, . . . but with precious blood, as of a lamb unblemished and spotless, the blood of Christ" (1 Pet. 1:18-19). No wonder John saw the four living creatures and the twenty-four elders singing, "Worthy art Thou to take the book, and to break its seals; for Thou wast slain, and didst purchase for God with Thy blood men from every tribe and tongue and people and nation. And Thou hast made them to be a kingdom and priests to our God; and they will reign upon the earth" (Rev. 5:8-10).

The "redemption which is in Christ Jesus . . . in His blood through faith" (Rom. 3:24-25) has paid the price for those enslaved by sin, bought them out of the slave market where they were in bondage, and set them free as liberated sons of God. In their freedom they are in union with Jesus Christ and receive every good thing that He is and has. His death frees believers from sin's guilt, condemnation, bondage, power, penalty, and—some glorious day—even from its presence.

THE REDEMPTIVE RESULTS

the forgiveness of our trespasses, according to the riches of His grace, which He lavished upon us. In all wisdom and insight He made known to us the mystery of His will, (7b-9a)

Redemption involves every conceivable good thing, "every spiritual blessing in the heavenly places in Christ" (v. 3). But here Paul focuses on two especially important aspects. One is negative, the **forgiveness of our trespasses,** and the other is positive, **wisdom and insight.**

Forgiveness. The primary result of redemption for the believer is **forgiveness,** one of the central salvation truths of both the Old and New Testaments. It is also the dearest truth to those who have experienced its blessing. At the Last Supper, Jesus explained to the disciples that the cup He then shared with them was His "blood of the covenant, which is poured out for many for forgiveness of sins" (Matt. 26:28). Redemption brings **forgiveness.**

Behaviorists and those from some other schools of psychology maintain that we cannot be blamed for our sin, that it is the fault of our genes, our environment, our parents, or something else external. But a person's sin is his own fault, and the guilt for it is his own. The honest person who has any understanding of his own heart knows that.

The gospel does not teach, as some falsely maintain, that men have no sin or guilt, but rather that Christ will take away both the sin and the guilt of those who trust Him. As Paul told the Jews in Pisidian Antioch, "Through Him [Christ] forgiveness of sins is proclaimed to you, and through Him everyone who believes is freed from all things" (Acts 13:38-39).

Israel's greatest holy day was Yom Kippur, the Day of Atonement. On that day the high priest selected two unblemished sacrificial goats. One goat was killed, and his blood was sprinkled on the altar as a sacrifice. The high priest placed his hands on the head of the other goat, symbolically laying the sins of the people on the animal. The goat was then taken out deep into the wilderness, so far that it could never find its way back. In symbol the sins of the people went with the goat, never to return to them again (Lev. 16:7-10).

But that enactment, beautiful and meaningful as it was, did not actually remove the people's sins, as they well knew. It was but a picture of what only God Himself in Christ could do. As mentioned above, *aphiēmi* (from which **forgiveness** comes) basically means to send away. Used as a legal term it meant to repay or cancel a debt or to grant a pardon. Through the shedding of His own blood, Jesus Christ actually took the sins of the world upon His own head, as it were, and carried them an infinite distance away from where they could never return. That is the extent of **the forgiveness of our trespasses.**

It is tragic that many Christians are depressed about their shortcomings and wrongdoing, thinking and acting as if God still holds their sins against them—forgetting that, because God has taken their sins upon Himself, they are separated from those sins "as far as the east is from the west" (Ps. 103:12). They forget God's promise through Isaiah that one day He would wipe out the transgressions of believers "like a thick cloud" and their "sins like a heavy mist. Return to Me," He said, "for I have redeemed you" (Isa. 44:22). Even before the Messiah came and paid the price for redemption, God spoke of it as already having taken place. Depressed Christians forget that God looked down the corridors of time even before He fashioned the earth and placed the sins of His elect on the head of His Son, who took them an eternal distance away. He dismissed our sins before we were born, and they can never return.

Hundreds of years before Calvary, Micah proclaimed, "Who is a God like Thee, who pardons iniquity and passes over the rebellious act of the remnant of His possession? He does not retain His anger forever, because He delights in unchanging love. He will again have compassion on us; He will tread our iniquities under foot. Yes, Thou wilt cast all their sins into the depths of the sea" (Mic. 7:18-19).

To ancient Israel the distance from east to west and "the depths of the sea" represented infinity. God's **forgiveness** is infinite; it takes away **our trespasses** to the farthest reaches of eternal infinity.

In Shakespeare's *King Richard III* (5.3.194) the king laments,

> My conscience hath a thousand several tongues,
> And every tongue brings in a several tale,
> And every tale condemns me for a villain.

That is not true of Christians. When Jesus comes into our lives as Savior and Lord, He says to us what He said to the woman caught in the act of adultery, "Neither do I condemn you; go your way" (John 8:11). "There is therefore now no condemnation for those who are in Christ Jesus. For the law of the Spirit of life in Christ Jesus has set you free from the law of sin and of death" (Rom. 8:1-2).

Forgiveness in Jesus Christ is undeserved, but it is free and it is complete. Those who have Him have freedom from sin, now and throughout eternity. In Christ our sins—past, present, and future—"are forgiven . . . for His name's sake" (1 John 2:12; cf. Eph. 4:32; Col. 2:13). They were forgiven countless ages before we committed them and will remain forgiven forever.

Because we continue to sin, we need the continued forgiveness of cleansing; but we do not need the continued forgiveness of redemption. Jesus told Peter, "He who has bathed needs only to wash his feet, but is completely clean" (John 13:10). Even though we continue to sin, Jesus "is faithful and righteous to forgive us our sins and to cleanse us from all unrighteousness" (1 John 1:9). He forgives all our sins in the sweeping grace of salvation. That does not mean we will no longer sin, nor that when we do our sins have no harmful effect. They have a profound effect on our growth, joy, peace, usefulness, and ability to have intimate and rich communion with the Father. Thus the believer is called on to ask for forgiveness daily so that he may enjoy not just the general forgiveness of redemption, but the specific forgiveness of daily cleansing, which brings fellowship and usefulness to their maximum. That is the issue in our Lord's teaching on prayer recorded in Matthew 6:12, 14-15.

There are no second class Christians, no deprived citizens of God's kingdom or children in His family. Every sin of every believer is forgiven forever. God knows how we were, how we now live, and how we will live the rest of our lives. He sees everything about us in stark-naked reality. Yet He says, "I am satisfied with you because I am satisfied with My Son, to whom you belong. When I look at you, I see Him, and I am pleased."

Because God accepts every believer as He accepts His own Son, every believer ought to accept himself in the same way. We do not accept ourselves for what we are in ourselves any more than God accepts us for that reason. We accept ourselves as forgiven and as righteous because that is what God Himself declares us to be. To think otherwise is not a sign of humility but of arrogance, because to think otherwise is to put our own judgment above God's Word and to belittle the redemption price paid for us by His own beloved Son. A Christian who denigrates himself and doubts full forgiveness denies the work of God and denigrates a child of God. If we matter to God, we certainly ought to matter to ourselves.

A person may have many friends in high places. He may know presidents, kings, governors, senators, and world leaders of every sort. But such friendships pale beside that of the most obscure Christian, who not only is a friend but a child of the Creator of the universe.

Philip Bliss wrote,

> I am so glad that our Father in heav'n
> Tells of His love in the Book He has giv'n.
> Wonderful things in the Bible I see;
> This is the dearest, that Jesus loves me.
>
> Oh, if there's only one song I can sing,
> When in His beauty I see the Great King,
> This shall my song in eternity be:
> "Oh, what a wonder that Jesus loves me!"

The vastness and comprehensiveness of our **forgiveness** is seen in Paul's statement that it is **according to the riches of His grace**. God's grace—like His love, holiness, power, and all His other attributes—is boundless. It is far beyond our ability to comprehend or describe, yet we know it is **according to the riches of** that infinite **grace** that He provides forgiveness.

If you were to go to a multimillionaire and ask him to contribute to a worthy ministry, and he gave you a check for twenty-five dollars, he would only be giving *out of* his riches. Many poor people give that much. But if, instead, he gave you a check for fifty thousand dollars, he would be giving *according to* his riches.

That is a small picture of God's generosity. His **forgiveness** not only is given **according to the riches of His grace** but is **lavished upon us**. We need never worry that our sin will outstrip God's gracious forgiveness. "Where sin increased," Paul assures us, "grace abounded all the more" (Rom. 5:20). Our heavenly Father does not simply give us subsistence forgiveness that will barely cover our sins if we are careful not to overdo. We *cannot* sin beyond God's grace, because as wicked and extensive as our sins might be or become, they will never approach the greatness of His grace. His **forgiveness** is infinite, and He lavishes it without measure upon those who trust in His Son. We therefore not only can enjoy future glory with God but present fellowship with Him as well.

Wisdom and Insight. The second result of redemption for the believer is his being given **wisdom and insight.** *Sophia* (**wisdom**) emphasizes understanding of ultimate things—such as life and death, God and man, righteousness and sin, heaven and hell, eternity and time. Paul is speaking of wisdom concerning the things of God. *Phronēsis* (**insight**), on the other hand, emphasizes practical understanding, comprehension of the needs, problems, and principles of everyday living. It is spiritual prudence in the handling of daily affairs.

God not only forgives us—taking away the sin that corrupts and distorts our lives—but also gives us all the necessary equipment to understand Him and to walk through the world day by day in a way that reflects His will and is pleasing to Him. He generously gives us the wherewithal both to understand His Word and to know how to obey it.

In Jesus Christ, God takes us into His confidence. "We do speak wisdom among those who are mature," Paul said; it is "a wisdom, however, not of this age, nor of the rulers of this age, who are passing away; but we speak God's wisdom in a mystery, the hidden wisdom, which God predestined before the ages to our glory. . . . Now we have received, not the spirit of the world, but the Spirit who is from God, that we might know the things freely given to us by God" (1 Cor. 2:6-7, 12). He concluded that amazing passage by declaring, "we have the mind of Christ" (v. 16).

The French philosopher André Maurois said, "The universe is indifferent. Who created it? Why are we on this puny mud-heap, spinning in infinite space? I have not the slightest idea, and I am convinced that no one has the least idea."

It is not surprising that those who do not even recognize that God exists, much less trust and serve Him, do not have the least idea of what life, the universe, and eternity are all about. Jesus said, "I praise Thee, O Father, Lord of heaven and earth, that Thou didst hide these things from the wise and intelligent and didst reveal them to babes" (Matt. 11:25). James said, "If any of you lacks wisdom, let him ask of God, who gives to all men generously and without reproach, and it will be given to him" (James 1:5). When God takes away sin, He does not leave us in a spiritual, moral, and mental vacuum where we must then work things out for ourselves. He lavishes **wisdom and insight** on us according to the riches of His grace just as He lavishes forgiveness on us according to those riches.

25

THE REDEMPTIVE REASON

according to His kind intention which He purposed in Him with a view to an administration suitable to the fulness of the times, that is, the summing up of all things in Christ, things in the heavens and things upon the earth. (1:9b-10)

Why has God done so much for us? Why has He blessed us with every spiritual blessing, chosen us in Christ before the foundation of the world, made us holy and blameless, predestined us to adoption as His children, redeemed us through His blood, and lavishly given us forgiveness, wisdom, and insight according to the infinite riches of His grace?

God redeems men in order that He might gather everything to Himself. The time of that gathering will be the millennial kingdom, which will be **an administration suitable to the fulness of the times.** When the completion of history comes, the kingdom arrives, eternity begins again, and the new heaven and new earth are established, there will be a **summing up of all things in Christ, things in the heavens and things upon the earth.** Jesus Christ is the goal of history, which finds its resolution in Him. The paradise lost in Adam is restored in Christ.

At that time, "at the name of Jesus every knee [will] bow, of those who are in heaven, and on earth, and under the earth, and . . . every tongue [will] confess that Jesus Christ is Lord, to the glory of God the Father" (Phil. 2:10-11). Christ will gather the entire universe into unity (see Ps. 2; Heb. 1:8-13). At the present time the universe is anything but unified. It is corrupted, divided, and splintered. Satan is now "the ruler of this world," but in that day he "shall be cast out" (John 12:31). He and his demon angels will be thrown into the pit during the Millennium, released for a short while, and then cast into the lake of fire for all eternity (Rev. 20:3, 10).

When every trace of evil has been disposed of, God will establish an incomparable unity in Himself of all things that remain. That is the inevitable goal of the universe.

Macbeth pessimistically declared that history is "a tale told by an idiot, full of sound and fury, signifying nothing" (Shakespeare, *Macbeth,* 5.5.19).

Apart from the wisdom and insight God provides His children, such a hopeless conclusion is inescapable. But history belongs to God, not to the puny plans of man or the perverse power of Satan. History is written and directed by its Creator, who will see it through to the fulfillment of His own ultimate purpose— **the summing up of all things in Christ.** He designed His great plan in the ages past; He now sovereignly works it out according to His divine will; and in **the fulness of the times** He will complete and perfect it in His Son, in whom it will forever operate in righteous harmony and glorious newness along with all **things in the heavens and things upon the earth.**

Divine Inheritance Guaranteed

4

In Him also we have obtained an inheritance, having been predestined according to His purpose who works all things after the counsel of His will, to the end that we who were the first to hope in Christ should be to the praise of His glory. In Him, you also, after listening to the message of truth, the gospel of your salvation—having also believed, you were sealed in Him with the Holy Spirit of promise, who is given as a pledge of our inheritance, with a view to the redemption of God's own possession, to the praise of His glory. (1:11-14)

Over the years I have had many conversations with people—young and old, educated and uneducated, privileged and underprivileged—who face life with a sense of foreboding, wondering if they will ever find fulfillment for their lives. They wonder if they will turn out to be what they could be if everything went just right. They wonder if life really has the potential to be wonderful, meaningful, and fulfilling—and, if it does, whether they can discover and achieve that potential.

Some years ago at a Christian camp in the mountains I met a young man with a severely withered arm and leg. He always stayed at the back of the group or in a corner by himself, never participating with the other campers. On the second day I went over to him, introduced myself, and asked his name. He responded with a bitter scowl, pulled up the sleeve that covered his deformed arm, and said, "Look what God did to me." After silently praying for God's wisdom I said, "Would you like to know something? That's not you." "What do you mean its not me?" he retorted. "It's just the house you live in," I said; "that's all. It's a very temporary house; but you are a forever person. God offers a forever plan for you and also a new and eternal body for your future." "You're kidding," he said. "No, I'm not kidding," I replied, and then shared the gospel with him.

He gave his heart to Jesus Christ, and his attitude and outlook immediately changed. One of the first things he did was ask me to play a game of Ping-Pong with him. He seemed in those moments not to be embarrassed or bitter about his physical handicap. As soon as Jesus Christ took control of his life he realized God had some things for him that far surpassed what, from his human perspective, had seemed to be so terribly important and valuable. When he knew he was part of God's eternal plan and had received God's eternal promises, his perspective dramatically changed.

In this passage Paul shows us the awesome and wonderful potential of Christian believers. That for which every person in one way or another yearns, the Christian already possesses or is one day assured of possessing. The apostle gives us a glimpse of the glorious blessings God has planned for and promised to those who come to Him through His Son, Jesus Christ.

It is human nature to break promises. Governments make and break promises. Advertisers and politicians make and break promises. Employers and employees, preachers and church members, parents and children, husbands and wives, and friends and relatives all make promises to each other which often are broken. Some are made with the best of intentions, and some are made in order to deceive and exploit. But all of us find ourselves both making and receiving promises that, for whatever reason, do not materialize.

We can be eternally thankful that God's promises are not like ours. Every promise He makes, He keeps. The promises Paul mentions here that our heavenly Father makes to His children not only are wonderful and exciting but absolute and certain. As the writer of Hebrews tells us, "He who promised is faithful" (Heb. 10:23). Like Abraham, every believer should be fully assured that what God promises He is able and certain to perform (Rom. 4:21). Ours is a God who will not and cannot lie (Titus 1:2).

At the completion of this longest sentence in the Bible (Eph. 1:3-14), in which Paul pours out his heart in praise to God for His immeasurable grace, he presents to us the Father's guarantee of His divine promise to His children. They are certain to receive the full, undiminished inheritance of Jesus Christ. Just as we have been blessed "with every spiritual blessing," chosen "in Him before the foundation of the world," "predestined . . . to adoption as sons," given "redemption through His blood," and shown "the mystery of His will" (vv. 3-5, 7, 9)—so we have also **obtained an inheritance**.

Our inheritance is the aspect of salvation which is primarily future. We were elected, or predestined, before the world or time existed; we have been redeemed in this present age; and we will receive our completed inheritance in the ages to come, when we enter fully into the Father's eternal heavenly kingdom.

Here we are shown the ground, the guarantee, and the goal of our incomparable inheritance in Jesus Christ.

THE GROUND OF OUR INHERITANCE

In Him also we have obtained an inheritance, having been predestined according to His purpose who works all things after the counsel of His will, to the end that we who were the first to hope in Christ should be to the praise of His glory. In Him, you also, after listening to the message of truth, the gospel of your salvation—having also believed, (1:11-13a)

In Him fits more appropriately at the beginning of verse 11 than at the end of verse 10. But in either place the phrase clearly refers to Jesus Christ (v. 10), who is the ground or source of our divine **inheritance.** Apart from Jesus Christ, the only ultimate and eternal thing a person can receive from God is condemnation. God bestows sunshine, rain, and many other good things on all men, the righteous and unrighteous alike (Matt. 5:45). But His spiritual blessings are bestowed only on those who are **in Him** (cf. vv. 1, 3-4, 6-7, 10). "There is salvation in no one else; for there is no other name under heaven that has been given among men, by which we must be saved" (Acts 4:12).

In Romans 6, Paul gives the spiritual biography of every believer. "Do you not know," he begins, "that all of us who have been baptized into Christ Jesus have been baptized into His death?" (v. 3). "Therefore," he continues, "we have been buried with Him through baptism into death, in order that as Christ was raised from the dead through the glory of the Father, so we too might walk in newness of life. For if we have become united with Him in the likeness of His death, certainly we shall be also in the likeness of His resurrection" (vv. 4-5). By a marvelous miracle that only God can comprehend, every believer has been to the cross of Calvary, been nailed there spiritually with the Savior, and been buried and raised with Him. Jesus Christ not only was crucified, buried, and raised *for* every believer but *with* every believer. Not only that, but "we know that, when He appears, we shall be like Him, because we shall see Him just as He is" (1 John 3:2). On that glorious day we will finally and fully "become conformed to the image of His Son" (Rom. 8:29).

We have obtained an inheritance translates a single compound word in the Greek *(eklērōthēmen).* When something in the future was so certain that it could not possibly fail to happen, the Greeks would often speak of it as if it had already occurred (as here, where Paul uses the aorist passive indicative).

In chapter two Paul uses a similar Greek tense (aorist active indicative) to speak of God's having "seated us with Him in the heavenly places" (v. 6), although the apostle and those to whom he wrote had not yet entered into that glorious experience. Their dwelling eternally with the Lord was just as certain as if they were already in heaven.

The passive form of the verb in 1:11a allows for two possible renderings, both of which are consistent with other Scripture. It can be translated "were made an inheritance" or, as here, **have obtained an inheritance.** The first rendering would indicate that **we,** that is, believers, are *Christ's* inheritance. Jesus repeatedly spoke of believers as gifts that the Father had given Him (John 6:37, 39; 10:29; 17:2, 24; etc.). Jesus won us at Calvary—as the spoils of His victory over Satan, sin, and death—and we now belong to Him. "'And they will be Mine,' says the Lord of hosts, 'on the day that I prepare My own possession'" (Mal. 3:17). From eternity past the Father planned and determined that every person who would trust in His Son for salvation would be given to His Son as a possession, a glorious inheritance.

Translated the other way, however, this word means just the opposite: it is *believers* who receive the inheritance. Peter speaks of our having been "born again to a living hope through the resurrection of Jesus Christ from the dead, to obtain an inheritance which is imperishable and undefiled and will not fade away, reserved in heaven for [us]" (1 Pet. 1:3-4).

Both of the translations are therefore grammatically and theologically legitimate. Throughout Scripture believers are spoken of as belonging to God, and He is spoken of as belonging to them. The New Testament speaks of our being in Christ and of His being in us, of our being in the Spirit and of His being in us. "The one who joins himself to the Lord is one spirit with Him" (1 Cor. 6:17). Paul could therefore say, "For me, to live is Christ" (Phil. 1:21).

The practical side of that truth is that, because we are identified with Christ, our lives should be identified with His life (cf. 1 John 2:6). We are to love as He loved, help as He helped, care as He cared, share as He shared, and sacrifice our own interests and welfare for the sake of others just as He did. Like our Lord, we are in the world to lose our lives for others.

Although either rendering of *eklērōthēmen* can be supported, Paul's emphasis in Ephesians 1:3-14 makes the second translation more appropriate here: **we have obtained an inheritance.** Our inheritance with Christ is yet another of the amazing and magnificent blessings with which the Father has blessed us in the Son. As Paul makes clear in verse 3, our inheritance includes "every spiritual blessing in the heavenly places in Christ." In Jesus Christ, believers inherit every promise God has ever made. Peter tells us that God's "divine power has granted to us everything pertaining to life and godliness" and "has granted to us His precious and magnificent promises" (2 Pet. 1:3-4). Paul says with absolute inclusiveness, "For as many as may be the promises of God, in Him they are yes" (2 Cor. 1:20).

Our every conceivable need is met by God's gracious provision in accordance with His divine promises. We are promised peace, love, grace, wisdom, eternal life, joy, victory, strength, guidance, power, mercy, forgiveness, righteousness, truth, fellowship with God, spiritual discernment, heaven, eternal riches, glory—those and every other good thing that comes from God. Paul says, "The world or life or death or things present or things to come; all things belong to you, and you belong to Christ, and Christ belongs to God" (1 Cor. 3:22-23). Because we have been made joint heirs with Christ, we are guaranteed possession of everything He possesses. We are "heirs of God and fellow heirs with Christ" (cf. Rom. 8:17).

Jesus Christ is therefore the ground of the **inheritance** that **we have obtained**. Paul first shows that **inheritance** from the divine perspective and then from the human.

THE DIVINE PERSPECTIVE

having been predestined according to His purpose who works all things after the counsel of His will, to the end that we . . . should be to the praise of His glory. (1:11, 12b)

Our discussion here will follow the order of the Greek text of verse 12, in which (as reflected in the King James Version) **should be to the praise of His glory** precedes "who were the first to hope in Christ" (which phrase will be discussed below in relation to the human perspective).

God's perspective on our inheritance in Christ is here shown in His predestination, His power, and His preeminence.

God's predestination. **having been predestined according to His purpose.** As Christians we are what we are because of what God chose to make us before any man was created. From eternity past He declared that every elect sinner—though vile, rebellious, useless, and deserving only of death—who trusted in His Son would be made as righteous as the One in whom they put their trust. As Paul has already established, "He chose us in Him before the foundation of the world, that we should be holy and blameless before Him" (v. 4).

William Hendriksen's comment on this passage is helpful and concise:

> Neither fate nor human merit determines our destiny. The benevolent purpose— that we should be holy and faultless (verse 4), sons of God (verse 5), destined to glorify him forever (verse 6, cf. verses 12 and 14)—is fixed, being part of a larger, universe-embracing plan. Not only did God *make* this plan that includes absolutely all things that ever take place in heaven, on earth, and in hell; past, present, *and even the future,* pertaining to both believers and unbelievers, to angels and devils, to physical as well as spiritual energies and units of existence both large and small; he also *wholly carries it out.* His providence in time is as comprehensive as is his decree from eternity. (*New Testament Commentary: Exposition of Ephesians* [Grand Rapids: Baker, 1967], p. 88)

God's power. **who works all things after the counsel of His will. Works** is from *energeō,* from which we get such English words as *energy, energetic,* and *energize.* God's creating and energizing are one in His divine mind. When He spoke each part of the world into existence it began immediately to operate precisely as He had planned it to do. Unlike the things we make, God's creations do not have to be redesigned, prototyped, tested, fueled, charged, and the like. They are not only created ready to function, they are created functioning.

Energizing is an indispensable part of His creative plan and work. Because in His wondrous grace God chose us to be His children, citizens of His kingdom, and joint heirs with His Son, He will bring all of that to pass. "For I am confident of this very thing," Paul declared, "that He who began a good work in you will perfect it until the day of Christ Jesus" (Phil. 1:6). God works out what He plans. He energizes every believer with all the power necessary for his spiritual completion. It is not sufficient to think that God only makes the plan. He also makes it work out.

God's preeminence. **should be to the praise of His glory.** As mentioned above, this phrase begins verse twelve in the Greek text, and that order fits logically with what Paul has been saying about God's perspective on our inheritance. The Lord's perspective and working are seen in His predestination, in His power, and, as we see here, in His preeminence. Man is redeemed for the purpose of restoring the divine image marred by sin. Because God's intention in creating men was that they should bear the divine image, salvation's goal is creation's goal. God desires creatures that will give Him glory by both proclaiming and displaying His glory. For that reason He redeems men.

Scripture always presents salvation from God's side, in order that He should have full credit. In our humanly-oriented society, God's wanting exclusive credit seems inappropriate—but only because men have no concept of His greatness, holiness, and glory. What views they may have of Him are simply projections of themselves. The praise and glory that men so much desire are totally undeserved, and their motives for wanting them are purely sinful. But God seeks glory for the right reasons and because He alone is deserving of it. His seeking glory is a holy desire of which He is supremely and singly worthy.

Our predestined salvation, including our attendant eternal and boundless blessings, are therefore designed that they **should be to the praise of His glory.**

THE HUMAN PERSPECTIVE

to the end that we who were first to hope in Christ . . . In Him, you also, after listening to the message of truth, the gospel of your salvation—having also believed, (12a, 13a)

In the Greek text this passage is continuous, the last part of verse 12 leading directly into verse 13. Here we see the believer's divine inheritance in Jesus Christ from our own human perspective. Throughout Scripture there is tension between God's sovereignty and man's will, a tension that, in his limited and imperfect knowledge, man is incapable of fully reconciling. As with all the other antinomies and paradoxes in God's Word, our responsibility is to believe both sides of them without reservation, just as they are revealed. We know the truths are in perfect accord in God's mind, and that knowledge should satisfy us.

Someone has pictured the divine and human sides of salvation in this way: When you look toward heaven you see a sign that reads, "Whosoever will may come," and after you enter heaven you look back to that same sign and read on the other side, "Chosen in Him before the foundation of the world."

Whatever God's reasons for designing such humanly irreconcilable truths, we should thank and praise Him for them. For the very reason that they are completely true while seeming to be contradictory, we are humbled in His presence as we stand in awe of that which to us is incomprehensible. To the trusting believer such truths are but further evidence that Scripture is God's doing, and not man's.

To the end that we who were first to hope in Christ is the first statement given here about the human side of our divine inheritance in Christ. The Greek has a definite article before **Christ**, and a more literal translation is **hope in** *the* **Christ**. The meaning is not changed, but the definite article emphasizes the uniqueness of our hope: it is in *the* one and only Savior, Jesus **Christ**. It also stresses the idea that the apostles and other first-generation Jewish believers were the first to receive the Messiah.

A rich factor in man's believing the gospel is the **hope** He is given in His Savior and Lord. Though Paul mentions **hope** before belief in this passage, the chronological as well as theological order is faith and then hope. In this context, however, **hope** is used primarily as a synonym for faith. The **first to hope in Christ** were the first to believe in Him.

Therefore, Paul continues, **In Him, you also, after listening to the message of truth, the gospel of your salvation—having also believed,** . . . As the apostle explains in his letter to the Romans, "Faith comes from hearing, and hearing by the word of Christ" (10:17). Faith comes from a positive response **to the message of truth, the gospel** (cf. Gal. 1:6-9)—the good news that God has provided a way of salvation through the atoning work of His Son, Jesus Christ. To "as many as received Him, to them He gave the right to become children of God, even to those who believe in His name" (John 1:12). Man-made systems of religion, which rely on ritual or works or both, not only do not lead to God but can become great barriers to finding Him. The only way to come is through His Son. "For with the heart man believes, resulting in righteousness, and with the mouth he confesses, resulting in salvation. For the Scripture says, 'Whoever believes in Him will not be disappointed'" (Rom. 10:10-11). **Having also believed** not only stresses the means by which salvation is appropriated but also the uniformity of such means by the use of **also**.

Faith is man's response to God's elective purpose. God's choice of men is election; men's choice of God is faith. In election God gives His promises, and by faith men receive them.

THE GUARANTEE OF OUR INHERITANCE

you were sealed in Him with the Holy Spirit of promise, who is given as a pledge of our inheritance, (1:13b-14a)

Men have always wanted assurances. Because the promises of other men are so often unreliable, we demand oaths, sworn affidavits, surety bonds, guarantees, warranties, and many other such means of trying to assure that what is promised is received.

God's simple word should be sufficient for us, but in His graciousness He makes His promises even more certain—if that were possible—by giving us His own guarantees. Here the Lord guarantees His promises with His seal and with His pledge. This is reminiscent of Hebrews 6:13-18, in which God gives His promise of blessing and then confirms it with an oath to provide what the Holy Spirit calls "strong encouragement" (v. 18) to all who hope in Christ.

GOD'S SEAL

Because we do not directly and immediately receive the fullness of all God's promises when we first believe (since it is "reserved in heaven for us," 1 Pet. 1:3-4), we may sometimes be tempted to doubt our salvation and wonder about the ultimate blessings that are supposed to accompany it. While we are still in this life our redemption is not complete, because we still await "the redemption of our body" (Rom. 8:23). Because we have not yet received full possession of our inheritance, we may question its reality or at least its greatness.

As one means of guaranteeing His promises to those who have received Jesus Christ, God has **sealed** [them] **in Him with the Holy Spirit of promise**. Every believer is given the very **Holy Spirit** of God the moment he trusts in Christ. "You are not in the flesh but in the Spirit, if indeed the Spirit of God dwells in you," Paul declares (Rom. 8:9a). Conversely, he goes on to say, "If anyone does not have the Spirit of Christ, he does not belong to Him" (v. 9b). Incredibly, the body of every true Christian is actually "a temple of the Holy Spirit who is in [him]" (1 Cor. 6:19).

When a person becomes a Christian, the Holy Spirit takes up residence in his life. Life in Jesus Christ is different because the Spirit of God is now within. He is there to empower us, equip us for ministry, and function through the gifts He has given us. The Holy Spirit is our Helper and Advocate. He protects and encourages us. He also guarantees our inheritance in Jesus Christ. "The Spirit Himself bears witness with our spirit that we are children of God, and if children, heirs also, heirs of God and fellow heirs with Christ" (Rom. 8:16-17). The Spirit of God is our securing force, our guarantee.

The sealing of which Paul speaks here refers to an official mark of identification that was placed on a letter, contract, or other important document. The seal usually was made from hot wax, which was placed on the document and then impressed with a signet ring. The document was thereby officially identified with and under the authority of the person to whom the signet belonged.

That is the idea behind our being **sealed in Him** [Christ] **with the Holy Spirit of promise**. The seal of God's Spirit in the believer signifies four primary things: security, authenticity, ownership, and authority.

Security. In ancient times the seal of a king, prince, or noble represented security and inviolability. When Daniel was thrown into the lion's den, King Darius, along with his nobles, placed their seals on the stone placed over the entrance to the den, "so that nothing might be changed in regard to Daniel" (Dan. 6:17). Any person but the king who broke or disturbed that seal would likely have forfeited his life. In a similar way the tomb where Jesus was buried was sealed. Fearing that Jesus' disciples might steal His body and falsely claim His resurrection, the Jewish leaders obtained Pilate's permission to place a seal on the stone and to guard it with soldiers (Matt. 27:62-66).

In an infinitely greater way, the Holy Spirit secures each believer, marking him with His own inviolable seal.

Authenticity. When King Ahab tried unsuccessfully to get Naboth to sell or trade his vineyard, Queen Jezebel volunteered to get the vineyard her way. "So she wrote letters in Ahab's name and sealed them with his seal" and sent the letters to various nobles who lived in Naboth's city, demanding that they arrange false accusations of blasphemy and treason against him. The nobles did as they were instructed, and Naboth was stoned to death because of the false charges. The king then simply confiscated the vineyard he had so strongly coveted (1 Kings 21:6-16). Despite the deceptions contained in the letters Jezebel sent, the letters themselves were authentically from the king, because they were sent with his approval and marked with his seal. The seal was his signature.

When God gives us His Holy Spirit, it is as if He stamps us with a seal that reads, "This person belongs to Me and is an authentic citizen of My divine kingdom and member of My divine family."

Ownership. While Jerusalem was under seige by Nebuchadnezzar and Jeremiah was under arrest by King Zedekiah for prophesying against the king and the nation, the Lord gave special instructions to His prophet. Jeremiah was told to buy some land in Anathoth for which he had redemption rights. The contract was agreed on, and the stipulated payment was made in the court of the palace guard before the required number of witnesses. In the presence of the witnesses the deed was signed and sealed, establishing Jeremiah as the new legal owner of the property (Jer. 32:10).

When the Holy Spirit seals believers, He marks them as God's divine possessions, who from that moment on entirely and eternally belong to Him. The Spirit's seal declares the transaction of salvation as divinely official and final.

Authority. Even after Haman had been hanged for his wicked plot to defame and execute Mordecai, Queen Esther was distressed about the decree that Haman had persuaded King Ahasuerus to make that permitted anyone in his kingdom to attack and destroy the Jews. Because the king could not even himself revoke the decree that was marked with his own seal, he issued and sealed another decree that permitted and even encouraged the Jews to arm and defend themselves (Esther 8:8-12). In both cases the absolute authority of the decrees was represented in the king's seal. Those who possessed the sealed decree of the king had the king's delegated authority set forth in the decree.

When Christians are sealed with the Holy Spirit they are delegated to proclaim, teach, minister, and defend God's Word and His gospel with the Lord's own authority.

GOD'S PLEDGE

who is given as a pledge of our inheritance, (1:14a)

The Holy Spirit not only guarantees **our inheritance** in Jesus Christ with His seal but also with His **pledge**. An *arrabōn* **(pledge)** originally referred to a down payment or earnest money given to secure a purchase. Later it came to represent any sort of pledge or earnest. A form of the word even came to be used for engagement ring.

As believers, we have the Holy Spirit as the divine **pledge of our inheritance**, God's first installment of His guarantee that the fullness of the promised spiritual blessings "in the heavenly places in Christ" (v. 3) will one day be completely fulfilled. They are assured and guaranteed with an absolute certainty that only God could provide. The Holy Spirit is the church's irrevocable **pledge**, her divine engagement ring, as it were, that, as Christ's bride, she will never be neglected or forsaken (cf. 2 Cor. 1:22; 5:5).

THE GOAL OF OUR INHERITANCE

with a view to the redemption of God's own possession, to the praise of His glory. (1:14b)

Although our divine inheritance in Christ is a marvelous, awesome, and guaranteed promise to us from the Lord, it is not the primary purpose of our salvation. Our salvation and all of the promises, blessings, and privileges we gain through salvation are first of all bestowed **with a view to the redemption of God's own possession, to the praise of His glory.**

The great, overriding purpose of God's **redemption** of men is the rescuing of what is His **own possession**. All creation belongs to God, and in His infinite wisdom, love, and grace He chose to provide redemption for the fallen creatures He had made in His own image—for His own sake even more than for their sakes, because they do not belong to themselves but to Him.

As Paul has already twice declared (vv. 6, 12), God's ultimate goal in redeeming men is **the praise of His glory**. We are not saved and blessed for our own glory but for God's (cf. Isa. 43:20-21). When we glorify ourselves we rob God of that which is wholly His. He saved us to serve Him and to **praise** Him. We are saved to be restored to the intended divine purpose of creation—to bear the image of God and bring Him greater glory.

This is fully accomplished at the believer's glorification, when we receive full glory and redemption and are made the perfect possession of God.

Our Resources in Christ

5

For this reason I too, having heard of the faith in the Lord Jesus which exists among you, and your love for all the saints, do not cease giving thanks for you, while making mention of you in my prayers; that the God of our Lord Jesus Christ, the Father of glory, may give to you a spirit of wisdom and of revelation in the knowledge of Him. I pray that the eyes of your heart may be enlightened, so that you may know what is the hope of His calling, what are the riches of the glory of His inheritance in the saints, and what is the surpassing greatness of His power toward us who believe. These are in accordance with the working of the strength of His might which He brought about in Christ, when He raised Him from the dead, and seated Him at His right hand in the heavenly places, far above all rule and authority and power and dominion, and every name that is named, not only in this age, but also in the one to come. And He put all things in subjection under His feet, and gave Him as head over all things to the church, which is His body, the fulness of Him who fills all in all. (1:15-23)

In verses 3-14 Paul has set forth the amazing and unlimited blessings believers have in Jesus Christ, blessings that amount to our personal inheritance of all that belongs to Him. In the remainder of the chapter (vv. 15-23) Paul prays that the believers to whom he writes will come to fully understand and appreciate those blessings. In this prayer he focuses on believers' comprehension of their resources in their Lord and Savior, Jesus Christ. In verses 15-16 he praises them, and in verses 17-23 he makes petitions to God for them.

PRAISE FOR BELIEVERS

For this reason I too, having heard of the faith in the Lord Jesus which exists among you, and your love for all the saints, do not cease giving thanks for you, while making mention of you in my prayers; (1:15-16)

In light of their marvelous inheritance in Jesus Christ (**For this reason**), Paul now intercedes for the possessors of that treasure. As mentioned in the Introduction, these initially included not only the believers in Ephesus but probably those in all the churches of Asia Minor. It had been about four years since Paul ministered there, and he was now in prison. But from letters, as well as through personal reports from friends who visited him in prison, he had received considerable information from and about the churches. He **heard** two things that indicated the genuineness of their salvation, and for those two cardinal marks of a true Christian—faith in Christ and love for other Christians—he affectionately praises them. Those two dimensions of spiritual life are inseparable (cf. 1 John 2:9-11).

PRAISE FOR THEIR FAITH

the faith in the Lord Jesus which exists among you, (1:15*b*)

The emphasis here is on true saving belief, with the lordship of Jesus as the object of that belief. Some Christians, perhaps intending to protect the gospel from any taint of works righteousness, underplay Christ's lordship almost to the point of denying it. Others would like to accept the term **Lord** only as a reference to deity, not sovereignty. But such a separation is artificial, because deity implies sovereignty. The One who alone is God rules alone. Yet those who teach that a person must believe in Christ as sovereign Lord in order to be saved are sometimes described derisively as "lordship salvationists." The New Testament, however, does not separate Jesus as Savior from Jesus as Lord. He is both, or He is neither. Paul says, "If you confess with your mouth Jesus as Lord, and believe in your heart that God raised Him from the dead, you shall be saved" (Rom. 10:9; cf. Acts 16:31). Jesus becomes Savior when He is accepted as Lord. "For to this end," Paul explains later in Romans, "Christ died and lived again, that He might be Lord both of the dead and of the living" (14:9). Believers say—in fact, only believers can say—"Jesus is Lord" because they possess the Holy Spirit (1 Cor. 12:3), who was given to them when they were saved (Rom. 8:9). To receive Jesus as Savior but not as Lord would be to divide His nature in two. When we receive Him, we receive Him wholly as He is.

Granted, no person receives Jesus Christ with a full understanding of all He is or all He requires as Lord of those He saves. Many Christians come to Christ with only the barest idea of His sovereign deity or of what it means to belong to and submit to Him. But they are willing to submit (cf. Matt. 8:19-22; 9:9; 10:37-39; Luke 9:57-62), to give up all they are and have (cf. Matt. 13:44-46; 18:3-4; 19:16-26), and to leave all and follow Him (Matt. 19:27). Once they have come to Him, some Christians lose their first love for Him as Savior and resist obeying Him as Lord. But their lovelessness makes Him no less Savior, and their resistance makes Him no less Lord. Christ is not accepted in parts, first as Savior and later as Lord. Jesus the Savior is Jesus the Lord, and Jesus the Lord is Jesus the Savior. He does not exist in parts or relate to believers in parts. Awareness, appreciation, and obedience to Him as Savior and Lord change. When we are faithful to Him those things increase, and when we are unfaithful they diminish. But the *fact* of Jesus' lordship begins the same moment He becomes Savior, and neither His lordship nor His saviorhood changes for believers from that time through all eternity. All the commands of Christ, which are to be taught to all believers (Matt. 28:19-20), assume His sovereign right to give orders and to be obeyed. That is precisely why Paul calls salvation "the obedience of faith" (Rom. 1:5).

Paul is not praising the Ephesians for some later, supplemental act of faith but for the original faith that brought them to saving submission to the sovereign Lord. **The faith in the Lord Jesus which exists among you** refers to this same saving faith with which they entered the Christian life and in which they were continuing to live.

PRAISE FOR THEIR LOVE

and your love for all the saints, (15c)

A second mark of genuine salvation is **love for all the saints**, and because of such love Paul offers thanks for the Ephesian believers.

Christian love is indiscriminate; it does not pick and choose which believers it will love. Christ loves all believers, and they are precious to Him. By definition, therefore, Christian love extends to all Christians. To the extent that it does not, it is less than Christian. Paul calls for believers to be "maintaining the same love" (Phil. 2:2), which is to love all believers the same.

Sometimes we hear Christians say, "I love him in the Lord," which seems to imply that they have no personal affection for nor commitment to the needs of the individual. They extend a certain spiritualized kind of love only because the other person is a fellow believer. But that is not genuine love. To truly love a person in the Lord is to love him as the Lord loves him—genuinely and sacrificially.

"We know that we have passed out of death into life," John says, "because we love the brethren. He who does not love abides in death" (1 John 3:14).

Important as it is, sound theology is no substitute for love. Without love the best doctrine is like "a noisy gong or a clanging cymbal" (1 Cor. 13:1). True salvation goes from the head and heart of the believer out to other believers and out to the world to touch unbelievers in Christ's name. True salvation produces true love, and true love does "not love with word or with tongue, but in deed and truth" (1 John 3:18). Always in the New Testament true spiritual love is defined as an attitude of selfless sacrifice that results in generous acts of kindness done to others. It is far more than a feeling, an attraction or emotion. When the Lord had washed the feet of the proud and self-seeking disciples, He told them that what He had done for them was the example of how they were to love each other (John 13:34). John emphasizes the same truth: "We know love by this, that He laid down His life for us; and we ought to lay down our lives for the brethren. But whoever has the world's goods, and beholds his brother in need and closes his heart against him, how does the love of God abide in him? Little children, let us not love with word or with tongue, but in deed and truth" (1 John 3:16-18).

That is the sort of love the Ephesian Christians then had **for all the saints.** Sadly, however, their love did not last. They kept the faith pure and persevered in it. Yet in His letter to the seven churches of Asia Minor the Lord says of the church at Ephesus, "I have this against you, that you have left your first love" (Rev. 2:2-4). They had lost the great love for Christ and their fellow believers for which only a few decades earlier Paul had so warmly praised them.

Faith and love must be kept in balance. Many monks, hermits, and countless others throughout the history of the church have endeavored to keep their faith pure but have not reached out to others in love as the Lord commands every believer to do. They often become heresy hunters, eager to tear down what is wrong but doing little to build up what is good, full of criticism but deficient in love.

It is unfortunate that some Christians have a loveless kind of faith. Because it is loveless there is reason to doubt that such faith is even genuine. True faith cannot exist apart from true love. We cannot love the Lord Jesus without loving those whom He loves. "Whoever believes that Jesus is the Christ is born of God; and whoever loves the Father loves the child born of Him" (1 John 5:1).

The Christians to whom Paul wrote his Ephesian letter had the right balance, and it was for their great faith and their great love that the apostle assured them, **I . . . do not cease giving thanks for you, while making mention of you in my prayers.**

PETITION FOR BELIEVERS

that the God of our Lord Jesus Christ, the Father of glory, may give to you a spirit of wisdom and of revelation in the knowledge of Him. I pray that the eyes of your heart may be enlightened, so that you may know what is the hope of His calling, what are the riches of the glory of His inheritance in the saints, and what is the surpassing greatness of His power toward us who believe. These are in

accordance with the working of the strength of His might which He brought about in Christ, when He raised Him from the dead, and seated Him at His right hand in the heavenly places, far above all rule and authority and power and dominion, and every name that is named, not only in this age, but also in the one to come. And He put all things in subjection under His feet, and gave Him as head over all things to the church, which is His body, the fulness of Him who fills all in all. (1:17-23)

The remainder of the chapter is a petition in which Paul prays for God to give believers true comprehension and appreciation of who they are in Jesus Christ, in order that they might begin to have some idea of how magnificent and unlimited are the blessings that already belonged to them in their Lord and Savior. The petition is directed to **the God of our Lord Jesus Christ, the Father of glory**, a designation of God which links God the Father to Christ the Son in terms of essential nature (see also Rom. 15:6; Eph. 1:3a, 17a; 2 Cor. 1:3; Phil. 2:9-11; 1 Pet. 1:3; 2 John 3). The One to whom all **glory** belongs is the same in essence as the **Lord Jesus Christ**. For the second time in three verses Christ is called Lord (see v. 15).

In essence Paul prayed that the Ephesians would be spared from frantically searching for what was already theirs, but rather would see that the great God who is their God is the source of all they need and has it ready for them if they are open to receive it. Such a receptive attitude requires that God Himself **give to you a spirit of wisdom and of revelation in the knowledge of Him.**

Warren Wiersbe tells the story of how William Randolph Hearst once read of an extremely valuable piece of art, which he decided he must add to his extensive collection. He instructed his agent to scour the galleries of the world to find the masterpiece he was determined to have at any price. After many months of pains-taking search, the agent reported that the piece already belonged to Mr. Hearst and had been stored in one of his warehouses for many years.

It is tragic that many believers become entangled in a quest for something more in the Christian life, for something special, something extra that the "ordinary" Christian life does not possess. They talk of getting more of Jesus Christ, more of the Holy Spirit, more power, more blessings, a higher life, a deeper life—as if the resources of God were divinely doled out one at a time like so many pharmaceutical prescriptions or were unlocked by some spiritual combination that only an initiated few can know.

To say, "I want to get all of Jesus there is," implies that when we were saved Christ did not give us all of Himself, that He held some blessings in reserve to be parceled out to those who meet certain extra requirements.

Peter explicitly says, "His divine power has granted to us everything pertaining to life and godliness, through the true knowledge of Him who called us by His own glory and excellence" (2 Pet. 1:3). The New Testament teaching of salvation is that the new birth grants every believer everything in Christ. There is consequently no need and no justification in searching for anything more. Though it does not do so intentionally, such searching undermines the essence of God's revealed truth about salvation. The germ of this great truth is found in the words of the Preacher: "I know that everything God does will remain forever; there is nothing to add to it and there is nothing to take from it, for God has so worked that men should [reverence] Him" (Eccles. 3:14).

The Colossian church apparently had been troubled by that sort of philosophy, thinking they were missing something from God that had to be supplied by some act, ritual, or other requirement in addition to salvation. For some of the members the idea had turned into actual heresy, which was taught and promulgated in place of apostolic teaching.

They were being taught that a person needs Christ plus human philosophy, the same approach to the gospel seen in modern liberalism, neoorthodoxy, existentialism, and other theological-philosophical systems that appear under the guise of Christianity. Of such heresy Paul says, "See to it that no one takes you captive through philosophy and empty deception, according to the tradition of men, according to the elementary principles of the world, rather than according to Christ" (Col. 2:8).

The false teachers in Colossae also taught Christ plus legalism. They advocated observance of special days, feasts, and various rituals in order to attain higher spiritual standing and favor with God. Of this heresy Paul said, "Let no one act as your judge in regard to food or drink or in respect to a festival or a new moon or a Sabbath day—things which are a mere shadow of what is to come; but the substance belongs to Christ" (2:16-17).

A third error taught by the Colossian heretics involved both the sin of pride and the seeking of mystical experiences and visions to supplement the finished work of Christ's atoning sacrifice on the cross. What they taught as something more really brought something less, Paul warned, because it took away from Christ's perfect work. "Let no one keep defrauding you of your prize by delighting in self-abasement and the worship of the angels, taking his stand on visions he has seen, inflated without cause by his fleshly mind, and not holding fast to the head, from whom the entire body, being supplied and held together by the joints and ligaments, grows with a growth which is from God" (2:18-19).

A fourth error promoted in the Colossian church was asceticism, the belief that one can gain special favor and reward from God through extreme self-denial, forsaking of physical pleasure and comfort, and avoiding contact with the "common" people by living in isolated and austere situations. That error, even more than the others, feeds human pride. Under the name of suppressing the flesh, such ideas and practices actually stimulate it. As Paul points out, the teachings "Do not handle, do not taste, do not touch . . . are matters which have, to be sure, the appearance of wisdom in self-made religion and self-abasement and severe treatment of the body, but are of no value against fleshly indulgence" (2:21, 23).

Paul's counsel to the Colossian believers in response to those serious threats to the faith is introduced in 1:12, where he says that "the Father . . . has qualified us to share in the inheritance of the saints in light," and is summarized in

2:9-10—"For in Him [Christ] all the fulness of Deity dwells in bodily form, and in Him you have been made complete." All of God's fullness is in Jesus Christ, and He keeps back none of that fullness from believers. "In Him . . . we have been made complete," because we are sufficient, authorized saints (as the use of *hikanoō* [to qualify, make sufficient] in 1:12 proves). John gives a warning about the same problem in his first letter, saying, "These things I have written to you concerning those who are trying to deceive you. And as for you, the anointing which you received from Him abides in you, and you have no need for anyone to teach you; but as His anointing teaches you about all things, and is true and is not a lie, and just as it has taught you, you abide in Him" (1 John 2:26-27).

Yet today many Christians spend a great deal of time and effort vainly looking for blessings already available to them. They pray for God's light, although He has already supplied light in abundance through His Word. Their need is to follow the light they already have. They pray for strength, although His Word tells them they can do all things through Christ who strengthens them (Phil. 4:13). They pray for more love, although Paul says that God's own love is already poured out within their hearts through the Holy Spirit (Rom. 5:5). They pray for more grace, although the Lord says the grace He has already given is sufficient (2 Cor. 12:9). They pray for peace, although the Lord has given them His own peace, "which surpasses all comprehension" (Phil. 4:7). It is expected that we pray for such blessings if the tone of the prayer is one of seeking the grace to appropriate what is already given, rather than one of pleading for something we think is scarcely available or is reluctantly shared by God.

The Christian's primary need is for wisdom and obedience to appropriate the abundance of blessings the Lord has already given. Our problem is not lack of blessings, but lack of insight and wisdom to understand and use them properly and faithfully. Our blessings are so vast that the human mind cannot comprehend them. In our own minds we cannot fathom the riches we have in our position in Jesus Christ. Such things are totally beyond the human mind to grasp. Only the Holy Spirit Himself can search the deep things of the mind of God, and only the Spirit can bring them to our understanding. "Just as it is written," Paul says, "'Things which eye has not seen and ear has not heard, and which have not entered the heart of man, all that God has prepared for those who love Him.' For to us God revealed them through the Spirit; for the Spirit searches all things, even the depths of God. For who among men knows the thoughts of a man except the spirit of the man, which is in him? Even so the thoughts of God no one knows except the Spirit of God. Now we have received, not the spirit of the world, but the Spirit who is from God, that we might know the things freely given to us by God" (1 Cor. 2:9-12).

God's deeper truths cannot be seen with our eyes, heard with our ears, or comprehended by our reason or intuition. They are revealed only to those who love Him.

Every Christian has many specific needs—physical, moral, and spiritual—for which He must ask the Lord's help. But no Christian needs, or can have, more of the Lord or of His blessing and inheritance than he already has. That is why Paul tells us, as he told the Ephesian believers, not to seek more spiritual resources but to understand and use those we were given in absolute completeness the moment we received Christ.

Paul prays specifically that God **may give** the faculty of understanding so that we can know our resources, which he calls **a spirit of wisdom and of revelation in the knowledge of Him.**

The **spirit of wisdom** is given *through* the Holy Spirit, but this **spirit** does not refer to the Holy Spirit Himself, as some interpreters suggest. *Pneuma* (**spirit**) is anarthrous here, meaning that it has no article before it. In such cases the indefinite article is usually supplied in English, as in our text: *a* **spirit.** Believers already possess the Holy Spirit (Rom. 8:9), for whom their bodies are temples (1 Cor. 6:19). Nor does it seem that Paul was speaking of the human spirit, which every person already possesses (1 Cor. 2:11).

The basic meaning of *pneuma* (from which we get such English words as pneumatic and pneumonia) is breath or air, and from that meaning is derived the connotation of spirit. But like our English *spirit, pneuma* sometimes was used of a disposition, influence, or attitude—as in "He is in high spirits today." Jesus used the word in that sense in the first beatitude: "Blessed are the poor in spirit" (Matt. 5:3). He was not referring to the Holy Spirit or to the human spirit but to the spirit, or attitude, of humility.

Paul prayed for God to give the Ephesians a special disposition of **wisdom,** the fullness of godly knowledge and understanding of which the sanctified human mind is capable of receiving. "Let them know how much they possess in your Son," he says, in effect. "Give them a keen, rich, deep, strong understanding of their inheritance in Christ." He prays for the Holy Spirit to give their spirits the right **spirit of wisdom and of revelation in the knowledge of Him.**

Revelation, though used here as a synonym of **wisdom,** deals with God's imparting knowledge to us, whereas **wisdom** could emphasize our use of that knowledge. We must know and understand our position in the Lord before we are capable of serving Him. We must know what we have before we can satisfactorily use it. This additional **wisdom** goes beyond intellectual knowledge. It is far richer; and Paul desired that the Ephesian Christians, like those in Colossae, would "keep seeking the things above, where Christ is" (Col. 3:1).

In his praying for the Ephesian believers Paul asks God to give them **revelation** and **wisdom** in three particular areas of God's magnificent, incomparable truth. He prays for them to come to a clearer understanding of the greatness of God's plan, the greatness of His power, and the greatness of His Person.

UNDERSTANDING THE GREATNESS OF GOD'S PLAN

I pray that the eyes of your heart may be enlightened, so that you may know what is the hope of His calling, what are the riches of the glory of His inheritance in the saints, (1:18)

In most modern cultures, the **heart** is thought of as the seat of emotions and feelings. But most ancients—Hebrews, Greeks, and many others—considered the **heart** (Greek *kardia*) to be the center of knowledge, understanding, thinking, and wisdom. The New Testament also uses it in that way. The heart was considered to be the seat of the mind and will, and it could be taught what the brain could never know. Emotions and feelings were associated with the intestines, or bowels (Greek *splanchnon;* cf. Acts 1:18, where the term clearly refers to physical organs, with Col. 3:12; Philem. 7, 12, 20; and 1 John 3:17, where it refers to affections and feelings).

One cause of immaturity in the church at Corinth was reliance on feelings above knowledge. Many believers were more interested in doing what felt right than in doing what God declared to be right. Paul therefore told them, "Our mouth has spoken freely to you, O Corinthians, our heart *[kardia]* is opened wide. You are not restrained by us, but you are restrained in your own affections *[splanchnon]*. Now in a like exchange—I speak as to children—open wide to us also" (2 Cor. 6:11-13). The apostle said, in effect, "I can't take God's truth from my mind and give it to your minds, because your emotions get in the way." Instead of their emotions being controlled by God's truth, their emotions distorted their understanding of His truth.

Paul therefore prays for the minds of the Ephesians to **be enlightened**. Emotions have a significant place in the Christian life, but they are reliable only as they are guided and controlled by God's truth—which we come to know and understand through our minds. That is why we are to "let the word of Christ richly dwell within [us]" (Col. 3:16). When the Holy Spirit works in the believer's mind, He enriches it to understand divine truth that is deep and profound, and then relates that truth to life—including those aspects of life that involve our emotions.

While Jesus talked with the two disciples on the Emmaus road, their hearts (that is, their minds) burned within them; but it was not until "their eyes were opened [that] they recognized Him" (Luke 24:31-32). Before the Spirit enlightened them they had the information but not the understanding; what they knew was true, but they could not in the power of their own minds grasp the meaning and significance of it.

The first thing for which Paul prays is that believers **be enlightened** about the greatness of God's plan. In the most comprehensive of terms, the apostle asks that they be given understanding of **the hope of His calling** and **the riches of the glory of His inheritance in the saints**. He prays for God to enlighten them about the magnificent truths of election, predestination, adoption, redemption, forgiveness, wisdom and insight, inheritance, and sealing and pledge of the Holy Spirit about which he has just been instructing them (vv. 3-14).

Those truths summarize God's master plan for the redemption of mankind, His eternal plan to bring men back to Himself through His own Son, thereby making them His children. Now that they belonged to Christ by faith (v. 13), Paul's supreme desire was for the Ephesian believers to fully realize what their new

45

identity meant. "You were no afterthought of God," he says. "God not only chose to save you, but He chose to save you eons before you existed, eons before you would have opportunity by His grace to choose Him. That is who you are!"

Until we comprehend who we truly are in Jesus Christ, it is impossible to live an obedient and fulfilling life. Only when we know who we really are can we live like who we are. Only when we come to understand how our lives are anchored in eternity can we have the right perspective and motivation for living in time. Only when we come to understand our heavenly citizenship can we live obedient and productive lives as godly citizens on earth.

It is God's great plan that every believer one day "become conformed to the image of His Son" (Rom. 8:29). That is **the hope of His calling**—the eternal destiny and glory of the believer fulfilled in the coming kingdom. The fullness of that hope will be experienced when we receive the supreme **riches of the glory of His inheritance in the saints.** It is truth too magnificent for words to describe, which is why even God's own revelation requires the illumination of His Spirit in order for believers even to begin to understand the marvelous magnitude of the blessings of salvation that exist in the sphere of the saints.

Our being glorious children of God and joint heirs with Jesus Christ of all God possesses is the consummation and end of salvation promised from eternity past and held in hope until the future manifestation of Christ. There is nothing more to seek, nothing more to be given or received. We have it all now, and we will have it throughout eternity.

UNDERSTANDING THE GREATNESS OF GOD'S POWER

and what is the surpassing greatness of His power toward us who believe. These are in accordance with the working of the strength of His might which He brought about in Christ, when He raised Him from the dead, and seated Him at His right hand in the heavenly places, (1:19-20)

Paul's second request is for the Lord to give the Ephesian believers understanding of His great **power** that will bring them to their inheritance in glory. In verse 19 Paul uses four different Greek synonyms to emphasize the greatness of that power.

First is *dunamis* **(power)**, from which we get *dynamite* and *dynamo*. This **power** is only for Christians, for those **who believe.** Not only that, but it is all the power we are ever offered or could ever have. There could be no more, and it is foolish and presumptuous to ask for more. **The surpassing greatness** of God's **power** is given to every believer, not just to those who believe and then have a mystical experience, second blessing, or some other supposed additional work of grace. When we are saved we receive all of God's grace and all of His power, and that assures us of the realization of our eternal hope.

Second is *energeia* **(working),** the energizing force of the Spirit that empowers believers to live for the Lord. Third is *kratos* (**strength**), which may also be translated "dominion" (1 Tim. 6:16) or "power" (Heb. 2:14). Fourth is *ischus* (**might**), which carries the idea of endowed power or ability. In all those ways the Holy Spirit empowers God's children.

Paul did not pray for power to be given to believers. How could they have more than what they had? He prayed first of all that they be given a divine awareness of the power they possessed in Christ. Later in the letter (chaps. 4-6) he admonished them to employ that power in faithful living for their Lord.

We need not pray for power to evangelize, to witness the gospel to others. Believers already have that power. The gospel itself "is the power of God for salvation to everyone who believes" (Rom. 1:16). Writing to the Thessalonians, Paul reminded them, "Our gospel did not come to you in word only, but also in power and in the Holy Spirit and with full conviction" (1 Thess. 1:5).

We need not pray for power to endure suffering. As an introduction to mentioning the many afflictions he had endured for the Lord, Paul commented, "But we have this treasure in earthen vessels, that the surpassing greatness of the power may be of God and not from ourselves" (2 Cor. 4:7).

Nor do we need to pray for power to do God's will. "It is God who is at work in you," Paul assures us, "both to will and to work for His good pleasure" (Phil. 2:13). Paul accomplished his work for the Lord through the strength the Lord supplied, "striving according to His power, which mightily works within me" (Col. 1:29). Just before His ascension Jesus assured the disciples, "You shall receive power when the Holy Spirit has come upon you" (Acts 1:8), an enduement every believer receives at the time he is saved. God "is able to do exceeding abundantly beyond all that we ask or think, according to the power that works within us" (Eph. 3:20). To ask God for more power is an affront to His gracious love which already has provided us everything.

The supernatural **power . . . working . . . strength** and **might** with which God supplies every believer and with **which He will glorify every believer is that which He brought about in Christ, when He raised Him from the dead, and seated Him at His right hand in the heavenly places.** Later in the letter Paul deals with the matter of using God's power in His service (3:20), but his prayer here is that we understand the power of His keeping, His securing us and His fulfilling the marvelous hope which is ours in Christ. The resurrection and ascension power— the divine energy that lifted Christ from the grave to the earth, and from the earth to heaven—is the power that will lift us to glory.

At times all of us are tempted to doubt, to wonder if God can do a certain thing for us or through us or ultimately bring us into His presence. But when we look at **what He brought about in Christ,** at what He faithfully accomplished on behalf of His Son—and at His assurance that He will just as faithfully accomplish His work on our behalf (through **the surpassing greatness of His power toward us**)—what ground do we have for doubting? In light of such assurance, how can a Christian feel insecure, forsaken, or powerless? The same unlimited divine power that **raised Him from the dead** will raise us from the dead, and the same power that

seated Him at His right hand in the heavenly places will seat us there with Him. In the meanwhile, that resurrection power is at our disposal for living to His glory (Eph. 1:19-20; 3:20). It is so certain that this power will bring us to glory that Paul spoke as if it has already occurred, because it has already occurred in God's eternal plan (2:6).

UNDERSTANDING THE GREATNESS OF GOD'S PERSON

far above all rule and authority and power and dominion, and every name that is named, not only in this age, but also in the one to come. And He put all things in subjection under His feet, and gave Him as head over all things to the church, which is His body, the fulness of Him who fills all in all. (1:21-23)

Moving from Christ's might to His majesty, Paul's third request is for the Lord to give believers understanding of the greatness of His Person who secures and empowers them.

Once when Timothy was intimidated by criticism from fellow Christians, he understandably became discouraged. Paul wrote to him, "Remember Jesus Christ, risen from the dead, descendant of David, according to my gospel, for which I suffer hardship even to imprisonment as a criminal; but the word of God is not imprisoned. For this reason I endure all things for the sake of those who are chosen, that they also may obtain the salvation which is in Christ Jesus and with it eternal glory" (2 Tim. 2:8-10). "Remember the greatness of the Person who lives within you," Paul says. "He was raised from the dead and seated at God's right hand. He was born of the seed of David, as a man just like us. He identifies with us, understands us, and sympathizes with us."

Every Christian should continually have that focus. When we look at Him, our physical problems, psychological problems, and even spiritual problems will not loom so all-important before us. We not only will be better able to see our problems as they really are, but will then, and only then, have the right motivation and power to work them out. It is sad that we read and hear so much about the peripheral things of the Christian life and so little about the Person who is the source of Christian life. How much happier and more productive we are when our primary attention is on His purity, greatness, holiness, power, and majesty. Paul calls the Corinthians to gaze intently on His glory with the clear vision provided in the New Covenant, and thus be made like Him by the Holy Spirit (1 Cor. 3:18).

What great blessing we can have when we take time to set our own concerns and needs aside and simply focus on the Lord of glory, allowing the Holy Spirit to do in us what Paul asked Him to do in the Ephesians—give us deep understanding of the truth that our Lord is **far above all rule and authority and power and dominion, and every name that is named, not only in this age, but also in the one to come.** The terms rule (*archē*, meaning leader or first one), **authority** (*exousia*), **power** (*dunamis*), and **dominion** (*kuriotēs*, lordship) were traditional

Jewish terms to designate angelic beings of great rank and might. The point here is that the power of Christ applied in the believer's behalf cannot be overthrown or negated or defeated, because it far surpasses that of the hosts of Satan who design to defeat it.

It should be noted that the matter of the cosmic war between God and His angelic hosts and Satan and his demons is a matter of great importance in Scripture. Redemption is a demonstration of God's power before the angels (3:10). Our conflict is with these fallen angels, who endeavor to halt our efforts for God (6:12; cf. 1 Pet. 3:18-22, which shows Christ's triumph over those fallen angels, accomplished in His death). Satan and his hosts have endeavored to thwart the plan of God from the beginning and are the constant enemy of the work of the kingdom, but they are destined to be overthrown and eternally banished (Rev. 20:10-15).

Our Lord not only is above, but **far above**, everything and everyone else. He is above Satan and above Satan's world system. He is above the holy angels and the fallen angels, above saved people and unsaved people, for time and for eternity. He is above all names, titles, ranks, levels, powers, and jurisdictions in the universe. God **put all things in subjection under His feet** (a quote from Ps. 8:6; cf. Heb. 2:8). There is no limit on time, as Paul said Christ will be supreme **not only in this age, but also in the one to come**—that is, in the eternal kingdom of the Lord Jesus Christ (cf. 2:7).

Most importantly, as far as believers are concerned, God **gave Him as head over all things to the church, which is His body, the fulness of Him who fills all in all.** Christ not only is the **head** of the church but its **fulness.** Since He has such a unique and intimate relationship with the redeemed whom He loves, all His power will be used in their behalf to fulfill His loving purpose for them. He is completely over us and completely in us, our supreme Lord and supreme power. The church is **the fulness** or complement (*plērōma*) of Christ. As a head must have a body to manifest the glory of that head, so the Lord must have the church to manifest His glory (3:10). Jesus Christ is the only One for whom the word *incomparable* truly applies; yet in a thrilling and securing wonder, He has chosen us to display His incomparable majesty. We are guaranteed to come to glory in order that we might forever manifest His praise.

The incomparable Christ is incomplete until **the church, which is His body,** is complete. Jesus Christ **fills all in all**, giving His fulness to believers. But in God's wisdom and grace, believers, as **the church**, are also **the fulness of Him**. John Calvin said, "This is the highest honor of the church that until He is united to us, the Son of God reckons Himself in some measure incomplete. What consolation it is for us to learn that not until we are in His presence does He possess all His parts, nor does He wish to be regarded as complete."

The point of this great petition is that we might comprehend how secure we are in Christ and how unwavering and immutable is our hope of eternal inheritance. The power of glorification is invincible and is presently operative to bring us to glory.

Coming Alive in Christ

6

And you were dead in your trespasses and sins, in which you formerly walked according to the course of this world, according to the prince of the power of the air, of the spirit that is now working in the sons of disobedience. Among them we too all formerly lived in the lusts of our flesh, indulging the desires of the flesh and of the mind, and were by nature children of wrath, even as the rest. But God, being rich in mercy, because of His great love with which He loved us, even when we were dead in our transgressions, made us alive together with Christ (by grace you have been saved), and raised us up with Him, and seated us with Him in the heavenly places, in Christ Jesus, in order that in the ages to come He might show the surpassing riches of His grace in kindness toward us in Christ Jesus. For by grace you have been saved through faith; and that not of yourselves, it is the gift of God; not as a result of works, that no one should boast. For we are His workmanship, created in Christ Jesus for good works, which God prepared beforehand, that we should walk in them. (2:1-10)

Some years ago I spoke to a group of actors and actresses, presenting to them the gospel of Jesus Christ. Afterward, a handsome young Indian came up to me and told me that he was a Muslim and that he wanted to have Jesus Christ. We went to a nearby room, and after I had explained the gospel in more detail, he prayed a prayer of acceptance. He opened his eyes and said, "Isn't it wonderful! Now I have Jesus and Mohammed." Considerably disappointed, I had to tell him that Jesus could not be taken from some shelf of divinities and added to whatever other gods one might have. When He is Lord, there can be no others beside Him. Such is an example of the many misunderstandings of the meaning of salvation.

In Ephesians 2:1-10 Paul clarifies what it means to receive salvation and to be a part of Christ's Body, the church. Here the apostle moves from eternity past into time. He describes the act and process of salvation, the miracle that draws men into the eternal plan portrayed in chapter 1. In context this section builds on the thought of 1:19, where Paul introduces the great power of Christ toward us who believe and then digresses to discuss that power in Christ's life. He returns now to show that power in our salvation.

In the first ten verses Paul presents the past, present, and future of the Christian: what he was (vv. 1-3), what he is (vv. 4-6, 8-9), and what he will be (vv. 7, 10). Within this framework he gives six aspects of salvation: It is from sin (vv. 1-3), by love (v. 4), into life (v. 5), with a purpose (vv. 6-7), through faith (vv. 8-9), and unto good works (v. 10). The first aspect is in the past, the next four aspects (except for the second part of "purpose," v. 7) pertain to the present, and the last aspect (including v. 7) is in the future.

SALVATION IS FROM SIN

And you were dead in your trespasses and sins, in which you formerly walked according to the course of this world, according to the prince of the power of the air, of the spirit that is now working in the sons of disobedience. Among them we too all formerly lived in the lusts of our flesh, indulging the desires of the flesh and of the mind, and were by nature children of wrath, even as the rest. (2:1-3)

First, salvation is from sin, which characterizes life before Christ. In these three verses there is perhaps no clearer statement in Scripture on the sinfulness of man apart from Christ.

The wages, or payment, for sin is death (Rom. 6:23), and because man is born in sin he is born to death. Man does not *become* spiritually dead because he sins; he *is* spiritually dead because by nature he is sinful. Except for Jesus Christ, that is the condition of every human being since the Fall, including every believer before he is saved. It is the past condition of believers and the present condition of everyone else.

Man's basic trouble is not being out of harmony with his heritage or his environment but being out of harmony with his Creator. His principal problem is not that he cannot make meaningful relationships with other human beings but that he has no right relationship to God, from whom he is alienated by sin (Eph. 4:18). His condition has nothing to do with the way he lives; it has to do with the fact that he is dead even while he is alive. He is spiritually dead while being physically alive. Because he is dead to God, he is dead to spiritual life, truth, righteousness, inner peace and happiness, and ultimately to every other good thing.

One of the first indications of physical death is the body's inability to respond to stimulus, no matter what it might be. A dead person cannot react. He no longer responds to light, sound, smell, taste, pain, or anything else. He is totally insensitive.

One day a young boy came up and pounded on my office door. When I opened the door, I saw he was breathless and crying. He said, "Are you the Reverend? Are you the Reverend?" When I answered yes, he said, "Come on. Please hurry." I ran after him for a block or two, and we went into a house. A young woman was standing inside, weeping uncontrollably. She said, "My baby is dead! My baby is dead!" Lying on a bed was the limp body of her three-month old infant. She had tried to revive him, and nothing I could do proved to be of help. He showed no sign of life. The mother caressed the baby, kissed it, spoke to it, and cried tears over its little head. But the child made no response. When the ambulance crew arrived they tried desperately to get the child breathing, but to no avail. He was dead, and nothing anyone could do had an effect or could bring any response. There was no life there to respond, not even to the powerful love of a mother.

That is the way of spiritual death as well. A person who is spiritually dead has no life by which he can respond to spiritual things, much less live a spiritual life. No amount of love, care, and words of affection from God can draw a response. A spiritually dead person is alienated from God and therefore alienated from life. He has no capacity to respond. As the great Scottish commentator John Eadie said, "It is a case of death walking." Men apart from God are spiritual zombies, the walking dead who do not know they are dead. They go through the motions of life, but they do not possess it.

After Jesus had called a certain man to follow Him, the man asked permission to first bury his father—a figure of speech that meant waiting until his father died in order to receive the inheritance. Indicating the condition of spiritual deadness and bringing both deaths together, Jesus responded, "Follow Me; and allow the dead to bury their own dead" (Matt. 8:21-22). The man's concern was not for his father, who was not likely dead, but for the things of the physical world. He wanted to take care of his physical welfare first and showed no genuine desire for the spiritual. When Paul counseled Timothy about widows in the church, he said of those who were profligate, "She who gives herself to wanton pleasure is dead even while she lives" (1 Tim. 5:6). Dead while they live is the sad state of every unredeemed human being.

Before we were saved we were like every other person who is apart from God—**dead in . . . trespasses and sins.** The Greek case is the locative of sphere, indicating the sphere, or realm, in which something or someone exists. We were not **dead** because we had committed sin but because we were **in** sin. In this context **trespasses and sins** do not refer simply to acts but first of all to the sphere of existence of the person apart from God. He does not become a liar when he tells a lie; he tells a lie because he already *is* a liar. He does not become a thief when he steals; he steals because he already *is* a thief. And so with murder, adultery, covetousness, and every other sin. Committing sinful acts does not make us sinners; we commit sinful acts because we *are* sinners. Jesus confirmed this when He said, "The evil man out of his evil treasure brings forth what is evil" (Matt. 12:35) and "the things that proceed out of the mouth come from the heart, and those defile the man. For out of the heart come evil thoughts, murders, adulteries, fornications, thefts, false witness, slanders" (Matt. 15:18-19).

Paraptōma (**trespasses**) means to slip, fall, stumble, deviate, or go the wrong direction. *Hamartia* (**sins**) originally carried the idea of missing the mark, as when hunting with a bow and arrow. It then came to represent missing or falling short of any goal, standard, or purpose. In the spiritual realm it refers to missing and falling short of God's standard of holiness, and in the New Testament it is the most common and general term for sin (used 173 times). Paul does not use the two terms here to point up different kinds of wrongdoing but simply to emphasize the breadth of the sinfulness that results from spiritual deadness.

Paul's statement that "all have sinned and fall short of the glory of God" (Rom. 3:23) does not give two truths but two views of the same truth. Sin is falling short of God's glory, and falling short of God's glory is sin. As Paul had explained two chapters earlier in Romans, in its most basic sense sin is failing to glorify God. Although fallen mankind "knew God, they did not honor Him as God" (1:21). Of all the epitaphs that could have been written for Herod, the words of Acts 12:23 are the most appropriate: "An angel of the Lord struck him because he did not give God the glory, and he was eaten by worms and died."

That all men apart from God are sinful does not mean that every person is equally corrupt and wicked. Twenty corpses on a battlefield might be in many different stages of decay, but they are uniformly dead. Death manifests itself in many different forms and degrees, but death itself has no degrees. Sin manifests itself in many different forms and degrees, but the state of sin itself has no degrees. Not all men are as evil as they could be, but all fail to measure up to God's perfect standard.

As a state of being, a sphere of existence, sin has more to do with what is not done than with what is done. God's standard is for men to be perfect just as He Himself is perfect (Matt. 5:48). Jesus did not give a new standard but restated a very old one. Nor had God's command to "be holy; for I am holy" (Lev. 11:44; cf. 1 Pet. 1:16) created a new standard for mankind or for His chosen people. God has never had any standard for man but perfect holiness.

It is because of that perfect standard of holiness that men apart from God cannot be anything but sinful. Because he is separated from God he cannot do anything but fall short of God's standard. No matter how much good he does or attempts to do, the standard of never doing or never having done evil at all is unattainable.

Man's common state of sin has often been compared to a diverse group of people standing on the bank of a wide river, perhaps a mile across. Each of them is trying to jump to the other side. The little children and old people can jump only a few feet. The larger children and agile adults can jump several times that far. A few athletes can jump several times farther still. But none of them gets near the other side. Their degrees of success vary only in relation to each other. In relation to achieving the goal they are equal failures.

Throughout history people have varied greatly in their levels of human goodness and wickedness. But in relation to achieving God's holiness they are equal failures. That is why the good, helpful, kind, considerate, self-giving person needs salvation as much as the multiple murderer on death row. The person who is a good parent, loving spouse, honest worker, and civic humanitarian needs Jesus Christ to save him from the eternal condemnation of hell as much as the skid row drunk or the heartless terrorist. They do not lead equally sinful lives, but they are equally in the state of sin, equally separated from God and from spiritual life.

Jesus said, "If you do good to those who do good to you, what credit is that to you? For even sinners do the same" (Luke 6:33). On another occasion He said, "You then, being evil, [nevertheless] know how to give good gifts to your children" (Luke 11:13). A person apart from God can do humanly good things. But as the Lord points out in both of those statements, the person is still a sinner, still evil by nature, and still operating on a motive less than that of glorifying God. When Paul and the others were shipwrecked on the island of Malta, Luke reports that "the natives showed us extraordinary kindness" (Acts 28:2); yet those natives remained superstitious pagans (v. 6). A sinner's doing good is good, but it cannot change his nature or his basic sphere of existence, and it cannot reconcile him to God.

Relational goodness is helpful to other people and is more pleasing to God. It is a step in the right direction. But a hundred thousand such steps cannot bring a person any nearer to God. Because it is a sinner's condition of sinfulness and not his particular sins that separate him from God, his particular acts of goodness cannot reconcile him to God.

During Jesus' second farewell discourse to His disciples He said, "He [the Holy Spirit], when He comes, will convict the world concerning sin" (John 16:8). The sin of which He will convict men is the sin of disbelief in Jesus Christ (v. 9). That is the sin of separation, the sin that both causes and reflects man's alienation from God. It is the sin of not accepting God as God and Christ as Savior, the sin of rejection. It is not particular acts or statements of rejection but the sphere of rejection in which the unsaved person exists that separates him from God. That is his state of spiritual death, his being **dead in . . . trespasses and sins.**

In the state of spiritual death, the only walking, or living, a person can do is **according to the course of this world, according to the prince of the power of the air, of the spirit that is now working in the sons of disobedience.** *Kosmos* (world) does not here represent simply the physical creation but the world order, the world's system of values and way of doing things—the world's **course.** And as Paul makes clear, the **course of this world** follows the leadership and design of Satan, **the prince of the power of the air.**

What we often call "the spirit of the times" reflects the wider **course of this world**, a course in which men are in basic agreement about what is right and wrong, valuable and worthless, important and unimportant. Sinful men have many different ideas and standards, but they are in total agreement that the network of things in **this world** is more important than the divine perspective of God. In this most basic world outlook they are of one mind. They resolutely work to fulfill the goals and values of their system, though it defies God and always self-destructs. Sinners are persistent in their rejection, and the worse their system becomes, the more they try to justify it and condemn those who speak the Word of God against it.

They are of one mind because they have a common leader and lord, **the prince of the power of the air.** Satan is now "the ruler of this world," and until the Lord casts him out (John 12:31) he will continue to rule. **The power** [or authority] **of the air** probably refers to Satan's host of demons who exist in the heavenly sphere. Paul has this in mind in Ephesians 6:12, where he warns of "the spiritual forces of wickedness in the heavenly places." During the present age he and his demon host dominate, pressure, and control every person who is unsaved. He is the personification of spiritual death because he is the personification of rebellion against God—and so is the system he designed.

The three elements that most characterize our present **world** system are humanism, materialism, and illicit sex. Humanism places man above all else. Man is the measure and end of all things. Each man is his own boss, his own standard of good, his own source of authority—in short, his own god. Materialism places high value in physical things, especially money, because money is a means of acquiring all the other things. Sexual perversion dominates modern western society as it has no other societies since the lowest periods of ancient Greece and Rome. Along with the humanistic appeal to self-interest and the materialistic appeal to self-aggrandizement, sexual vice is used to promote and persuade in virtually every field of marketing, pandering to self-pleasure. That triumvirate represents the spirit of our age, the current **course of this world.**

Satan is the *archōn,* **the prince** and ruler over this world system. Not all unsaved people are necessarily indwelt at all times by Satan or are demon-possessed. But knowingly or unknowingly they are subject to Satan's influence. Because they share his nature of sinfulness and exist in the same sphere of rebellion against God, they respond naturally to his leading and to the influence of his demons. They are on the same spiritual wavelength.

As with the **world,** the **air** over which Satan has controlling **power** represents the sphere where demons move. The air could be used metaphorically, as when we speak of an "air of expectancy." In this context **world** and **air** would be almost synonymous, both of them representing a realm, or sphere, of influence. In that case it would be a reference to the realm of ideas, beliefs, and convictions over which Satan now operates as **prince.** But it is not that which is in Paul's mind here or in 6:12. He has in mind the fact that Satan rules the **power** (demons) who occupy the air (the heavenly sphere around the earth). Men are not free and independent;

they are totally dominated by the hosts of hell.

To walk **according to the course of this world, according to the power of the prince of the power of the air**, is to think and live according to the presuppositions, ideologies, and standards over which sin and Satan have control and to be dominated by evil supernatural beings. Satan's supreme purpose for men is not to get them only to do evil things (the flesh will see to that, as is made clear in Gal. 5:19-21) but to think and believe evil things, especially about God (cf. 2 Cor. 11:13-15). Because fallen mankind and Satan's hosts exist in the same **spiritual realm, it is quite natural that his spirit is the same spirit that is now working in the sons of disobedience.** The **prince** of disobedience works in (the use of *en* emphasizes the intimate relationship) willing followers, those who have no regard for the Word and will of God, called **the sons of disobedience** (a Semitic term that describes a person characterized by disobedience), of whom he is the spiritual father (John 8:38-44). Paul makes clear this identifying characteristic of disobedience to God when he states absolutely that "you are slaves of the one whom you obey, either of sin resulting in death, or of obedience resulting in righteousness" (Rom. 6:16). He then characterizes the believer as one who obeys God: "you became obedient from the heart" (v. 17).

Paul's primary purpose here is not to show how unsaved people now live—though the teaching is valuable for that purpose—but to remind believers how they themselves **formerly walked** and **formerly lived.** All of us once **lived in the lusts of our flesh, indulging the desires of the flesh and of the mind, and were by nature children of wrath, even as the rest.**

Epithumia **(lusts)** refers to strong inclinations and desires of every sort, not simply to sexual lust. *Thelēma* **(desires)** emphasizes strong willfulness, wanting and seeking something with great diligence. As with **trespasses and sins, lusts** and **desires** are not given to show their distinctiveness but their commonness. They are used synonymously to represent fallen man's complete orientation to his own selfish way. By nature he is driven to fulfill the **lusts** and **desires** of his sinful **flesh and . . . mind.** The **flesh** (*sarx*) refers to the dissipation of life that comes when one is abandoned to doing whatever feels good. The **mind** (*dianoia*) indicates the deliberate choices that defy the will of God.

Every believer was once totally lost in the system of the **world**, the **flesh**, and the devil, who is **the prince** over the demons, who are **the power of the air.** Those are fallen man's three great arenas where he is in a losing battle with spiritual enemies—yet they are enemies with whom, by nature, he is now allied (cf. 1 John 2:16). Rather than all men being children of God, as most of the world likes to think, those who have not received salvation through Jesus Christ are **by nature children of wrath** (cf. John 3:18). Apart from reconciliation through Christ, every person by nature (through human birth) is the object of God's **wrath**, his eternal judgment and condemnation. They are characterized most accurately not only as **sons of disobedience** but consequently as **children of wrath**—objects of God's condemning judgment.

But though we were once **even as the rest**, through faith in the Savior we are not like them any longer. Because of Christ's past work of salvation in us, we are presently and eternally under His love and delivered from the natural human condition of death, sin, alienation, disobedience, demon control, lust, and divine judgment.

SALVATION IS BY LOVE

But God, being rich in mercy, because of His great love with which He loved us, (2:4)

Salvation is *from* sin and *by* love. God's **mercy** is *plousios,* rich, overabounding, without measure, unlimited. The problem with reconciliation is not on the Lord's side. The two words **but God** show where the initiative was in providing the power of salvation. His great desire is to be rejoined with the creatures He made in His own image and for His own glory. The rebellion and rejection is on man's side. Because He was **rich in mercy** toward us and had **great love** for us, He provided a way for us to return to Him. In Romans 11:32 the apostle Paul focuses on this same issue in saying, "God has shut up all in disobedience that He might show mercy to all." His purpose in so doing is given in verse 36: "For from Him and through Him and *to* Him are all things. To Him be the glory forever. Amen" (emphasis added).

Salvation for God's glory is by the motivation and power of God's **great love.** God is intrinsically kind, merciful, and loving. And in His love He reaches out to vile, sinful, rebellious, depraved, destitute, and condemned human beings and offers them salvation and all the eternal blessings it brings. Man's rebellion is therefore not only against God's lordship and law but against His **love.**

If a person were driving down the street and carelessly ran down and killed a child, he probably would be arrested, tried, fined, and imprisoned for involuntary manslaughter. But after he paid the fine and served the sentence he would be free and guiltless before the law in regard to that crime. But paying his penalty before the law would do nothing to restore the life of the child or alleviate the grief of the parents. The offense against them was on an immeasurably deeper level. The only way a relationship between the parents and the man who killed their child could be established or restored would be for the parents to offer forgiveness. No matter how much the man might want to do so, he could not produce reconciliation from his side. Only the one offended can offer forgiveness, and only forgiveness can bring reconciliation.

Though greatly offended and sinned against (as depicted in the parable of Matt. 18:23-35), because of God's **rich . . . mercy** and His **great love** He offered forgiveness and reconciliation to us as He does to every repentant sinner. Though in their sin and rebellion all men participated in the wickedness of Jesus' crucifixion, God's **mercy** and **love** provide a way for them to participate in the righteousness of His crucifixion. "I know what you are and what you have done,"

He says; "but because of My **great love** for you, your penalty has been paid, My law's judgment against you has been satisfied, through the work of My Son on your behalf. For His sake I offer you forgiveness. To come to Me you need only to come to Him." Not only did He love enough to forgive but also enough to die for the very ones who had offended Him. "Greater love has no one than this, that one lay down his life for his friends" (John 15:13). Compassionate love for those who do not deserve it makes salvation possible.

SALVATION IS INTO LIFE

even when we were dead in our transgressions, [God] made us alive together with Christ (by grace you have been saved), (2:5)

Above all else, a **dead** person needs to be made **alive**. That is what salvation gives—spiritual life. To encourage believers who doubt the power of Christ in their lives, Paul reminds them that if God was powerful and loving enough to give them spiritual life **together with Christ,** He is certainly able to sustain that life. The power that raised us out of sin and death and **made us alive** (aorist tense) **together with Christ** (cf. Rom. 6:1-7) is the same power that continues to energize every part of our Christian living (Rom. 6:11-13). The **we** may emphasize the linking of the Jew with the Gentile "you" in verse 1. Both are in sin and may receive mercy to be made alive in Christ.

When we became Christians we were no longer alienated from the life of God. We became spiritually **alive** through union with the death and resurrection of Christ and thereby for the first time became sensitive to God. Paul calls it walking in "newness of life" (Rom. 6:4). For the first time we could understand spiritual truth and desire spiritual things. Because we now have God's nature, we now can seek godly things, "the things above" rather than "the things that are on earth" (Col. 3:2). That is what results from being **alive together with Christ.** "We shall also live with Him" (Rom. 6:8) says the apostle, and our new life is indistinguishable from His life lived in us (Gal. 2:20). In Christ we cannot help but be pleasing to God.

SALVATION IS WITH A PURPOSE

and raised us up with Him, and seated us with Him in the heavenly places, in Christ Jesus, in order that in the ages to come He might show the surpassing riches of His grace in kindness toward us in Christ Jesus. (2:6-7)

Salvation has a purpose, in regard to us and in regard to God. The most immediate and direct result of salvation is to be **raised up with Him, and** [to be] **seated with Him in the heavenly places.** Not only are we dead to sin and alive to righteousness through His resurrection in which we are raised, but we also enjoy

His exaltation and share in His preeminent glory.

When Jesus raised Lazarus from the dead His first instruction was, "Unbind him, and let him go" (John 11:44). A living person cannot function while wrapped in the trappings of death. Because our new citizenship through Christ is in heaven (Phil 3:20), God seats us **with Him in the heavenly places, in Christ Jesus.** We are no longer of this present world or in its sphere of sinfulness and rebellion. We have been rescued from spiritual death and given spiritual life in order to be **in Christ Jesus** and to be **with Him in the heavenly places.** Here, as in 1:3, **heavenly places** refers to the supernatural sphere where God rules, though in 6:12 it refers to the supernatural sphere where Satan rules.

The Greek verb behind **seated** is in the aorist tense and emphasizes the absoluteness of this promise by speaking of it as if it had already fully taken place. Even though we are not yet inheritors of all that God has for us in Christ, to be **in the heavenly places** is to be in God's domain instead of Satan's, to be in the sphere of spiritual life instead of the sphere of spiritual death. That is where our blessings are and where we have fellowship with the Father, the Son, the Holy Spirit, and with all the saints who have gone before us and will go after us. That is where all our commands come from and where all our praise and petitions go. And some day we will receive the "inheritance which is imperishable and undefiled and will not fade away, reserved in heaven for [us]" (1 Pet. 1:4).

The phrase **in order that** indicates that the purpose of our being exalted to the supernatural sphere of God's preserve and power is that we may forever be blessed. But it is not only for our benefit and glory. God's greater purpose in salvation is for His own sake, **in order that in the ages to come He might show the surpassing riches of His grace in kindness toward us in Christ Jesus.** That, too, is obviously for our benefit, but it is first of all for God's, because it displays for all eternity **the surpassing riches of His grace** (cf. 3:10). Through His endless **kindness toward us in Christ Jesus** the Father glorifies Himself even as He blesses us. From the moment of salvation throughout **the ages to come** we never stop receiving the **grace** and **kindness** of God. **The ages to come** is different from the age to come in 1:21 and refers to eternity. He glorifies Himself by eternally blessing us with "every spiritual blessing in the heavenly places in Christ" (1:3) and by bestowing on us His endless and limitless **grace** and **kindness.** The whole of heaven will glorify Him because of what He has done for us (Rev. 7:10-12).

SALVATION IS THROUGH FAITH

For by grace you have been saved through faith; and that not of yourselves, it is the gift of God; not as a result of works, that no one should boast. (2:8-9)

Our response in salvation is **faith,** but even that is **not of ourselves** [but is] **the gift of God. Faith** is nothing that we do in our own power or by our own resources. In the first place we do not *have* adequate power or resources. More than that, God would not want us to rely on them even if we had them. Otherwise salvation would be in part by our own **works**, and we would have some ground to **boast** in ourselves. Paul intends to emphasize that even faith is not from us apart from God's giving it.

Some have objected to this interpretation, saying that **faith** (*pistis*) is feminine, while **that** (*touto*) is neuter. That poses no problem, however, as long as it is understood that **that** does not refer precisely to the noun **faith** but to the act of believing. Further, this interpretation makes the best sense of the text, since if **that** refers to **by grace you have been saved through faith** (that is, to the whole statement), the adding of **and that not of yourselves, it is the gift of God** would be redundant, because grace is defined as an unearned act of God. If salvation is of grace, it has to be an undeserved gift of God. Faith is presented as a gift from God in 2 Peter 1:1, Philippians 1:29, and Acts 3:16.

The story is told of a man who came eagerly but very late to a revival meeting and found the workmen tearing down the tent in which the meetings had been held. Frantic at missing the evangelist, he decided to ask one of the workers what he could do to be saved. The workman, who was a Christian, replied, "You can't do anything. It's too late." Horrified, the man said, "What do you mean? How can it be too late?" "The work has already been accomplished," he was told. "There is nothing you need to do but believe it."

Every person lives by faith. When we open a can of food or drink a glass of water we trust that it is not contaminated. When we go across a bridge we trust it to support us. When we put our money in the bank we trust it will be safe. Life is a constant series of acts of faith. No human being, no matter how skeptical and self-reliant, could live a day without exercising faith.

Church membership, baptism, confirmation, giving to charity, and being a good neighbor have no power to bring salvation. Nor does taking Communion, keeping the Ten Commandments, or living by the Sermon on the Mount. The only thing a person can do that will have any part in salvation is to exercise faith in what Jesus Christ has done for him.

When we accept the finished work of Christ on our behalf, we act by the **faith** supplied by God's **grace**. That is the supreme act of human faith, the act which, though it is ours, is primarily God's—His **gift** to us out of His **grace**. When a person chokes or drowns and stops breathing, there is nothing he can do. If he ever breathes again it will be because someone else starts him breathing. A person who is spiritually dead cannot even make a decision of faith unless God first breathes into him the breath of spiritual life. **Faith** is simply breathing the breath that God's **grace** supplies. Yet, the paradox is that we must exercise it and bear the responsibility if we do not (cf. John 5:40).

Obviously, if it is true that salvation is all by God's grace, it is therefore **not as a result of works**. Human effort has nothing to do with it (cf. Rom. 3:20; Gal. 2:16). And thus, **no one should boast**, as if he had any part. All boasting is eliminated in salvation (cf. Rom. 3:27; 4:5; 1 Cor. 1:31). Nevertheless, good works have an important place, as Paul is quick to affirm.

SALVATION IS UNTO GOOD WORKS

For we are His workmanship, created in Christ Jesus for good works, which God prepared beforehand, that we should walk in them. (2:10)

Although they have no part in gaining salvation, **good works** have a great deal to do with living out salvation. No **good works** can produce salvation, but many **good works** are produced by salvation.

"By this is My Father glorified," Jesus said, "that you bear much fruit, and so prove to be My disciples" (John 15:8). Good works do not bring discipleship, but they prove it is genuine. When God's people do good deeds they bear fruit for His kingdom and bring glory to His name.

The Bible has much to say about works. It speaks of the works of the law, which are good but cannot save a person (Gal. 2:16). It speaks of dead works (Heb. 6:1) and of works, or deeds, of darkness and of the flesh, all of which are inherently evil (Rom. 13:12; Gal. 5:19-21; Eph. 5:11). All of those works are done in man's own strength and have nothing to do with salvation.

Before we can do any good work for the Lord, He has to do His good work in us. By God's grace, made effective through our faith, we become **His workmanship, created in Christ Jesus for good works.** God has ordained that we then live lives of **good works,** works done in His power and for His glory.

> I am the true vine, and My Father is the vinedresser. Every branch in Me that does not bear fruit, He takes away; and every branch that bears fruit, He prunes it, that it may bear more fruit. You are already clean because of the word which I have spoken to you. Abide in Me, and I in you. As the branch cannot bear fruit of itself, unless it abides in the vine, so neither can you, unless you abide in Me. I am the vine, you are the branches; he who abides in Me, and I in him, he bears much fruit; for apart from Me you can do nothing. If anyone does not abide in Me, he is thrown away as a branch, and dries up; and they gather them, and cast them into the fire, and they are burned. If you abide in Me, and My words abide in you, ask whatever you wish, and it shall be done for you. By this is My Father glorified, that you bear much fruit, and so prove to be My disciples. (John 15:1-8)

The same power that **created us in Christ Jesus** empowers us to do the **good works** for which He has redeemed us. These are the verifiers of true salvation. Righteous attitudes and righteous acts proceed from the transformed life now living in the heavenlies. To the Corinthians Paul said there was in them "an abundance for every good deed" (2 Cor. 9:8). To Timothy he instructed that the believer is "equipped for every good work" (2 Tim. 3:17). Christ died to bring to Himself a people "zealous for good deeds" (Titus 2:14). Even this is the work of God, as Paul says: While you "work out your salvation . . . it is God who is at work in you, both to will and to work for His good pleasure" (Phil. 2:12-13).

Paul's primary message here is still to believers, many of whom had experienced salvation years earlier. He is not showing them how to be saved, but how they *were* saved, in order to convince them that the power that saved them is the same power that keeps them. Just as they already had been given everything necessary for salvation, they also had been given everything necessary for faithfully living the saved life. The greatest proof of a Christian's divine empowerment is his own salvation and the resulting good works that God produces in and through him (cf. John 15). These **good works** are expected because **God prepared beforehand, that we should walk in them,** and that is why James says faith is illegitimate if works are not present (James 2:17-26).

It is from *poiēma* (**workmanship**) that we get poem, a piece of literary workmanship. Before time began, God designed us to be conformed to the image of His Son, Jesus Christ (Rom. 8:29). Paul could therefore say to the Philippians, "For I am confident of this very thing, that He who began a good work in you will perfect it until the day of Christ Jesus" (1:6).

The story is often told of the rowdy, disruptive young boy in a Sunday school class who continually frustrated his teacher. One morning the teacher asked him, "Why do you act like that? Don't you know who made you?" To which the boy replied, "God did, but He ain't through with me yet."

All of us are still imperfect, uncut diamonds being finished by the divine Master Craftsman. He is not finished with us yet, but His work will not cease until He has made us into the perfect likeness of His Son (1 John 3:2).

A famous actor was once the guest of honor at a social gathering where he received many requests to recite favorite excerpts from various literary works. An old preacher who happened to be there asked the actor to recite the Twenty-third Psalm. The actor agreed on the condition that the preacher would also recite it. The actor's recitation was beautifully intoned with great dramatic emphasis, for which he received lengthy applause. The preacher's voice was rough and broken from many years of preaching, and his diction was anything but polished. But when he finished there was not a dry eye in the room. When someone asked the actor what made the difference, he replied, "I know the psalm, but he knows the Shepherd."

Salvation does not come from knowing about the truth of Jesus Christ but from intimately knowing Christ Himself. This coming alive can be accomplished by the power of God because of His love and mercy.

The Unity of the Body

7

Therefore remember, that formerly you, the Gentiles in the flesh, who are called "Uncircumcision" by the so-called "Circumcision," which is performed in the flesh by human hands—remember that you were at that time separate from Christ, excluded from the commonwealth of Israel, and strangers to the covenants of promise, having no hope and without God in the world. But now in Christ Jesus you who formerly were far off have been brought near by the blood of Christ. For He Himself is our peace, who made both groups into one, and broke down the barrier of the dividing wall, by abolishing in His flesh the enmity, which is the Law of commandments contained in ordinances, that in Himself He might make the two into one new man, thus establishing peace, and might reconcile them both in one body to God through the cross, by it having put to death the enmity. And He came and preached peace to you who were far away, and peace to those who were near; for through Him we both have our access in one Spirit to the Father. So then you are no longer strangers and aliens, but you are fellow citizens with the saints, and are of God's household, having been built upon the foundation of the apostles and prophets, Christ Jesus Himself being the corner stone, in whom the whole building, being fitted together is growing into a holy temple in the Lord; in whom you also are being built together into a dwelling of God in the Spirit. (2:11-22)

It is a part of sinful human nature to build barriers that shut out other people. In New Testament times one of the greatest barriers was between slaves and freemen, especially between slaves and their owners. Those who were free looked down on slaves as being inferior, slightly above animals. Many slaves looked on their masters with contempt and resentment. Consequently, one of the greatest problems of the early church was in getting Christian slave owners and Christian slaves to treat each other as spiritual equals.

For the most part, women were also looked down on as inferior beings. Husbands often treated their wives little better than they did their slaves. When a wife became a Christian, her entire life, outlook, and value system changed. An unbelieving husband would likely divorce her simply because she had made such a radical decision without his consent.

The Greeks were so proud of their culture and supposed racial superiority that they considered everyone else to be barbarians, a belief to which Paul alludes in Romans 1:14 and Colossians 3:11. The Greek language was considered to be the language of the gods. The Roman statesman Cicero wrote, "As the Greeks say, 'All men are divided into two classes, Greeks and barbarians.'" Livy, another ancient Roman, wrote that Greeks constantly waged a truceless war against people of other races, all of whom they held to be barbarians. Because of such feelings, the early church faced continuing barriers not only between believing Gentiles and Jews but between believing Greeks and other Gentile believers.

In his book *The Cross of Peace* Sir Philip Gibbs writes,

> The problem of fences has grown to be one of the most acute that the world must face. Today there are all sorts of zig-zag and criss-crossing fences running through the races and peoples of the world. Modern progress has made the world a neighborhood and God has given us the task of making it a brotherhood. In these days of dividing walls of race and class we must shake the earth anew with the message of Christ, in whom there is neither bond nor free, Jew nor Greek, Scythian nor Barbarian, but all are one.

Disunity among His own people has always been a special heartache to God. In His intercessory prayer for His disciples in John 17, Jesus prayed three times that they would be one (vv. 11, 21, 22) and again "that they may be perfected in unity" (v. 23). Jesus' prayers were always answered because He always prayed according to His Father's will. His prayer for the unity of His people has already been answered positionally, because every person who has believed in Him has been spiritually made one with Him and with every other believer from every age. Positionally we *are* one in Jesus Christ. "The one who joins himself to the Lord is one spirit with Him" (1 Cor. 6:17). "For even as the body is one and yet has many members, and all the members of the body, though they are many, are one body, so also is Christ. For by one Spirit we were all baptized into one body" (12:12-13).

Just as a physical body has a common principle of life flowing through it, so does the Body of Christ, His church. The Spirit of God puts the life of God in the soul of every person who trusts in Jesus Christ and unites that person with every other believer in the same eternal realm. In the kingdom of Jesus Christ all barriers come down. In Him there are no walls, no classes, no castes, no races, no gender, no distinctions of any sort.

Practically, however, the truth is often tragically different. In the same letter to Corinth in which Paul so strongly declared the positional unity of believers he also strongly rebuked the Corinthians for their practical disunity. "And I, brethren, could not speak to you as to spiritual men, but as to men of flesh, as to babes in Christ. . . . for you are still fleshly. For since there is jealousy and strife among you, are you not fleshly, and are you not walking like mere men?" (1 Cor. 3:1, 3; cf. 1:11-13).

Only about twenty years ago the pastor of prosperous white church in a southern U. S. town became burdened for the community at large. The black janitor of his church was a gracious and obedient Christian, and the two men began a weekly Bible study and prayer time together. After a few months the church board approached the pastor and told him he had to stop having fellowship with "that man" because it was bad for the church's image. When he told them he could not do that because he felt fellowshiping with and ministering to him was the Lord's will, virtually no store in town would do business with him. He could not buy clothes, gas, or even groceries. Before long he had a nervous breakdown and was taken to the psychiatric ward of a hospital in a nearby large city, where on the second day he dived out of the window and killed himself.

A far different story, however, is that of a contemporary African church, composed of believers from various tribes who had been the bitterest of enemies for countless generations. A missionary who was officiating at a communion service in the church was deeply moved when he looked around him. He saw the chief of the Ngoni, along with many other members of that tribe. He also saw members of the Senga and Tumbuka tribes—singing, praying, and participating in the Lord's Supper together. In former years each of these tribes loved to brag about how many men, women, and children of the other tribes they had killed, raped, or maimed. The old chief could remember the days when the young Ngoni warriors had gone out to attack their enemies. They had left behind a trail of burned and devastated villages and had come home with their spears bloodied with the death of Senga and Tumbuka people. But as they once were divided by the spilling of each other's blood, they are now united by the blood of their common Savior, Jesus Christ.

That is the kind of unity Jesus Christ gives to His people and that He commands them to maintain, "being diligent to preserve the unity of the Spirit in the bond of peace" (Eph. 4:3). "There is one body and one Spirit," Paul goes on to say, "just as also you were called in one hope of your calling; one Lord, one faith, one baptism, one God and Father of all who is over all and through all and in all" (vv. 4-6). The church is to manifest that oneness "until we all attain to the unity of the faith, and of the knowledge of the Son of God, to a mature man, to the measure of the stature which belongs to the fulness of Christ" (v. 13).

ALIENATION APART FROM CHRIST

Therefore remember, that formerly you, the Gentiles in the flesh, who are called "Uncircumcision" by the so-called "Circumcision," which is performed in the flesh by human hands—remember that you were at that time separate from Christ, excluded from the commonwealth of Israel, and strangers to the covenants of promise, having no hope and without God in the world. (2:11-12)

The disunity within the Ephesian church was primarily between Jewish and Gentile believers. But, as Paul later reminded them, the very "mystery of Christ" that had "been revealed to His holy apostles and prophets in the Spirit" is "that the Gentiles are fellow heirs and fellow members of the body, and fellow partakers of the promise in Christ Jesus through the gospel" (3:4-6). All differences were set aside in favor of common unity in the Holy Spirit of God. "For you are all sons of God through faith in Christ Jesus. For all of you who were baptized into Christ have clothed yourselves with Christ. There is neither Jew nor Greek, there is neither slave nor free man, there is neither male nor female; for you are all one in Christ Jesus" (Gal. 3:26-28; cf. Rom. 10:12). The church's unity is not organizational but spiritual. This passage focuses on the idea of that spiritual oneness. The terms "both . . . one" (Eph. 2:14), "one new man" (v. 15), "one body" (v. 16), "both" (vv. 14, 16, 18), and "together" (vv. 21-22) all indicate the apostle's emphasis.

It is often helpful, and sometimes necessary, to focus on particular national, racial, religious, or ethnic groups for evangelistic work and to devise approaches for a given group that are somewhat unique. But it is unfortunate that believers who come from such groups are often never assimilated into existing churches.

God sovereignly chose the Jews to be His special people. "You only," He told Israel, "have I chosen among all the families of the earth" (Amos 3:2). God chose the Jews not only to receive His special blessings but also to be a channel of those blessings to others. From the beginning it was God's plan that through Abraham and his descendants, the Jews, "all the families of the earth shall be blessed" (Gen. 12:3). Israel was called to be a vessel through which the knowledge of God would be spread to the entire world.

Unfortunately, Israel never fulfilled that calling. She preferred to condemn the Gentiles rather than witness to them. A rabbinic writer tells of an incident that explains the common Jewish attitude toward Gentiles. A certain Gentile woman came to Rabbi Eleazar, confessed that she was sinful, and told him that she wanted to become righteous. She wanted to be accepted into the Jewish faith because she had heard that the Jews were near to God. The rabbi is said to have responded, "No. You cannot come near," and then shut the door in her face.

Peter had such an attitude of disdain for Gentiles before he had the vision of the unclean animals that the Lord commanded him to eat (Acts 10:9-16). Peter later explained to the Roman centurion Cornelius and his household: "You yourselves know how unlawful it is for a man who is a Jew to associate with a foreigner or to visit him; and yet God has shown me that I should not call any man unholy or unclean" (v. 28; cf. Gal. 2:11-14).

God commanded the church to "go into all the world and preach the gospel to all creation" (Mark 16:15), to "make disciples of all the nations" (Matt. 28:19), and to be His "witnesses both in Jerusalem, and in all Judea and Samaria, and even to the remotest part of the earth" (Acts 1:8). It has always been God's plan to extend His love, grace, forgiveness, and mercy to every person on earth.

God made Israel distinct for two reasons. First, He wanted the world to see and notice them, to realize that they did not live and act like other men. Second, He wanted them to be so distinct that they would never be amalgamated with other peoples. He gave them such strict dietary, clothing, marriage, ceremonial, and other laws that they could never fit easily into another society. Those distinctions, like the special blessings God gave them, were intended to be a tool for witness. But Israel continually perverted them into a source for pride, isolation, and self-glory.

As Paul reminds the Ephesian Christians later in this letter, the church has a similar calling to be distinct from the world: to "walk no longer just as the Gentiles also walk, in the futility of their mind," but to "lay aside the old self, which is being corrupted in accordance with the lusts of deceit," and to "be renewed in the spirit of your mind, and put on the new self, which in the likeness of God has been created in righteousness and holiness of the truth" (4:17, 22-24). Yet the church also faces the danger of proudly perverting special blessing into a means for pride, isolation, and self-satisfaction instead of using it humbly to witness God's grace and goodness to the world.

Jonah typified the common Jewish attitude toward Gentiles. When God called him to preach to Nineveh, the prophet fled in the opposite direction. After he finally obeyed the Lord and saw the whole city repent because of his preaching, "it greatly displeased Jonah, and he became angry," because God, in His grace and compassion, spared the wicked Gentiles of Nineveh—just as Jonah knew God would do if they repented (Jonah 4:1-2).

Like Jonah, most Jews did not want to share their gracious and loving God with anyone else. They accepted their divine blessings but not their divine mission—to be a light to the Gentile nations (Isa. 42:6; 49:6; 60:3; 62:1-2).

Jewish contempt for Gentiles often had justification from a human standpoint, because throughout their history they suffered recurrent oppression and persecution from Gentiles—who frequently looked on Jews as a slave people to be exploited. As in our own day under the Nazis, Jews have often been derided as enemies of the human race.

But instead of reflecting the gracious love and forgiveness of the God who called and blessed them, the Jews most often vented their own resentment and hatred back against their persecutors. Like Jonah, they wanted Gentiles to be judged, not forgiven. Some Jews believed that God created the Gentiles to use as fuel for hell. Many believed that He loved Israel and hated every other nation.

Consequently, some Jewish women refused to help a non-Jewish woman give birth, because to do so would make them responsible for bringing another despised Gentile into the world.

When a Jew entered Palestine he would often shake the dust off his sandals and clothing in order not to contaminate the Holy Land with Gentile dust. Because Samaritans were partly Gentile, most Jews would go far out of their way to avoid traveling through Samaria. If a young Jewish man or woman married a Gentile, their families would have a funeral service, symbolizing the death of their child as far as religion, race, and family were concerned. For fear of contamination, many Jews would not enter a Gentile home or allow a Gentile to enter theirs.

For many hundreds of years the animosity between Jew and Gentile had festered and grown. Although they were not always in open conflict, their mutual contempt continued to widen the gulf between them.

Traces of that animosity were found in the early church. The practical outworking of positional unity was not easy. Many Jewish believers thought it inconceivable that a Gentile could be saved unless he first became a proselyte Jew—by keeping the laws of Moses and by becoming circumcised if he were a man. These Judaizers became so influential in the church that a special council was called in Jerusalem to deal with their teaching (see Acts 15). Even after the clear decision of the council that a Gentile did *not* have to become a Jew to be saved, many Jewish Christians continued to believe otherwise. Despite God's special revelation to him in this regard (Acts 10) and his own participation in the Jerusalem council, Peter was intimidated by certain Judaizers to compromise the gospel. For that reason, Paul "opposed him to his face, because he stood condemned" (Gal. 2:11). There is only one gospel, the gospel of grace. Therefore, as Paul had warned, "Even though we, or an angel from heaven, should preach to you a gospel contrary to that which we have preached to you, let him be accursed" (Gal. 1:8).

Converted Jews had difficulty breaking from the ceremonial laws such as Sabbath observance and the eating of unclean animals. Converted Gentiles had difficulty with such things as eating meat that had been offered as a sacrifice to a pagan deity. In many such ways, Jewish and Gentile believers stumbled over their former traditions and beliefs, and in doing so they also stumbled over each other. What was of extreme importance to one group was inconsequential to the other. In Ephesians 2:11-22 Paul confronts that problem from two sides. First, he describes the former social and spiritual alienation of Jews and Gentiles, and then he describes their new spiritual unity in Jesus Christ.

This important section begins with the word **therefore**, indicating that the next line of thought regarding the new identity of these Gentile Christians is built on what Christ has done to give them life and eternal blessing, as described in verses 1-10. It is as if Paul is calling them to be so grateful for their deliverance from their old situation that they come to fully appreciate their new situation of union with all other believers. Nothing more inspires gratitude in a saved sinner than a look back to the pit from which he has come.

SOCIAL ALIENATION

The first kind of alienation was social: **formerly you, the Gentiles in the flesh, who are called "Uncircumcision" by the so-called "Circumcision," which is performed in the flesh by human hands.** Paul calls his readers **the Gentiles in the flesh** in order to emphasize the physical, external nature of the distinction, and he calls on them to **remember** who they had been before coming to Christ. As far as Jews were concerned they were outcasts, referred to as the **Uncircumcision**, a term of derision, defamation, and reproach. David called Goliath an "uncircumcised Philistine" (1 Sam. 17:26). Because Gentiles did not have the physical mark of circumcision to set them apart as the people of God, many Jews had come to consider them to be inferior and, in fact, of no concern to God. Paul carries a tone of disdain for such Jewish hatred, as evidenced in his choice of words to describe Jews—**the so-called "Circumcision"** (lit., "in the flesh, made by hand"). He thereby takes exception to Jewish boasting by emphasizing that circumcision is also only external (cf. Lev. 26:41; Deut. 10:16; Jer. 4:4; Ezek. 44:7).

But circumcision had never been a mark of personal relationship to God, for Jews or anyone else. Paul makes much of that truth in the book of Romans. "For he is not a Jew who is one outwardly; neither is circumcision that which is outward in the flesh. But he is a Jew who in one inwardly; and circumcision is that which is of the heart, by the Spirit, not by the letter; and his praise is not from men, but from God" (Rom. 2:28-29; cf. Gal. 5:6; 6:15). Later in the Romans epistle he points out that Abraham, the father of the Jewish people, was saved before he was circumcised (4:9-12). The separation of the two groups from each other was symbolized by the mark of circumcision, a purely physical distinction.

SPIRITUAL ALIENATION

A much more important Gentile alienation was spiritual: **remember that you were at that time separate from Christ, excluded from the commonwealth of Israel, and strangers to the covenants of promise, having no hope and without God in the world.** Although there was no moral difference between Jew and Gentile (as vv. 1-10 show), there was a difference in God's dealing with them as men. Before Christ came, the Jews were the people of promise from God, but the Gentiles as a people were cut off from God in five different ways.

First, they were Christless, **separate from Christ**, the Messiah. They therefore had no messianic hope of a Savior and Deliverer. Their history had no purpose, no plan, and no destiny—except the ultimate judgment of God, of which they were unaware. The popular Stoic philosophers taught that history repeated itself in three-thousand-year cycles. At the end of each cycle the universe is burned up and then reborn to repeat the same futile pattern.

Pagan deities were but extensions of men's own weaknesses and sins. The goddess Diana, or Artemis, who was the patron deity of Ephesus, was not depicted as a beautiful and gracious creature but as an ugly beast, with nipples hanging down on which her brood of little beasts suckled. Without exception, pagan idolatry has always been forbidding and repulsive when shown in its true form. It thrives on fear and despair rather than trust and hope, because its demonic gods are wicked and capricious rather than holy and faithful. Although God had them in His eternal, sovereign plan to be united with Christ through faith, they had no such relationship as yet.

Second, the Gentiles were spiritually alienated because they were **excluded from the commonwealth of Israel.** God had made His chosen people into a theocracy, a nation of whom He Himself was King and Lord. He gave that nation His special blessing, protection, and love. He gave them His covenants, His law, His priesthood, His sacrifices, His promises, and His guidance (see Deut. 32:9-14; 33:27-29; Isa. 63:7-9; Amos 3:2). The psalmist said that God "has not dealt thus with any nation; and as for His ordinances, they have not known them" (147:20). Ezekiel's description of God's special care of Israel is powerful:

> "As for your birth, on the day you were born your navel cord was not cut, nor were you washed with water for cleansing; you were not rubbed with salt or even wrapped in cloths. No eye looked with pity on you to do any of these things for you, to have compassion on you. Rather you were thrown out into the open field, for you were abhorred on the day you were born.
>
> "When I passed by you and saw you squirming in your blood, I said to you while you were in your blood, 'Live!' I said to you while you were in your blood, 'Live!' I made you numerous like plants of the field. Then you grew up, became tall, and reached the age for fine ornaments; your breasts were formed and your hair had grown. Yet you were naked and bare. Then I passed by you and saw you, and behold, you were at the time for love; so I spread My skirt over you and covered your nakedness. I also swore to you and entered into a covenant with you so that you became Mine," declares the Lord God. "Then I bathed you with water, washed off your blood from you, and anointed you with oil. I also clothed you with embroidered cloth, and put sandals of porpoise skin on your feet; and I wrapped you with fine linen and covered you with silk. And I adorned you with ornaments, put bracelets on your hands, and a necklace around your neck. I also put a ring in your nostril, earrings in your ears, and a beautiful crown on your head. Thus you were adorned with gold and silver, and your dress was of fine linen, silk, and embroidered cloth. You ate fine flour, honey, and oil; so you were exceedingly beautiful and advanced to royalty. Then your fame went forth among the nations on account of your beauty, for it was perfect because of My splendor which I bestowed on you," declares the Lord God. (Ezek. 16:4-14)

Had the Gentiles accepted the true God they, too, could have been a part of that blessed nation. But because they rejected God, they forfeited His national blessing. They had no God-blessed community or kingdom and no divine benefactor. They received no special blessing or protection, because they were outside the dominion of God.

Third, the Gentiles were spiritually alienated because they were without a covenant with God, **strangers to the covenants of promise**. The supreme covenant of promise was the one given to Abraham: "I will make you a great nation, and I will bless you, and make your name great; and so you shall be a blessing; and I will bless those who bless you, and the one who curses you I will curse. And in you all the families of the earth shall be blessed" (Gen. 12:2-3; 17:7; 26:3-5; 28:13-15). Inherent within that one great covenant were the Mosaic, Palestinian, and Davidic covenants—and even the New Covenant (Jer. 31:33). The covenant with Abraham surrounded and determined all of God's dealing with Israel (Rom. 9:4).

It should be clarified that a divine covenant is an agreement in which God binds Himself to carry out His personal promise to His people, to redeem them from sin and bless them forever. Faith and obedience are the marks of the person who experiences the fulfillment of the covenant.

Within the covenants God gave and renewed His promises to bless, prosper, multiply, save, and redeem Israel. Within them He promised to give His people a land, a kingdom, and a King; and to those who believed in Him He promised eternal life and heaven.

Fourth, the Gentiles were spiritually alienated because they were hopeless, **having no hope**. Those who have no **Christ**, no **commonwealth**, and no **covenants of promise** also have **no hope**. True hope can be based only on a true promise, on confidence in someone who can perform what he promises. Hope is a profound blessing that gives meaning and security to life. Living without hope of future joy and enrichment reduces man to a piece of meaningless protoplasm. Hope is the consummation of life, the confident assurance that we have a blessed future in the plan of God. The saddest feature of Job's great lament is found in these words: "My days are swifter than a weaver's shuttle, and come to an end without hope" (Job 7:6). The opposite of that pessimistic outlook is the joyous truth celebrated among the Jews and stated succinctly in Psalm 146:5—"How blessed is he whose help is the God of Jacob, whose hope is in the Lord his God!" "The hope of Israel" (Acts 28:20) was the hope of eternal salvation and glory. Jeremiah uses the term "the hope of Israel" as a title for God, parallel in meaning to Savior (Jer. 14:8; 17:13). The Gentiles had no hope such as that expressed by the psalmist: "For Thou art my hope; O Lord God, Thou art my confidence from my youth" (71:5).

If someone offered you a million-dollar business loan, you would want to be sure he actually had that much money to lend. You would also want to be sure he was a man of his word, that he was credible. If he did not have sufficient money or if he did not keep his word, his promise would be worthless, and no reasonable person would take hope in it.

Israel was able to have complete hope in God's promises because He had every resource at His disposal and because He cannot lie. They had God's promises, and they knew He was able and trustworthy to fulfill them. The fact that they often failed to hope in those promises was due to their own unfaithfulness, not God's.

The Gentiles, however, had no such promises and therefore had no ground for hope. Most Gentiles of Paul's day either thought that death ended all existence or that it released the spirit to wander aimlessly in some nether world throughout the rest of eternity. Death brought only nothingness or everlasting despair. The Greek philosopher Diogenes said, "I rejoice in sport in my youth. Long enough will I lie beneath the earth bereft of life, voiceless as a stone, and shall leave the sunlight which I love, good man though I am. Then shall I see nothing more. Rejoice, O my soul, in thy youth." That is the basic philosophy of many people in our own day, reflected in such sayings as, "Grab all the gusto you can" and "You only go around once."

Fifth, and most importantly, the Gentiles were spiritually alienated because they were **without God** *[atheos]* **in the world**. It was not that they were intellectual atheists, because most of them believed in many gods. Some were pantheists, believing that divinity was in everything, animate and inanimate. On Mars Hill Paul noted that the Greeks of Athens were "very religious in all respects. For while I was passing through and examining the objects of your worship, I also found an altar with this inscription, 'TO AN UNKNOWN GOD'" (Acts 17:22-23). That shrine was erected in case they had missed a god!

The problem was not that the Gentiles had no god but that they did not have the true God. Though believers have many hardships and trials in the present sinful world and are continually surrounded by Satan's system, they have the sure hope of a future world that is sinless and perfect. But to be caught in that evil system without God is to be hopeless. Paul reminded the Gentile converts in Galatia that, before they came to know the Lord, they "were slaves to those which by nature are no gods" (Gal. 4:8), which is why every person without Christ is without hope (1 Thess. 4:13).

The Gentiles were **without God in the world** because they did not want Him. The Lord did not reject the Gentiles, "for there is no partiality with God" (Rom. 2:11). They did not have God's law given to them on stone tablets as did the Jews, but they had it written in their hearts and consciences (Rom. 2:15). They had the revelation of His nature "evident within them; for God made it evident to them. For since the creation of the world His invisible attributes, His eternal power and divine nature, have been clearly seen, being understood through what has been made, so that they are without excuse" (Rom. 1:19-20). The Gentiles rejected God by suppressing the truth about Himself that He had made abundantly evident. The problem was that, "even though they knew God, they did not honor Him as God, or give thanks; but they became futile in their speculations, and their foolish heart was darkened" (v. 21).

God's purpose in calling the Jews as His holy people was to send them as His missionaries to the Gentiles, to call all nations back to Himself in grace and love. The Jews, however, were no more faithful to their greater light than the Gentiles were to their lesser. Sadly, many Christians are not faithful to their still greater Light, "the true light which, coming into the world, enlightens every man" (John 1:9; cf. Rom. 1:18-21).

There will never be an end to alienation until Christ returns and by His own power breaks down the barriers of separation. Apart from Christ there not only can be no harmony with God but no harmony among men.

UNITY IN CHRIST

But now in Christ Jesus you who formerly were far off have been brought near by the blood of Christ. For He Himself is our peace, who made both groups into one, and broke down the barrier of the dividing wall, by abolishing in His flesh the enmity, which is the Law of commandments contained in ordinances, that in Himself He might make the two into one new man, thus establishing peace, and might reconcile them both in one body to God through the cross, by it having put to death the enmity. And He came and preached peace to you who were far away, and peace to those who were near; for through Him we both have our access in one Spirit to the Father. (2:13-18)

Those **who formerly were far off** were the Gentiles who had come to Christ. **Far off** was a common Jewish term used in rabbinical writings to describe Gentiles, those who were far away from the true God (cf. Isa. 57:19; Acts 2:39). Jews, on the other hand, considered themselves and their converts to be **brought near** to God because of their covenant relation to Him and the presence of His Temple in Jerusalem. But **in Christ** every person, Jew and Gentile alike, is **brought near** to God **by the blood of Christ.** And that nearness is not an external, dispensational, national, geographic, or ceremonial nearness—but is a spiritual intimacy of union with the Lord Jesus Christ (cf. 1 Cor. 1:24).

The root cause of strife, discord, antagonism, enmity, hate, bitterness, fighting, war, conflict, and every other form of disunity and division is sin. The reason there is always perfect harmony in the Godhead is that there is no sin in the Godhead. Perfect holiness produces perfect harmony. And the only solution for divisions among men is the removal of sin, which Jesus **Christ** accomplished by the shedding of His own **blood.** Those who trust in His atoning work are freed from sin now in their new nature and will be practically and permanently freed from sin in their new bodies when they meet the Lord. The cleansing value of **the blood of Christ** immediately washes away the penalty of sin and ultimately washes away even its presence.

Because **in Christ** the great foundational barrier of sin has been removed, every other barrier has been removed as well. Those who are one in Christ are one in each other—whether they realize it or act like it or not (1 Cor. 6:17). The purpose of the Lord's Table is to remind us of the sacrifice our Lord made not only to bring us to Himself but also to each other.

By removing our sin, Christ gives us peace with each other and access to God.

PEACE WITH GOD AND WITH HIS PEOPLE

For He Himself is our peace, who made both groups into one, and broke down the barrier of the dividing wall, by abolishing in His flesh the enmity, which is the Law of commandments contained in ordinances, that in Himself He might make the two into one new man, thus establishing peace, and might reconcile them

both in one body to God through the cross, by it having put to death the enmity. And He came and preached peace to you who were far away, and peace to those who were near; (2:14-17)

The Greek text here has only one pronoun, *autos* **(He)**, but it is in the emphatic position, as reflected by the addition of **Himself** in many English translations. The writer emphasizes that Jesus alone **is our peace** (cf. Isa. 9:6); there is no other source. What laws, ordinances, ceremonies, sacrifices, and good deeds could not do to make peace between men and God, Jesus did. Those things could neither bring men into harmony with God or with each other. In the sacrifice of **Himself** on the cross, Jesus accomplished both.

Just as sin is the cause of all conflict and division, it is also the enemy of all **peace** and harmony. Built into wickedness is the impossibility of **peace**. Sin is basically selfishness, and selfishness is basically divisive and disruptive. We cannot always have what we want without infringing on what someone else wants or needs. We cannot always have our own way without interfering with someone else's way.

James said, "What is the source of quarrels and conflicts among you? Is not the source your pleasures that wage war in your members? You lust and do not have; so you commit murder. And you are envious and cannot obtain; so you fight and quarrel. You do not have because you do not ask. You ask and do not receive, because you ask with wrong motives, so that you may spend it on your pleasures" (James 4:1-3).

Peace comes only when self dies, and the only place self truly dies is at the foot of Calvary. "I have been crucified with Christ," Paul said; "and it is no longer I who live, but Christ lives in me; and the life which I now live in the flesh I live by faith in the Son of God, who loved me, and delivered Himself up for me" (Gal. 2:20).

During World War II a group of American soldiers was exchanging fire with some Germans who occupied a farm house. The family who lived in the house had run to the barn for protection. Suddenly their little three-year-old daughter became frightened and ran out into the field between the two groups of soldiers. When they saw the little girl, both sides immediately ceased firing until she was safe. A little child brought peace, brief as it was, as almost nothing else could have done.

Jesus Christ came as a babe to earth, and in His sacrifice on the cross **He Himself** became **peace** for those who trust in Him. His peace is not temporary but permanent. He **made both groups**, Jews (those who were "near") and Gentiles (those who were "far off"), **into one, and broke down the barrier of the dividing wall.**

In Jesus Christ, a Jew is no longer distinct from a Gentile as far as religion is concerned. In fact, since A.D. 70, when the Temple was destroyed, true religious Judaism ceased to exist. Not only was the place of sacrifice destroyed, but so were all the genealogical records on which priestly descent was based. Likewise, a Gentile in Christ is no longer distinct as far as his spiritual condition is concerned. His paganism is gone, his unbelief is gone, his hopelessness is gone, and his godlessness is gone.

For those in Christ, the only identity that matters is their identity in Him. There is no Jewish or Gentile Christianity, black or white Christianity, male or female Christianity, or free or slave Christianity. There is only Christianity. Our one Lord has only one church.

The barrier of the dividing wall alludes to the separation of the Court of the Gentiles from the rest of the Temple. Between that court and the Court of the Israelites was a sign that read, "No Gentile may enter within the barricade which surrounds the sanctuary and enclosure. Anyone who is caught doing so will have himself to blame for his ensuing death." This physical barrier illustrated the barrier of hostility and hate that also separated the two groups. As we learn from the book of Acts, even a Jew who brought a Gentile into the restricted part of the Temple risked being put to death. Although Paul had not done so, certain Jews from Asia accused him of taking Trophimus, a Gentile from Ephesus, into the Temple. They would have stoned Paul to death had he not been rescued by Roman soldiers (Acts 21:27-32).

God had originally separated Jews from Gentiles (cf. Isa. 5:1-7; Matt. 21:33) for the purpose of redeeming both groups, not for saving the Jews alone. He placed the Court of the Gentiles in the Temple for the very purpose of winning Gentiles to Himself. It was meant to be a place for Jewish evangelism of Gentiles, a place for winning proselytes to Judaism and of thereby bringing them "near." It was that court, however, that the Jewish leaders of Jesus' day used as "a robbers' den" (Mark 11:17) rather than as a place of witness.

Christ forever **broke down** (the Greek aorist tense signifies completed action) every dividing wall **by abolishing in His flesh the enmity, which is the Law of commandments contained in ordinances.** When Jesus died on the cross He abolished every barrier between man and God and between man and his fellow man. The greatest barrier between Jew and Gentile was the ceremonial law, **the Law of commandments contained in ordinances.** The feasts, sacrifices, offerings, laws of cleanliness and purification, and all other such distinctive outward **commandments** for the unique separation of Israel from the nations were abolished.

That God's moral law was not abolished is clear from the phrase **contained in ceremonies.** His moral law reflects His own holy nature and therefore can never change (cf. Matt. 5:17-19). That is the law which for the Jews was summarized in the Ten Commandments and which for all men is written on their hearts (Rom. 2:15) and still commanded of them (Matt. 22:37-40; Rom. 13:8-10). Jesus summarized God's moral law still further by declaring, "A new commandment I give to you, that you love one another, even as I have loved you" (John 13:34). The Ten Commandments, like all of God's moral laws, are but the structured and particularized love that God still requires (James 2:8).

All the ceremonial laws which distinguished and separated Jews from

Gentiles were obliterated. Before Christ those groups could not eat together because of restricted foods, required washings, and ceremonial contamination. Now they could eat anything with anyone. Before Christ they could not worship together. A Gentile *could not* fully worship in the Jewish Temple, and a Jew *would not* worship in a pagan temple. In Christ they now worshiped together and needed no temple or other sacred place to sanctify it. All ceremonial distinctions and requirements were removed (cf. Acts 10:9-16; 11:17-18; Col. 2:16-17), **that in Himself He might make the two into one new man, thus establishing peace.** The emphasis is again on **in Himself**, affirming that this new unity can occur only when men are united in the person of the Lord Jesus Christ.

Kainos (**new**) does not refer to something recently completed, such as a new car rolling off the assembly line—one of many other cars just like it. This **new** refers to a difference in kind and quality, to a completely new model, unlike anything that existed before. The **new** person in Christ is not simply a Jew or Gentile who now happens to be a Christian. He is no longer a Jew or Gentile but only a Christian. Every other characteristic is "former" (see v. 11). Paul summed it up when he said, "For there is no distinction between Jew and Greek; for the same Lord is Lord of all, abounding in riches for all who call upon Him; for 'Whoever will call upon the name of the Lord will be saved'" (Rom. 10:12-13).

Another story from World War II is that of a group of American soldiers who lost their buddy in battle. They carried his body to the only cemetery in the area, which happened to be Catholic. When the priest was told that the dead man was not Catholic he said, "I am sorry, but he cannot be buried here." The disheartened and discouraged soldiers decided to do what they thought was next best, and during the night they buried their comrade just outside the cemetery fence. They returned the next morning to pay their last respects, but they could not find a grave outside the fence. When they told the priest of their quandary, he said, "The first part of the night I stayed awake sorry for what I told you. And the second part of the night I spent moving the fence."

When Jesus Christ **broke down the barrier of the dividing wall, by abolishing in His flesh the enmity,** He moved the fence, in order **that in Himself He might make the two into one new man.** No person who comes to Him will be excluded, and no person who is included will be spiritually distinct from any other. **In His flesh** points specifically to Jesus' death on the cross, through which He nullified, annulled, made of no effect, and invalidated (**abolished**, *katargeō*) the feud, discord, and alienation (**enmity**, *echthra*), **thus establishing peace**, as already indicated in verse 14.

The words **and might reconcile them both in one body to God through the cross** demonstrate not only that Jew and Gentile (**both** is masculine, clearly referring to men) are brought together but that together they are brought to God. Reconciliation to each other is inseparable from reconciliation to God. As **both** are brought to God, they are brought to each other. The death of Christ accomplished perfectly what God intended—bringing men to Himself. Verse 13 points to the blood of Christ, verse 15 focuses on the flesh of the dying Savior, and now in verse

16 Paul specifically mentions the place **(the cross)** where the blood was shed and the flesh was slain. How did **the cross** accomplish such reconciliation? It **put to death the enmity** between men and God (cf. Rom. 5:1, 10).

The hostility between men and God was ended in the sacrifice of Christ. He was the One who received the judicial sentence of God for sin. He paid the price of death which God required and thereby satisfied divine justice (cf. 2 Cor. 5:20). He became "a curse" for sinners (Gal. 3:13) and provided reconciliation of the believing sinner to God and to all other repentant sinners, regardless of race.

Reconcile is a rich term (*apokatallassō*) which holds the idea of turning from hostility to friendship. The double use of prepositions as prefixes (*apo, kata*) emphasizes the totality of this reconciliation (cf. Col. 1:19-23).

Man cannot even reconcile himself to his fellow man, much less to God. "God demonstrates His own love toward us, in that while we were yet sinners, Christ died for us. Much more then, having now been justified by His blood, we shall be saved from the wrath of God through Him. For if while we were enemies, we were reconciled to God through the death of His Son, much more, having been reconciled, we shall be saved by His life" (Rom. 5:8-10). Apart from Christ every person is helpless, sinful, and an enemy of God. As Paul says in another epistle, "It was the Father's good pleasure for all the fulness to dwell in [Christ], and through Him to reconcile all things to Himself, having made peace through the blood of His cross" (Col. 1:19-20). The Scottish commentator John Eadie wrote, "The cross which slew Jesus slew also the hostility between man and God. His death was the death of that animosity." The cross is God's answer to Judaizing, racial discrimination, segregation, apartheid, anti-Semitism, bigotry, war, and every other cause and result of human strife. This is the great mystery of Ephesians 3:6, "that the Gentiles are fellow heirs and fellow members of the body, and fellow partakers of the promise in Christ Jesus through the gospel."

The One who "Himself is our peace" (v. 14) **came and preached peace to you who were far away, and peace to those who were near.** *Euangelizō* (preached) literally means to bring or announce good news, and is almost always used in the New Testament of proclaiming the gospel, the good news of salvation through Jesus Christ. From that and related Greek terms we get such English words as evangelize, evangelist, and evangelical. The phrase in our text might therefore be rendered, **He came and** gospeled, or evangelized, **peace.**

The heavenly announcement of Jesus' birth was, "Glory to God in the highest, and on earth peace among men with whom He is pleased" (Luke 2:14). Those with whom the Lord is pleased are those who trust in His Son, Jesus Christ. As stated in verse 13 and explained above, those **who were far away** are Gentiles and **those who were near** are Jews. Every person, Jew and Gentile alike, has access to God's **peace** through Christ.

Jesus is the Prince of Peace (Isa. 9:6), who promised His disciples, "Peace I leave with you; My peace I give to you" (John 14:27). Like their Master, His disciples are also to be peacemakers (Matt. 5:9) and proclaimers of peace. When He sent out the seventy He commissioned them: "Whatever house you enter, first say, 'Peace be to this house.' And if a man of peace is there, your peace will rest upon him; but if not, it will return to you" (Luke 10:5-6). Peace surrounded the ministry of Jesus as an aura that continually blessed those who believed in Him. Among His last words' to His disciples were, "These things I have spoken to you, that in Me you may have peace" (John 16:33). The ministry of the apostles and other preachers of the early church was characterized by "preaching peace through Jesus Christ" (Acts 10:36). The ministry of the Holy Spirit is characterized by the giving of "love, joy, peace," and the other spiritual fruit mentioned in Galatians 5:22-23. God's kingdom itself is characterized by "righteousness and peace and joy in the Holy Spirit" (Rom. 14:17). The God of peace (1 Cor. 14:33; Heb. 13:20) calls His people to peace (1 Cor. 7:15).

ACCESS TO GOD

for through Him we both have our access in one Spirit to the Father. (2:18)

When we have Jesus Christ **(Him)** we also have access by the **Spirit to the Father.** The resources of the entire Trinity are ours the moment we receive Christ. It is not just a judicial reconciliation but an actual intimate relationship with practical value as we bring our needs to the Father.

Prosagōgē **(access)** is used only three times in the New Testament, in each case referring to the believer's access to God (see also Rom. 5:2; Eph. 3:12). In ancient times a related word was used to describe the court official who introduced persons to the king. They gave **access** to the monarch. The term itself carries the idea not of possessing access in our own right but of being granted the right to come to God with boldness, knowing we will be welcomed. It is only through our Savior's shedding of His blood in sacrificial death on Calvary and by faith in Him that we have union **in** His Holy **Spirit** and have **access** to the **Father.** The **Spirit** is at work to draw us continually to God (Rom. 8:15-17; Gal. 4:6-7). **Both** and **one spirit** emphasize again the commonality of Jew and Gentile. The work of Christ and the establishment of His church reach to all men.

Although in John 10 Jesus spoke of Himself both as the Good Shepherd and as the door to the sheepfold (vv. 1-14), He was not mixing metaphors. A Palestinian shepherd brought his sheep into the pen at night or erected a temporary fence of stones, wood, or mud if he was away from home. After he put the sheep inside, counted them carefully, and put oil on their wounds from briars or sharp rocks, he lay across the narrow opening that served as a door. The shepherd himself was the door.

The only **access** into God's presence, the only door into the sheepfold of His kingdom, is through His Son. But it is a wonderful and glorious **access** that can never be taken from us. We can always "draw near with confidence to the throne of grace, that we may receive mercy and may find grace to help in time of need" (Heb. 4:16). Through God's divine Son we, too, become His sons. Consequently we "have not received a spirit of slavery leading to fear again, but . . . a spirit of adoption as sons by which we cry out, 'Abba! Father!'" (Rom. 8:15).

Those who once were socially and spiritually alienated are in Christ united with God and with each other. Because they have Christ they have both peace and **access in one Spirit to the Father.** They have an Introducer who presents them at the heavenly throne of God, before whom they can come at any time. They can now come to God as their own **Father**, knowing that He no longer judges or condemns but only forgives and blesses. Even His discipline is an act of love, given to cleanse and restore His precious children to purity and spiritual richness.

Closing Summary

So then you are no longer strangers and aliens, but you are fellow citizens with the saints, and are of God's household, having been built upon the foundation of the apostles and prophets, Christ Jesus Himself being the corner stone, in whom the whole building, being fitted together is growing into a holy temple in the Lord; in whom you also are being built together into a dwelling of God in the Spirit. (2:19-22)

Paul closes his discussion of the marvelous unity of the Body of Christ by giving three metaphors to illustrate it. In the picture of **fellow citizens** he shows how Jew and Gentile have become part of the same kingdom. In the picture of **God's household** he shows how all believers are one spiritual family in Christ. In the picture of **a holy temple in the Lord** he shows that all believers are together a habitation for God.

UNITED IN GOD'S KINGDOM

So then you are no longer strangers and aliens, but you are fellow citizens with the saints, (2:19a)

Whether believers were previously apart from God and His people or whether they were previously nearby, they became one in Jesus Christ. Whether they were former **strangers** and outcasts or former **aliens** and guests, all believers in Christ become **fellow citizens** of God's kingdom **with the saints**—the believers from every age who have trusted in God. God's kingdom has no **strangers** or **aliens**, no second-class **citizens**. "Our citizenship is in heaven" (Phil. 3:20), Paul declares, and the only **citizens** of heaven are God's **saints**.

UNITED IN GOD'S FAMILY

and are of God's household, (2:19b)

As if being members of His divine kingdom were not enough, God's gracious work in Christ draws us even closer and makes us members of **God's household**. Because we have identified ourselves with His Son by faith, God now sees us and treats us exactly as He sees and treats His Son—with infinite love. Because the Father cannot give anything but His best to the Son, He cannot give anything but His best to those who are in His Son. "Both He who sanctifies and those who are sanctified are all from one Father," the writer of Hebrews tells us, "for which reason He is not ashamed to call them brethren. . . . Christ was faithful as a Son over His house whose house we are" (2:11; 3:6; Rom. 8:17).

Heavenly citizenship and family membership are not distinct roles or positions but simply different views of the same reality, because every kingdom citizen is a family member and every family member is a kingdom citizen.

If believers have no distinctions before God, they should have no distinctions among themselves. We are fellow citizens and fellow family members, equal in every spiritual way before God. If God accepts each one of us, how can we not accept each other?

UNITED IN GOD'S TEMPLE

having been built upon the foundation of the apostles and prophets, Christ Jesus Himself being the corner stone, in whom the whole building, being fitted together is growing into a holy temple in the Lord; in whom you also are being built together into a dwelling of God in the Spirit. (2:20-22)

The **foundation of the apostles and prophets** refers to the divine revelation that they taught, which in its written form is the New Testament. Because the Greek genitive case appears to be used in the subjective sense, signifying the originating agency, the meaning is not that the **apostles and prophets** were themselves the **foundation**—though in a certain sense they were— but that they laid the foundation. Paul spoke of himself as "a wise master builder" who "laid a foundation" and went on to say, "For no man can lay a foundation other than the one which is laid, which is Jesus Christ" (1 Cor. 3:10-11; cf. Rom. 15:20). These are New Testament **prophets**, as indicated by the facts that they are listed after **the apostles** and are part of the building of the church of Jesus Christ (cf. 3:5; 4:11). Their unique function was to authoritatively speak the word of God to the church in the years before the New Testament canon was complete. The fact that they are identified with the foundation reveals that they were limited to that formative period. As 4:11 shows, they completed their work and gave way to "evangelists, and . . . pastors and teachers."

The **corner stone** of the foundation is **Christ Jesus Himself** (see Isa. 28:16; Ps. 118:22; Matt. 21:42; Acts 4:11). The cornerstone was the major structural part of ancient buildings. It had to be strong enough to support what was built on it, and it had to be precisely laid, because every other part of the structure was oriented to it. The cornerstone was the support, the orienter, and the unifier of the entire building. That is what Jesus Christ is to God's kingdom, God's family, and God's building.

Through Isaiah, God declared, "Behold, I am laying in Zion a stone, a tested stone, a costly cornerstone for the foundation, firmly placed. He who believes in it will not be disturbed" (Isa. 28:16). After quoting that passage, Peter says, "This precious value, then, is for you who believe. . . . you are a chosen race, a royal priesthood, a holy nation, a people for God's own possession" (1 Pet. 2:7, 9).

It is **Christ Jesus Himself** as the corner stone, in whom the whole build-ing, being fitted together is growing into a holy temple in the Lord. *Sunarmologeō* (**fitted together**) refers to the careful joining of every component of a piece of furniture, wall, building, or other structure. Every part is precisely cut to fit snugly, strongly, and beautifully with every other part. Nothing is out of place, defective, misshapen, or inappropriate. Because it is Christ's **building**, the church is perfect, spotless, without defect or blemish. And that is how He will one day present the church, His own **holy temple**, to Himself (Eph. 5:27).

Christ's Body, however, will not be complete until every person who will believe in Him has done so. Every new believer is a new stone in Christ's **building**, His **holy temple**. Thus Paul says the temple **is growing** because believers are continually being added.

Many cathedrals in Europe have been under construction for hundreds of years. In a continuing process, new rooms, alcoves, chapels, and so forth are built. That is the way with the church of Jesus Christ. It is in a continual state of con-struction as each new saint becomes a new stone. "You also, as living stones," Peter said, "are being built up as a spiritual house for a holy priesthood, to offer up spiritual sacrifices acceptable to God through Jesus Christ" (1 Pet. 2:5). As kingdom citizens, family members, and living stones, believers in Jesus Christ are a holy priesthood who offer up spiritual sacrifices in God's **holy temple**. As a living, functioning, and precious part of that **temple**, we **also are being built together into a dwelling of God in the Spirit** (see also 2 Cor. 6:16).

The term **a dwelling** (*katoikētērion*) carries the idea of a permanent home. **God in the Spirit** makes His earthly sanctuary in the church, where He takes up permanent residence as Lord. This would be a vivid perception for people living amid temples in which pagan deities were believed to dwell, as in the temple to Artemis in Ephesus (see Acts 19:23-41). But the church is no small physical chamber in which an idol is kept; it is the vast spiritual body of the redeemed, wherein resides His Spirit. (It should be noted that this is a distinct truth from that of each believer being the individual temple of the Holy Spirit, as taught in 1 Cor. 6:19-20.)

Through the blood, the suffering flesh, the cross, and the death of the Lord Jesus Christ, aliens become citizens, strangers become family, idolaters become the temple of the true God, the hopeless inherit the promises of God, those without Christ become one in Christ, those far off are brought near, and the godless are reconciled to God. Therein is the reconciliation of men to God and of men to men.

The Mystery Revealed

8

For this reason I, Paul, the prisoner of Christ Jesus for the sake of you Gentiles—if indeed you have heard of the stewardship of God's grace which was given to me for you; that by revelation there was made known to me the mystery, as I wrote before in brief. And by referring to this, when you read you can understand my insight into the mystery of Christ, which in other generations was not made known to the sons of men, as it has now been revealed to His holy apostles and prophets in the Spirit; to be specific, that the Gentiles are fellow heirs and fellow members of the body, and fellow partakers of the promise in Christ Jesus through the gospel, of which I was made a minister, according to the gift of God's grace which was given to me according to the working of His power. To me, the very least of all saints, this grace was given, to preach to the Gentiles the unfathomable riches of Christ, and to bring to light what is the administration of the mystery which for ages has been hidden in God, who created all things; in order that the manifold wisdom of God might now be made known through the church to the rulers and the authorities in the heavenly places. This was in accordance with the eternal purpose which He carried out in Christ Jesus our Lord, in whom we have boldness and confident access through faith in Him. Therefore I ask you not to lose heart at my tribulations on your behalf, for they are your glory. (3:1-13)

This passage is largely a parenthesis, which runs from verse 2 through verse 13. Paul begins a prayer for believers to understand their resources as one in Christ and then decides to reemphasize and expand some of the truths he has already mentioned. He does not actually get into the prayer until verse 14, where he repeats the phrase "For this reason" in order to pick up the thought originally introduced in verse 1. He seems to have felt that the Ephesians were not ready to hear his prayer in their behalf until they better understood—and were therefore better able to apply—the truths he wanted to pray about. And it seemed essential for Paul to affirm his authority for teaching such a new and far-reaching truth as the oneness of Jew and Gentile in Christ, which he does by saying that God Himself gave him the truth and the commission to proclaim it (vv. 2-7).

The primary reemphasis is on the great mystery now revealed by God that Gentiles and Jews are one in Christ and that there is no longer any distinction. The revelation of the mystery is discussed in vv. 1-3, the explanation of it in vv. 4-6, the proclamation of it in vv. 7-9, and finally the intention of it in vv. 10-13. "To be specific," he says in verse 6, the sacred secret never before revealed is that "the Gentiles are fellow heirs and fellow members of the body, and fellow partakers of the promise in Christ Jesus through the gospel." That verse is essentially a summary of 2:11-22.

In 3:1-13 the apostle leads us to focus on five aspects of this divine mystery: its prisoner, its plan, its preaching, its purpose, and its privileges.

THE PRISONER OF THE MYSTERY

For this reason I, Paul, the prisoner of Christ Jesus for the sake of you Gentiles—if indeed you have heard of the stewardship of God's grace which was given to me for you; that by revelation there was made known to me the mystery, as I wrote before in brief. And by referring to this, when you read you can understand my insight into the mystery of Christ, (3:1-4)

For this reason introduces the cause of Paul's prayer (which really begins in v. 14) and refers back to the group of unifying truths Paul has just discussed in chapter 2—including the truths that the person in Christ becomes new (v. 15); that all believers are in one body (v. 16); that the Gentiles, who were once far away, now become near when they believe (v. 17); that all believers are equally citizens of God's kingdom and members of His family (v. 19); and that all believers are being built into God's temple and dwelling (vv. 21-22).

As already mentioned, however, before beginning his prayer, Paul decided to go over again some of those truths which prompted it, emphasizing their divine source. The apostle knew the value of repetition in teaching and the importance of establishing authority when teaching such new and non-traditional doctrine. None of us understands everything about a truth when we first hear it. God's truths are so marvelous and vast that we will never comprehend them fully in this life, no matter how many times we hear and study them. Even things we come to understand to some extent, we often forget and need to be reminded of, and some truths would be unacceptable to our human minds if we did not know they came from God (cf. John 6:60; 2 Pet. 3:16).

The first truth Paul mentions is about his own situation and God-given ministry. Outside of the Lord Jesus Himself, **Paul** is by far the dominant figure in the New Testament. He wrote at least thirteen of its 27 books. He is also the dominant human instrument of the Spirit in the book of Acts. And more than any other apostle he delineated the mysteries of the gospel, the truths hidden even to the most faithful believers of former ages but made known to the church of Jesus Christ.

In the opening of the letter Paul gives his credentials as Christ's apostle (1:1), but here he speaks of himself as **the prisoner of Christ Jesus**. He had been a prisoner for some five years, two years in Caesarea and the rest in Rome. He had been arrested on false charges made by Jews from the province of Asia who were visiting in Jerusalem. They had accused him of taking the Gentile Trophimus into forbidden areas of the Temple, though he had not done so. Paul had faced hearings before the Sanhedrin, before the Roman governor Felix, before Felix's successor, Festus, and even before King Agrippa. Had Paul not appealed to Caesar while defending himself before Festus, Agrippa would have released him. From Caesarea the apostle was taken to Rome, where he was allowed to stay in private quarters with a soldier to guard him (see Acts 21:27—28:16).

Although arrested on Jewish charges, Paul did not consider himself a prisoner of the Jews. Although imprisoned by Roman authority, he did not consider himself a prisoner of Rome. Although he had appealed to Caesar, he did not consider himself Caesar's prisoner. He was a minister of Jesus Christ, bought with a price, and given the special mission of preaching the gospel to the Gentiles. He was therefore **the prisoner of Christ Jesus**. Whatever he did and wherever he went were under Christ's control. Without his Lord's consent, he was not subject to the plans, power, punishment, or imprisonment of any man or government. The Greek form of the phrase has been called a genitive of originating cause, to identify Paul as a prisoner belonging to Jesus Christ, who was the cause of his imprisonment.

Perspective is all-important. How we view and react to circumstances is more important than the circumstances themselves. If all we can see is our immediate situation, then our circumstances control us. We feel good when our circumstances are good but miserable when they are not. Had Paul been able to see only his circumstances, he would quickly have given up his ministry. Had he thought that his life was ultimately in the hands of his persecutors, his jailers, his guards, or the Roman government, he would long since have given up in despair.

But Paul's perspective was a divine perspective, and he lived with total trust in God's purposes. It was not that he himself knew his future or fully *understood* the divine purposes behind his afflictions, but that he knew his future, his afflictions, and every other aspect of his life were totally in His Lord's hands. Despite his apostleship and his many revelations from the Lord, Paul lived and worked by faith, not by sight. He knew—not because of what he could see but because of the Lord's own Word—"that God causes all things to work together for good to those who love God, to those who are called according to His purpose" (Rom. 8:28). That is why as believers we are to "consider it all joy" when we "encounter various trials." We know that those trials, or testings, produce faith, that faith produces endurance, and that endurance leads to the perfection and completion of our preparation for living a godly life (James 1:2-4; cf. Acts 16:19-25; 1 Pet. 4:12-19).

Paul knew that his circumstances had "turned out for the greater progress of the gospel," so that his "imprisonment in the cause of Christ [had] become well known throughout the whole praetorian guard and to everyone else, and that most of the brethren, trusting in the Lord because of [his] imprisonment, [had] far more courage to speak the word of God without fear" (Phil. 1:12-14).

Paul was imprisoned for Christ's saving purpose, which was **for the sake of you Gentiles.** Just as Christ was not crucified for His own sake, Paul was not imprisoned for his own sake, but for the sake of his Lord and the sake of those he had been given a special calling to serve (Acts 9:15; 15:7; 20:20-24; 22:21; Rom. 11:13; etc.). "Now I rejoice in my sufferings for your sake," he told the Colossian believers, "and in my flesh I do my share on behalf of His body (which is the church) in filling up that which is lacking in Christ's afflictions" (Col. 1:24). In the next verses he told the Colossian Gentiles, "I was made a minister according to the stewardship from God bestowed on me for your benefit, that I might fully carry out the preaching the word of God, that is, the mystery which has been hidden from the past ages and generations; but has now been manifested to His saints" (vv. 25-26).

Paul knew he was in the ministry because he had been called by God to minister. He was not in it for his own purposes, and he did not try to carry it out in his own power. He made the supreme sacrifices of unselfish service for the sake of bringing others to glory (Eph. 3:13). In 2 Corinthians Paul expands our understanding of this commitment:

> We are afflicted in every way, but not crushed; perplexed, but not despairing; persecuted, but not forsaken; struck down, but not destroyed; always carrying about in the body the dying of Jesus, that the life of Jesus also may be manifested in our body. For we who live are constantly being delivered over to death for Jesus' sake, that the life of Jesus also may be manifested in our mortal flesh. So death works in us, but life in you. But having the same spirit of faith, according to what is written, "I believed, therefore I spoke," we also believe, therefore also we speak; knowing that He who raised the Lord Jesus will raise us also with Jesus and will present us with you. For all things are for your sakes, that the grace which is spreading to more and more people may cause the giving of thanks to abound to the glory of God. (4:8-15)

The words **if indeed you have heard of the stewardship of God's grace which was given to me for you** begin Paul's parenthesis to emphasize his divine authority for this teaching. The Greek first-class conditional clause indicates that the condition (if indeed you have heard . . .) is assumed to be true. Paul is therefore saying, "As I am sure you have already heard . . . ."

That about which they had heard was the stewardship of God's grace which was given to Paul on their behalf as Gentiles. *Oikonomia* (stewardship) primarily referred to the management of a household, business, or other concern on behalf of someone else. A steward was responsible for taking care of that which belonged to someone else. He supervised such things as buying, selling, bookkeeping, planting, harvesting, storing, the preparation of meals, the assignment of duties to slaves, and whatever else needed to be done.

Paul did not choose his apostleship or his ministry; he was appointed. "I thank Christ Jesus our Lord, who has strengthened me, because He considered me faithful, putting me into service; even though I was formerly a blasphemer and a persecutor and a violent aggressor" (1 Tim. 1:12-13; cf. Rom. 15:15-16; Gal. 2:9). Paul was chosen and commissioned purely by God's grace. He was appointed a steward *by* God's grace and then became a steward *of* God's grace. In 1 Corinthians 9:16-17 Paul articulates the sense of divine compulsion behind his ministry: "For if I preach the gospel, I have nothing to boast of, for I am under compulsion; for woe is me if I do not preach the gospel. For if I do this voluntarily, I have a reward; but if against my will [the sovereign act of God on the Damascus road], I have a stewardship entrusted to me." He therefore requested that men "regard us in this manner, as servants of Christ, and stewards of the mysteries of God" (1 Cor. 4:1).

Every believer is a steward of the calling, spiritual gifts, opportunities, skills, knowledge, and every other blessing he has from the Lord. Everything we have belongs to the Lord, and we are therefore entrusted as stewards to manage our lives and everything we possess in behalf of the One to whom they belong. We are faithful stewards when we use what we have to minister to those within the family of God and witness to those who are without. "As each one has received a special gift," Peter admonishes us, "employ it in serving one another, as good stewards of the manifold grace of God" (1 Pet. 4:10).

Paul's stewardship was unique even for an apostle, and it was so revolutionary that he found it necessary to add that **by revelation there was made known to me the mystery, as I wrote before in brief.** Obviously the mystery is that of Jew and Gentile being one in Christ, about which he **wrote before in brief** in 1:9-12 and 2:11-12. It was unknowable, incomprehensible truth hidden from all men until revealed by God (cf. 2 Tim. 3:16-17; 2 Pet. 1:19-21). **And by referring to this, when you read you can understand my insight into the mystery of Christ.** Paul was instrumental in revealing many mysteries to the church, but the particular mystery in view here is the one he has already mentioned in general and is about to state specifically—namely, that in Christ, Jew and Gentile become one in God's sight and in His kingdom and family (3:6).

It was Paul's intention not simply to declare the mystery but to explain and clarify it. When Ephesian believers, and every subsequent believer, would **read** his explanations (here stated as an assumed part of Christian living), Paul's hope was that they would come to **understand** his God-given **insight into the mystery of**

Christ. *Sunesis* (**insight**) literally means to bring together and metaphorically refers to comprehension and understanding, mentally bringing knowledge together in order to grasp its full meaning and significance. Spiritual **insight** must always precede practical application, because what is not properly understood cannot be properly applied.

The opposite of spiritual **insight** is "foolishness" (*asunetos,* Rom. 1:21), lack of spiritual discernment. As is made clear from the first part of that verse, lack of discernment existed even though the necessary spiritual facts were known—"For even though they knew God, they did not honor Him as God, or give thanks; but they became futile in their speculations."

Paul did not get his zeal for the gospel and his passion for souls from high emotional experiences, though he may have had many of them. His love, passion, and energetic zeal to win the lost and to build up the saved came from his great **insight** into the gospel. The more he comprehended God's fathomless love and grace, the more he was compelled to share and exemplify that love and that grace.

Paul was so filled with understanding of **the mystery of Christ** that he sacrificed his health, his freedom, and his very life in the ministry of imparting that understanding to others so that they, too, could **understand**. And for him, such sacrifice was supreme joy.

The Plan of the Mystery

which in other generations was not made known to the sons of men, as it has now been revealed to His holy apostles and prophets in the Spirit; to be specific, that the Gentiles are fellow heirs and fellow members of the body, and fellow partakers of the promise in Christ Jesus through the gospel, (3:5-6)

In verse 5 Paul defines the general meaning of mystery as it is used in the New Testament, and in verse 6 he identifies the particular mystery he is explaining to the Ephesians.

The antecedent of **which** is "the mystery of Christ," about which the apostle had been given special revelation and insight (vv. 3-4). **In other generations** this mystery **was not made known to the sons of men. Sons of men** refers to mankind in general, not just to God's chosen people, Israel. Before the church age no person, not even the greatest of God's prophets, had anything but a glimpse of the truth that Paul now discloses. The Old Testament teachings that relate to this mystery can only be understood clearly in light of New Testament revelation. We know the meaning of many Old Testament passages *only* because they are explained in the New (cf. Heb. 11:39-40; 1 Pet. 1:10-12).

No one knew the full meaning of God's promise to Abraham that "in you all the families of the earth shall be blessed" (Gen. 12:3) until Paul wrote, "And the Scripture, foreseeing that God would justify the Gentiles by faith, preached the gospel beforehand to Abraham, saying, 'All the nations shall be blessed in you'"

(Gal. 3:8). No one knew the full meaning of Isaiah's prediction, "I will also make You a light of the nations so that My salvation may reach to the end of the earth" (Isa. 49:6), until it was explained by Paul to mean the offering of the gospel of Jesus Christ (the Messiah) to the Gentiles as well as the Jews (Acts 13:46-47).

Old Testament saints had no vision of the church, the assembling together of all the saved into one united Body, in which there were absolutely no racial distinctions. The clues they had in the Old Testament were a mystery to them because too much information was lacking. That is why Jews in the early church— even the apostle Peter (see Acts 10)—had such a difficult time accepting Gentile believers as being completely on the same spiritual level as Jews. And that is why Paul was concerned in this letter to the Ephesians to state and restate, to explain and explain again, that great truth.

That truth **has now been revealed to His holy apostles and prophets in the Spirit.** The Greek behind **has . . . been revealed** is in the aorist tense, which refers to specific acts or events. Coupled with **now**, it here indicates the present immediacy of the revelation, which was given exclusively to New Testament **holy apostles and prophets**, and not to any other persons before or after them. These men were the instruments of writing Scripture, and 1 John 1:1-3 describes their unique function. The last time they met was at the Jerusalem Council, and the man who officiated there (James, the half brother of Jesus; see Acts 15:13) was not an apostle. They were soon scattered and died, but not before the revelation was complete. They are referred to in Ephesians 2:20 and 4:11, but only here are they called **holy**, to affirm that they were fit for such revelation and were authentic.

Some have noted that the personal pronoun (*autou*, **His**) is linked with **apostles** and that there is no such pronoun with **prophets.** This would be an emphasis on both the primacy and chronological priority of the **apostles** over the **prophets** who followed them. The distinction will be treated in connection with the discussion of 4:11.

The **Spirit** is the divine agency of God's revelation through these men. "Know this first of all," Peter explains, "that no prophecy of Scripture is a matter of one's own interpretation, for no prophecy was ever made by an act of human will, but men moved by the Holy Spirit spoke from God" (2 Pet. 1:20-21). This was the fulfillment of our Lord's promise in John 14:25-26 and 15:26-27.

To be specific, Paul goes on to say, the mystery is that **the Gentiles are fellow heirs and fellow members of the body, and fellow partakers of the promise in Christ Jesus through the gospel.**

As mentioned before, it is difficult for us to realize how incredibly revolutionary that truth was to Jews of Paul's day. In spite of the fact that the Old Testament teaches that Gentiles will be blessed by God (Gen. 12:3; 22:18; 26:4; 28:14), that Gentiles will bless God (Psalm 72), that the Messiah will come to Gentiles (Isa. 11:10; 49:6; 54:1-3; 60:1-3), that they will be saved by the Messiah (Hos. 1:10; Amos 9:11ff.), and that they will receive the Holy Spirit (Joel 2:28-29), the idea of including Gentiles in one body with Jews was the spiritual equivalent of saying that lepers were no longer to be isolated, that they were now perfectly free to intermingle and associate with everyone else as normal members of society. In the minds of most Jews, their spiritual separation from Gentiles was so absolute and so right that the thought of total equality before God was inconceivable and little short of blasphemy.

Yet Paul declares that, first of all, the **Gentiles are fellow heirs.** Those who once were "excluded from the commonwealth of Israel, and strangers to the covenants of promise" (2:12) now have exactly the same legal status before God as His chosen people, the Jews. They have the same marvelous, boundless inheritance in Christ that Paul has already mentioned (1:11, 14, 18). *Every* believer is blessed "with every spiritual blessing in the heavenly places in Christ" (1:3). As the apostle told the Galatians, regardless of your racial or other heritage, "If you belong to Christ, then you are Abraham's offspring, heirs according to promise" (Gal. 3:29). The Gentiles are not boarders or strangers but sons (cf. 1:11, 14, 18; 2:19), having the same legal status as all other believers.

Gentiles are also now **fellow members of the body.** They are now equally blessed as outsiders, as joint heirs who have the same benefits as Jews but who experience those benefits in some sort of separate but equal existence. They are full **members of the body,** linked by common life with every other person in God's holy family. They are not second-class in-laws, begrudgingly acknowledged as distant relatives. They are **fellow members,** indistinguishable in God's eyes from any other member. Every child of God is *only* God's child. Spiritually, he has no genes but divine genes. "For even as the body is one and yet has many members, and all the members of the body, though they are many, are one body, so also is Christ. For by one Spirit we were all baptized into one body, whether Jews or Greeks, whether slaves or free, and we were all made to drink of one Spirit" (1 Cor. 12:12-13).

In addition to having the same legal and family status, Gentiles also are **fellow partakers of the promise in Christ through the gospel.** That is not so much a third status as it is a summary of the other two. All Christians, regardless of their status or position before being saved, are now **fellow partakers** of everything that pertains to **Christ through the gospel**—which is everything that pertains to Christ. The essence of the **gospel** is that, through faith in Jesus Christ, believers are made everything He is and given everything He has. The phrase "the mystery of Christ" (v. 4) is also used in Col. 4:3 as the very essence of Paul's message. It carries the truth of Colossians 1:27, that Christ is in believing Gentiles as well as believing Jews as "the hope of glory" for both. It also carries the truth of Colossians 2:2, that the mystery is "Christ Himself," in whom believers have everything (v. 3). So the mystery is fully understood to be Jew and Gentile in Christ—Christ in Jew and Gentile, so that there is the intimate shared union of eternal life as they both become immersed in the Lord Jesus Christ (Gal. 2:20). God predestines every believer "to become conformed to the image of His Son" (Rom. 8:29). This is in answer to the prayer of our Lord recorded in John 17:

> I do not ask in behalf of these alone, but for those also who believe in Me through their word; that they may all be one; even as Thou, Father, art in Me, and I in Thee,

that they also may be in Us; that the world may believe that Thou didst send Me. And the glory which Thou hast given Me I have given to them; that they may be one, just as We are one; I in them, and Thou in Me, that they may be perfected in unity, that the world may know that Thou didst send Me, and didst love them, even as Thou didst love Me." (vv. 20-23)

Being **in Christ** through acceptance of **the gospel** is what creates among believers their perfect and absolutely new society. There can never be true oneness apart from that reality. And there can never be practical unity in the church until Christians realize and live by the positional unity they already have **in Christ,** their one Lord and Savior.

THE PREACHING OF THE MYSTERY

of which I was made a minister, according to the gift of God's grace which was given to me according to the working of His power. To me, the very least of all saints, this grace was given, to preach to the Gentiles the unfathomable riches of Christ, and to bring to light what is the administration of the mystery which for ages has been hidden in God, who created all things; (3:7-9)

The gospel is spread by men whom God calls to proclaim it, and it is the gospel of which Paul **was made a minister.** "How then shall they call upon Him in whom they have not believed?" Paul asks in Romans. "And how shall they believe in Him whom they have not heard? And how shall they hear without a preacher?" (Rom. 10:14). Although they had heard God's truth, many Israelites did not "heed the glad tidings; for Isaiah says, 'Lord, who has believed our report?'" (v. 16)—just as many who hear the gospel do not heed it. But it must be heard before it can be heeded, and Paul's calling, like the calling of every preacher, was to proclaim God's good news as a **minister, according to the gift of God's grace.** In a similar line of thought in 1 Corinthians, Paul emphasizes this calling of grace: "But by the grace of God I am what I am, and His grace toward me did not prove vain; but I labored even more than all of them, yet not I, but the grace of God with Me" (1 Cor. 15:10).

Minister is from *diakonos,* the basic meaning of which is servant, in particular a servant who waits on tables. It later came to refer to servants in general. By definition, a servant is one who acts on the commands of others, who recognizes and submits to a higher power. His primary responsibility is to do what he is told to do. Paul's single responsibility was to faithfully be a servant, **according to the gift of God's grace which was given to** [him] **according to the working of His power.** "What then is Apollos?" Paul asked the factious Corinthians. "And what is Paul? Servants through whom you believed, even as the Lord gave opportunity to each one" (1 Cor. 3:5). The Lord is the power behind the servant. To the Colossians the apostle said, "I labor, striving according to His power, which mightily works within me" (Col. 1:29).

Paul emphasizes the fact that he did not make himself a minister but that he **was made a minister** (cf. Col. 1:23, 25). The calling, the message, the work, and the empowering were all God's. When he was first saved on the Damascus Road, and while he was still blinded from the great light, Paul was given his commission by Jesus. "Arise, and stand on your feet; for this purpose I have appeared to you, to appoint you a minister and a witness" (Acts 26:16). It was not Paul's education, natural abilities, experience, power, personality, influence, or any other such thing that qualified him to be a **minister** of Jesus Christ. He **was made** an apostle, a preacher, and a servant by the will and power of His Lord. He felt unworthy of any reward, as if he had sought sacrificially to serve in this way. The choice was not his at all, so he deserved no commendation (1 Cor. 9:16-18). He did not want accolades but prayers, because he was in serious trouble if he failed to fulfill a calling he had not even chosen!

Any person in the ministry of the church whom God has not appointed is a usurper. No matter how seemingly good his intentions, he can do nothing but harm to the work of the Lord and to the Lord's people. Jeremiah speaks to this matter when he writes the Lord's word: "I did not send these prophets, but they ran. I did not speak to them, but they prophesied. . . . I did not send them or command them" (Jer. 23:21, 32). No man should enter the ministry unless he is absolutely certain of the Lord's calling.

The key for present knowledge of a divine call is given in 1 Timothy 3, where Paul speaks of the pastor or spiritual overseer as a man who "aspires to the office" and who is verified and approved by those who know him as one who is "above reproach" (vv. 3-7). The present call, then, is bound up in a man's strong desire and affirmation as to a godly life. God calls through desire and church verification.

Then or now, the man who is genuinely called by God is in constant danger of losing his effectiveness by coming to think of himself as more than a servant. When he loses his sense of servanthood, at that same time he loses his spiritual power and usefulness. When he exalts himself and begins to work in his own human power and according to his own plans, he competes with God and forfeits his spiritual power. To lose dependence is to lose everything, because everything that is of any value in our lives, including power for effective service, comes only from the Lord. Among the greatest dangers to the ministry, and to all faithful Christian living, are things that in the world's eyes are of supreme value—personal ambition, prestige, recognition, honor, reputation, and success. God not only chooses weak and foolish people to save (1 Cor. 1:26-29), but weak and foolish preachers through whom to save them (2 Cor. 11:30; 12:7-10). For those not willing to pay that price, their seeking the position is illegitimate.

Unholiness is also a disqualification, prompting Paul to say, "I buffet my body and make it my slave, lest possibly, after I have preached to others, I myself should be disqualified" (1 Cor. 9:27).

Paul's calling to the ministry of the gospel, like everything else he received from the Lord, was **the gift of God's grace. To me, the very least of all the saints,** he goes on to say, **this grace was given.** Though an apostle and a specially chosen minister of the mysteries of the gospel, Paul considered himself **the very least of all the saints**. The term **very least** is a comparative, indicating less than the least. That was not mock humility but his honest assessment of himself. Because he had such an unusually clear comprehension of God's righteousness, he also had an unusually clear understanding of how far short he himself fell of that righteousness. Paul claimed no second work of grace by which he was perfected in holiness, love, or anything else. To the end of his life he considered himself the foremost of sinners (1 Tim. 1:15) and was overwhelmed by his sense of unworthiness. That attitude does not limit a man's service but rather is the key to his usefulness (cf. Gideon in Judges 6:15-16 and Isaiah in Isa. 6:1-9).

The unfathomable riches of Christ include all His truths and all His blessings, all that He is and has. The purpose of every preacher is to declare those **riches**, to tell believers how rich they are in **Christ**. That is why it is so important for Christians to understand the greatness of their position in the Lord. The obedient, productive, and happy Christian life cannot be lived apart from understanding that glorious position. Before we can do what the Lord wants us to do for Him, we must understand what He already has done for us. We have riches beyond measure in the One of whom it was said, "in whom are hidden all the treasures of wisdom and knowledge" (Col. 2:3) and in the One in whom we have "everything pertaining to life and godliness" (2 Pet. 1:3).

Among the **unfathomable riches** with which Christ has blessed us are "His kindness and forbearance and patience" (Rom. 2:4), His "wisdom and knowledge" (11:33), His mercy and great love (Eph. 2:4), "His glory" (3:16), His supplying us with "all things to enjoy" (1 Tim. 6:17), His assurance (Col. 2:2), His word (3:16), and even our being reproached for His sake (Heb. 11:26). Little wonder that Paul triumphantly reminds us that "in Him you have been made complete" (Col. 2:10).

Simply knowing about the **riches of Christ** is not enough, however. When we fall into sin and disobedience we forfeit the present blessing of those riches, just as did the fleshly, disobedient Corinthian believers. "You are already filled," Paul told them sarcastically. "You have already become rich, you have become kings without us; and I would indeed that you had become kings so that we also might reign with you" (1 Cor. 4:8). Like the Laodiceans, they thought they were rich and in need of nothing, not realizing that they were really "wretched and miserable and poor and blind and naked" (Rev. 3:17).

Paul's ministry was also **to bring to light what is the administration of the mystery which for ages has been hidden in God, who created all things**. **Administration** is from the same Greek word (*oikonomia*) as "stewardship" in verse 2. Paul is saying, in effect, "I am not only called in the vertical area to preach the unfathomable riches of Christ, but in the horizontal area to teach about the **administration**, the stewardship or dispensation, of the mystery of the church age." The first area deals with our relationship to God and the second with our daily living and our ministry to each other as fellow believers.

Paul's mission was **to bring to light**, or reveal, the full expression of the operation of this great truth of Gentile and Jews being one, a truth hidden for so long in the mind of God the Creator.

THE PURPOSE OF THE MYSTERY

in order that the manifold wisdom of God might now be made known through the church to the rulers and the authorities in the heavenly places. This was in accordance with the eternal purpose which He carried out in Christ Jesus our Lord, (3:10-11)

The purpose (*hina* with subjunctive verb) of God's revealing the mystery of the church is **that the manifold wisdom of God might now be made known through the church to the rulers and the authorities in the heavenly places,** namely, the angels. Angels are also spoken of in such terms in Ephesians 1:21 and Colossians 1:16. In Ephesians 6:12 Paul uses similar words in regard to fallen angels. God has brought the church into being for the purpose of manifesting His great wisdom before the angels, both holy and unholy. The New Testament emphasis is on the holy angels' concern with the church, but it is obvious that the fallen angels can also to some extent see what is going on, though they have no desire or capacity for praise.

This was in accordance with the eternal purpose which He carried out in Christ Jesus our Lord, Paul continues to explain. Everything God has ever done has had the ultimate purpose of giving Himself glory. As Paul declares elsewhere, "There is but one God, the Father, from whom are all things, and we exist for Him; and one Lord, Jesus Christ, by whom are all things, and we exist through Him" (1 Cor. 8:6), and "All things have been created by Him and for Him" (Col. 1:16).

The church does not exist simply for the purpose of saving souls, though that is a marvelous and important work. The supreme purpose of the church, as Paul makes explicit here, is to glorify God by manifesting His **wisdom** before the angels, who can then offer greater praise to God. The purpose of the universe is to give glory to God, and that will be its ultimate reality after all evil is conquered and destroyed. Even now, "The heavens are telling of the glory of God; and their expanse is declaring the work of His hands" (Ps. 19:1). The church is not an end in itself but a means to an end, the end of glorifying God. The real drama of redemption can only be understood when we realize that the glory of God is the supreme goal of creation. Holy angels are especially made and confirmed in purity and praise as creatures who will forever give God glory (Ps. 148:2; Heb. 1:6), and the redemption of fallen men enriches their praise. Redeemed people, then, are to enhance angelic praise and some day in heaven to join in it (Rev. 4:8-11; 5:8-14; 7:9-12; 14:1-3; 19:1-8).

Even the fallen angels glorify God, though they do not intend to do so. It was their very rejection of His glory and the seeking of their own glory that caused them to be cast out of heaven in the first place. Yet Jesus said, "I will build My church; and the gates of Hades shall not overpower it" (Matt. 16:18). God is glorified through the fallen angels by continually frustrating their rebellious plans and showing the futility of their evil intentions to destroy His church. His holy wrath also displays His glory, since it is a revelation of who He is (cf. Rom. 9:19-22).

The angels can see the power of God in creation, the wrath of God at Sinai, and the love of God at Calvary. But above all they see His **manifold** [multi-colored, multi-faceted] **wisdom** that is **made known through the church.** They see Him taking Jew and Gentile, slave and free, male and female—who together murdered the Messiah and were worthy only of hell—and making them, by that very cross of murder, one spiritual Body in Jesus Christ. They see Him breaking down every barrier, every wall that divides and making all believers one in an indivisible, intimate, and eternal union with the Father, the Son, the Holy Spirit, and every other believer from every other age and circumstance. "There is joy in the presence of the angels of God over one sinner who repents," Jesus said (Luke 15:10). Every sinner who repents and turns to Christ adds another spiritual stone to God's temple, another member to His Body, and becomes another forgiven and cleansed sinner who is made eternally one with every other forgiven and cleansed sinner. The holy angels not only are interested in the salvation of men (1 Pet. 1:12) but constantly watch the face of God in heaven to see His reaction to the treatment of His saved earthly children (Matt. 18:10, 14), standing ready to carry out any mission in their behalf.

When Paul admonished the Corinthian women to show submission to their husbands through the custom of wearing long hair, he reinforced the command by saying it was given "because of the angels" (1 Cor. 11:10), so as not to offend their sense of submissiveness and to give them greater cause to glorify God by the obedience of the church in the matter of proper male and female responses. They are led to praise the Lord when they see the right relationship in the church overruling the perversion of man's relationship engineered by Satan and sin. After Paul had stated certain principles regarding elders in the church, he wrote, "I solemnly charge you in the presence of God and of Christ Jesus and of His chosen angels, to maintain these principles without bias" (1 Tim. 5:21). Angels are exceedingly concerned about the discipline needed to produce holy behavior and pure living in the church as well as godly leadership (vv. 17-25). After all, says the writer of Hebrews, "Are they not all ministering spirits, sent out to render service for the sake of those who will inherit salvation?" (Heb. 1:14). They minister to and watch over the church.

In the classroom of God's universe, He is the Teacher, the angels are the students, the church is the illustration, and the subject is **the manifold wisdom of God.**

The Privilege of the Mystery

in whom we have boldness and confident access through faith in Him. Therefore I ask you not to lose heart at my tribulations on your behalf, for they are your glory. (3:12-13)

When we put our **faith in** Jesus Christ we can freely come to God and share in all of heaven's unfathomable riches. In Judaism only the high priest could enter the presence of God in the Holy of Holies, and that but briefly once a year on the Day of Atonement. For anyone else to come into God's presence meant instant death. But now, Paul says, every person who comes to Christ in faith can come before God at any time and with **boldness and confident access.** That is the privilege within the mystery of the church. "For we do not have a high priest who cannot sympathize with our weaknesses, but one who has been tempted in all things as we are, yet without sin. Let us therefore draw near with confidence to the throne of grace, that we may receive mercy and may find grace to help in time of need" (Heb. 4:15-16).

We are not to be flippant or irreverent but are to come to the Lord with an honest, open heart—in freedom of speech and freedom of spirit. **Confident access** is trust that knows no fear of rejection, because we belong to Him (cf. 1 Tim. 3:13).

In light of such great privilege, Paul says, **I ask you not to lose heart at my tribulations on your behalf, for they are your glory.** In and through every circumstance of His children, God works His goodness, blessing, and **glory.** Apparently many believers grieved over Paul's extended years of imprisonment and over the almost continual suffering he endured because of his ministry. But "I consider that the sufferings of this present time," he explained to the Roman believers, "are not worthy to be compared with the glory that is to be revealed to us" (Rom. 8:18). And Paul's suffering turned out for the honor rather than the disgrace of those to whom he ministered (cf. Phil. 1:12).

The Fullness of God

For this reason, I bow my knees before the Father, from whom every family in heaven and on earth derives its name, that He would grant you, according to the riches of His glory, to be strengthened with power through His Spirit in the inner man; so that Christ may dwell in your hearts through faith; and that you, being rooted and grounded in love, may be able to comprehend with all the saints what is the breadth and length and height and depth, and to know the love of Christ which surpasses knowledge, that you may be filled up to all the fulness of God.

Now to Him who is able to do exceeding abundantly beyond all that we ask or think, according to the power that works within us, to Him be the glory in the church and in Christ Jesus to all generations forever and ever. Amen. (3:14-21)

It is possible to know a great deal about an automobile—to know exactly how the engine, the ignition, the transmission, and so on operate—and yet never use it to go anywhere. It is also possible to know very little about an automobile and yet use it every day to travel hundreds of miles. In the same way it is possible to know a great deal about the Bible—its doctrines, interpretations, moral standards, promises, warnings, and so on—and yet not live by those truths.

In Ephesians 1:1—3:13 Paul gives the basic truths about the Christian life—who we are in Christ and the great, unlimited resources we have in Him. From 3:14 through the rest of the letter we are exhorted to claim and to live by those truths. In 3:14-21 Paul gives his prayer requests on behalf of the Ephesian believers. In sharing his requests with them, he urges them to live in the full power and effectiveness of "every spiritual blessing in the heavenly places in Christ" (1:3). This second prayer in the book of Ephesians (see also 1:15-23) is a prayer for enablement. The first prayer is for believers to *know* their power; the second is for them to *use* it.

Two things a pastor should be most concerned about are telling his people who they are in Christ and then urging them to live like it. In other words, the pastor helps members of the flock understand their spiritual power, and then he motivates them to use it. Like the apostle Paul in this letter, the faithful pastor seeks to bring his people to the place of maximum power as full-functioning Christians.

The prayer of Ephesians 3:14-21 is a plea to God that also serves as a plea to believers. Paul pleads with believers to respond to God's sovereign provision, and he pleads with God to motivate them to do it—because God not only is the provider but is also the initiator and motivator. Paul calls on God to activate believers' power so that they can become faithful children and thereby glorify their heavenly Father.

In this great prayer of entreaty to God and exhortation to His children, Paul prays specifically for the inner strength of the Spirit, for the indwelling of Christ in the believer's heart, for incomprehensible love to permeate their lives, for them to have God's own fullness, and for God's glory thereby to be manifested and proclaimed. Each element builds on the previous ones, making a grand progression of enablement.

THE SPIRIT'S POWER

For this reason, I bow my knees before the Father, from whom every family in heaven and on earth derives its name, that He would grant you, according to the riches of His glory, to be strengthened with power through His Spirit in the inner man; (3:14-16)

For this reason picks up after the parenthesis of 3:2-13, and begins by repeating the words of verse one. The **reason** about which Paul speaks is therefore found in chapter 2. Christ makes us spiritually alive in Him (2:5), we are "His workmanship" (v. 10), "no longer strangers and aliens, but . . . fellow citizens with the saints, and are of God's household" (v. 19), "built upon the foundation of the apostles and prophets" (v. 20), and "are being built together into a dwelling of God in the Spirit" (v. 22). **For this reason,** therefore (that our new identity makes us the dwelling place of God), Paul prays for the Ephesians to use the power that their great status in Christ provides. Because God's power is in those believers, Paul prays that God would enable them to employ the fullness of that power. Because believers are the habitation of the triune, all-powerful God of the universe, Paul prays that their unlimited energy from Him would be manifested.

The truth that omnipotence dwells within impotence is so majestic, grandiose, and elevated that we would expect Paul to address God as the eternal King of glory or by some other such exalted title. But he says rather, **I bow my knees before the Father. Father** is the same appellation Jesus always used in prayer, and the one He used in teaching His disciples to pray (Matt. 6:9). Because God is our heavenly **Father**, we do not come to Him in fear and trembling, afraid that He will rebuff us or be indifferent. We do not come to God to appease Him as the pagans do to their deities. We come to a tender, loving, concerned, compassionate, accepting **Father.** A loving human father always accepts the advances of his children, even when they have been disobedient or ungrateful. How much more does our heavenly Father accept His children, regardless of what they have done or not done? Paul approaches the **Father** with boldness and confidence, knowing that He is more willing for His children to come to Him than they ever are of going to Him. He knows that God has been waiting all the while with a Father's heart of love and anticipation.

In saying, **I bow my knees,** Paul is not prescribing a required posture for prayer. He did not always pray while kneeling, and Scripture tells of God's faithful people praying in many different positions, as shown in the following passages in which emphasis is added. As he interceded for Sodom and Gomorrah, "Abraham was still *standing* before the Lord" (Gen. 18:22). When David prayed about the building of the Temple, he "went in and *sat* before the Lord" (1 Chron. 17:16). As Jesus prayed in the Garden of Gethsemane on the night of His betrayal, He "*fell on His face* and prayed" (Matt. 26:39).

But in Scripture, bowing the knees signifies several things that may have prompted Paul to mention that position here. First, it represents an attitude of submission, of recognition that one is in the presence of someone who is of much higher rank, dignity, and authority. After proclaiming the Lord as "the rock of our salvation, . . . a great God, and a great King above all gods," and as the Creator of all the earth, the psalmist says, "Come, let us worship and bow down; let us kneel before the Lord our Maker" (Ps. 95:1-6).

Second, we see references to bowing the knee before God in times of intense passion and emotion. Appalled and heartbroken over hearing of the intermarriage of Israelites with their pagan neighbors, Ezra fell on his knees and stretched out his hands in confession to the Lord on their behalf (Ezra 9:5-6). When Daniel heard that King Darius had signed the edict devised by the jealous commissioners and satraps forbidding the worship of any god besides the king, "he continued kneeling on his knees three times a day, praying and giving thanks before his God" (Dan. 6:10)—knowing that his continued worship of the true God would result in his being thrown into a den of lions. As Paul met for the last time with the elders from Ephesus, "he knelt down and prayed with them all" on the seashore at Miletus (Acts 20:36).

As he prayed for the Ephesians while writing this letter to them, the apostle felt led to **bow [his] knees before the Father** on their behalf, not because that position or any other is especially sacred, but because it spontaneously reflected his reverence for God's glory in the midst of his passionate prayer.

From whom every family in heaven and on earth derives its name does not teach that God is the spiritual **Father** of every being in the universe. It does not, as claimed by modern liberalism, teach the universal fatherhood of God and the universal brotherhood of man. Scripture clearly teaches two spiritual fatherhoods, God's and Satan's. God is the heavenly Father of those who trust in Him and Satan is the spiritual father of those who do not. Nowhere are these two opposite fatherhoods more explicitly distinguished than in John 8. To the unbelieving Jews who rejected Him but presumed to claim Abraham as their spiritual forefather, Jesus said, "If you are Abraham's children, do the deeds of Abraham. But as it is, you are seeking to kill Me, a man who has told you the truth, which I heard from God; this Abraham did not do. You are doing the deeds of your father. . . . If God were your Father, you would love Me; . . . You are of your father the devil" (vv. 39-42, 44). In his first epistle, John declares, "By this the children of God and the children of the devil are obvious: anyone who does not practice righteousness is not of God, nor the one who does not love his brother" (3:10).

Every family in heaven and on earth refers to the saints of every age— those now **in heaven** and those still remaining **on earth.** They are the only ones who legitimately derive their names from God the Father. Christians are no more or less the children of God than were believing Israelites, as well as believing Gentiles, before the coming of Christ. **Every family** of believers is a part of the one spiritual family of God, in which there are many members but only one **Father** and one brotherhood.

Paul's first and central request for this divine family is that **God would grant [them], according to the riches of His glory, to be strengthened with power through His Spirit in the inner man.**

In a previous chapter the illustration was used of a wealthy person who gives *according to,* rather than simply *out of,* his riches. For a millionaire to give fifty or a hundred dollars would be simply to give out of his wealth, but to give twenty-five thousand dollars would be to give according to his wealth. The greater a person's wealth, the greater his gift must be to qualify for giving according to his wealth. For God to give **according to the riches of His glory** is absolutely staggering, because His **riches** are limitless, completely without bounds! Yet that is exactly the measure by which Paul implores God to empower the Ephesians.

Almost every prayer of Paul's that is recorded in Scripture was for the spiritual welfare of others. Even when he was persecuted, imprisoned, and in need of many things for his own welfare, he prayed primarily for fellow believers that they might be spiritually protected and strengthened. Even when he prayed for himself it was most often for the purpose of being better able to serve his Lord and the Lord's people. Later in this letter the apostle asked the Ephesians to "pray on my behalf, that utterance may be given to me in the opening of my mouth, to make known with boldness the mystery of the gospel" (6:19).

Paul prayed that the Philippians' love would "abound still more and more in real knowledge and all discernment, so that [they would] be sincere and blameless until the day of Christ" (Phil. 1:9-10). He did not cease to pray for the Colossian believers to "be filled with the knowledge of His will in all spiritual wisdom and understanding, so that [they might] walk in a manner worthy of the Lord, to please Him in all respects, bearing fruit in every good work and increasing in the knowledge of God; strengthened with all power [lit., being empowered with all power], according to His glorious might" (Col. 1:9-11; cf. Phil. 1:4; 1 Thess. 1:2).

All of God's people are to be like Paul in having an overriding sensitivity to the spiritual needs of others, for the salvation of the unsaved and the spiritual protection and growth of the saved. We are to be sensitive to the spiritual needs of our wives, husbands, children, pastors, fellow church members, neighbors, fellow students, friends, and co-workers. We are to pray for everyone with whom we have any contact at all, as well as for many others—such as government officials, Christian leaders, and missionaries—whom we may never have met or known.

Prayer is to be a constant effort of our daily living. Jesus said, "Keep on the alert at all times, praying in order that you may have strength" (Luke 21:36). Paul often mentioned that he prayed continually for others (Eph. 1:16; Phil. 1:4; Col. 1:3, 9) and repeatedly encouraged others to do the same (Rom. 12:12; Eph. 6:18; Col. 4:2; cf. Phil. 4:6). At least two of Jesus' parables focus on persistent prayer—the parable of the man who knocks on his neighbor's door at midnight asking for food to give an unexpected guest (Luke 11:5-10) and the parable of the importunate widow who eventually obtained help from a wicked judge because she refused to stop petitioning him (Luke 18:1-8).

As the rest of the prayer indicates, Paul's petition for the Ephesian believers was bold, confident, and inclusive. He asked God to give them every spiritual enablement they did not already use to apply their available resources. Jacques Ellul, the contemporary Christian philosopher, is convinced that prayer for persons living in the technological age must be combative—and prayer, he says, is not just combat with Satan, corrupted society, and one's own divided self, but is combat with God. We must struggle with the Lord just as Jacob did at Peniel (Gen. 32:24-30), as Abraham boldly interceded for Sodom and Gomorrah (Gen. 18:23-32), and as Moses interceded for his fellow Israelites (Ex. 32:11-13; Num. 14:13-19).

In 1540 Luther's good friend and assistant, Friedrich Myconius, became sick and was expected to die within a short time. From his bed he wrote a tender farewell letter to Luther. When Luther received the message, he immediately sent back a reply: "I command thee in the name of God to live because I still have need of thee in the work of reforming the church. . . . The Lord will never let me hear that thou art dead, but will permit thee to survive me. For this I am praying, this is my will, and may my will be done, because I seek only to glorify the name of God."

Those words seem harsh and insensitive to modern ears, but God apparently honored the prayer. Although Myconius had already lost the ability to speak when Luther's reply came, he soon recovered. He lived six more years and died two months after Luther.

In our daily living and in our prayer, it is more difficult to appreciate spiritual riches than it is to appreciate material riches. Whether we have a lot of money or not, we have some comprehension of what material wealth is like. We have a taste of it in the things we do possess and we can vicariously enjoy the expensive homes, cars, boats, jewelry, clothes, and other such things that we see rich people enjoying. Spiritual riches, on the other hand, are not so obvious—and are not even attractive to the natural man or to disobedient Christians.

But to the spiritual believer, **the riches of His glory** are rich indeed. From the beginning of the letter Paul has been exulting over those divine riches—God blessing us with every spiritual blessing in the heavenly places (1:3), His choosing us for Himself before the foundation of the world (1:4), His redemption and forgiveness (1:7), His making known to us the mystery of His will (1:9), His giving us an inheritance with His Son, Jesus Christ (1:11), and so on throughout the first two and a half chapters. The phrase **of His glory** testifies that these riches belong to God because of who He is. They belong innately to His Person, which is to say, His glory (cf. 1:17, where Paul calls God, "the Father of glory" and Ex. 33:18ff., where God reveals His personal attributes as glory).

Those, and many others, are the riches that every believer has in Jesus Christ. Paul is not praying for God to *give* these **riches** to believers, but **that He would grant** believers **to be strengthened** by God **according to** the **riches** they already possess. He wants them to live lives that correspond to the spiritual wealth they have in Christ.

A certain rich English eccentric named Julian Ellis Morris liked to dress like a tramp and sell razor blades, soap, and shampoo door-to-door. After a day's work he would return to his beautiful mansion, put on formal attire and have his chauffeur drive him to an exclusive restaurant in his limousine. Sometimes he would catch a flight to Paris and spend the evening there.

Many Christians live something like Mr. Morris, spending their day-by-day lives in apparent spiritual poverty and only occasionally enjoying the vast **riches of His glory** that their heavenly Father has given them. How tragic to go around in the tattered rags of our own inadequacy when we could be living sumptuously in the superabundance of God's unspeakable riches.

The first step in living like God's children is to be **strengthened with power through His Spirit in the inner man.** Yet most Christians never seem to get to this first step, not knowing what it is to see God's power fully at work in them. They suffer, the church suffers, and the world suffers because **the inner man** of most believers is never **strengthened with power through His Spirit.**

Paul was concerned for the physical health of believers and was used by God to bring healing to many. He was concerned for the destitute saints in Jerusalem and worked tirelessly to raise money for them to buy food and other physical necessities. But he knew that the outer man was destined to perish. It is only a temporary housing for the real person, **the inner man.** "Therefore we do not lose heart," Paul could say, "but though our outer man is decaying, yet our inner man is being renewed day by day" (2 Cor. 4:16). Paul told Timothy, "But the Lord stood with me, and strengthened me, in order that through me the proclamation might be fully accomplished, and that all the Gentiles might hear; and I was delivered out of the lion's mouth" (2 Tim. 4:17).

In *The Psychological Society* Martin Gross questions the very foundations of psychology and psychiatry, suggesting that prestige and financial gain are the real driving forces behind them. Even more significantly, however, he asserts that psychology and psychiatry have no answers to the mental and emotional ills they are used to treat. His conclusion is that every person is incurably neurotic by nature and should be left alone with his neurosis. From the purely human standpoint from which he writes, Gross's pessimistic conclusion is perfectly sound, because man's basic nature is indeed universally and incurably flawed. But the flaw is sin, of which neuroses and all other problems are but symptoms. The flaw is in **the inner man**, where man himself cannot perform a cure.

Only God can reach and cure **the inner man**, and that is where He most wants to work. His work begins with salvation, and after that His main field of work is still **the inner man**, because that is where spiritual life exists and where it must grow. The "divine nature," imparted to the believer at salvation (1 Pet. 1:3), is at the core of the **inner man** and is the base from which the Holy Spirit changes the thinking of the believer.

Although the outer, physical man becomes weaker and weaker with age, the **inner**, spiritual man should continually grow stronger and stronger **with power through His Spirit**. Only God's Spirit can strengthen our spirits. He is the one who energizes, revitalizes, and empowers us (cf. Acts 1:8). In Romans 7:22-23 we hear Paul expressing the strong desire of a regenerated man to do the will of God but being hampered by the sin that dwells in his fleshly body, whereas in chapter 8 we hear him express the truth that victory in this conflict is in the Holy Spirit. "For those who are according to the flesh set their minds on the things of the flesh, but those who are according to the Spirit, the things of the Spirit. For the mind set on the flesh is death, but the mind set on the Spirit is life and peace" (8:5-6). "Those who are in the flesh cannot please God," he goes on to say. "However, you are not in the flesh but in the Spirit, if indeed the Spirit of God dwells in you" (vv. 8-9). In fact, the promise comes that through the power of the Spirit the believer can "kill" the evil deeds of his unredeemed flesh (v. 13).

To the Galatians he wrote, "Walk by the Spirit, and you will not carry out the desire of the flesh" (Gal. 5:16). The obedient, effective, and productive Christian must be Spirit conscious, Spirit filled, and Spirit controlled.

When the **inner man** is fed regularly on the Word of God and seeks the Spirit's will in all the decisions of life, the believer can be sure he will be **strengthened with power through His Spirit**. Spiritual power is not the mark of a special class of Christian but is the mark of every Christian who submits to God's Word and Spirit. Like physical growth and strength, spiritual growth and strength do not come overnight. As we discipline our minds and spirits to study God's Word, understand it, and live by it, we are nourished and strengthened. Every bit of spiritual food and every bit of spiritual exercise add to our strength and endurance.

Spiritual growth can be defined as the decreasing frequency of sin. The more we exercise our spiritual muscles, yielding to the Spirit's control of our lives, the less sin is present. Where the strength of God increases, sin necessarily decreases. The nearer we come to God, the further we go from sin.

As that occurs, what happens to the outer man matters less and less. Paul could tell the Corinthians,

> We are handicapped on all sides but we are never frustrated: we are puzzled, but never in despair. We are persecuted, but we never have to stand it alone: we may be knocked down but we are never knocked out! Every day we experience something of the death of the Lord Jesus, so that we may also know the power of the life of Jesus in these bodies of ours. We are always facing death, but this means that you know more and more of life. . . . This is the reason why we never collapse. The outward man does indeed suffer wear and tear, but every day the inward man receives fresh strength. (2 Cor. 4:8-12, 16, Phillips)

CHRIST'S INDWELLING

so that Christ may dwell in your hearts through faith; (3:17a)

So that translates *hina,* a Greek word used to introduce purpose clauses. The purpose of our being "strengthened with power through His Spirit in the inner man" is **that Christ may dwell in** [our] **hearts through faith.**

The proper order seems to be reversed, because every believer at salvation is indwelt by Christ (2 Cor. 13:5; Col. 1:27) and cannot have "the Holy Spirit in the inner man" until he has received Christ as Savior (Rom. 8:9, 11; 1 Cor. 3:16; 6:19). Paul has already made clear that all believers are in Christ (1:1, 3, 10, 12; 2:6, 10, 13). He is therefore not here referring to Christ's indwelling believers in salvation but in sanctification.

Katoikeō (**dwell**) is a compound word, formed from *kata* (down) and *oikeō* (to inhabit a house). In the context of this passage the connotation is not simply that of being inside the house of our **hearts** but of being at home there, settled down as a family member. Christ cannot be "at home" in our hearts until our inner person submits to the strengthening of His Spirit. Until the Spirit controls our lives, Jesus Christ cannot be comfortable there, but only stays like a tolerated visitor. Paul's teaching here does not relate to the *fact* of Jesus' presence in the hearts of believers but to the *quality* of His presence.

When the Lord came with two angels to visit them, Abraham and Sarah immediately made preparations to entertain their guests in the best possible way. From the rest of the passage (Gen. 18) it is evident that Abraham and Sarah knew they were hosting the Lord Himself. It is also evident that the Lord felt at home with

Abraham and Sarah. It seems significant that when, a short while later, the Lord warned Lot to take his family and flee for their lives, He did not go Himself but only sent the two angels (19:1). Lot was a believer, but the Lord did not feel at home in Lot's house as He did in Abraham's tent.

In his booklet *My Heart Christ's Home,* Robert Munger pictures the Christian life as a house, through which Jesus goes from room to room. In the library, which is the mind, Jesus finds trash and all sorts of worthless things, which He proceeds to throw out and replace with His Word. In the dining room of appetite He finds many sinful desires listed on a worldly menu. In the place of such things as prestige, materialism, and lust He puts humility, meekness, love, and all the other virtues for which believers are to hunger and thirst. He goes through the living room of fellowship, where He finds many worldly companions and activities, through the workshop, where only toys are being made, into the closet, where hidden sins are kept, and so on through the entire house. Only when He had cleaned every room, closet, and corner of sin and foolishness could He settle down and be at home.

Jesus enters the house of our hearts the moment He saves us, but He cannot live there in comfort and satisfaction until it is cleansed of sin and filled with His will. God is gracious beyond comprehension and infinitely patient. He continues to love those of His children who insist on spurning His will. But He cannot be happy or satisfied in such a heart. He cannot be fully at home until He is allowed to **dwell in** our **hearts** through the continuing **faith** that trusts Him to exercise His lordship over every aspect of our lives. We practice as well as receive His presence by **faith**.

How awesome and wonderful that the almighty and holy God wants to live in our **hearts**, be at home there, and rule there! Yet Jesus said, "If anyone loves Me, he will keep My word; and My Father will love him, and We will come to him, and make Our abode with him" (John 14:23).

Love's Abundance

and that you, being rooted and grounded in love, may be able to comprehend with all the saints what is the breadth and length and height and depth, and to know the love of Christ which surpasses knowledge, (3:17b-19a)

Being made strong inwardly by God's Spirit leads to Christ's being at home in our hearts, which leads to love that is incomprehensible. The result of our yielding to the Spirit's power and submitting to Christ's lordship in our hearts is **love**. When Christ settles down in our lives He begins to display His own love in us and through us. When He freely indwells our hearts, we become **rooted and grounded in love**, that is, settled on a strong foundation of love.

"A new commandment I give to you," Jesus said, "that you love one another, even as I have loved you" (John 13:34). Peter wrote, "Since you have in obedience to the truth purified your souls for a sincere love of the brethren, fervently love one another from the heart" (1 Pet. 1:22). It is God's supreme desire that His children sincerely and fully love each other, just as He loves us. Love is the first fruit of the Spirit, of which joy, peace, patience, kindness, goodness, faithfulness, gentleness, and self-control are essentially subcategories (Gal. 5:22-23).

Love is an attitude of selflessness. Biblical *agapē* **love** is a matter of the will and not a matter of feeling or emotion, though deep feelings and emotions almost always accompany love. God's loving the world was not a matter simply of feeling; it resulted in His sending His only Son to redeem the world (John 3:16). Love is selfless giving, always selfless and always giving. It is the very nature and substance of love to deny self and to give to others. Jesus did not say, "Greater love has no one than to have warm feelings for his friends," but rather, "Greater love has no one than this, that one lay down his life for his friends" (John 15:13).

In obeying the Father's loving will to redeem the world, Jesus willingly and lovingly gave Himself to accomplish that redemption. "Although He existed in the form of God, [He] did not regard equality with God a thing to be grasped, but emptied Himself, taking the form of a bond-servant, and being made in the likeness of men. And being found in appearance as a man, He humbled Himself by becoming obedient to the point of death, even death on a cross" (Phil. 2:6-8). That is love in its most perfect form, and it is this divine attitude of self-sacrificing love that every believer should have in himself (v. 5).

We can only have such love when Christ is free to work His own love through us. We cannot fulfill any of Christ's commands without Christ Himself, least of all His command to love. We can only love as Christ loves when He has free reign in our hearts. "By this," John says, "the love of God was manifested in us, that God has sent His only begotten Son into the world so that we might live through Him. In this is love, not that we loved God, but that He loved us and sent His Son to be the propitiation for our sins. Beloved, if God so loved us, we also ought to love one another. No one has beheld God at any time; if we love one another, God abides in us, and His love is perfected in us. . . . We love, because He first loved us" (1 John 4:9-12, 19).

When the Spirit empowers our lives and Christ is obeyed as the Lord of our hearts, our sins and weaknesses are dealt with and we find ourselves *wanting* to serve others, *wanting* to sacrifice for them and serve them—because Christ's loving nature has truly become our own. Loving is the supernatural attitude of the Christian, because love is the nature of Christ. When a Christian does not love he has to do so intentionally and with effort—just as he must do to hold his breath. To become habitually unloving he must habitually resist Christ as the Lord of his heart. To continue the analogy to breathing, when Christ has his proper place in our hearts, we do not have to be told to love—just as we do not have to be told to breathe. Eventually it must happen, because loving is as natural to the spiritual person as breathing is to the natural person.

Though it is unnatural for the Christian to be unloving, it is still possible to be disobedient in regard to love. Just as loving is determined by the will and not by circumstances or other people, so is *not* loving. If a husband fails in his love for his wife, or she for him, it is never because of the other person, regardless of what the other person may have done. You do not fall either into or out of *agapē* love, because it is controlled by the will. Romantic love can be beautiful and meaningful, and we find many favorable accounts of it in Scripture. But it is *agapē* love that God commands husbands and wives to have for each other (Eph. 5:25, 28, 33; Titus 2:4)—the love that each person controls by his own act of will. Strained relations between husbands and wives, between fellow workers, between brothers and sisters, or between any others is never a matter of incompatibility or personality conflict but is always a matter of sin.

The principle applies to everyone with whom the Christian has contact, especially his fellow Christians. Loving others is an act of obedience, and not loving them is an act of disobedience. "If someone says, 'I love God,' and hates his brother, he is a liar; for the one who does not love his brother whom he has seen, cannot love God whom he has not seen. And this commandment we have from Him, that the one who loves God should love his brother also" (1 John 4:20-21). In the deepest sense, love is the *only* commandment of God. The greatest commandment, Jesus said, is to love God with all our heart, soul, and mind; and the second greatest is to love our neighbor as ourselves (Matt. 22:37-39). And "he who loves his neighbor," Paul said, "has fulfilled the law. For this, 'You shall not commit adultery, You shall not murder, You shall not steal, You shall not covet,' and if there is any other commandment, it is summed up in this saying, 'You shall love your neighbor as yourself.' Love does no wrong to a neighbor; love therefore is the fulfillment of the law" (Rom. 13:8-10).

The absence of love is the presence of sin. The absence of love has nothing at all to do with what is happening to us, but everything to do with what is happening in us. Sin and love are enemies, because sin and God are enemies. They cannot coexist. Where one is, the other is not. The loveless life is the ungodly life; and the godly life is the serving, caring, tenderhearted, affectionate, self-giving, self-sacrificing life of Christ's love working through the believer.

When we are **rooted and grounded in love**, we then become **able to comprehend with all the saints what is the breadth and length and height and depth** of love. We cannot **comprehend** the fulness of love unless we are totally immersed in love, unless it is the very root and ground of our being. When someone asked the famed jazz trumpeter Louis Armstrong to explain jazz, he replied, "Man, if I've got to explain it, you ain't got it." In some ways that simplistic idea applies to love. It cannot truly be understood and comprehended until it is experienced. Yet the experience and working of love that Paul is talking about in this passage is not emotional or subjective. It is not nice feelings or warm sentiments that bring such comprehension, but the actual working of God's Spirit and God's Son in our lives to *produce* a love that is pure and sincere, selfless and serving. To be **rooted and grounded in love** requires being rooted and grounded in God. When we are saved, God's love is "poured out within our hearts through the Holy Spirit who was given to us" (Rom. 5:5). It is the Lord Himself who directs our "hearts into the love of God and into the steadfastness of Christ" (2 Thess. 3:5).

Love is available to every Christian because Christ is available to every Christian. Paul prays that we will become **able to comprehend with all the saints.** Love is not simply for the even-tempered Christian or the naturally pleasant and agreeable Christian. Nor is it for some supposed special class of Christians who have an inside spiritual track. It is for, and commanded of, every Christian—**all the saints.**

Comprehension of love comes from being continually immersed in the things of God, especially His Word. "Thy words were found and I ate them," Jeremiah declared, "and Thy words became for me a joy and the delight of my heart; for I have been called by Thy name, O Lord God of hosts" (Jer. 15:16). Job testified, "I have treasured the words of His mouth more than my necessary food" (Job 23:12), and the psalmist tells us that the delight of the righteous person "is in the law of the Lord, and in His law he meditates day and night" (Ps. 1:2; cf. 19:9b-10; 119:167; etc.).

To comprehend . . . what is the breadth and length and height and depth of love is to understand it in its fullness. Love goes in every direction and to the greatest distance. It goes wherever it is needed for as long as it is needed. The early church Father Jerome said that the love of Christ reaches up to the holy angels and down to those in hell. Its length covers the men on the upward way and its breadth reaches those drifting away on evil paths.

I do not think that **breadth and length and height and depth** represent four specific types or categories of love but simply suggest its vastness and completeness. In whatever spiritual direction we look we can see God's love. We can see love's **breadth** reflected in God's acceptance of Gentile and Jew equally in Christ (Eph. 2:11-18). We can see love's **length** in God's choosing us before the foundation of the world (1:4-5) for a salvation that will last through all eternity. We can see love's **height** in God's having "blessed us with every spiritual blessing in the heavenly places in Christ" (1:3) and in His raising us up and seating us "with Him in the heavenly places, in Christ Jesus" (2:6). We can see love's **depth** in God's reaching down to the lowest levels of depravity to redeem those who are dead in trespasses and sins (2:1-3). God's love can reach any person in any sin, and it stretches from eternity past to eternity future. It takes us into the very presence of God and sits us on His throne.

In what may at first seems a self-contradiction, Paul says that **to know the love of Christ . . . surpasses knowledge.** Knowing Christ's **love** takes us beyond human **knowledge,** because it is from an infinitely higher source. Paul is not speaking here of our knowing the love we are to have *for* Christ but the **love of Christ,** His very own love that He must place in our hearts before we can love Him or anyone else. We are commanded to love because we are given love. God always gives before He commands anything in return, and love is one of Christ's greatest gifts to His church. Throughout John 14-16 Jesus promises to give love, joy, peace, power, and comfort without measure to those who belong to Him.

The world cannot comprehend the great love that Christ gives because it cannot understand Christ. Worldly love is based on attraction and therefore lasts only as long as the attraction. Christ's love is based on His own nature and therefore lasts forever. Worldly love lasts until it is offended or rebuffed. Christ's love lasts despite every offense and every rebuff. Worldly love loves for what it can get. Christ's love loves for what it can give. What is incomprehensible to the world is to be normal living for the child of God.

GOD'S FULLNESS

that you may be filled up to all the fulness of God. (3:19*b*)

The inner strengthening of the Holy Spirit leads to the indwelling of Christ, which leads to abundant love, which leads to God's fullness in us. To **be filled up to all the fulness of God** is indeed incomprehensible, even to God's own children. It is incredible and indescribable. There is no way, this side of heaven, we can fathom that truth. We can only believe it and praise God for it.

J. Wilbur Chapman often told of the testimony given by a certain man in one of his meetings:

> I got off at the Pennsylvania depot as a tramp, and for a year I begged on the streets for a living. One day I touched a man on the shoulder and said, "Hey, mister, can you give me a dime?" As soon as I saw his face I was shocked to see that it was my own father. I said, "Father, Father, do you know me?" Throwing his arms around me and with tears in his eyes, he said, "Oh my son, at last I've found you! I've found you. You want a dime? Everything I have is yours." Think of it. I was a tramp. I stood begging my own father for ten cents, when for 18 years he had been looking for me to give me all that he had.

That is a small picture of what God wants to do for His children. His supreme goal in bringing us to Himself is to make us like Himself by filling us with Himself, with all that He is and has.

Even to begin to grasp the magnitude of that truth, we must think of every attribute and every characteristic of God. We must think of His power, majesty, wisdom, love, mercy, patience, kindness, longsuffering, and every other thing that God is and does. That Paul is not exaggerating is clear from the fact that in this letter he repeatedly mentions the fullness of God's blessings to those who belong to Him through Christ. He tells us that the church is Christ's "body, the fulness of Him who fills all in all" (Eph. 1:23). He tells us that "He who descended is Himself also He who ascended far above all the heavens, that He might fill all things" (4:10). And he tells us that God wants every believer to "be filled with the Spirit" (5:18).

Plēroō means to make full, or fill to the full, and is used many times in the New Testament. It speaks of total dominance. A person filled with rage is totally dominated by hatred. A person filled with happiness is totally dominated by joy. To **be filled up to all the fulness of God** therefore means to be totally dominated by

Him, with nothing left of self or any part of the old man. By definition, then, to be filled with God is to be emptied of self. It is not to have much of God and little of self, but all of God and none of self. This is a recurring theme in Ephesians. Here Paul talks about **the fulness of God**; in 4:13 it is "the fulness of Christ"; and in 5:18 it is the fulness of the Spirit.

What a God, who loves us so much that He will not rest until we are completely like Him! We can only sing with David, "The Lord is my rock and my fortress and my deliverer; my God, my rock, in whom I take refuge; my shield and the horn of my salvation, my stronghold and my refuge; my Savior" (2 Sam. 22:2-3). Throughout the rest of that magnificent hymn, David stacks praise upon praise in declaring God's greatness and goodness.

In the same way Job seems to be almost at a loss for words to properly extol the wonders of God. "What a help you are to the weak! How you have saved the arm without strength! What counsel you have given to one without wisdom! What helpful insight you have abundantly provided! . . . He stretches out the north over empty space, and hangs the earth on nothing. He wraps up the waters in His clouds; and the cloud does not burst under them. . . . The pillars of heaven tremble, and are amazed at His rebuke. . . . By His breath the heavens are cleared; His hand has pierced the fleeing serpent. Behold, these are the fringes of His ways" (Job 26:2-3, 7-8, 11, 13-14).

From our human, earthly perspective we can never see more than "the fringes of His ways." No wonder David said that he would not be satisfied until he awoke in the likeness of God (Ps. 17:15). Only then will we know fully as we have been fully known (1 Cor. 13:12).

The Lord's Glory

Now to Him who is able to do exceeding abundantly beyond all that we ask or think, according to the power that works within us, to Him be the glory in the church and in Christ Jesus to all generations forever and ever. Amen. (3:20-21)

In culmination of all he has been declaring about God's limitless provision for His children, Paul gives this great doxology, a paean of praise and glory, introduced by **Now unto Him.**

When the Holy Spirit has empowered us, Christ has indwelt us, love has mastered us, and God has filled us with His own fullness, then He **is able to do exceeding abundantly beyond all that we ask or think.** Until those conditions are met, God's working in us is limited. When they are met, His working in us is unlimited. "Truly, truly, I say to you, he who believes in Me, the works that I do shall he do also; and greater works than these shall he do; because I go to the Father. And whatever you ask in My name, that will I do, that the Father may be glorified in the Son. If you ask Me anything in My name, I will do it" (John 14:12-14).

There is no situation in which the Lord cannot use us, provided we are submitted to Him. As is frequently pointed out, verse 20 is a pyramid progression of God's enablement: He is able; He is able to do; He is able to do exceeding abundantly; He is able to do exceeding abundantly beyond all that we ask; He is able to do exceeding abundantly beyond all that we ask or think. There is no question in the minds of believers that God **is able** to do more than we can conceive, but too few Christians enjoy the privilege of seeing Him do that in their lives, because they fail to follow the pattern of enablement presented in these verses.

Paul declared that the effectiveness of his own ministry was that "my message and my preaching were not in persuasive words of wisdom, but in demonstration of the Spirit and of power" (1 Cor. 2:4), because "the kingdom of God does not consist in words, but in power" (4:20). Throughout his ministry the apostle was concerned about "giving no cause for offense in anything, in order that the ministry be not discredited, but in everything commending ourselves as servants of God, in much endurance, in afflictions, in hardships, in distresses, in beatings, in imprisonments, in tumults, in labors, in sleeplessness, in hunger, in purity, in knowledge, in patience, in kindness, in the Holy Spirit, in genuine love, in the word of truth, in the power of God" (2 Cor. 6:3-7). Everything Paul did was in the power of God, and in the power of God there was nothing within the Lord's will that he could not see accomplished. That same power **works within us** by the presence of the Spirit (Acts 1:8).

When by our yieldedness God **is able to do exceeding abundantly beyond all that we ask or think, according to the power that works within us**, only then are we truly effective and only then is He truly glorified. And He deserves **glory in the church and in Christ Jesus**, not only now, but **to all generations forever and ever**. The **Amen** confirms that worthy goal.

The Lowly Walk

10

I, therefore, the prisoner of the Lord, entreat you to walk in a manner worthy of the calling with which you have been called, with all humility and gentleness, with patience, showing forbearance to one another in love, being diligent to preserve the unity of the Spirit in the bond of peace. There is one body and one Spirit, just as also you were called in one hope of your calling; one Lord, one faith, one baptism, one God and Father of all who is over all and through all and in all. (4:1-6)

When a person joins an organization, he obligates himself to live and act in accordance with the standards of the group. He accepts its aims, objectives, and standards as his own. A citizen is obligated to abide by the laws of his country. An employee is obligated to work according the rules, standards, and purposes of his company. Members of service clubs obligate themselves to promote the goals of the club and to abide by its standards. When someone joins an athletic team he is obligated to play as the coach orders and according to the rules of the sport. Human society could not operate without such obligation.

We have a natural desire to be accepted and to belong, and many people will go to almost any lengths to qualify for acceptance in a fraternal order, social club, athletic team, or other group. Many people will also go to great lengths to keep from being rejected by a group. The parents of the man born blind were afraid to tell the Jewish leaders that Jesus had healed their son, because they were afraid of being thrown out of the synagogue (John 9:22). Although they had seen the result of a miracle that had healed their own son of his life-long blindness, they would not credit Jesus with the miracle for fear of being socially ostracized. For the same reason, "many even of the rulers believed in Him, but because of the Pharisees they were not confessing Him, lest they should be put out of the synagogue; for they loved the approval of men rather than the approval of God" (12:42-43).

Sometimes in the church such loyalties to standards and fear of ostracism do not operate with the same force. Too many Christians are glad to have the spiritual security, blessings, and promises of the gospel but have too little sense of responsibility in conforming to its standards and obeying its commands.

In the first three chapters of Ephesians Paul has set forth the believer's position with all the blessings, honors, and privileges of being a child of God. In the next three chapters he gives the consequent obligations and requirements of being His child, in order to live out salvation in accordance with the Father's will and to His glory. The first three chapters set forth truth about the believer's identity in Christ, and the last three call for the practical response.

When we received Christ as Savior we became citizens of His kingdom and members of His family. Along with those blessings and privileges we also received obligations. The Lord expects us to act like the new persons we have become in Jesus Christ. He expects His standards to become our standards, His purposes our purposes, His desires our desires, His nature our nature. The Christian life is simply the process of becoming what you are.

God expects conformity within the church, the Body of Christ. It is not a forced legalistic conformity to external rules and regulations, but a willing inner conformity to the holiness, love, and will of our heavenly Father, who wants His children to honor Him as their Father. "Conduct yourselves in a manner worthy of the gospel of Christ," Paul admonished the Philippians, "so that whether I come and see you or remain absent, I may hear of you that you are standing firm in one spirit, with one mind striving together for the faith of the gospel" (Phil. 1:27).

The **therefore** of Ephesians 4:1 marks the transition from positional to practical truth, from doctrine to duty, principle to practice. Paul makes a similar transition in the book of Romans. After laying down eleven chapters of doctrine, he devotes the remainder of the book to urging Christians to live in accordance with that doctrine—to present their bodies as "a living and holy sacrifice, acceptable to God, which is your spiritual service of worship" (12:1). In Galatians Paul devotes the first four chapters to explaining Christian liberty and the last two chapters to exhorting Christians to live by that liberty. That sort of division is found in many of Paul's epistles (see also Phil. 2:1-2; Col. 3:5; 1 Thess. 4:1). Right practice must always be based on right principle. It is impossible to have a Christian life-style without knowing the realities of the life that Christ has provided.

Right doctrine is essential to right living. It is impossible to live a faithful Christian life without knowing biblical doctrine. Doctrine simply means teaching, and there is no way that even the most sincere believer can live a life pleasing to God without knowing what God Himself is like and knowing the sort of life God wants him to live. Those who set biblical theology aside also set aside sound Christian living.

Church renewal does not come with new programs, buildings, organization, educational methods, or anything else external. Church renewal comes first of all through the renewal of the mind. Later in this letter Paul prays that the Ephesians would "be renewed in the spirit of your mind, and put on the new self, which in the likeness of God has been created in righteousness and holiness of the truth" (4:23-24). It is only when in the spirit of their minds they grasp the righteousness and holiness of God's truth that God's people are renewed. At the beginning of this letter Paul prayed "that the God of our Lord Jesus Christ, the Father of glory, may give to you a spirit of wisdom and of revelation in the knowledge of Him" (1:17). Growing in grace, Peter tells us, is linked with growing in the "knowledge of our Lord and Savior Jesus Christ" (2 Pet. 3:18). Along with his ministry of proclaiming Christ, Paul also was "admonishing every man and teaching every man with all wisdom, that we may present every man complete in Christ" (Col. 1:28). In his well-known words to Timothy, Paul declares that "All Scripture is inspired by God and profitable for teaching, for reproof, for correction, for training in righteousness; that the man of God may be adequate, equipped for every good work" (2 Tim. 3:16-17). It is impossible to do good works without knowledge of the Word of God.

In Ephesians 4:1-6 Paul appeals to believers to walk worthily of their high position in Jesus Christ. In describing that walk he discusses its call, its characteristics, and its cause.

THE CALL TO THE WORTHY WALK

I, therefore, the prisoner of the Lord, entreat you to walk in a manner worthy of the calling with which you have been called, (4:1)

Before giving his appeal, Paul once again refers to himself as **the prisoner of the Lord** (see 3:1). By mentioning his imprisonment he gently reminds his readers that he knows the worthy Christian walk can be costly and that he has paid considerable cost himself because of his obedience to the Lord. He would not ask them to walk in a way in which he had not himself walked or pay a price that he himself was not willing to pay. His present physical circumstance seemed extremely negative from a human perspective, but Paul wanted his readers to know that this did not change his commitment to or his confidence in **the Lord**.

The apostle was not seeking sympathy or using his Roman confinement as a means for shaming the Ephesians into compliance with his request. He was reminding them again of his own complete subservience to Christ, his being **the prisoner of the Lord** whether he was in jail or not. He became the Lord's **prisoner** on the road to Damascus and never sought to be free of that divine imprisonment.

Paul had the ability to see everything in the light of how it affected Christ. He saw everything vertically before he saw it horizontally. His motives were Christ's, his standards were Christ's, his objectives were Christ's, his vision was Christ's, his entire orientation was Christ's. Everything he thought, planned, said, and did was in relation to his Lord. He was in the fullest sense a captive of the Lord Jesus Christ.

Most of us will admit that we tend to be so self-oriented that we see many things first of all—and sometimes only—in relation to ourselves. But the person who has the Word of Christ abiding in him richly, the one who saturates his mind with divine wisdom and truth will ask, "How does this affect God? How will it reflect on Him? What does he want me to do with this problem or this blessing? How can I most please and honor Him in this?" He tries to see everything through God's divine grid. That attitude is the basis and the mark of spiritual maturity. With David, the mature Christian can say, "I have set the Lord continually before me; because He is at my right hand" (Ps. 16:8).

Paul made no apology for pleading with people to do what he knew was right. **I . . . entreat you**, he says. *Parakaleō* **(entreat)** means to call to one's side, with the idea of wanting to help or be helped. It connotes intense feeling, strong desire. In this context it is not simply a request but a plea, an imploring or begging. Paul was not giving suggestions to the Ephesians but divine standards, standards apart from which they could not live in a way that fittingly corresponded to their being children of God. Paul never exhorted on a take-it-or-leave-it basis. He could not rest until all those given into his spiritual care walked **in a manner worthy of the calling with which** they had **been called.**

Paul pleaded with King Agrippa to listen to his testimony (Acts 26:3), he strongly urged the Corinthians to reaffirm their love for a repentant brother (2 Cor. 2:8), and pleaded with the Galatians to stand in the liberty of the gospel as he did (Gal. 4:12). He pleaded out of an intense love for others, saved and unsaved. Of unsaved fellow Jews, he wrote, "I am telling the truth in Christ, I am not lying, my conscience bearing me witness in the Holy Spirit, that I have great sorrow and unceasing grief in my heart. For I could wish that I myself were accursed, separated from Christ for the sake of my brethren, my kinsmen according to the flesh" (Rom. 9:1-3).

Christians should not resent a pastor's entreating them in the faith as Paul did those to whom he ministered. A pastor who approaches his ministry with detachment or indifference is not worthy of his office. Loving concern for the spiritual welfare of others is costly, and apart from God's strength it is frustrating and demoralizing.

Surveys of pastors over the past decade or so have revealed widespread discouragement and even depression—what one writer described as battle fatigue. A large percentage of those interviewed said that the most depressing part of their ministry was the sense of never being through, of always having more to do, and of seeing much of their "success" turn out to be superficial and temporary. They reported that there never seems to be enough time to prepare sermons as carefully as they should, to visit and counsel everyone who needs them, to attend all the meetings, or to accomplish the many other things expected of the pastor by his congregation and by himself. His work is never done, and the more he cares the more he sees to do. Paul, who himself did the work of a pastor and was an apostle and an evangelist, spoke of believers in Galatia as, "My children, with whom I am again in labor until Christ is formed in you" (Gal. 4:19). He suffered perpetual birth pains from his great desire for the spiritual growth and maturity of those to whom he ministered.

Not only pastors but every believer should have a loving concern to entreat, implore, beg, and plead with others to respond in obedience to the gospel. Like Paul, they should have a passion to **entreat** their fellow believers **to walk in a manner worthy of** their **calling**—to be everything the Lord desires of them.

Walk is frequently used in the New Testament to refer to daily conduct, day-by-day living, and it is the theme of the last three chapters of Ephesians. In the first sixteen verses of chapter 4, Paul emphasizes the unity and in the rest of the chapter the uniqueness of the Christian walk. In chapters 5 and 6 he stresses the moral purity, the wisdom, the Spirit control, the family manifestations, and the warfare of the Christian walk.

Axios (**worthy**) has the root meaning of balancing the scales—what is on one side of the scale should be equal in weight to what is on the other side. By extension, the word came to be applied to anything that was expected to correspond to something else. A person worthy of his pay was one whose day's work corresponded to his day's wages. The believer who walks **in a manner worthy of the calling with which** he has **been called** is one whose daily living corresponds to his high position as a child of God and fellow heir with Jesus Christ. His practical living matches his spiritual position.

The calling with which you have been called is the sovereign, saving calling of God (cf. 1 Thess. 2:12). "No one can come to Me," Jesus said, "unless the Father who sent Me draws him" (John 6:44; cf. v. 65). On another occasion, He said, "And I, if I be lifted up from the earth, will draw all men to Myself" (John 12:32). Paul tells us that those whom God "predestined, these He also called; and whom He called, these He also justified; and whom He justified, these He also glorified" (Rom. 8:30). As the apostle mentioned in the opening of this letter, "He chose us in Him before the foundation of the world, that we should be holy and blameless before Him" (Eph. 1:4). No person can be saved apart from receiving Jesus Christ as his Savior. But no person can choose Christ who has not already been chosen by the Father and the Son. "You did not choose Me," Jesus explained to the disciples, "but I chose you, and appointed you, that you should go and bear fruit, and that your fruit should remain" (John 15:16).

Paul makes many references to the believer's **calling** *(klēsis)*, which, as in this case, refers to the Lord's sovereign, effectual call to salvation (Rom. 11:29; 1 Cor. 1:26; Eph. 1:18; 4:1, 4; Phil. 3:14; 2 Thess. 1:11; 2 Tim. 1:9; cf. Heb. 3:1; 2 Pet. 1:10).

Without God's **calling**, without His choosing us, our choosing Him would be futile. In fact, if God did not call men to Himself no man would *want* to come to Him, because the natural man—every natural man—is at enmity with God (Rom. 8:7). The marvelous truth of the gospel is that God not only sent His Son to *provide* the way of salvation (Rom. 5:8) but that He sent Him to *seek* the lost in order to save them (Luke 19:10). God was not content simply to make salvation available. He has called the redeemed elect to Himself.

That is why our **calling** is a high calling, a "heavenly calling" (Heb. 3:1), and "a holy calling" (2 Tim. 1:9). And that is why the faithful, responsive Christian is determined to "press on toward the goal for the prize of the upward call of God in Christ Jesus" (Phil. 3:14).

THE CHARACTERISTICS OF THE WORTHY WALK

with all humility and gentleness, with patience, showing forbearance to one another in love, being diligent to preserve the unity of the Spirit in the bond of peace. (4:2-3)

Here Paul gives five essentials for faithful Christian living, five attitudes on which walking worthily in the Lord's call are predicated.

HUMILITY

These characteristics, of which **humility** is the foundation, form a progression, the genuine exercise of one leading to the exercise of those that follow. *Tapeinophrosunē* (**humility**) is a compound word that literally means to think or judge with lowliness, and hence to have lowliness of mind. John Wesley observed that "neither the Romans nor the Greeks had a word for humility." The very concept was so foreign and abhorrent to their way of thinking that they had no term to describe it. Apparently this Greek term was coined by Christians, probably by Paul himself, to describe a quality for which no other word was available. To the proud Greeks and Romans, their terms for ignoble, cowardly, and other such characteristics were sufficient to describe the "unnatural" person who did not think of himself with pride and self-satisfaction. When, during the first several centuries of Christianity, pagan writers borrowed the term *tapeinophrosunē,* they always used it derogatorily—frequently of Christians—because to them humility was a pitiable weakness.

But **humility** is the most foundational Christian virtue. We cannot even begin to please God without humility, just as our Lord Himself could not have pleased His Father had He not willingly "emptied Himself, taking the form of a bond-servant, and . . . humbled Himself by becoming obedient to the point of death, even death on a cross" (Phil. 2:7-8).

Yet **humility** is terribly elusive, because if focused on too much it will turn into pride, its very opposite. Humility is a virtue to be highly sought but never claimed, because once claimed it is forfeited. Only Jesus Christ, as the perfectly obedient Son, could justifiably claim humility for Himself. "Take My yoke upon you," He said, "for I am gentle and humble in heart" (Matt. 11:29). He came to earth as God's Son, yet was born in a stable, raised in a peasant family, never owned property except the garments on His back, and was buried in a borrowed tomb. At any time He could have exercised His divine rights, prerogatives, and glory, but in obedience and humility He refused to do so because it would have been to go outside His Father's will. If the Lord of glory walked in humility while He was on earth, how much more are His imperfect followers to do so? "The one who says he abides in Him ought himself to walk in the same manner as He walked" (1 John 2:6).

Although humility is at the heart of Christian character, no virtue is more foreign to the world's ways. The world exalts pride, not humility. Throughout history, fallen human nature, ruled by Satan, the prince of this world, has shunned humility and advocated pride. For the most part humility has been looked on as weakness and impotence, something ignoble to be despised. People unashamedly claim to be proud of their jobs, their children, their accomplishments, and on and on. Society loves to recognize and praise those who have accomplished something outstanding. Ostentation, boasting, parading, and exalting are the world's stock in trade.

Unfortunately the church often reflects that worldly perspective and pattern, building many programs and organizations around the superficial enticements of awards, trophies, and public recognition. We seem to have found a way to encourage boasting that is "acceptable," because such boasting is done in the name of the gospel. But in doing so we contradict the very gospel we claim to promote, because the hallmark of the gospel is humility, not pride and self-exaltation. God's work cannot be served by the world's ways. God's call is *to* humility and His work is only accomplished *through* humility.

The first sin was pride, and every sin after that has been in some way an extension of pride. Pride led the angel Lucifer to exalt himself above his Creator and Lord. Because the bright "star of the morning" continually said, "I will, I will, I will" in opposition to God's will, he was cast out of heaven (Isa. 14:12-23). Because he said, "I am a god," the Lord cast him "from the mountain of God" (Ezek. 28:11-19). The original sin of Adam and Eve was pride, trusting in their own understanding above God's (Gen. 3:6-7). The writer of Proverbs warns, "When pride comes, then comes dishonor" (11:2), "Pride goes before destruction, and a haughty spirit before stumbling" (16:18), and again "Haughty eyes and a proud heart, the lamp of the wicked, is sin" (21:4).

Isaiah warned, "The proud look of man will be abased, and the loftiness of man will be humbled, and the Lord alone will be exalted in that day" (Isa. 2:11; cf. 3:16-26). "Behold, I am against you, O arrogant one," God declared against Babylon, "For your day has come, the time when I shall punish you. And the arrogant one will stumble and fall with no one to raise him up" (Jer. 50:31-32). The last chapter of the Old Testament begins, "For behold, the day is coming, burning like a furnace; and all the arrogant and every evildoer will be chaff" (Mal. 4:1). The

Beatitudes begin with "Blessed are the poor in spirit" (Matt. 5:3), and James assures us that "God is opposed to the proud, but gives grace to the humble" (James 4:6; cf. Ps. 138:6).

Pride is the supreme temptation from Satan, because pride is at the heart of his own evil nature. Consequently, Satan makes sure that the Christian is never entirely free from the temptation of pride. We will always be in a battle with pride until the Lord takes us to be with Himself. Our only protection against pride, and our only source of humility, is a proper view of God. Pride is the sin of competing with God, and humility is the virtue of submitting to His supreme glory.

Pride comes in many forms. We may be tempted to be proud of our abilities, our possessions, our education, our social status, our appearance, our power, and even our biblical knowledge or religious accomplishments. But throughout Scripture the Lord calls His people to humility. "Before honor comes humility" (Prov. 15:33); "The reward of humility and the fear of the Lord are riches, honor and life" (22:4); "Let another praise you, and not your own mouth; a stranger, and not your own lips" (27:2).

Humility is an ingredient of all spiritual blessing. Just as every sin has its roots in pride, every virtue has its roots in humility. Humility allows us to see ourselves as we are, because it shows us before God as He is. Just as pride is behind every conflict we have with other people and every problem of fellowship we have with the Lord, so humility is behind every harmonious human relationship, every spiritual success, and every moment of joyous fellowship with the Lord.

During the days of slavery in the West Indies, a group of Moravian Christians found it impossible to witness to the slaves because they were almost totally separated from the ruling class—many of whom felt it beneath them even to speak to a slave. Two young missionaries, however, were determined to reach those oppressed peoples at any cost. In order to fulfill God's calling they joined the slaves. They worked and lived beside the slaves, becoming totally identified with them—sharing their overwork, their beatings, and their abuse. It is not strange that the two missionaries soon won the hearts of those slaves, many of whom accepted for themselves the God who could move men to such loving selflessness.

A person cannot even become a Christian without humility, without recognizing himself as a sinner and worthy only of God's just condemnation. "Truly I say to you," Jesus said, "unless you are converted and become like children, you shall not enter the kingdom of heaven. Whoever then humbles himself . . ." (Matt. 18:3-4). At the height of his own fame and recognition as a prophet, John the Baptist said of Jesus, "I am not fit to remove His sandals" (Matt. 3:11) and "He must increase, but I must decrease" (John 3:30). Martha was busy doing many things supposedly for Jesus' sake, but on three different occasions we see Mary simply sitting humbly at Jesus' feet. In all four gospels the writers hide themselves and focus attention on Jesus. How easy it would have been for them to subtly include accounts favorable to themselves. Matthew identifies himself as a despised tax-collector, which none of the other gospel writers does. On the other hand, he does not mention the feast that he gave for his fellow tax-collectors to meet Jesus.

Because of Matthew's humility, it was left to Luke to write about that.

Mark probably wrote under the tutelage of Peter, and possibly because of that apostle's influence he does not report two of the most amazing things that happened to Peter during Jesus' ministry—his walking on water and his confession of Jesus as the Christ, the Son of the living God. John never mentions his own name, referring to himself simply as "the disciple whom Jesus loved."

In a compilation of old quotes is an excellent paragraph written by Thomas Guthrie:

> The grandest edifices, the tallest towers, the loftiest spires rest on deep foundations. The very safety of eminent gifts and preeminent graces lies in their association with deep humility. They are dangerous without it. Great men do need to be good men. Look at the mighty ship. A leviathan into the sea, with her towering masts and carrying a cloud of canvas. How she steadies herself on the waves and walks erect on the rolling waters like a thing with inherent, self-regulating life. . . . Why is she not flung on her beam's end, sent down floundering into the deep? Because unseen beneath the surface a vast well-ballasted hull gives her balance and takes hold of the water, keeps her steady under a pressive sail and on the bosom of a swelling sea. Even though to preserve the saint upright, to preserve the saint erect and safe from falling, God gives him balance and ballast bestowing on the man to whom He has given lofty endowments, the tendant grace of a proportionate humility.

Humility begins with proper self-awareness, "the virtue," said Bernard of Clairvaux, "by which a man becomes conscious of his own unworthiness." It begins with an honest, unadorned, unretouched view of oneself. The first thing the honest person sees in himself is sin, and therefore one of the surest marks of true humility is daily confession of sin. "If we say that we have no sin, we are deceiving ourselves, and the truth is not in us. If we confess our sins, He is faithful and righteous to forgive us our sins and to cleanse us from all unrighteousness" (1 John 1:8-9). "We are not bold to class or compare ourselves with some of those who commend themselves," Paul says; "but when they measure themselves by themselves, and compare themselves with themselves, they are without understanding" (2 Cor. 10:12). It is not only unspiritual but unintelligent to judge ourselves by comparison with others. We all tend to exaggerate our own good qualities and minimize the good qualities of others. Humility takes off our rose-colored glasses and allows us to see ourselves as we really are. We are not "adequate in ourselves to consider anything as coming from ourselves," says Paul, "but our adequacy is from God" (2 Cor. 3:5).

Second, **humility** involves Christ-awareness. He is the only standard by which righteousness can be judged and by which pleasing God can be judged. Our goal should be no less than "to walk in the same manner as He walked" (1 John 2:6), and Jesus Christ walked in perfection. Only of Jesus has God ever said, "This is My beloved Son, in whom I am well-pleased" (Matt. 3:17).

Third, **humility** involves God-awareness. As we study His life in the gospels we come to see Jesus more and more in His human perfection—His perfect humility, His perfect submission to the Father, His perfect love, compassion, and wisdom. But beyond His human perfection we also come to see His divine perfection—His limitless power; His knowing the thoughts and heart of every person; and His authority to heal diseases, cast out demons, and even forgive sins. We come to see Jesus Christ as Isaiah saw the Lord, "sitting on a throne, lofty and exalted" and we want to cry out with the seraphim, "Holy, Holy, Holy, is the Lord of hosts, the whole earth is full of His glory," and with the prophet himself, "Woe is me, for I am ruined! For I am a man of unclean lips, and I live among a people of unclean lips; for my eyes have seen the King, the Lord of hosts" (Isa. 6:1, 3, 5).

When Paul looked at himself in self-awareness, he saw the foremost of sinners (1 Tim. 1:15). When Peter looked at himself in Christ awareness, he said, "Depart from me, for I am a sinful man, O Lord" (Luke 5:8). When Job looked at himself in God awareness, he said, "Therefore I retract, I repent in dust and ashes" (Job 42:6).

Our business success, fame, education, wealth, personality, good works, or anything else we are or have in ourselves counts for nothing before God. The more we rely on and glory in such things, the greater barrier they become to our communion with God. Every person comes before the Lord with nothing to commend him and everything to condemn him. But when he comes with the spirit of the penitent tax-collector, saying, "God, be merciful to me, the sinner," God will willingly and lovingly accept him. "For everyone who exalts himself shall be humbled, but he who humbles himself shall be exalted" (Luke 18:13-14).

GENTLENESS

Humility always produces **gentleness**, or meekness. Meekness is one of the surest signs of true humility. You cannot possess meekness *without* humility, and you cannot possess meekness *with* pride. Because pride and humility are mutually exclusive, so are pride and meekness, or **gentleness.**

Many dictionaries define meekness in terms such as "timid," or "a deficiency in courage or spirit"; but that is far from the biblical meaning. *Praotēs* (here translated **gentleness**) refers to that which is mild-spirited and self-controlled, the opposite of vindictiveness and vengeance. Jesus used the adjective form in giving the third beatitude ("Blessed are the gentle," Matt. 5:5) and to describe His own character ("For I am gentle," Matt. 11:29). **Gentleness** is one of the fruits of the Spirit (Gal. 5:23) and should characterize every child of God (Col. 3:12; cf. Phil. 4:5).

The meaning of *praotēs* has nothing to do with weakness, timidity, indifference, or cowardice. It was used of wild animals that were tamed, especially of horses that were broken and trained. Such an animal still has his strength and spirit, but its will is under the control of its master. The tamed lion is still powerful, but his power is under the control of his trainer. The horse can run just as fast, but he runs only when and where his master tells him to run.

Meekness is power under control. Biblical meekness, or **gentleness**, is power under the control of God. A meek person is normally quiet, soothing, and mild mannered, and he is never avenging, self-assertive, vindictive, or self-defensive. When the soldiers came to arrest Him in the Garden of Gethsemane and Peter drew his sword to defend His Lord, Jesus said, "Do you think that I cannot appeal to My Father, and He will at once put at My disposal more than twelve legions of angels?" (Matt. 26:53). Even in His humanity Jesus had access to infinite divine power, which He could at any time have used in His own defense. Yet not once did He choose to do so. His refusal to enlist divine resources for anything but obeying His Father's will is the supreme picture of meekness—power under control.

David displayed such meekness when he refused to kill King Saul in the cave near Engedi, although he had easy opportunity and considerable justification from the human point of view (1 Sam. 24:1-7). After David himself became king, he again showed the restraint of meekness when he refused to retaliate against the malicious taunts, curses, and stone throwing of Shimei (2 Sam. 16:5-14).

Moses is described as, "very humble, more than any man who was on the face of the earth" (Num. 12:3). Yet he fearlessly confronted Pharaoh in the Lord's name (see Ex. 5-12), angrily confronted Israel with her rebelliousness and idolatry (32:19-29), and even boldly confronted the Lord to forgive the people's sin (32:11-13, 30-32). Yet Moses' confidence was not in himself but in the Lord's character and promises. When God first called him, Moses replied, "Please, Lord, I have never been eloquent, neither recently nor in time past, nor since Thou hast spoken to Thy servant; for I am slow of speech and slow of tongue" (4:10). As he served the Lord throughout his life, Moses had God's rod to remind him that the great work to which the Lord had called him could be accomplished only in the Lord's own power. That he himself was nothing and God was everything were the marks of Moses' meekness. As Martyn Lloyd-Jones has observed, "To be meek means you have finished with yourself altogether."

Yet the meek person is also capable of righteous anger and action when God's Word or name is maligned, as Jesus was when His Father's house was made into a robber's den and He forcibly drove out the offenders (Matt. 21:13). As Paul affirms later in this letter, it is possible to be angry and not sin (Eph. 4:26). Like the Lord Himself, the meek person does not revile in return when he is reviled (1 Pet. 2:23). When the meek person becomes angry, he is aroused by that which maligns God or is harmful to others, not by what is done against himself. And his anger is controlled and carefully directed, not a careless and wild venting of emotion that spatters everyone who is near.

One of the marks of true meekness is self-control. People who are angered at every nuisance or inconvenience to themselves know nothing of meekness or **gentleness.** "He who is slow to anger is better than the mighty, and he who rules his spirit, than he who captures a city" (Prov. 16:32). Two other marks of meekness, already mentioned, are anger at God's name or work being maligned and *lack* of anger when we ourselves are harmed or criticized.

The meek person responds willingly to the Word of God, no matter what the requirements or consequences, humbly receiving "the word implanted" (James 1:21). He is also a peacemaker, who readily forgives and helps to restore a sinning brother (Gal. 6:1). Finally, the person who is truly meek and gentle according to God's standards has the right attitude toward the unsaved. He does not look down on them with a feeling of superiority but longs for their salvation, knowing that he himself was once lost—and would still be lost but for God's grace. We are to be "ready to make a defense to everyone who asks [us] to give an account for the hope that is in [us], yet with gentleness *(praotēs)* and reverence" (1 Pet. 3:15). Not only Christian women but all believers should be adorned "with the imperishable quality of a gentle and quiet spirit" (1 Pet. 3:4).

PATIENCE

A third attitude that characterizes the Christian's worthy walk is **patience**, which is an outgrowth of humility and gentleness. *Makrothumia* (**patience**) literally means long-tempered, and is sometimes translated longsuffering. The patient person endures negative circumstances and never gives in to them.

Abraham received the promise of God but had to wait many years to see its fulfillment. "Thus," the writer of Hebrews tells us, "having patiently waited, he obtained the promise" (Heb. 6:15). God had promised that Abraham's descendants would be a great nation (Gen. 12:2) and yet he was not given Isaac, the child of promise, until after Abraham was nearly a hundred years old. "Yet, with respect to the promise of God, he did not waver in unbelief, but grew strong in faith, giving glory to God" (Rom. 4:20).

God told Noah to build a ship in the wilderness, far from any body of water and before there had ever been rain on earth. For 120 years Noah worked at that task, while preaching to his neighbors of God's coming judgment.

In the chronicle of faithful Old Testament saints in the book of Hebrews, Moses' patient endurance is mentioned twice. He chose rather "to endure ill-treatment with the people of God, than to enjoy the passing pleasures of sin; considering the reproach of Christ greater riches than the treasures of Egypt; for he was looking to the reward. By faith he left Egypt, not fearing the wrath of the king; for he endured, as seeing Him who is unseen" (Heb. 11:25-27).

James said, "As an example, brethren, of suffering and patience, take the prophets who spoke in the name of the Lord" (James 5:10). When God called Jeremiah, He told the prophet that no one would believe his message and that he would be hated, maligned, and persecuted (Jer. 1:5-19). Yet Jeremiah served the Lord faithfully and patiently until the end of his life. Similarly, when the Lord called Isaiah he was told that the nation would not listen to him nor turn from their sin (Isa. 6:9-12). Like Jeremiah, however, he preached and ministered with patient faithfulness.

Paul was willing to endure any hardship, affliction, ridicule, or persecution in order to patiently serve his Master. "What are you doing, weeping and breaking my heart?" he asked the Christians at Caesarea after the prophet Agabus predicted the apostle's arrest and imprisonment. "For I am ready not only to be bound, but even to die at Jerusalem for the name of the Lord Jesus" (Acts 21:13).

When H. M. Stanley went to Africa in 1871 to find and report on David Livingstone, he spent several months in the missionary's company, carefully observing the man and his work. Livingstone never spoke to Stanley about spiritual matters, but Livingstone's loving and patient compassion for the African people was beyond Stanley's comprehension. He could not understand how the missionary could have such love for and patience with the backward, pagan people among whom he had so long ministered. Livingstone literally spent himself in untiring service for those whom he had no reason to love except for Christ's sake. Stanley wrote in his journal, "When I saw that unwearied patience, that unflagging zeal, and those enlightened sons of Africa, I became a Christian at his side, though he never spoke to me one word."

Aristotle said that the greatest Greek virtue was refusal to tolerate any insult and readiness to strike back. But that is not God's way for His people. The patient saint accepts whatever other people do to him. He is "patient with all men" (1 Thess. 5:14), even those who try his patience to the limit. He is patient with those who slander him and who question his motives for serving the Lord.

The patient saint accepts God's plan for everything, without questioning or grumbling. He does not complain when his calling seems less glamorous than someone else's or when the Lord sends him to a place that is dangerous or difficult. He remembers that God the Son left His heavenly home of love, holiness, and glory to come to earth and be hated, rejected, spat upon, and crucified—without once returning evil for evil or complaining to His Father.

FORBEARING LOVE

A fourth characteristic element of the worthy Christian walk is **forbearance to one another in love**. Peter tells us that such "love covers a multitude of sins" (1 Pet. 4:8). It throws a blanket over the sins of others, not to justify or excuse them but to keep the sins from becoming any more known than necessary. "Hatred stirs up strife, but love covers all transgressions" (Prov. 10:12). Forbearing love takes abuse from others while continuing to love them.

Forbearing **love** could only be *agapē* love, because only *agapē* love gives continuously and unconditionally. *Erōs* love is essentially self-love, because it cares for others only because of what it can get from them. It is the love that takes and never gives. *Philia* love is primarily reciprocal love, love that gives as long as it receives. But *agapē* love is unqualified and unselfish love, love that willingly gives whether it receives in return or not. It is unconquerable benevolence, invincible goodness—love that goes out even to enemies and prays for its persecutors (Matt. 5:43-44). That is why the **forbearance** of which Paul speaks here could only be expressed in *agapē* **love**.

UNITY

The ultimate outcome of humility, gentleness, patience, and forbearance is **being diligent to preserve the unity of the Spirit in the bond of peace**. *Spoudazō* (to be **diligent**) basically means to make haste, and from that come the meanings of zeal and diligence. One commentator describes it as a holy zeal that demands full dedication. Paul used the word in telling Timothy, "Be diligent to present yourself approved to God as a workman who does not need to be ashamed, handling accurately the word of truth" (2 Tim. 2:15; cf. Titus 3:12-13).

Preservation of the **unity of the Spirit in the bond of peace** should be the **diligent** and constant concern of every believer. Paul is not speaking of organizational unity, such as that promoted in many denominations and in the ecumenical movement. He is speaking of the inner and universal **unity of the Spirit** by which every true believer is bound to every other true believer. As Paul makes clear, this is **the unity of the Spirit** working in the lives of believers. It does not come from the outside but the inside, and is manifested through the inner qualities of humility, gentleness, patience, and forbearing love.

Spiritual **unity** is not, and cannot be, created by the church. It is already created by the Holy **Spirit**. "For by one Spirit we were all baptized into one body, whether Jews or Greeks, whether slaves or free, and we were all made to drink of one Spirit. . . . There are many members, but one body" (1 Cor. 12:13, 20; cf. Rom. 8:9). It is this very **unity of the Spirit** for which Jesus so earnestly prayed in the Upper Room shortly before His betrayal and arrest: "Holy Father, keep them in Thy name, the name which Thou hast given Me, that they may be one, even as We are, . . . that they may all be one; even as Thou, Father, art in Me, and I in Thee, that they also may be in Us. . . . And the glory which Thou hast given Me I have given to them; that they may be one, just as We are one; I in them, and Thou in Me, that they may be perfected in unity" (John 17:11, 21-23).

The church's responsibility, through the lives of individual believers, is **to preserve the unity** by faithfully walking in a manner worthy of God's calling (v. 1), manifesting Christ to the world by oneness in Him (cf. Rom. 15:1-6; 1 Cor. 1:10-13; 3:1-3; Phil. 1:27). The world is always seeking but never finding unity. All the laws, conferences, treaties, accords, and agreements fail to bring unity or peace. Someone has reported that throughout recorded history every treaty made has been broken. There is not, and cannot be, any peace for the wicked (Isa. 48:22). As long as self is at the center; as long as our feelings, prestige, and rights are our chief concern, there will never be unity.

The **bond** that preserves **unity** is **peace**, the spiritual belt that surrounds and binds God's holy people together. It is the **bond** that Paul described in Philippians as "being of the same mind, maintaining the same love, united in spirit, intent on one purpose" (2:2). Behind this **bond of peace** is love, which Colossians 3:14 calls "the perfect bond of unity."

Humility gives birth to gentleness, gentleness gives birth to patience, patience gives birth to forbearing love, and all four of those characteristics **preserve the unity of the Spirit in the bond of peace**. These virtues and the supernatural unity to which they testify are probably the most powerful testimony the church can have, because they are in such contrast to the attitudes and the disunity of the world. No program or method, no matter how carefully planned and executed, can open the door to the gospel in the way individual believers can do when they are genuinely humble, meek, patient, forbearing in love, and demonstrate peaceful unity in the Holy Spirit.

THE CAUSE OF THE WORTHY WALK

There is one body and one Spirit, just as also you were called in one hope of your calling; one Lord, one faith, one baptism, one God and Father of all who is over all and through all and in all. (4:4-6)

Everything that relates to salvation, the church, and the kingdom of God is based on the concept of unity, as reflected in Paul's use of seven **one**'s in these three verses. The cause, or basis, of outward oneness is inner oneness. Practical oneness is based on spiritual oneness. To emphasize the unity of the Spirit, Paul recites the features of oneness that are germane to our doctrine and life.

Paul does not develop the particular areas of oneness, but simply lists them: **body, Spirit, hope, Lord, faith, baptism,** and **God and Father.** His focus is on the oneness of those and every other aspect of God's nature, plan, and work as a basis for our commitment to live as one. It is obvious that verse 4 centers on the Holy Spirit, verse 5 on the Son, and verse 6 on the Father.

UNITY IN THE SPIRIT

There is one body and one Spirit, just as also you were called in one hope of your calling; (4:4)

There is only **one body** of believers, the church, which is composed of every saint who has trusted or will trust in Christ as Savior and Lord. There is no denominational, geographical, ethnic, or racial body. There is no Gentile, Jewish, male, female, slave, or freeman body. There is only Christ's **body,** and the unity of that **body** is the heart of the book of Ephesians.

Obviously there is but **one Spirit,** the Holy Spirit of God, who is possessed by every believer and who is therefore the inner unifying force in the **body.** Believers are individual temples of the Holy Spirit (1 Cor. 3:16-17) that are collectively "being fitted together [and are] growing into a holy temple in the Lord, . . . being built together into a dwelling of God in the Spirit" (Eph. 2:21-22). The **Spirit** "is given as a pledge of our inheritance, with a view to the redemption of God's own possession, to the praise of His glory" (Eph. 1:14). He is the divine engagement ring (pledge), as it were, who guarantees that every believer will be at the marriage supper of the Lamb (Rev. 19:9).

If all Christians were walking in obedience to and in the power of the Holy

Spirit, first our doctrine and then our relationships would be purified and unified. The spiritual unity that already exists would be practically manifested in complete harmony among the people of God.

Believers are also unified in the **one hope of** their **calling.** Our calling to salvation is ultimately a calling to Christlike eternal perfection and glory. In Christ we have different gifts, different ministries, different places of service, but only **one . . . calling,** the calling to "be holy and blameless before Him" (Eph. 1:4) and "to become conformed to the image of His Son" (Rom. 8:29), which will occur when we see the glorified Christ (1 John 3:2). It is the Spirit who has placed us in the one Body and who guarantees our future glory.

UNITY IN THE SON

one Lord, one faith, one baptism, (4:5)

Just as obviously, there is but **one Lord,** Jesus Christ our Savior. "There is salvation in no one else; for there is no other name under heaven that has been given among men, by which we must be saved" (Acts 4:12). Paul told the Galatians, "Even though we or an angel from heaven, should preach to you a gospel contrary to that which we have preached to you, let him be accursed" (Gal. 1:8). "For the same Lord is Lord of all, abounding in riches for all who call upon Him" (Rom. 10:12).

Consequently there can only be **one faith.** Paul is not referring here to the act of faith by which a person is saved or the continuing faith that produces right living, but rather the body of doctrine revealed in the New Testament. In true Christianity there is only **one faith,** "the faith which was once for all delivered to the saints" and for which we are to contend (Jude 3). Our **one faith** is the content of the revealed Word of God. Lack of faithful and careful study of His Word, unexamined tradition, worldly influences, carnal inclinations, and many other things fragment doctrine into many varying and even contradictory forms. God's Word contains many truths, but its individual truths are but harmonious facets of His one truth, which is our **one faith.**

There is but **one baptism** among believers. Spiritual baptism, by which all believers are placed into the Body by the Holy Spirit, is implied in verse 4. The **one baptism** of verse 5 is best taken to refer to water baptism, the common New Testament means of a believer's publicly confessing Jesus as Savior and Lord. This is preferred because of the way Paul has spoken specifically of each member of the Trinity in succession. This is the Lord Jesus Christ's verse, as it were.

Water baptism was extremely important in the early church, not as a means of salvation or special blessing but as a testimony of identity with and unity in Jesus Christ. Believers were not baptized in the name of a local church, a prominent evangelist, a leading elder, or even an apostle, but only in the name of Christ (see 1 Cor. 1:13-17). Those who by **one Lord** are in **one faith** testify to that unity in **one baptism.**

UNITY IN THE FATHER

one God and Father of all who is over all and through all and in all. (4:6)

The basic doctrine of Judaism has always been, "The Lord is our God, the Lord is one!" (Deut. 6:4; see also 4:35; 32:39; Isa. 45:14; 46:9), and God's oneness is just as foundational to Christianity (see 1 Cor. 8:4-6; Eph. 4:3-6; James 2:19). Yet the New Testament also reveals the more complete truth that the **one God** is in three Persons—**Father**, Son, and Holy Spirit (Matt. 28:19; John 6:27; 20:28; Acts 5:3-4).

God the **Father** is often used in Scripture as the most comprehensive and inclusive divine title, though it is clear from many New Testament texts that He is never separated in nature or power from the Son or the Holy Spirit. Paul's point here is not to separate the Persons of the Godhead but to note their unique roles and yet focus on their unity in relation to each other and in relation to the church—manifested in the several different aspects mentioned in these three verses.

Our **one God and Father**, along with the Son and the Holy Spirit, **is over all and through all and in all**. That comprehensive statement points to the glorious, divine, eternal unity that the Father gives believers by His Spirit and through the Son. We are God created, God loved, God saved, God Fathered, God controlled, God sustained, God filled, and God blessed. We are one people under one sovereign (**over all**), omnipotent (**through all**), and omnipresent (**in all**) God.

The Gifts of Christ
to His Church

11

But to each one of us grace was given according to the measure of Christ's gift. Therefore it says, "When He ascended on high, He led captive a host of captives, and He gave gifts to men." (Now this expression, "He ascended," what does it mean except that He also had descended into the lower parts of the earth? He who descended is Himself also He who ascended far above all the heavens, that He might fill all things.) And He gave some as apostles, and some as prophets, and some as evangelists, and some as pastors and teachers, (4:7-11)

The essence of the gospel is not in what men should do for God but in what He has done for men. The New Testament, like the Old, contains many commands and requirements, many standards to be met and obligations to be fulfilled. But important as those things are, they are not the heart of Christianity. They are simply what God calls and enables us to do for His glory in response to what He has done for us through our Lord Jesus Christ. Every New Testament book teaches what Christ has done for believers, and every New Testament exhortation is built on that foundation of God's gracious provision through the Savior. God gave the supreme gift of grace and His children are to respond in faithful obedience (see Eph. 2:10).

Paul begins this passage by referring to what God has done for those who have trusted in His Son. The worthy Christian walk he has just described (4:1-6) is carried out through the ministry of the gift He has given us. In verses 7-11 the apostle first assures us that every believer has been individually gifted; then he shows us how Christ obtained the right to give gifts; and finally he mentions some of the specially gifted men through whom the Lord blesses the whole church.

THE GIFTS OF CHRIST TO INDIVIDUAL BELIEVERS

But to each one of us grace was given according to the measure of Christ's gift. **(4:7)**

It is important to note that the term **but**, with which this verse begins, is used here as an adversative rather than as a simple conjunction. It could be translated "in spite of that" or "on the other hand," contrasting the previous subject matter with what is about to be said.

This interpretation of **but** brings together the emphasis of unity that has been the echoing theme of verses 3-6 with the parallel emphasis of diversity, which is the theme of verses 7-11. It sets the individual (**each one**) over against the "all" (v. 6) in regard to unity in the Body of Christ. The reading of **but** as adversative is strengthened by the emphatic use of *hekastos* (**each one**). Unity is not uniformity and is perfectly consistent with diversity of gifts. God's gracious relation to "all" is also a personal relation *to* **each one** (cf. 1 Cor. 12:7, 11) and a personal ministry *through* **each one**. Thus Paul moves from the unity of believers to the uniqueness of believers.

Grace is a single-word definition of the gospel. The gospel is the good news of God's grace to sinful mankind. The nature of grace is giving, and the Bible tells us much more about giving than getting, because God's nature is to give. God is a God of grace because He is a God who freely gives. It has nothing to do with anything we have done or have failed to do; it can only be received.

God is gracious because of who He is, not because of who or what we are. His **grace** is therefore unmerited, unearned, undeserved. It depends entirely on the One who gives it, not on those who receive it. **Grace** is God's self-motivated, self-generated, sovereign act of giving.

God's **grace** has another dimension that places it still further above every other kind of giving. The greatest gift of grace is self. **Grace** is therefore God's Self donation, His Self giving. He not only gives blessings to men, He gives Himself. Infinitely more important and precious than any blessing God gives us is that gift of Himself. The incomprehensible and staggering truth of the gospel is that the holy God of the universe has given *Himself* to sinful mankind! God grants us His salvation, His kingdom, His inheritance, His Spirit, His throne, His wisdom, His love, His power, His peace, His glory, and every other "spiritual blessing in the heavenly places in Christ" (Eph. 1:3). But far more than all of those blessings, He blesses us with His personal presence. God owes nothing to sinful men except judgment for their sin. He does not owe men the smallest blessing or favor. Yet in His grace He has given us the blessing of all blessings, the immeasurable blessing of intimate shared life (cf. 2 Pet. 1:3-4).

When we choose a partner with whom we plan to spend the rest of our life in marriage, we are careful to pick someone who is worthy of the self-giving that marriage demands. That person is the one above all others to whom we will give our love, our time, our thoughts, our devotion, our loyalty, and our resources—in short, all that we have.

Yet when God "chose us in Him before the foundation of the world" (Eph. 1:4), He did so out of pure grace and not for anything He saw in us that made us worthy of His care. "For God so loved the world, that He gave His only begotten Son" (John 3:16). All God can see in the world is sin, yet He gave Himself to that sinful world through His own Son in order that the world might be redeemed. The Son also gave Himself, emptying Himself of His own glory that He might offer glory to fallen men and giving His own life that spiritually dead men might live.

Throughout His earthly ministry Jesus continually gave Himself to others. He gave Himself to His disciples, to those He healed, to those He raised from the dead, released from demons, and forgave of sins. To the woman at the well in Sychar He offered the water of eternal life (John 4:14), and He Himself was that water (6:35; 7:38). "You know the grace of our Lord Jesus Christ, that though He was rich, yet for your sake He became poor, that you through His poverty might become rich" (2 Cor. 8:9). To those who receive His **grace** God will continue to "show the surpassing riches of His grace in kindness toward us in Christ Jesus" throughout the ages to come (Eph. 2:7).

The **grace** in which we stand (Rom. 5:2) not only saves but enables (cf. Eph. 6:10; Phil. 4:13; 1 Tim. 1:12; 2 Tim. 4:17), and that is the sense of the term here. Paul makes it clear that **grace was given** to every believer. The definite article *(hē)* is used in the original text, indicating that this is *the* grace, that is, the grace unique to Christ. The term for **grace** is *charis* and signifies that what is given is not the *charismata* (the special gifts indicated by this word in Rom. 12:6-8 and 1 Cor. 12:4-10) but the subjective grace that works in and shows itself through the life of a believer. This **grace** is the enabling power that makes the special gifts function to the glory of God.

This distinction is clear for the rest of Paul's statement, **according to the measure of Christ's gift.** Enabling grace is measured out to be consistent with what is necessary for the operation of **Christ's gift.** The term *dōrea* (gift) does not focus on the undeservedness of the gift as does *charismata* (the special "gifts"; cf. Rom. 12:6; 1 Cor. 12:4; 1 Pet. 4:10) nor on the spiritual source of the gift as does *pneumatikōn* ("spiritual gifts," lit., spiritual things; cf. 1 Cor. 12:1), but on the freeness of the gift (cf. Matt. 10:8; Rom. 3:24).

And each believer's **gift** is unique. **The measure** or specific portion given is by sovereign design from the Head of the church. The Lord has measured out the exact proportion of each believer's gift (compare Paul's use of the phrase "the measure of faith" in Rom. 12:3). The exact proportion of enabling grace on the part of God is linked with the exact proportion of enacting faith on the part of each believer; and God is the source of both. The sum of this is that God gives both the grace and the faith to energize whatever gift He gives to the full intent of His purpose.

In light of the truth just stated it is clear that since they are sovereignly given (cf. 1 Cor. 12:4-7, 11), no gifts should be sought; that since they are essential elements in God's plan (cf. 1 Cor. 12:18, 22, 25), no gifts should be unused; and that since they come from the Lord, no gifts should be exalted (cf. Rom. 12:3).

We each have a **gift** that is measured out to us—with certain distinct capabilities, parameters, and purposes. Each of us is given a specific **gift** (singular) through which we are to minister in Christ's name. "As each one has received a special gift," Peter says, "employ it in serving one another, as good stewards of the manifold grace of God" (1 Pet. 4:10).

In Romans 12 Paul gives a more detailed explanation of spiritual gifts, which he introduces by emphasizing, as he does in Ephesians 4, that "we have gifts that differ according to the grace given to us" (v. 6). By definition, gifts are something we receive, and we receive spiritual gifts through the working of God's grace. Believers' gifts are not determined by their preferences, inclinations, natural abilities, merit, or any other personal consideration, but solely by God's sovereign and gracious will. We are gifted according to His plan, His purpose, and His **measure**. We have no more to do with determining our gift than we did with determining what color of skin, hair, or eyes we would be born with. God is the source of electing grace, equipping grace, and enabling grace.

In 1 Corinthians 12 we see a similar explanation and emphasis. "Now there are varieties of gifts, but the same Spirit. And there are varieties of ministries, but the same Lord. And there are varieties of effects, but the same God who works all things in all persons. But to each one is given the manifestation of the Spirit for the common good" (vv. 4-7). God is the sole giver and determiner of spiritual gifts.

The lists of specific gifts in Romans 12:6-8, 1 Corinthians 12:8-10, and Ephesians 4:11 are not narrow and strict delineations of the spiritual gifts. There is not, for instance, a *single kind* of prophetic gift, teaching gift, or serving gift. A hundred believers with the gift of teaching will not all have the same degrees or areas of teaching ability or emphasis. One may excel in public teaching in the classroom or church. Another's teaching gift will be for instructing children, another's for teaching one-on-one, and so on. Each believer is given the measure of grace and faith to operate his gift according to God's plan. Add individual personality, background, education, influences in life, and needs in the area of service and it becomes obvious that each believer is unique.

Nor is it that a believer's single **gift** will be restricted to only one category of giftedness. An individual gift may include a number of specific areas of giftedness, in a limitless variety of combinations. Someone with a major gift of administration may also have something of the gifts of helps and of teaching. Believers' gifts are like snowflakes and fingerprints—each one is completely distinct from all others. Some teachers may emphasize knowledge, some instruction, some mercy, and others exhortation. From the palette of gift colors the Holy Spirit uses the brush of His sovereign design to paint the mixture of each believer so that no two are like.

Christians are not assembly-line productions, with every unit being exactly like every other unit. Consequently, no Christian can replace another in God's plan. He has His own individualized plan for each of us and has individually gifted us accordingly. We are not interchangeable parts in Christ's Body, but "individually members one of another" (Rom. 12:5). "One and the same Spirit works all these things, distributing to each one *individually* just as He wills" (1 Cor. 12:11, emphasis added). When a believer does not minister his gift properly as God's steward (1 Pet. 4:10), God's work suffers to that degree—because God has not called or gifted another Christian in exactly the same way or for exactly the same work. That is why no Christian is to be a spectator. Every believer is on the team and is strategic in God's plan, with his own unique skills, position, and responsibilities.

At weddings, birthdays, Christmas, and other such occasions, we often get gifts for which we have no use. We put them in a drawer, store them in the garage, or later give them to someone else. But God never gives such gifts. Each of His gifts is exactly what we need to fulfill our work for Him. We never get the wrong gift, or too much or too little of it. When the Holy Spirit gave us our gift, He presented us with precisely the right blend of abilities and enablement we need to serve God. Not only does our unique giftedness make us an irreplaceable member of Christ's Body but it is a mark of God's great love to single each of us out for unique blessing and ministry.

Not to use our gift is an affront to God's wisdom, a rebuff of His love and grace, and a loss to His church. We did not determine our gift, deserve it, or earn it. But we all have a gift from the Lord, and if we do not use it, His work is weakened and His heart is grieved. The intent of the text before us is to reveal the balanced relationship between the oneness of believers and their individuality which contributes to that oneness. (For further explanation of spiritual gifts, see the author's commentary on 1 Corinthians, noting the material on 12:1-31; cf. Rom. 12:3-8.)

HOW CHRIST WON THE RIGHT TO GIVE GIFTS

Therefore it says, "When He ascended on high, He led captive a host of captives, and He gave gifts to men." (Now this expression, "He ascended," what does it mean except that He also had descended into the lower parts of the earth? He who descended is Himself also He who ascended far above all the heavens, that He might fill all things.) (4:8-10)

Paul is set to delineate some of the gifts Christ has given, but before mentioning specific gifts bestowed on the whole church, he uses Psalm 68:18 as a comparison passage to show how Christ received the right to bestow those gifts. The obvious differences between both the Hebrew and Greek (Septuagint) Old

Testament texts of Psalm 68:18 and Paul's citation of it suggest that he is probably making only a general allusion to the passage for the sake of analogy, rather than specifically identifying it as a direct prediction of Christ.

Psalm 68 is a victory hymn composed by David to celebrate God's conquest of the Jebusite city and the triumphant ascent of God (represented by the Ark of the Covenant) up Mount Zion (cf. 2 Sam. 6-7; 1 Chron. 13). After a king won such a victory he would bring home the spoils and enemy prisoners to parade before his people. An Israelite king would take his retinue through the holy city of Jerusalem and up Mount Zion. Another feature of the victory parade, however, would be the display of the king's own soldiers who had been freed after being held prisoner by the enemy. These were often referred to as recaptured captives—prisoners who had been taken prisoner again, so to speak, by their own king and given freedom.

The phrase **when He ascended on high** depicts a triumphant Christ returning from battle on earth back into the glory of the heavenly city with the trophies of His great victory.

In His crucifixion and resurrection, Jesus Christ conquered Satan, sin, and death (cf. Col. 2:15), and by that great victory He **led captive a host of captives**, who once were prisoners of the enemy but now are returned to the God and the people with whom they belong. The picture is vivid in its demonstration that God has yet-unsaved people who belong to Him—though they are naturally in Satan's grasp and would remain there had not Christ by His death and resurrection made provision to lead them into the captivity of His kingdom into which they had been called by sovereign election "before the foundation of the world" (Eph. 1:4). Compare Acts 18:10, where the Lord tells Paul to stay in Corinth and preach because there were people in that city who belonged to Him but were not yet saved from bondage to the king of darkness (see also John 10:16; 11:51-52; Acts 15:14-18).

Upon arriving in heaven, **He gave gifts to men.** Paul here uses yet another term for **gifts** (*domata*) to express the comprehensiveness of this gracious provision. Like a triumphant conqueror distributing the spoils to his subjects, so Christ takes the trophies He has won and distributes them in His kingdom. After His ascension came all the gifts empowered by the Holy Spirit (John 7:39; 14:12; Acts 2:33). When the Savior was exalted on high, He sent the Spirit (Acts 1:8), and with the coming of the Spirit also came His gifts to the church. Before Paul identifies the gifts he has in mind, he first gives a brief parenthetical explanation of the analogy he has just used.

In explaining the application of the Old Testament passage, Paul says, **Now this expression, "He ascended," what does it mean except that He also descended into the lower parts of the earth?** The **He** of whom Paul is speaking is the One who will **fill all things**—Jesus Christ, "who fills all in all" (1:23). **Ascended** refers to Jesus' ascension from earth to heaven (Acts 1:9-11). He **ascended** from earth to heaven to forever reign with His Father.

Paul is quick to explain that the expression **He ascended** cannot mean anything **except that He . . . also descended.** If, as seems clear, **ascended** refers to our Lord's being taken up to heaven, then **descended** must refer to His coming down from heaven to earth. The captain of our salvation was first abased and then exalted. Divestiture came before investiture, incarnation before glorification (see Phil. 2:4-11). This truth is repeated in proper chronological sequence in verse 10: **He who descended is Himself also He who ascended.**

The depth of Christ's descent in incarnation is said to be **into the lower parts of the earth.** This reference is presented to provide a striking contrast in terms of His ascent **far above all the heavens,** emphasizing the extreme range of our Lord's condescension and exaltation. To understand the phrase **the lower parts of the earth** we need only examine its use elsewhere in Scripture. In Psalm 63:9 it has to do with death, being related to falling by the sword (v. 10). In Matthew 12:40 a similar phrase, "the heart of the earth," refers to the belly of a great fish where the prophet Jonah was kept. In Isaiah 44:23 the phrase refers to the created earth containing mountains, forests, and trees. Psalm 139:15 uses it in reference to the womb of a woman where God is forming a child. The sum of these uses indicates that the phrase relates to the created earth as a place of life and death. In the majority of the uses it appears in contrast to the highest heavens, as here and in Psalm 139:8, 15 and Isaiah 44:23.

The intent of the phrase in this letter is not to point to a specific place, but to refer to the depth of the incarnation. It is interesting that each of the uses of the phrase outside Ephesians can also relate to the depth of Christ's incarnation. He was formed in the womb (Psa. 139:15), lived on the earth (Isa. 44:23), referred to His own burial as a parallel to Jonah's being in the fish (Matt. 12:40), and His death is consistent with the use of the phrase in Psalm 63:9.

It should be noted further that our Lord's descent went even beyond the womb, the earth, the grave, and death—to a descent into the very pit of the demons. Peter sheds light on the meaning of **He also descended into the lower parts of the earth.** In his first letter he says, "For Christ also died for sins once for all, the just for the unjust, in order that He might bring us to God, having been put to death in the flesh, but made alive in the spirit; in which also He went and made proclamation to the spirits now in prison" (1 Pet. 3:18-19). Between Jesus' death on Calvary and His resurrection in the garden tomb, He was "put to death in the flesh, but made alive in the spirit." He was physically dead but spiritually alive. During the three days He was in that state **He also descended** "and made proclamation [from *kērussō*) to the spirits now in prison." This does not refer to preaching the gospel (from *euangelizō*) but to making a triumphant announcement—in this case Christ's announcement of His victory over the demons even while they tried to hold Him in death.

The Old Testament refers to the place of the departed dead as Sheol (Deut. 32:22; Job 26:6; Ps. 16:10; etc.). Part of Sheol was a place of torment and evil, occupied by the unrighteous dead and by the demons who had been confined and bound there because of their wicked cohabitation with women during the period before the Flood (see Gen. 6:2-5; 2 Pet. 2:4; Jude 6). When Christ **descended** to Sheol, He proclaimed His victory, because "He had disarmed the rulers and authorities [and] made a public display of them, having triumphed over them"

(Col. 2:15; cf. 1 Pet. 3:19). At that time came the announcement to the demons, both bound and loose (the "angels and authorities and powers"), that they all were subject to Christ (1 Pet. 3:22; Eph. 1:20-21). To ascend to heaven, He also passed through the territory of Satan and his demons in the air (Heb. 4:14 uses *dia,* through) and no doubt celebrated His triumph over them. Whether or not Paul had this event in mind in his reference here is difficult to establish; nonetheless, it does demonstrate the depth of Christ's descent.

Another part of Sheol, though not clearly distinguished from the other by Old Testament writers, was believed to be a place of happiness and bliss, inhabited by the righteous dead who had believed in God. "Abraham's bosom" (Luke 16:22-23) and "Paradise" (Luke 23:43) apparently were common designations for Sheol at the time of Christ. Early church dogma taught that the righteous dead of the Old Testament could not be taken into the fullness of God's presence until Christ had purchased their redemption on the cross, and that they had waited in this place for His victory on that day. Figuratively speaking, the early church Fathers said that, after announcing His triumph over demons in one part of Sheol, He then opened the doors of another part of Sheol to release those godly captives. Like the victorious kings of old, He recaptured the captives and liberated them, and henceforth they would live in heaven as eternally free sons of God.

It must be suggested that such a view seems strained in the Ephesian context, because **the lower parts of the earth** is a general phrase and cannot be proven to refer to Sheol.

Paul's point in Ephesians 4:8-10 is to explain that Jesus' paying the infinite price of coming to earth and suffering death on our behalf qualified Him to be exalted **above all the heavens** (that is, to the throne of God), in order that He might rightfully have the authority to give gifts to His saints. By that victory He gained the right to rule His church and to give gifts to His church, **that He might fill all things**.

Does **all things** mean all prophecies, all assigned tasks, all universal sovereignty? Surely the answer is yes in regard to each of those aspects. But the context would dictate that His filling **all things** primarily has to do with His glorious divine presence and power expressed in universal sovereignty. He fills the entire universe with blessing, particularly His church, as the next verse illustrates.

THE GIFTS OF CHRIST TO THE WHOLE CHURCH

And He gave some as apostles, and some as prophets, and some as evangelists, and some as pastors and teachers, (4:11)

After his parenthetical analogy (vv. 9-10) from Psalm 68:18, Paul continues his explanation of spiritual gifts. Christ not only gives gifts to individual believers but to the total Body. To each believer He gives special gifts of divine enablement, and to the church overall He gives specially gifted men as leaders (see v. 8, "He gave gifts to men")—**as apostles, . . . prophets, . . . evangelists, and . . . pastors and teachers**.

He gave emphasizes the sovereign choice and authority given to Christ because of His perfect fulfillment of the Father's will. Not only **apostles** and **prophets** but also **evangelists**, . . . **pastors and teachers** are divinely called and placed.

APOSTLES AND PROPHETS

In 1 Corinthians 12:28, Paul says, "God has appointed in the church, first apostles, second prophets, third teachers." That statement adds weight not only to the idea of divine calling but also to the chronological significance ("first, . . . second, . . . third") in the giving of these gifted men to the church.

The first two classes of gifted men, **apostles** and **prophets**, were given three basic responsibilities:

(1) to lay the foundation of the church (Eph. 2:20); (2) to receive and declare the revelation of God's Word (Acts 11:28; 21:10-11; Eph. 3:5); and (3) to give confirmation of that Word through "signs and wonders and miracles" (2 Cor. 12:12; cf. Acts 8:6-7; Heb. 2:3-4).

The first of the gifted men in the New Testament church were the apostles, of whom Jesus Christ Himself is foremost (Heb. 3:1). The basic meaning of apostle *(apostolos)* is simply that of one sent on a mission. In its primary and most technical sense *apostle* is used in the New Testament only of the twelve, including Matthias, who replaced Judas (Acts 1:26), and of Paul, who was uniquely set apart as apostle to the Gentiles (Gal. 1:15-17; cf. 1 Cor. 15:7-9; 2 Cor. 11:5). The qualifications for that apostleship were having been chosen directly by Christ and having witnessed the resurrected Christ (Mark 3:13; Acts 1:22-24). Paul was the last to meet those qualifications (Rom. 1:1; etc.). It is not possible therefore, as some claim, for there to be apostles in the church today. Some have observed that the apostles were like delegates to a constitutional convention. When the convention is over, the position ceases. When the New Testament was completed, the office of apostle ceased.

The term *apostle* is used in a more general sense of other men in the early church, such as Barnabas (Acts 14:4), Silas and Timothy (1 Thess. 2:6), and a few other outstanding leaders (Rom. 16:7; 2 Cor. 8:23; Phil. 2:25). The false apostles spoken of in 2 Cor. 11:13 no doubt counterfeited this class of apostleship, since the others were limited to thirteen and were well known. The true apostles in the second group were called "messengers *(apostoloi)* of the churches" (2 Cor. 8:23), whereas the thirteen were apostles of Jesus Christ (Gal. 1:1; 1 Pet. 1:1; etc.).

Apostles in both groups were authenticated "by signs and wonders and miracles" (2 Cor. 12:12), but neither group was self-perpetuating. In neither sense is the term *apostle* used in the book of Acts after 16:4. Nor is there any New Testament record of an apostle in either group being replaced when he died.

. . . Prophets were also appointed by God as specially gifted men, and differ from those believers who have the gift of prophecy (1 Cor. 12:10). Not all such believers could be called prophets. It seems that the office of prophet was exclusively for work within a local congregation, whereas that of apostleship was a much broader ministry, not confined to any area, as implied in the word *apostolos* ("one who is sent on a mission"). Paul, for example, is referred to as a prophet when he ministered locally in the Antioch church (Acts 13:1), but elsewhere is always called an apostle.

The prophets sometimes spoke revelation from God (Acts 11:21-28) and sometimes simply expounded revelation already given (as implied in Acts 13:1, where they are connected with teachers). They always spoke for God but did not always give a newly revealed message from God. The prophets were second to the apostles, and their message was to be judged by that of the apostles (1 Cor. 14:37). Another distinction between the two offices may have been that the apostolic message was more general and doctrinal, whereas that of the prophets was more personal and practical.

Like the apostles, however, their office ceased with the completion of the New Testament, just as the Old Testament prophets disappeared when that testament was completed, some 400 years before Christ. The church was established "upon the foundation of the apostles and prophets, Christ Jesus Himself being the corner stone" (Eph. 2:20). Once the foundation was laid, the work of the apostles and prophets was finished. (*First Corinthians,* The MacArthur New Testament Commentary [Chicago: Moody, 1984], pp. 322-24)

There is no mention of the latter two gifted offices replacing the first two, because in New Testament times all were operative. But the fact is that, as they continued to serve the church, the **evangelists** and **pastors and teachers** did pick up the baton from the first generation **apostles** and **prophets**.

From its inception at Pentecost the church has been indebted to the **apostles**, through whom Christ established the fullness of New Testament doctrine (see Acts 2:42). Those uniquely called and empowered men recorded God's final revelation as He revealed it to them.

The **prophets**, though they did not usually receive direct revelation from God, nevertheless were greatly instrumental in building up and strengthening the early church. Both **apostles** and **prophets** have passed from the scene (Eph. 2:20), but the foundation they laid is that on which all of Christ's church has been built.

EVANGELISTS

Evangelists and **pastors and teachers** are now in place in God's plan for the advancement of the kingdom. **Evangelists** (*euangelistēs*) are men who proclaim good news. The specific term *evangelist* is used only in this text in Ephesians; in Acts 21:8, where Philip is called an "evangelist" (see Acts 8:4-40 for details on one of Philip's evangelistic efforts); and in 2 Timothy 4:5, where Timothy is told to "do the work of an evangelist." But these limited references describe a vital, extensive, and far-reaching ministry, indicated by the use of the verb *euangelizō* (to proclaim the good news) 54 times and the noun *euangelion* (good news) 76 times. God was the first evangelist, since He "preached the gospel beforehand" (from *proeuangelizomai;* Gal. 3:8). Even the angel evangelized ("I bring . . . good news," [from *euangelizomai*]) in announcing the birth of Christ (Luke 2:10). Jesus Himself evangelized in "preaching the gospel" (Luke 20:1), as did the apostles in "preaching the word" (Acts 8:4).

The work of the evangelist is to preach and explain the good news of salvation in Jesus Christ to those who have not yet believed. He is a proclaimer of salvation by grace through faith in the Son of God.

Philip demonstrates that the evangelist is not a man with ten suits and ten sermons who runs a road show. New Testament evangelists were missionaries and church planters (much like the apostles, but without the title and miraculous gifts), who went where Christ was not named and led people to faith in the Savior. They then taught the new believers the Word, built them up, and moved on to new territory.

Timothy illustrates the fact that an evangelist can be identified with local churches in a prolonged ministry for the purposes of preaching and expounding the true gospel, in order to counter false teachers and their damning message and to establish sound doctrine and godliness.

These gifted men are uniquely designed and given to the church to reach the lost with the saving gospel, and every church should consider this ministry as high priority. It is my conviction that each local assembly should raise up evangelists, to send some out in mission enterprises and to have others remain permanently in the church fellowship—to teach, mobilize, and lead others out to fulfill the commission of winning the lost to Christ. Every church should be led by a combination of evangelists and teaching shepherds—men gifted to bring the lost in and men gifted for feeding believers and leading them in the Word to build them up.

PASTORS AND TEACHERS

Pastors translates *poimēn,* whose normal meaning is shepherd. It emphasizes the care, protection and leadership of the man of God for the flock. **Teachers** (*didaskaloi*) has to do with the primary function of **pastors.**

Though teaching can be identified as a ministry on its own (1 Cor. 12:28), **pastors and teachers** are best understood as one office of leadership in the church. Often the word **and** (*kai*) means "that is" or "in particular," making **teachers** in this context explanatory of **pastors.** That meaning cannot be conclusively proven in this text, but the text of 1 Timothy 5:17 clearly puts the two functions together when it says: "Let the elders who rule well be considered worthy of double honor, especially those who work hard at preaching and teaching" (lit., "labor to exhaustion in word and teaching"). Those two functions define the teaching shepherd. To fully understand this ministry, some key questions need to be answered about the identity of the elder in the New Testament, and some detail is necessary for proper understanding.

How is the pastor-teacher related to the bishop and elder? Pastors are not distinct from bishops and elders; the terms are simply different ways of identifying the same people. As explained above, the Greek word for pastor (*poimēn*) has the basic meaning of shepherd. The Greek word for bishop is *episkopos,* from which we derive Episcopalian, and its basic meaning is "overseer." The Greek word for elder is *presbuteros,* from which we get Presbyterian, and denotes an older person.

Textual evidence indicates that all three terms refer to the same office. In the qualifications for a bishop, listed in 1 Timothy 3:7, and those for an elder, in Titus, Paul uses both terms to refer to the same man (1:5, 7). First Peter 5:1-2 brings all three terms together. Peter instructs the elders to be good bishops as they pastor: "Therefore, I exhort the elders *[presbuteros]* among you, as your fellow elder and witness of the sufferings of Christ, and a partaker also of the glory that is to be revealed, shepherd *[poimainō]* the flock of God among you, exercising oversight *[episkopeo]* not under compulsion, but voluntarily, according to the will of God."

Acts 20 also uses all three terms interchangeably. In verse 17, Paul assembles all the elders *(presbuteros)* of the church to give them his farewell message. In verse 28, he says, "Be on guard for yourselves and for all the flock, among which the Holy Spirit has made you overseers *[episkopos],* to shepherd *[poimainō]* the church of God."

Elder emphasizes who the man is, *bishop* speaks of what he does, and *pastor* deals with his attitude and character. All three terms are used of the same church leaders, and all three identify those who feed and lead the church; yet each term has a unique emphasis.

Episkopos means "overseer," or "guardian," and is used five times in the New Testament. In 1 Peter 2:25, Jesus Christ is called the "Guardian *[episkopos]* of your souls." That is, He is the one who has the clearest overview of us and who therefore understands us best. The other four uses of *episkopos* refer to leaders in the church.

Episkopos was the secular Greek culture's equivalent to the historic Hebrew idea of elder. Overseers, or bishops, were those appointed by the emperors to govern captured or newly-founded city-states. The bishop was responsible to the emperor, but oversight was delegated to him. He functioned as a commissioner, regulating the affairs of the new colony or acquisition. *Episkopos* therefore suggested two ideas to the first-century Greek mind: responsibility to a superior power, and introduction to a new order of things. Gentile converts would immediately understand those concepts in the term.

It is interesting to trace the biblical uses of *episkopos.* It appears in the book of Acts only once and near the end (Acts 20:28). At that time there were relatively few Gentiles in the church, and so the term was not commonly used in Christian circles. But as more and more Gentiles were saved and the church began to lose its Jewish orientation, the Greek word *episkopos* was apparently used more frequently to describe those who functioned as elders (see 1 Tim. 3:1).

The New Testament bishop, or overseer, was in a unique leadership role in the church and was specifically responsible for teaching (1 Tim. 3:2), feeding, protecting, and generally nurturing the flock (Acts 20:28). Biblically, there is no difference in the role of an elder and that of a bishop. The two terms refer to the same group of leaders, *episkopos* emphasizing function and *presbuteros* emphasizing character.

Poimēn (pastor, or shepherd) is used a number of times in the New Testament, but Ephesians 4:11 is the only place in the King James Version where it is translated "pastor." Every other time it is translated "shepherd."

Two of the three times is appears in the epistles, poimēn refers to Christ. Hebrews 13:20-21 is a benediction: "Now the God of peace, who brought up from the dead the great Shepherd [poimēn]) of the sheep through the blood of the eternal covenant, even Jesus our Lord, equip you in every good thing to do His will." First Peter 2:25 says, "For you were continually straying like sheep, but now you have returned to the Shepherd [poimēn] and Guardian [episkopos] of your souls."

In Ephesians 4:11, pastor (poimēn) is used with the word teacher. The Greek construction there indicates that the two terms go together, and we might hyphenate them in English as pastor-teacher. The emphasis is on the pastor's ministry of teaching.

Poimēn, then, emphasizes the pastoral role of caring and feeding, although the concept of leadership is also inherent in the picture of a shepherd. The focus of the term poimēn is on the leader's attitude. To be qualified as a pastor, a man must have a shepherd's caring heart.

The word elder is of Old Testament Jewish origin. The primary Hebrew word for elder (zaqen) is used, for example, in Numbers 11:16 and Deuteronomy 27:1 of the seventy tribal leaders who assisted Moses. There it refers to a special category of men who, much like a senate, were set apart for leadership in Israel. Deuteronomy 1:9-18 indicates that these men were charged with responsibility for judging the people, and Moses communicated through them to the people (Ex. 19:7-9; Deut. 31:9). They led the Passover (Ex. 12:21) and perhaps other elements of worship.

Later, the elders of Israel were specifically involved in leadership of cities (1 Sam. 11:3; 16:4; and 30:26). Their function was still decision making—applying wisdom to the lives of the people in resolving conflicts, giving direction, and generally overseeing the details of an orderly society.

The Old Testament refers to them as "elders of the congregation" (Judg. 21:16), "elders of Israel" (1 Sam. 4:3), "elders of the land" (1 Kings 20:7), "elders of Judah" (2 Kings 23:1), and "elders . . . of each city" (Ezra 10:14). They served as local magistrates and as governors over the tribes (Deut. 16:18; 19:12; 31:28).

Another Hebrew word for elder is sab, used only five times in the Old Testament, all in the book of Ezra, where it refers to the group of Jewish leaders in charge of rebuilding the Temple after the Exile.

The Greek word for elder (presbuteros) is used about seventy times in the New Testament. Like zaqen (which means "aged," or "bearded"), sab (which means "gray-headed") and our English word elder, the term presbuteros refers to mature age. In Acts 2:17, Peter quotes Joel 2:28—"And your old men shall dream dreams." The Hebrew word for "old men" in Joel is zaqen, and the Greek word used in Acts is presbuteros. Used in that sense, elder does not constitute an official title but simply means an older man.

In 1 Timothy 5:2, the feminine form of presbuteros is used to refer to older women, who are there contrasted with younger ones: "[Appeal to] the older women as mothers, and the younger women as sisters, in all purity." In that context the term again simply signifies mature age, not an office in the church.

First Peter 5:5 contains a similar usage: "You younger men, likewise, be subject to your elders." As in 1 Timothy 5:2, the word is here used to contrast age and youth. In such a context *presbuteros* is generally understood to mean only "an older person," not necessarily an officeholder of any kind, and that was the primary meaning of the term in general Greek usage.

In the time of Christ *presbuteros* was a familiar term. It is used twenty-eight times in the New Testament to refer to a group of ex officio spiritual leaders of Israel. See, for example: "the chief priests and elders" (Matt. 27:3); "the scribes and elders" (27:41); "officers of the temple and elders" (Luke 22:52); and "rulers and elders of the people" (Acts 4:8). In each of those instances, and in every similar usage, *presbuteros* refers to recognized Jewish religious leaders who were not defined as priests of any kind. Those elders seem to have been members of the Sanhedrin, the highest ruling body in Judaism in Jesus' time.

Matthew 15:2 and Mark 7:3, 5 use the phrase "tradition(s) of the elders." There *presbuteros* refers to an ancestry of leaders who passed down principles governing religious practice. They were the teachers who determined Jewish tradition, and in that sense *elder* is equivalent to rabbi and may or may not have signified official status.

Presbuteros occurs twelve times in the book of Revelation, each time referring to the twenty-four elders who appear to be unique representatives of the redeemed people of God from all ages.

The New Testament church was initially Jewish, and it was natural that the concept of elder rule was adopted. Elder was the only commonly used Jewish term for leadership that was free of any connotation of either the monarchy or the priesthood. That is significant for the New Testament use of the term, because in the church each believer is a co-regent with Christ and there could therefore be no earthly king. And, unlike national Israel, the church has no specially designated earthly priesthood, because all believers are priests (1 Pet. 2:5, 9; Rev. 1:6). Therefore, of all the Jewish concepts of leadership, that of elder best transfers to the kind of leadership ordained for the church.

The elders of Israel were mature men, heads of families (Ex. 12:21); able men of strong moral character who feared God and were known for their truthfulness and integrity (Ex. 18:20-21); men full of the Holy Spirit (Num. 11:16-17); capable men of wisdom, discernment, and experience -- impartial and courageous men who would intercede, teach, and judge righteously and fairly (Deut. 1:13-17). All those characteristics were involved in the Jewish understanding of *presbuteros*. The use of that term to describe church leaders likewise emphasizes maturity of spiritual experience, shown in the strength and consistency of moral character.

Presbuteros is used nearly twenty times in Acts and the epistles in reference to a unique group of leaders in the church. From the earliest beginnings of the church it was clear that a group of mature spiritual leaders was designated to have responsibility for the church. The church at Antioch, for example, where believers were first called Christians, sent Barnabas and Saul to the elders at Jerusalem with a gift to be distributed to the needy brethren in Judea (Acts 11:29-30). It is therefore clear both that elders existed in the church at that very early date and that the believers at Antioch recognized their authority.

Since the church at Antioch grew out of the ministry at Jerusalem, elders probably existed there as well. It is likely that Paul himself functioned as an elder at Antioch before he stepped out in the role of apostle. He is listed in Acts 13:1 as one of that church's teachers. Elders played a dominant role in the Council of Jerusalem (see Acts 15: 2, 4, 6, 22, 23; 16:4) and they were obviously very influential in the foundational life of the early church.

As Paul and Barnabas began to preach in new areas, and as the church began to extend itself, the process of identifying church leaders became more clearly defined. And throughout the New Testament, as the church developed, leaders were called elders.

In general usage, therefore, *elder* seems to be the most appropriate term for our day, since it is free of many of the unbiblical connotations and nuances of meaning imposed on *bishop* and even *pastor* throughout much of church history.

As early in the biblical narrative as Acts 14, we see that one of the key steps in establishing a new church was to identify and appoint elders for church leadership. "And when they had appointed elders for them in every church, having prayed with fasting, they commended them to the Lord in whom they had believed" (Acts 14:23).

Nearly every church we know of in the New Testament is specifically said to have elders. We are told, for example, that "from Miletus [Paul] sent to Ephesus and called to him the elders of the church" (Acts 20:17). It is significant that the church at Ephesus had elders, because all the churches of Asia Minor—such as those listed in Revelation 1:11—were extensions of the ministry at Ephesus. We can assume that those churches established their leadership after the pattern in Ephesus, namely, that of a plurality of elders.

Peter wrote to the scattered believers in "Pontus, Galatia, Cappadocia, Asia, and Bithynia, . . . I exhort the elders among you . . . shepherd the flock of God" (1 Pet. 1:1; 5:1-2). Pontus, Galatia, Cappadocia, and Bithynia were not cities, but rather territories. Peter was therefore writing to a number of churches scattered all over Asia—all of which had elders.

What is the role of a pastor-teacher? As the apostolic era came to a close, the office of pastor-teacher emerged as the highest level of local church leadership. Thus it carried a great amount of responsibility. Elders were charged with the care and feeding, as well as the spiritual guidance, of the entire church. There was no higher court of appeal, and no greater resource for knowing the mind and heart of God with regard to issues in the church.

First Timothy 3:1 says, "It is a trustworthy statement: if any man aspires to the office of overseer [*episkopos*], it is a fine work he desires to do." In verse 5, Paul says that the work of an *episkopos* is to "take care of the church of God." The clear implication is that a bishop's primary responsibility is that of being caretaker for the church.

That general responsibility involves a number of more specific duties, perhaps the most obvious of which is to oversee the affairs of the local church. First Timothy 5:17 says, "Let the elders who rule well be considered worthy of double honor." The Greek word translated "rule" (*proistēmi*) is used to speak of the elders' responsibilities four times in 1 Timothy (3:4, 5, 12; 5:17), once in 1 Thessalonians 5:12 (where it is translated, "have charge over"), and once in Romans 12:8, where ruling is listed as a spiritual gift. *Proistēmi* literally means "to stand first," and it speaks of the duty of general oversight common to all elders.

As those who rule in the church, pastoral elders are not subject to any higher earthly authority outside the local assembly. But their authority over the church is not by force or dictatorial power but by precept and example (see Heb. 13:7).

Elders are not to operate by majority rule or vote. If all the elders are guided by the same Spirit and all have the mind of Christ, there should be unanimity in the decisions they make (see 1 Cor. 1:10; cf. Eph. 4:3; Phil. 1:27; 2:2). If there is division, all the elders should study, pray, and seek the will of God together until consensus is reached. Unity and harmony in the church begin with this principle.

With elders lies the responsibility to preach and teach (1 Tim. 5:17). They are to determine doctrinal issues for the church and have the responsibility of proclaiming the truth to the congregation. In listing the spiritual qualifications of the overseer, 1 Timothy 3:2-7 gives only one qualification that relates to a specific function: he must be "able to teach." All the other qualifications relate to personal character.

Titus 1:7-9 also emphasizes the significance of the elder's responsibility as a teacher: "For the overseer must . . . be able both to exhort in sound doctrine and to refute those who contradict." The threat of false teachers in the church was already so great that a key qualification for leadership was the ability to understand and teach sound doctrine. "Exhort" in that verse is the Greek *parakaleō*, which literally means "to call near." From its uses in the New Testament, we see that the ministry of exhortation has several elements. It involves persuasion (Acts 2:14; 14:22; Titus 1:9), pleading (2 Cor. 8:17), comforting (1 Thess. 2:11), encouraging (1 Thess. 4:1), and patient reiterating of important doctrine (2 Tim. 4:2).

Elders are to be a resource for those who seek partnership in prayer. James wrote, "Is anyone among you sick? Let him call for the elders of the church, and let them pray over him, anointing him with oil in the name of the Lord" (James 5:14).

From Acts 20:28 we learn that another function of an elder is shepherding: "Be on guard for yourselves and for the flock, among which the Holy Spirit has made you overseers, to shepherd the church of God." Involved in the concept of shepherding are the twin responsibilities of feeding and protecting the flock. Verses 29-30 reemphasize the fact that the protecting ministry of the overseer is essential for countering the threat of false teachers.

The elder acts as a caring and loving shepherd over the flock, but never in

Scripture is a congregation spoken of as "his flock" or "your flock." Believers are the "flock of God" (1 Pet. 5:2), and the elder is merely a steward and caretaker for those precious possessions of God.

As spiritual overseers of the church, teaching shepherds are to determine church polity (Acts 15:22); to oversee (Acts 20:28); to ordain others (1 Tim. 4:14); to rule, teach, and preach (1 Tim. 5:17); to exhort and refute (Titus 1:9); and to act as shepherds, setting an example for all (1 Pet. 5:1-3). Those responsibilities put elders at the core of the work of the New Testament church. (For further study regarding elders, see the author's book, *Answering the Key Questions About Elders* [Panorama City, CA: Word of Grace Communications, 1984].)

Every believer today is indebted directly or indirectly to these specially gifted men God has given to His church. Through their preaching, teaching, writing, exhortation, and other ministries, they lead the lost to Christ, enrich our knowledge of God and His Word, and encourage us "to walk in a manner worthy of the calling with which [we] have been called" (4:1). They are "worthy of double honor, especially those who work hard at preaching and teaching" (1 Tim. 5:17). "Obey your leaders, and submit to them," the writer of Hebrews tells us, "for they keep watch over your souls, as those who will give an account. Let them do this with joy and not with grief, for this would be unprofitable for you" (Heb. 13:17).

All of the gifts that Christ gives to individuals and to the church as a whole are gifts which He Himself perfectly exemplified. If ever there was a preacher it was Christ, if ever there was a teacher, ruler, administrator, servant, helper, or giver it was Christ. He is the perfect illustration and example of every gift, because His gifts to us are gracious gifts of Himself.

Building the Body of Christ

for the equipping of the saints for the work of service, to the building up of the body of Christ; until we all attain to the unity of the faith, and of the knowledge of the Son of God, to a mature man, to the measure of the stature which belongs to the fulness of Christ. As a result, we are no longer to be children, tossed here and there by waves, and carried about by every wind of doctrine, by the trickery of men, by craftiness in deceitful scheming; but speaking the truth in love, we are to grow up in all aspects into Him, who is the head, even Christ, from whom the whole body, being fitted and held together by that which every joint supplies, according to the proper working of each individual part, causes the growth of the body for the building up of itself in love. (4:12-16)

The past decade or so has witnessed the development of what is called the church growth movement. Seminars, conferences, books, programs, and even special organizations are devoted exclusively to teaching and discussing principles and methods for church growth. Many of the efforts are helpful, but only to the extent they are consistent with the principles Paul teaches in Ephesians 4:12-16. Here in its most succinct form is God's plan by which Christ produces church growth. Since the Lord said, "I *will* build My church" (Matt. 16:18, emphasis added), it is obvious that the building must be according to His plan. Attempting to build the church by human means only competes with the work of Christ.

As discussed in the previous chapter, God's spiritual gifts to His church include both the individual gifting of every believer as well as the gifted men called apostles and prophets, who were given strictly for New Testament times and were followed by the gifted men called evangelists and pastor-teachers, who are given for continuing ministry to the church (Eph. 4:11). It is God's plan for the last two groups of gifted men—the evangelists and pastor-teachers—to equip, build up, and develop His church by the general operational procedure set forth in verses 12-16. In this passage we are shown the progression, the purpose, and the power of God's divine pattern for the building and function of His church.

THE PROGRESSION OF GOD'S PATTERN

for the equipping of the saints for the work of service, to the building up of the body of Christ; (4:12)

In the simplest possible terms Paul here sets forth God's progressive plan for His church: **equipping** to **service** to **building up.**

EQUIPPING

The first task within God's design is for the evangelists and pastor-teachers to be properly equipping the **saints** (a title used for all those set apart to God by salvation; cf. 1 Cor. 1:2). The evangelist's work is to bring men and women to understanding of the gospel of salvation, to lead them to receive Jesus Christ as Lord and Savior and thereby become children in His spiritual family and citizens of His divine kingdom. In the early years the objective was to establish a local church. This begins the equipping. The pastor-teacher's subsequent work, then, is to provide the leadership and spiritual resources to cause believers to be taking on the likeness of their Lord and Savior through continual obedience to His Word and to provide a pattern, or example, of godliness (1 Thess. 1:2-7; 1 Pet. 5:3).

Katartismos (**equipping**) basically refers to that which is fit, is restored to its original condition, or is made complete. The word was often used as a medical term for the setting of bones. Paul used the verb form in his closing admonition to the Corinthian believers: "Finally, brethren, rejoice, *be made complete*" (2 Cor. 13:11, emphasis added). The writer of Hebrews used the term in his closing prayer: "Now the God of peace, who brought up from the dead the great Shepherd of the sheep through the blood of the eternal covenant, even Jesus our Lord, *equip* you in every good thing to do His will, working in us that which is pleasing in His sight" (Heb. 13:20-21).

Not only is the matter of individual equipping implied in these texts but also the collective equipping expressed in 1 Corinthians 1:10—"Now I exhort you, brethren, by the name of our Lord Jesus Christ, that you all agree, and there be no divisions among you, but you be made *complete* (from *katartizō*) in the same mind and in the same judgment" (emphasis added). The equipping of each believer results in the unity of all.

God has given four basic tools, as it were, for the spiritual **equipping of the saints.** These are spiritual means, because the flesh cannot make anyone perfect (Gal. 3:3). The first and most important is His Word, the Bible. "All Scripture is inspired by God and profitable for teaching, for reproof, for correction, for training in righteousness; that the man of God may be adequate, equipped for every good work" (2 Tim. 3:16-17). Jesus said, "You are already clean because of the word which I have spoken to you" (John 15:3). The first purpose of the pastor-teacher, therefore, is to feed himself, to feed his people, and to lead them to feed themselves on the Word of God.

The example of the apostles, who gave themselves continually to teaching the Word and to prayer (Acts 6:4) indicates that a second tool of **equipping** is prayer, and the pastor-teacher is responsible to prepare himself and to lead his people to prepare themselves in prayer. Epaphras was committed to this spiritual means for building up believers. Paul characterized the ministry of Epaphras by saying that he is "always laboring earnestly for you in his prayers, that you may stand *perfect* and fully assured in all the will of God. For I bear him witness that he has a deep concern for you" (Col. 4:12-13, emphasis added).

It is essential to note that this **equipping,** completing, or perfecting of the saints is attainable here on earth, because Paul uses *katartizō* (the verb form of **equipping**) to refer to what spiritually strong believers are to do for fellow believers who have fallen into sin. The text strongly teaches that the ministry of **equipping** is the work of leading Christians from sin to obedience.

A third tool of **equipping** is testing and a fourth is suffering. These are primary, purging experiences by which the believer is refined to greater holiness. James tells us to "consider it all joy . . . when [we] encounter various trials, knowing that the testing of [our] faith produces endurance. And let endurance have its perfect result," he goes on to say, "that you may be perfect and complete, lacking in nothing" (James 1:2-4). When we respond to God's testing in trust and continued obedience, spiritual muscles are strengthened and effective service for Him is broadened.

Suffering is also a means of spiritual **equipping.** Peter uses this word near the close of his first letter: "And after you have suffered for a little while, the God of all grace, who called you to His eternal glory in Christ, will Himself *perfect,* confirm, strengthen and establish you" (1 Pet. 5:10, emphasis added). Knowing and following Christ in the deepest sense not only involves being raised with Him but also sharing in "the fellowship of His sufferings" (Phil. 3:10). Paul rejoiced in his sufferings for Christ's sake. God "comforts us in all our affliction," he says, "so that we may be able to comfort those who are in any affliction with the comfort with which we ourselves are comforted by God. For just as the sufferings of Christ are ours in abundance, so also our comfort is abundant through Christ" (2 Cor. 1:4-5).

The sending of tests and suffering are entirely God's operation, and He gives them to His **saints** according to His loving and sovereign will. But the other two agents of spiritual **equipping**—prayer and knowledge of Scripture—are the tasks of the gifted men.

Like the apostles in Jerusalem, the pastor-teacher is to devote himself above all else "to prayer, and to the ministry of the word" (Acts 6:4). Like Paul, he should be able to say that his supreme effort is given to "admonishing every man and teaching every man with all wisdom, that we may present every man complete in Christ" (Col. 1:28). As Paul said of Epaphras, it should be said of every pastor-teacher that he labors earnestly in prayer for those given into his care, in order that they "may stand perfect and fully assured in all the will of God" (Col. 4:12). The devoted pastor-teacher is "a good servant of Christ Jesus, constantly nourished on the words of the faith and of the sound doctrine," which he then prescribes, teaches, reads publicly, and exhorts (1 Tim. 4:6, 11, 13). He is called to "preach the word; be ready in season and out of season; reprove, rebuke, exhort, with great patience and instruction" (2 Tim. 4:2).

Even the most biblical and efficient of church organizations will not produce spiritual maturity without the leadership of God's gifted ministers who are continually in prayer and in His Word. Administration and structure has its place, but it is far from the heart of spiritual church growth. The great need of the church has always been spiritual maturity rather than organizational restructuring. All the books on leadership, organization, and management offer little help to the dynamics of the church of Jesus Christ.

Even less does the church need entertaining. God's people can use their talents in ways that glorify the Lord and give testimony of His grace, but when testimony turns to vaudeville, as it often does, God is not glorified and His people are not edified. Religious entertainment neither comes from nor leads to spiritual maturity. It comes from self and can only promote self.

The study and teaching of God's Word takes time. The evangelist or pastor-teacher therefore cannot fulfill his God-given responsibility if he is encumbered with the planning and administration of a multitude of programs—no matter how worthy and helpful they are. Again, like the apostles in Jerusalem, he cannot "serve tables" and also be faithful "to prayer, and to the ministry of the word" (Acts 6:2, 4).

The surest road to a church's spiritual stagnation, to the pastor's burnout, or to both is for the pastor to become so engulfed in activities and programs that he has too little time for prayer and the Word. And programs that "succeed" can be even more destructive than those that fail if they are done in the flesh and for human satisfaction rather than the Lord's glory. It is lack of knowledge of God's Word and obedience to it (Hos. 4:6), not lack of programs and methods, that destroy His people. When they fail it is not because of weak programs but because of weak teaching.

The first concern of the leadership of the church should be for the filled seats, not the empty ones. When a young preacher complained to Charles Spurgeon that his own congregation was too small, Spurgeon replied, "Well, maybe it is as large as you'd like to give account for in the day of judgment."

Spiritual growth does not always involve learning something new. Our most important growth often is in regard to truth we have already heard but have not fully applied. Peter wrote, "I shall always be ready to remind you of these things, even though you already know them, and have been established in the truth which is present with you. And I consider it right, as long as I am in this earthly dwelling, to stir you up by way of reminder, . . . that at any time after my departure you may be able to call these things to mind" (2 Pet. 1:12-13, 15). The great truths of the Word of God can never be mastered or overlearned. The battle with our unredeemed flesh necessitates constant reminding. As long as a pastor has breath he should preach those truths, and as long his congregation has breath it should hear them.

During the Arab-Israeli war of 1967 an American reporter was flying over the Sinai desert with an Israeli officer, and they spotted some fifty thousand stranded Egyptian soldiers who obviously were dying of thirst. When the situation was reported in the newspapers, a number of world leaders and organizations tried to do something to help. But every time a plan was suggested, some military, diplomatic, or bureaucratic obstacle prevented its being carried out. By the time help came, thousands of the soldiers had died.

How equally tragic it is for churches to spin their wheels in programs and committees while thousands around them are desperately in need of the spiritual water of the Word.

SERVICE

The second aspect of God's plan for the operation of His church is **service**. Paul's language indicates that it is not the gifted men who have the most direct responsibility to do the **work of service**. No pastor, or even a large group of pastors, can do everything a church needs to do. No matter how gifted, talented, and dedicated a pastor may be, the work to be done where he is called to minister will always vastly exceed his time and abilities. His purpose in God's plan is not to try to meet all those needs himself but to equip the people given into his care to meet those needs (cf. v. 16, where this idea is emphasized). Obviously the leaders share in serving, and many of the congregation share in equipping, but God's basic design for the church is for the equipping to be done so that the **saints** can serve each other effectively. The entire church is to be aggressively involved in the work of the Lord (cf. 1 Cor. 15:58; 1 Pet. 2:5, 9; 4:10-11; and contrast 2 Thess. 3:11).

When the gifted men are faithful in prayer and in teaching the Word, the people will be properly equipped and rightly motivated to do the **work of service**. From the **saints** who are equipped God raises up elders, deacons, teachers, and every other kind of worker needed for the church to be faithful and productive. Spiritual **service** is the **work** of *every* Christian, *every* **saint** of God. Attendance is a poor substitute for participation in ministry.

BUILDING UP

The third element and the immediate goal of God's plan for the operation of His church is its being built up. Proper **equipping** by the evangelists and pastor-teachers leading to proper **service** by the congregation results inevitably in the **building up of the body of Christ.** *Oikodomē* (**building up**) literally refers to the building of a house, and was used figuratively of any sort of construction. It is the spiritual edification and development of the church of which Paul is speaking here. **The body** is built up externally through evangelism as more believers are added, but the emphasis here is on its being built up internally as all believers are nurtured to fruitful service through the Word. Paul's exhortation to the Ephesian elders emphasizes this process: "I commend you to God and to the word, . . . which is able to build you up" (Acts 20:32). The maturation of the church is tied to learning of and obedience to the holy revelation of Scripture. Just as newborn babes desire physical milk, so should believers desire the spiritual nourishment of the Word (1 Pet. 2:2).

THE PURPOSE OF GOD'S PATTERN

until we all attain to the unity of the faith, and of the knowledge of the Son of God, to a mature man, to the measure of the stature which belongs to the fulness of Christ. As a result, we are no longer to be children, tossed here and there by waves, and carried about by every wind of doctrine, by the trickery of men, by craftiness in deceitful scheming; but speaking the truth in love, (4:13-15a)

The building up of the redeemed involves a two-fold ultimate objective, which Paul identifies as **the unity of the faith** and **the knowledge of the Son of God**, out of which flow spiritual maturity, sound doctrine, and loving testimony.

Some commentators advocate the view that such an ultimate objective is only attainable at glorification, believing that Paul is describing our final heavenly unity and knowledge. But that idea does not fit the context at all, because the apostle is not describing the final work of Christ on behalf of the church in heaven but the work of gifted men in the church on earth. These results could only apply to the church in its earthly dimension.

UNITY OF THE FAITH

The ultimate spiritual target for the church begins with **the unity of the faith** (cf. v. 3). As in verse 5, **faith** does not here refer to the act of belief or of obedience but to the body of Christian truth, to Christian doctrine. **The faith** is the content of the gospel in its most complete form. As the church at Corinth so clearly illustrates, disunity in the church comes from doctrinal ignorance and spiritual immaturity. When believers are properly taught, when they faithfully do the work of service, and when the body is thereby built up in spiritual maturity, **unity of the faith** is an inevitable result. Oneness in fellowship is impossible unless it is built on the foundation of commonly believed truth. The solution to the divisions in Corinth was for everyone to hold the same understandings and opinions and to speak the same truths (1 Cor. 1:10).

God's truth is not fragmented and divided against itself, and when His people are fragmented and divided it simply means they are to that degree apart from His truth, apart from **the faith** of right knowledge and understanding. Only a biblically equipped, faithfully serving, and spiritually maturing church can **attain to the unity the faith.** Any other unity will be on a purely human level and not only will be apart from but in constant conflict with **the unity of the faith.** There can never be unity in the church apart from doctrinal integrity.

KNOWLEDGE OF CHRIST

The second result of following God's pattern for building His church is attaining **the knowledge of the Son of God.** Paul is not talking about salvation knowledge but about the deep knowledge (*epignōsis,* full knowledge that is correct and accurate) through a relationship with Christ that comes only from prayer and faithful study of and obedience to God's Word. After many years of devoted apostleship Paul still could say, "I count all things to be loss in view of the surpassing value of knowing Christ Jesus my Lord, for whom I have suffered the loss of all things, and count them but rubbish in order that I may gain Christ, and may be found in Him, . . . that I may know Him, and the power of His resurrection and the fellowship of His sufferings. . . . Not that I have already obtained it, or have already become perfect, but I press on in order that I may lay hold of that for which also I was laid hold of by Christ Jesus" (Phil. 3:8-10, 12). Paul prayed that the Ephesians would have that "knowledge of Him" (1:17; cf. Phil. 1:4; Col. 1:9-10; 2:2). Growing in the deeper **knowledge of the Son of God** is a life-long process that will not be complete until we see our Lord face-to-face. That is the knowing of which Jesus spoke when He said, "My sheep hear My voice, and I know them" (John 10:27). He was not speaking of knowing their identities but of knowing them intimately, and that is the way He wants His people also to know Him.

SPIRITUAL MATURITY

The third result of following God's pattern for His church is spiritual maturity, a maturity **to the measure of the stature which belongs to the fulness of Christ.** God's great desire for His church is that every believer, without exception, come to be like His Son (Rom. 8:29), manifesting the character qualities of the One who is the only **measure** of the full-grown, perfect, **mature man.** The church in the world is Jesus Christ in the world, because the church is now the fullness of His incarnate Body in the world (cf. 1:23). We are to radiate and reflect Christ's perfections. Christians are therefore called to "walk in the same manner as He walked" (1 John 2:6; cf. Col. 4:12), and He walked in complete and continual fellowship with and obedience to His Father. To walk as our Lord walked flows from a life of prayer and of obedience to God's Word. "We all, with unveiled face beholding as in a mirror the glory of the Lord, are being transformed into the same image from glory to glory, just as from the Lord, the Spirit" (2 Cor. 3:18). As we grow into deeper fellowship with Christ, the process of divine sanctification through His Holy Spirit changes us more and more into His image, from one level of glory to the next. The agent of spiritual maturity, as well as of every other aspect of godly living, is God's own Spirit—apart from whom the sincerest prayer has no effectiveness (Rom. 8:26) and even God's own Word has no power (John 14:26; 16:13-14; 1 John 2:20).

It is obvious that believers, all of whom have unredeemed flesh (Rom. 7:14; 8:23), cannot in this life fully and perfectly attain the **measure of the stature which belongs to the fulness of Christ**. But they must and can reach a degree of maturity that pleases and glorifies the Lord. The goal of Paul's ministry to believers was their maturity, as indicated by his labors to "present every man complete (*teleios,* mature) in Christ" (Col. 1:28-29; cf. Phil. 3:14-15).

SOUND DOCTRINE

The fourth result of following God's pattern for His church is sound doctrine. The Christian who is properly equipped and mature is **no longer** a child who is **tossed here and there by waves, and carried about by every wind of doctrine, by the trickery of men, by craftiness in deceitful scheming.**

Kubia (**trickery**) is the term from which we get *cube,* and was used of dice-playing. Just as today, the dice were often "loaded" or otherwise manipulated by professional gamblers to their own advantage. The term for dice therefore became synonymous with dishonest **trickery** of any sort. **Craftiness** (*panourgia;* see Luke 20:23; 1 Cor. 3:19; 2 Cor. 12:16) is a similar term, carrying the idea of clever manipulation of error made to look like truth. *Methodia* (**scheming**) is used later in the letter to refer to "the schemes of the devil" (6:11). No doubt it has reference to planned, subtle, systematized error. Paul's point is that neither the **trickery of men** nor the **deceitful scheming** of the devil will mislead the spiritually equipped and mature believer.

It is spiritual **children** (*nēpios,* lit., one who does not talk), such as were many of the Corinthian believers (1 Cor. 3:1; 14:20), who are in constant danger of falling prey to every new religious fad or novel interpretation of Scripture that comes along. Having no thorough knowledge of God's Word, they are **tossed here and there by waves** of popular sentiment and are **carried about by every wind of** new **doctrine** that seems appealing. Because they are not anchored in God's truth, they are subject to every sort of counterfeit truth—humanistic, cultic, pagan, demonic, or whatever. The New Testament is replete with warnings against this danger (see Acts 20:30-31; Rom. 16:17-18; 2 Cor. 11:3-4; Gal. 1:6-7; 3:1; Col. 2:4-8; 1 Tim. 4:1, 6-7; 2 Tim. 2:15-18; 3:6-9; 4:3; Heb. 13:9; 2 Pet. 2:1-3; 1 John 2:19, 26).

The immature Christian is gullible; and in the history of the church no group of believers has fallen into more foolishness in the name of Christianity than has much of the church today. Despite our unprecedented education, sophistication, freedom, and access to God's Word and sound Christian teaching, it seems that every religious huckster (cf. 2 Cor. 2:17; 4:2; 11:13-15) can find a ready hearing and financial support from among God's people. The number of foolish, misdirected, corrupt, and even heretical leaders to whom many church members willingly give their money and allegiance is astounding and heartbreaking.

The cause of this spiritual plight is not hard to find. A great many evangelists have presented an easy-believism gospel and a great many pastors have taught an almost contentless message. In many places the Body of Christ has not been built up in sound doctrine or in faithful obedience. Consequently there is little doctrinal solidarity ("unity of faith") and little spiritual maturity ("knowledge of the Son of God . . . to the measure of the stature which belongs to the fulness of Christ").

Just as many families today are dominated by their children, so are many churches. It is tragic when the church's **children**—spiritually immature believers (cf. 1 John 2:13-14) who change their views with **every wind of doctrine** and continually fall prey to men's **trickery** and Satan's **craftiness** and **deceitful scheming**—are found among its most influential teachers and leaders.

AUTHENTIC LOVING TESTIMONY

The fifth and final feature that is primarily a requirement and yet also a result of following God's pattern for His church will be in direct opposition to being tossed, carried away, tricked, and deceived by the schemes of Satan—namely, **speaking the truth in love**, a principle that applies to every aspect of Christian life and ministry. The verb translated **speaking the truth** is *alētheuō,* which means to speak, deal, or act truthfully. Some have translated it "truthing it," while others say it conveys the idea of walking in a truthful way. The verb refers to being true in the widest sense and is hard to translate into English. Yet in Galatians 4:16 it seems to especially emphasize preaching the gospel truth. Since the reference in Galatians is the only other use of the verb in the New Testament, it seems safe to say that the emphasis in Ephesians 4 is also on the preaching of the truth (within the context of a truthful and authentic Christian life). Authentic, mature believers whose lives are marked by **love** will not be victims of false teaching (v. 14) but will be living authentically and proclaiming the true gospel to a deceived and deceiving world. The work of the church goes full swing, from evangelism to edification to evangelism, and so on and on until the Lord returns. The evangelized are edified, and they, in turn, evangelize and edify others.

The spiritually equipped church, whose members are sound in doctrine and mature in their thinking and living, is a church that will reach out in **love** to proclaim the saving gospel. God does not give us knowledge, understanding, gifts, and maturity to keep but to share. He does not equip us to stagnate but to serve. We are not gifted and edified in order to be complacent and self-satisfied but in order to do the Lord's work of service in building up and expanding the Body of Christ. **In love** is the attitude in which we evangelize (cf. 3:17-19; 4:2; 5:1-2). Paul was an example for such love, as seen in the following testimony:

> But we proved to be gentle among you, as a nursing mother tenderly cares for her own children. Having thus a fond affection for you, we were well-pleased to impart

to you not only the gospel of God but also our own lives, because you had become very dear to us. For you recall, brethren, our labor and hardship, how working night and day so as not to be a burden to any of you, we proclaimed to you the gospel of God. You are witnesses, and so is God, how devoutly and uprightly and blamelessly we behaved toward you believers; just as you know how we were exhorting and encouraging and imploring each one of you as a father would his own children, so that you may walk in a manner worthy of the God who calls you into His own kingdom and glory. (1 Thess. 2:7-12; cf. 2 Cor. 12:15; Phil. 2:17; Col. 1:24-29)

John Bunyan said of Christians, "When all their garments are white the world will count them His," and the skeptical German poet Heinrich Heine said to Christians, "You show me your redeemed life and I might be inclined to believe in your Redeemer." The authentic life that speaks the gospel with a spirit of loving sacrifice will be eminently convincing.

Speaking the truth in love seems deceptively easy, but it is extremely difficult. It is possible only for the believer who is thoroughly equipped in sound doctrine and in spiritual maturity. For the immature believer, right doctrine can be no more than cold orthodoxy and love can be no more than sentimentality. Only the **mature man**, the man who is growing up **to the measure of the stature which belongs to the fulness of Christ** is consistent in having sufficient wisdom to understand God's **truth** and effectively present it to others; and only he has the continual humility and grace to present it in **love** and in power. The combination of truth and love counteracts the two great threats to powerful ministry—lack of truth and lack of compassion.

we are to grow up in all aspects into Him, who is the head, even Christ (4:15b)

This loving, authentic testimony assists believers in growing into the very likeness of Jesus Christ. The phrase **in all aspects** calls for a comprehensive Christlikeness such as that described in verse 13 (cf. 1 Cor. 11:1; 2 Cor. 3:18; Gal. 4:19; Eph. 5:2; 1 Pet. 2:21; 1 John 2:6).

The head . . . Christ expresses a familiar Pauline analogy indicating Christ's authority (Eph. 1:22; Col. 1:18), leadership (Eph. 5:23), and here, as in Colossians 2:19, controlling power. He not only is the sovereign Head and the ruling Head but also the organic Head. He is the source of power for all functions. Human beings are declared officially dead when the EKG is flat, signifying brain death. As the brain is the control center of physical life, so the Lord Jesus Christ is the organic source of life and power to His Body, the church.

To grow into His likeness is to be completely subject to His controlling power, obedient to His every thought and expression of will. It is to personify Paul's prayers "For to me, to live is Christ" (Phil. 1:21) and "It is no longer I who live, but Christ lives in me" (Gal. 2:20).

THE POWER FOR GOD'S PATTERN

from whom the whole body, being fitted and held together by that which every joint supplies, according to the proper working of each individual part, causes the growth of the body for the building up of itself in love. (4:16)

The power for being equipped and matured into lovingly authentic proclaimers is not in believers themselves, in their leaders, or in church structure. The Body receives its authority, direction, and power as it grows "up in all aspects into . . . Christ," **from whom the whole body [is] fitted and held together.** The two present passive participles that these phrases translate are synonymous and are meant to express that the close, tight, compacted correlation of function in the Body as an organism is the result of Christ's power. That does not negate the efforts of believers, as proved by the phrases **by that which every joint supplies** and **according to the proper working of each individual part.** Each of these phrases is extremely significant in conveying truth about the function of the Body. Christ holds the Body together and makes it function **by that which every joint supplies.** That is to say, the joints are points of contrast, the joining together or union where the spiritual supply, resources, and gifts of the Holy Spirit pass from one member to another, providing the flow of ministry that produces growth.

The **proper working of each individual part** recalls the importance of each believer's gift (v. 7; cf. 1 Cor. 12:12-27). The growth of the church is not a result of clever methods but of every member of the Body fully using his spiritual gift in close contact with other believers. Christ is the source of the life and power and growth of the church, which He facilitates through each believer's gifts and mutual ministry in **joints** touching other believers. The power in the church flows from the Lord through individual believers and relationships between believers.

Where His people have close relationships of genuine spiritual ministry, God works; and where they are not intimate with each other and faithful with their gifts, He cannot work. He does not look for creativity, ingenuity, or cleverness but for willing and loving obedience. The physical body functions properly only as each member in union with every other member responds to the direction of the head to do exactly what it was designed to do.

In Colossians 2:19 Paul gives a priceless insight when he warns against "not holding fast to the head, from whom the entire body, being supplied and held together by the joints and ligaments, grows with a growth which is from God." The key idea in that verse is for every member of the Body to remain close and intimate, holding tightly to fellowship with Christ, the Head, and thus not be led astray by that which is false and destructive.

The sum of all that these truths affirm is that every individual believer is to stay close to Jesus Christ, faithfully using his spiritual gift in close contact with every believer he touches, and that through such commitment and ministry the Lord's power will flow for the **building up** of the Body **in love.**

The noun **growth** (*auxēsis,* used only here and in Col. 2:19) is present middle in form, indicating that the body produces its own growth through resident dynamics. As with all living organisms, spiritual growth in the church does not come from forces outside but from the vital power within that **causes the growth of the body for the building up of itself.** All of this is **in love**, which is always to be the spirit of the fellowship of believers. Above all things, the Body is to manifest **love,** and when it is built up according to this plan, the world will know it is the Body of Christ (John 13:34-35).

Off with the Old, On with the New

13

This I say therefore, and affirm together with the Lord, that you walk no longer just as the Gentiles also walk, in the futility of their mind, being darkened in their understanding, excluded from the life of God, because of the ignorance that is in them, because of the hardness of their heart; and they, having become callous, have given themselves over to sensuality, for the practice of every kind of impurity with greediness. But you did not learn Christ in this way, if indeed you have heard Him and have been taught in Him, just as truth is in Jesus, that, in reference to your former manner of life, you lay aside the old self, which is being corrupted in accordance with the lusts of deceit, and that you be renewed in the spirit of your mind, and put on the new self, which in the likeness of God has been created in righteousness and holiness of the truth. (4:17-24)

When a person believes and confesses Jesus Christ as Lord and is thereby born again, a transformation takes place in his basic nature. The change is even more basic and radical than the change that will take place at death. When a believer dies, he has already been fitted for heaven, already been made a citizen of the kingdom, already become a child of God. He simply begins to perfectly experience the divine nature he has had since his spiritual birth, because for the first time he is free from the unredeemed flesh. The future receiving of his glorified body (cf. 1 Cor. 15:42-54) will not make him better, since he is already perfected; but it will give him the full capacity for all that eternal resurrection life involves.

Salvation is not a matter of improvement or perfection of what has previously existed. It is total transformation. The New Testament speaks of believers having a new mind, a new will, a new heart, a new inheritance, a new relationship, new power, new knowledge, new wisdom, new perception, new understanding, new righteousness, new love, new desire, new citizenship, and many other new things—all of which are summed up in newness of life (Rom. 6:4).

At the new birth a person becomes "a new creature; the old things passed away; behold, new things have come" (2 Cor. 5:17). It is not simply that he receives something new but that he *becomes* someone new. "I have been crucified with Christ," Paul said; "and it is no longer I who live, but Christ lives in me; and the life which I now live in the flesh I live by faith in the Son of God, who loved me, and delivered Himself up for me" (Gal. 2:20). The new nature is not added to the old nature but replaces it. The transformed person is a completely new "I." In contrast to the former love of evil (cf. John 3:19-21; Rom. 1:21-25; 28-32), that new self—the deepest, truest part of the Christian—now loves the law of God, longs to fulfill its righteous demands, hates sin, and longs for deliverance from the unredeemed flesh, which is the house of the eternal new creation until glorification (see Rom. 7:14-25; 8:22-24).

Why, then, do we continue to sin after we become Christians? As Paul explains in Romans 7, "No longer am I the one doing it, but sin which indwells me. For I know that nothing good dwells in me, that is, in my flesh; for the wishing is present in me, but the doing of the good is not" (vv. 17-18; cf. 20). Sin is still resident in the flesh, so that we are inhibited and restrained from being able to give full and perfect expression to the new nature. Possessing the fullness of the divine nature without the corruption of our unredeemed flesh is a promise we will realize only in the future (cf. Rom. 8:23; Phil. 3:20-21; 2 Pet. 1:3-4).

Biblical terminology, then, does not say that a Christian has two different natures. He has but one nature, the new nature in Christ. The old self dies and the new self lives; they do not coexist. It is not a remaining old nature but the remaining garment of sinful flesh that causes Christians to sin. The Christian is a single new person, a totally new creation, not a spiritual schizophrenic. It is the filthy coat of remaining humanness in which the new creation dwells that continues to hinder and contaminate his living. The believer as a total person is transformed but not yet wholly perfect. He has residing sin but no longer reigning sin (cf. Rom. 6:14). He is no longer the old man corrupted but is now the new man created in righteousness and holiness, awaiting full salvation (cf. Rom. 13:11).

In Ephesians 4 Paul makes two appeals based on the fact that believers are new creations. The first begins the chapter: "I, therefore, . . . entreat you to walk in a manner worthy of the calling with which you have been called" (v. 1). The second (v. 17) introduces the present text, in which Paul contrasts the walk of the wicked unbeliever with the walk of the spiritual Christian. He follows that contrast with more "therefores" (v. 25; 5:1, 7, 15), showing the Christian's proper response to being a new creation. All of this points to the fact that a changed nature demands changed behavior. It is as if the apostle is saying, "Since God has created a marvelous new entity in the world called the church, and because of this unique creation, with its unique character of humility, its unique empowerment with spiritual gifts, its unique unity as the Body of Christ, and its need to be built up in love, here is how every believer should live as a member of that church."

In verses 17-24, Paul moves from the general to the specific, first giving four characteristics of the walk of the old man and then four characteristics of the walk of the new.

The Walk of the Old Self

This I say therefore, and affirm together with the Lord, that you walk no longer just as the Gentiles also walk, in the futility of their mind, being darkened in their understanding, excluded from the life of God, because of the ignorance that is in them, because of the hardness of their heart; and they, having become callous, have given themselves over to sensuality, for the practice of every kind of impurity with greediness. (4:17-19)

The **therefore** refers back to what Paul has been saying about our high calling in Jesus Christ. Because we are called to salvation, unified in the Body of Christ, gifted by the Holy Spirit, and built up by the gifted men (vv. 1-16), we should **therefore . . . walk no longer just as the Gentiles also walk.** We cannot accomplish the glorious work of Christ by continuing to live the way the world lives.

Ethnos (**Gentiles**) is not in all of the ancient Greek texts, and may have been a later addition. But its presence here is perfectly consistent with its use elsewhere in the New Testament, including Paul's other letters. The term basically refers to a multitude of people in general, and then to a group of people of a particular kind. It is this secondary meaning that we see in our derived English word *ethnic*. Jews used the term in two common ways, first to distinguish all other people from Jews and second to distinguish all religions from Judaism. **Gentiles** therefore referred racially and ethnically to all non-Jews and religiously to all pagans.

In his first letter to the Thessalonians Paul uses the term in its pagan meaning when he refers to "the Gentiles who do not know God" (1 Thess. 4:5), and that is the sense in which he uses it in our present text. **Gentiles** here represent all ungodly, unregenerate, pagan persons.

Like the church in our own day, the churches at Ephesus and in almost every non-Palestinian area in New Testament times were surrounded by rank paganism and its attendant immorality. Ephesus was a leading commercial and cultural city of the Roman empire. It boasted the great pagan temple of Artemis, or Diana, one of the seven wonders of the ancient world. But it was also a leading city in debauchery and sexual immorality. Some historians rank it as the most lascivious city of Asia Minor.

The temple of Artemis was the center of much of the wickedness. Like those in most pagan religions, its rituals and practices were but extensions of man's vilest and most perverted sins. Male and female roles were interchanged, and orgiastic sex, homosexuality, and every other sexual perversion were common. Artemis was herself a sex goddess, represented by an ugly, repulsive black female idol that looked something like a cross between a cow and a wolf. She was served by thousands of temple prostitutes, eunuchs, singers, dancers, and priests and priestesses. Idols of Artemis and other deities were to be seen everywhere, in every size and made out of many different materials. Of special popularity were silver idols and religious artifacts. It was because Paul's preaching cut deeply into that trade that the Ephesian silversmiths rallied the populace against him and his fellow believers (Acts 19:24-28).

The temple of Artemis contained one of the richest art collections then in existence. It was also used as a bank, because most people feared stealing from within its walls lest they incur the wrath of the goddess or other deities. A quarter mile-wide perimeter served as an asylum for criminals, who were safe from apprehension and punishment as long as they remained within the temple confines. For obvious reasons, the presence of hundreds of hardened criminals added still further to Ephesus's corruption and vice. The fifth-century B.C. Greek philosopher Heraclitus, himself a pagan, referred to Ephesus as "the darkness of vileness. The morals were lower than animals and the inhabitants of Ephesus were fit only to be drowned." There is no reason to believe that the situation had changed much by Paul's day. If anything, it may have been worse.

The church at Ephesus was a small island of despised people in a giant cesspool of wickedness. Most of the believers had themselves once been a part of that paganism. They frequently passed by places where they once caroused and ran into friends with whom they once indulged in debauchery. They faced continual temptations to revert to the old ways, and the apostle therefore admonished them to resist. **This I say therefore, and affirm together with the Lord, that you walk no longer just as the Gentiles walk.** Peter gave a similar word when he wrote, "For the time already past is sufficient for you to have carried out the desire of the Gentiles, having pursued a course of sensuality, lusts, drunkenness, carousals, drinking parties and abominable idolatries. And in all this, they are surprised that you do not run with them into the same excess of dissipation, and they malign you" (1 Pet. 4:3-4).

On the basis of what we are in Christ and of all that God now purposes for us as His redeemed and beloved children, we are to be absolutely distinct from the rest of the world, which does not know or follow Him. Spiritually we have already left the world and are now citizens of heaven. We are therefore not to "love the world, nor the things in the world. If anyone loves the world, the love of the Father is not in him. For all that is in the world, the lust of the flesh and the lust of the eyes and the boastful pride of life, is not from the Father, but is from the world. And the world is passing away, and also its lusts; but the one who does the will of God abides forever" (1 John 2:15-17). The world's standards are wrong, its motives are wrong, its aims are wrong. Its ways are sinful, deceitful, corrupt, empty, and destructive.

The warning Paul gives did not originate from his own personal tastes or preferences. **This I say . . . and affirm together with the Lord.** The matter of forsaking sin and following righteousness is not the whim of isolated, narrow-minded preachers and teachers. It is God's own standard and His only standard for those who belong to Him. It is the very essence of the gospel and is set in bold contrast to the standards of the unredeemed.

Paul proceeds to give four specific characteristics of the ungodly, pagan life-style that believers are to forsake. The worldly life is intellectually futile, ignorant of God's truth, spiritually and morally calloused, and depraved in mind.

INTELLECTUALLY FUTILE

The first characteristic of unregenerate people is that they live **in the futility of their mind.** It is significant that the basic issue of life-style centers in the **mind.** Paul continues to speak of understanding and ignorance (v. 18), learning and teaching (vv. 20-21), and the mind and truth (vv. 23-24)—all of which are related to the intellect. Because unbelievers and Christians *think differently* they are therefore to *act* differently. As far as spiritual and moral issues are concerned, an unbeliever cannot think straight. His rational processes in those areas are warped and inadequate (cf. Rom. 1:28; 8:7; 1 Cor. 2:14; Col. 2:18; Titus 1:15).

In their two-volume book *The Criminal Personality,* Samuel Yochelson and Stanton Samenow maintain that criminal behavior is the result of warped thinking. Three entire sections (pp. 251-457) are devoted to "The thinking errors of the criminal." By studying what criminals think, rather than trying to probe their feelings and backgrounds, these researchers use these sections to share their conclusions. "It is remarkable," they write, "that the criminal often derives as great an impact from his activities during nonarrestable phases as he does from crime. The criminal's thinking patterns operate everywhere; they are not restricted to crime." That is a description of the depraved, reprobate mind. "Sociological explanations have been unsatisfactory," the authors declare. "The idea that a man becomes a criminal because he is corrupted by his environment has proved to be too weak an explanation. We have indicated that criminals come from a broad spectrum of homes, both disadvantaged and privileged within the same neighborhood. Some are violators and most are not. It is not the environment that turns a man into a criminal, it is a series of choices that he makes starting at a very early age." The researchers also conclude that the criminal mind eventually "will decide that everything is worthless." "His thinking is illogical," they affirm in summary.

Because man's sinfulness flows out of his reprobate mind, the transformation must begin with the mind (v. 23). Christianity is cognitive before it is experiential. It is our thinking that makes us consider the gospel and our thinking that causes us to believe the historic facts and spiritual truths of the gospel and to receive Christ as Lord and Savior. That is why the first step in repentance is a change of mind about oneself, about one's spiritual condition, and about God.

To the Greeks the mind was all-important. They prided themselves in their great literature, art, philosophy, politics, and science. They were so advanced in their learning that Greek slaves were prized by the Romans and other conquerors as tutors for their children and as managers of their households and businesses. Greeks believed that almost any problem could be reasoned to a solution.

Yet Paul says that spiritually the operation of the natural mind is futile and unproductive. *Mataiotēs* (**futility**) refers to that which fails to produce the desired result, that which never succeeds. It was therefore used as a synonym for empty, because it amounts to nothing. The spiritual thinking and resulting life-style of **the Gentiles**—here representing all the ungodly—is inevitably empty, vain, and void of substance. The life of an unbeliever is bound up in thinking and acting in an arena of ultimate trivia. He consumes himself in the pursuit of goals that are purely selfish, in the accumulation of that which is temporary, and in looking for satisfaction in that which is intrinsically deceptive and disappointing.

The unregenerate person plans and resolves everything on the basis of his own thinking. He becomes his own ultimate authority and he follows his own thinking to its ultimate outcome of futility, aimlessness, and meaninglessness—to the self-centered emptiness that characterizes our age (cf. Ps. 94:8-11; Acts 14:15; Rom. 1:21-22).

After a life of experiencing every worldly advantage and pleasure, the wisest, wealthiest, and most favored man of the ancient world concluded that the worldly life is "vanity and striving after wind" (Eccles. 2:26; cf. 1:2; 14; 2:11; etc.). Yet century after century, millennia after millennia, men go on seeking the same futile goals in the same futile ways.

IGNORANT OF GOD'S TRUTH

The second characteristic of ungodly persons is ignorance of God's truth. Their thinking not only is futile but spiritually uninformed. They are **darkened in their understanding, excluded from the life of God, because of the ignorance that is in them, because of the hardness of their heart.**

General education and higher learning are more widespread today than ever in history. College graduates number in the tens of millions, and our society, like ancient Greece, prides itself in its science, technology, literature, art, and other achievements of the mind. For many people, to be called ignorant is a greater offense than to be called sinful. Yet Paul's point in this passage is that ignorance and sin are inseparable. The ungodly may be "always learning," but they are "never able to come to the knowledge of the truth" (2 Tim. 3:7). Fallen mankind has a built-in inability to know and comprehend the things of God—the only things that ultimately are worth knowing. When men rejected God, "they became futile in their speculations, and their foolish heart was darkened" (Rom. 1:21). Intellectual futility and foolishness combine as part of sin's penalty.

The Greek word behind **being darkened** is a perfect participle, indicating a continuing condition of spiritual darkness. This darkness implies both ignorance and immorality. And darkness of **understanding** is coupled with exclusion **from the life of God** (cf. John 1:5). The cause of their darkness, ignorance, and separation from God is **the hardness of their heart**, their willful determination to remain in sin. Because men determine to reject Him, God judicially and sovereignly determines to blind their minds, exclude them from His presence, and confirm them in their spiritual ignorance. "For even though they knew God, they did not honor Him as God, or give thanks," Paul explains of fallen mankind. "Professing to be wise, they became fools. . . . Therefore God gave them over in the lusts of their hearts to impurity" (Rom. 1:21-22, 24).

Because of the hardness of their heart, the ungodly are unresponsive to truth (cf. Isa. 44:18-20; 1 Thess. 4:5). Just as a corpse cannot hear a conversation in the mortuary, the person who is spiritually "dead in [his] trespasses and sins" (Eph. 2:1) cannot hear or understand the things of God, no matter how loudly or clearly they may be declared or evidenced in his presence. *Pōrōsis* (**hardness**) carries the idea of being rock-hard. It was used by physicians to describe the calcification that forms around broken bones and becomes harder than the bone itself. It was also used of the hard formations that sometimes occur in joints and cause them to become immobile. It could therefore connote the idea of paralysis as well as of hardness. Sin has a petrifying effect, and the **heart** of the person who continually chooses to sin becomes hardened and paralyzed to spiritual truth, utterly insensitive to the things of God.

Leroy Auden of the University of Chicago has written, "We hide a restless lion under a cardboard box, for while we may use other terms than guilt to describe this turbulence in our souls, the fact remains that all is not right within us." By one way or another—by psychological game playing, rationalization, self-justification, transferring the blame, or by denying sin and eliminating morality—men try futilely to get rid of the lion of guilt. But it will not go away.

Satan plays a part in the blindness of those who refuse to believe, because "the god of this world has blinded the minds of the unbelieving, that they might not see the light of the gospel of the glory of Christ, who is the image of God" (2 Cor. 4:4). They refuse to see Christ because they refuse to see God, and their refusal is readily confirmed and reinforced by the god of this world.

And when men continually persist in following their own way, they will also eventually be confirmed in their choice by the God of heaven. The Jews who heard Jesus teach and preach had the great advantage of having had God's Word given to them through Moses, the prophets, and other Old Testament writers. They had the even greater advantage of seeing and hearing God's own incarnate Son. But "though He had performed so many signs before them," John tells us, "yet they were not believing in Him. . . . For this cause they could not believe, for Isaiah said again, 'He has blinded their eyes, and He hardened their heart; lest they see with their eyes, and perceive with their heart, and be converted, and I heal them'" (John 12:37, 39-40). Because they would not believe, they could not believe. God one day says,

"Let the one who does wrong, still do wrong; and let the one who is filthy, still be filthy" (Rev. 22:11).

When men choose to petrify their hearts by constant rejection of the light (John 12:35-36), they became **darkened in their understanding, excluded from the life of God, because of the ignorance that is in them, because of the hardness of their heart.** That is the unspeakable tragedy of unbelief, the tragedy of the person who makes himself his own god.

SPIRITUALLY AND MORALLY CALLOUSED

The third characteristic of the unregenerate person is spiritual and moral callousness—**they . . . become callous.** When people continue in sin and turn themselves away from the life of God, they become apathetic and insensitive about moral and spiritual things. They reject all standards of righteousness and do not care about the consequences of their unrighteous thoughts and actions. Even conscience becomes scarred with tissue that is not sensitive to wrong (1 Tim. 4:2; Titus 1:15).

According to an ancient Greek story, a Spartan youth stole a fox but then inadvertently came upon the man from whom he had stolen it. To keep his theft from being discovered, the boy stuck the fox inside his clothes and stood without moving a muscle while the frightened fox tore out his vital organs. Even at the cost of his own painful death he would not own up to his wrong.

Our wicked society is so determined not to be discovered for what it is that it stands unflinching as its very life and vitality is ripped apart by the sins and corruption it holds so dear. It has **become callous** both to the reality and to the consequences of sin, and will endure any agony rather than admit that its way of "living" is the way of death.

On the other hand, sins that were once hidden or excused are now indulged in openly and blatantly. Often not even the semblance of morality is maintained. When self-desire rules, indecency runs wild and proceeds to cauterize the conscience, the God-given warning light and pain center of the soul. Those who are dying are desensitized to that which is killing them—because they choose it that way. Even when held up shamefully in full view of the world, their sins are not recognized as sinful or as the cause of increasing meaninglessness, hopelessness, and despair (cf. Rom. 1:32).

DEPRAVED IN MIND

Futile, self-centered thinking, ignorance of the truth, and spiritual and moral callousness lead inevitably **to sensuality, for the practice of every kind of impurity with greediness.**

Aselgeia **(sensuality)** refers to total licentiousness, the absence of all moral restraint, especially in the area of sexual sins. One commentator says the term relates to "a disposition of the soul incapable of bearing the pain of discipline." The idea is that of unbridled self-indulgence and undisciplined obscenity.

Sensuality characterizes the people Peter describes as "those who indulge the flesh in its corrupt desires and despise authority. Daring, self-willed, they do not tremble when they revile angelic majesties, whereas angels who are greater in might and power do not bring a reviling judgment against them before the Lord. But these, like unreasoning animals, born as creatures of instinct to be captured and killed, reviling where they have no knowledge, will in the destruction of those creatures also be destroyed" (2 Pet. 2:10-12).

All people initially recognize at least some standard of right and wrong and have a certain sense of shame when they act against that standard. Consequently, they usually try to hide their wrongdoing. They may continually fall back into it but still recognize it as wrong, as something they should not be doing; and conscience will not let them remain comfortable. But as they continue to overrule conscience and train themselves to do evil and to ignore guilt, they eventually reject those standards and determine to live solely by their own desires, thereby revealing an already seared conscience. Having rejected all divine guidelines and protection, they become depraved in mind and give themselves over **to sensuality.** Such a person cares nothing about what other people think—not to mention about what God thinks—but only about what gratifies the cravings of his own warped mind.

Ungodliness and its attendant immorality destroy the mind as well as the conscience and the spirit. Rejection of God and of His truth and righteousness finally results in what Paul refers to in Romans as a "depraved mind" (1:28)—a mind that is no mind, that cannot reason, that cannot think clearly, that cannot recognize or understand God's truth, and that loses contact with spiritual reality. In its extreme, the depraved mind loses contact with *all* reality. That is the mindlessness of the self-indulgent, profligate celebrity who loses his career, his sanity, and often his life because of wanton **sensuality.** When indecency becomes a way of life, every aspect of life is corrupted, distorted, and eventually destroyed.

The rapid increase in mental illness today can be laid in large measure at the feet of increased **sensuality** of every sort. Man is made for God and designed according to His standards. When he rejects God and His standards he destroys himself in the process. The corruptions of our present society are not the result of psychological or sociological circumstances but the result of personal choices based on principles that are specifically and purposely against God and His way. Homosexuality, sexual perversion, abortion, lying, cheating, stealing, murder, and every other type of moral degeneration have become unabashed and calloused ways of life through the conscious choices of those who indulge in them.

Ergasia **(practice)** can refer to a business enterprise, and that idea could apply here. The ungodly person often makes business out of **every kind of impurity.** A Christian leader commented some years ago that many of the books published in the United States today rival the drippings of a broken sewer. Yet pornography, prostitution, X-rated films, suggestive TV programs, and **every kind of impurity** form perhaps the largest industry in our country. The vast majority of it is open, unashamed, and legally protected.

An article in *Forbes* magazine (Sept. 18, 1978, pp. 81-92) entitled "The X-Rated Economy" began by stating the obvious—pornography is no longer an illegal business. The market for pornography is not confined to perverts or other emotional cripples. To the contrary, the largest part of the market is middle class people. In an increasingly permissive society those who enjoy pornography are free to revel in it. The surprising revelation was that, according to one official estimate, the nation's pornographers do more than four billion dollars worth of business a year—more than the combined incomes of the often supportive movie and music industries! Other estimates place the total pornographic business—including a large segment of the burgeoning home video market—at three times that much.

Impurity is inseparable from **greediness**. *Pleonexia* (**greediness**) is unbounded covetousness, uninhibited lust for that which is wanted. Immorality has no part in love, and anything the sensual person does under the guise of caring and helpfulness is but a ruse for exploitation. The world of **sensuality** and **impurity** is the world of **greediness**. The person given over to godlessness and immorality greedily takes whatever he can from those around him. He evaluates life only in material terms (Luke 12:15), uses other people to his own advantage (1 Thess. 2:5; 2 Pet. 2:3), and turns his back on God in order to fulfill his own evil desires (Rom. 1:29). And his **greediness** is no less than idolatry (Col. 3:5).

When a person determines to think his own way, do things his own way, and pursue his own destiny, he cuts himself off from God. When that happens, he cuts himself off from truth and becomes spiritually blind and without standards of morality. Without standards of morality, immorality becomes a shameless and calloused way of life. When that is continued it destroys the mind's ability to distinguish good from evil, truth from falsehood, and reality from unreality. The godless life becomes the mindless life.

That process characterizes every unbeliever. It is the direction that every ungodly person is headed, although some are further along than others. "Evil men and impostors will proceed from bad to worse, deceiving and being deceived" (2 Tim. 3:13). That some people may not reach the extremes Paul mentions in Ephesians 4:17-19 is due only to the protective shield of God's common grace that He showers both on the righteous and the unrighteous (see Matt. 5:45) and to the preserving influence of the Holy Spirit (Job 34:14-15) and of the church (Matt. 5:13).

THE WALK OF THE NEW SELF

But you did not learn Christ in this way, if indeed you have heard Him and have been taught in Him, just as truth is in Jesus, that, in reference to your former manner of life, you lay aside the old self, which is being corrupted in accordance with the lusts of deceit, and that you be renewed in the spirit of your mind, and put on the new self, which in the likeness of God has been created in righteousness and holiness of the truth. (4:20-24)

The new walk in Christ is the exact opposite of the old walk of the flesh. Whereas the old is self-centered and futile, the new is Christ-centered and purposeful. Whereas the old is ignorant of God's truth, the new knows and understands it. Whereas the old is morally and spiritually calloused and shameless, the new is sensitive to sin of every sort. Whereas the old is depraved in its thinking, the new is renewed.

CHRIST-CENTERED

But you did not learn Christ in this way, (4:20)

After reviewing the evils of the pagan world and the self-centered, purposeless, standardless wickedness that both comes from and leads to spiritual darkness and ignorance, Paul declared to believers who had fallen back into such degradation, **But you did not learn Christ in this way.** That is not the way of Christ or of His kingdom or family. "You are not to have any part of such things," He insisted, "whether by participation or association."

You did not learn Christ is a direct reference to salvation. To learn Christ is to be saved. While it is true that the verb *manthanō* can be used in reference to the process of learning truth (see Rom. 16:17; Phil. 4:9), it can also mean "to come to know" (Walter Bauer, *A Greek-English Lexicon of the New Testament.* Translated and edited by W. F. Arndt and F. W. Gingrich. 5th ed. [Chicago; U. of Chicago, 1958], p. 490), as a one-time act, particularly when the verb is aorist active indicative, as in this case. The aorist is also used in John 6:45, where Jesus spoke to those who had "learned from the Father"—indicating a reference to the saving act of faith under the Old Covenant which would lead them now to Him.

In Matthew 11:29, Jesus offered one of the loveliest of all salvation invitations: "Take my yoke upon you, and learn of me" (KJV). This use of *manthanō* is also in the aorist tense, indicating a single unrepeated act.

Both the context and the use of the aorist tense of the verb "to learn" in these passages lead to the conclusion that this learning refers to the moment of saving faith.

"Friendship with the world is hostility toward God" (James 4:4), and the person who makes a profession of Christ but makes no effort to break with his worldly and sinful habits has reason to doubt his salvation. "The one who says, 'I have come to know Him' and does not keep His commandments, is a liar, and the truth is not in him," and "If anyone loves the world, the love of the Father is not in him" (1 John 2:4, 15).

The ways of God and the ways of the world are not compatible. The idea, promoted by some who claim to be evangelicals, that a Christian does not have to give up anything or change anything when he becomes a Christian is nothing less than diabolical. That notion, under the pretense of elevating God's grace and of protecting the gospel from works righteousness, will do nothing but send many people confidently down the broad way that Jesus said leads to destruction (Matt. 7:13).

From the human side, salvation begins with repentance, a change of mind and action regarding sin, self, and God. John the Baptist (Matt. 3:2), Jesus (Matt. 4:17), and the apostles (Acts 2:38; 3:19; 5:31; 20:21; 26:20) began their ministries with the preaching of repentance. The very purpose of receiving Christ is to "be saved from this perverse generation" (Acts 2:40), and no one is saved who does not repent and forsake sin. Repentance does not save us, but God cannot save us from sin of which we are unwilling to let go. To hold on to sin is to refuse God, to scorn His grace, and to nullify faith. No Christian is totally free from the presence of sin in this life, but in Christ he is willingly freed from his orientation to sin. He slips and falls many times, but the determined direction of his life is *away from* sin.

One of the first things a Christian should learn is that he cannot trust his own thinking or rely on his own way. "They who live should no longer live for themselves, but for Him who died and rose again on their behalf" (2 Cor. 5:15). The Christian has the mind of Christ (1 Cor. 2:16), and Christ's is the only mind on which he can rely. The obedient, faithful Christian is the one for whom Christ thinks, acts, loves, feels, serves, and lives in every way. He says with Paul, "I have been crucified with Christ; and it is no longer I who live, but Christ lives in me; and the life which I now live in the flesh I live by faith in the Son of God, who loved me, and delivered Himself up for me" (Gal. 2:20).

Because we have the mind of Christ, we are to "have this attitude in [ourselves] which was also in Christ Jesus," who "humbled Himself by becoming obedient to the point of death, even death on a cross" (Phil. 2:5, 8). Although Christ was one with His Father, while on earth He did absolutely nothing but His Father's will (Matt. 26:39, 42; John 4:34; 5:30; 6:38; etc.). If the incarnate Lord sought the mind of His heavenly Father in everything He did, how much more should we? The mark of the Christian life is to think like Christ, act like Christ, love like Christ, and in every possible way to be like Christ—in order that "whether we are awake or asleep, we may live together with Him" (1 Thess. 5:10).

God has a plan of destiny for the universe, and as long as Christ is working in us He is working out a part of that plan through us. The Christ-centered life is the most purposeful and meaningful life conceivable—it is part of the divine plan and work of God!

KNOWS GOD'S TRUTH

if indeed you have heard Him and have been taught in Him, just as truth is in Jesus, (4:21)

Instead of being ignorant of God's truth, the Christian has **heard** Christ and is **taught in Him**. Both verbs are in the aorist tense, again pointing to a one-time past act, and in this context referring to the time when the readers were taught and came to believe the gospel—here called the **truth . . . in Jesus**. These terms describe the moment of salvation-conversion. When a person receives Christ as Savior and Lord, he comes into God's truth.

If indeed you have heard Him and have been taught in Him (cf. Matt. 17:5) could not possibly refer to hearing Jesus' physical voice on earth, because there is no way that could have been true of all the believers in Asia Minor to whom Paul was writing. It must refer to the hearing of His spiritual call to salvation (cf. John 8:47; 10:27; Acts 3:22-23; Heb. 3:7-8). Many New Testament references speak of this hearing and being taught as the call of God (see, e.g., Acts 2:39). *En autoi* (**in Him**) means in union with Christ and further emphasizes the fact that at conversion we received the truth embodied in Christ, because we came to be **in Him**.

Life without God leads to cynicism about truth. The ungodly person may ask rhetorically with Pilate, "What is truth?" (John 18:38), but he expects no satisfactory answer. The Christian, however, can say, "The truth of Christ is in me" (2 Cor. 11:10) and "We know that the Son of God has come, and has given us understanding, in order that we might know Him who is true, and we are in Him who is true, in His Son Jesus Christ" (1 John 5:20).

The **truth** that **is in Jesus**, then, is first of all the truth about salvation. This idea is parallel to 1:13, where Paul says hearing the truth and being in Him are synonymous with conversion: "In Him, you also, after listening to the message of truth, the gospel of your salvation—having also believed, you were sealed in Him with the Holy Spirit of promise." The **truth . . . is in Jesus** and it leads to the fullness of truth about God, man, creation, history, sin, righteousness, grace, faith, salvation, life, death, purpose, meaning, relationships, heaven, hell, judgment, eternity, and everything else of ultimate consequence.

John summed up this relationship with truth when he wrote: "And we know that the Son of God has come, and has given us understanding, in order that we might know Him who is true, and we are in Him who is true, in His Son Jesus Christ. This is the true God and eternal life" (1 John 5:20).

DELIVERED FROM THE OLD SELF

that, in reference to your former manner of life, you lay aside the old self, which is being corrupted in accordance with the lusts of deceit, (4:22)

To demonstrate the transforming nature of regeneration, the apostle further describes and defines the inherent realities of the truth in Jesus that his readers heard and were taught at conversion. He uses three infinitives (in the original Greek) to summarize what they heard in the call of the gospel: **lay aside**, "be renewed" (v. 23), and "put on" (v. 24).

It is important to note that Paul is not here exhorting believers to do these things. These three infinitives describe the saving truth in Jesus and are not imperatives directed to Christians. They are done at the point of conversion, and are mentioned here only as a reminder of the reality of that experience.

Lay aside the old self is related to "have heard . . . and have been taught" in the gospel (v. 21). It should also be noted that, although it is essential to affirm that salvation is a divine and sovereign miracle apart from any human contribution, it must also be affirmed that men do hear and believe and lay aside the old while putting on the new. The saving act of God effects such responses in the believing soul. These are not human works required for divine salvation but inherent elements of the divine work of salvation. Paul's terms here are basically a description of repentance from sin and submission to God, so often taught as elements of regeneration (see Isa. 55:6-7; Matt. 19:16-22; Acts 2:38-40; 20:21; 1 Thess. 1:9; et al.).

In contrast to the unregenerate person who continually resists and rejects God and lives in the sphere of dominating sin **(the former manner of life)**, the Christian has heard the call to **lay aside the old self.** The verb means to strip off, as in the case of old filthy clothes. The tense (aorist middle) indicates a once-and-forever action done by the believer at salvation.

Paul's reference to **the old self** (old in the sense of worn out and useless) is consistent with gospel terminology in his other epistles. For example, Colossians 3 describes the fact of salvation using four verbs: "for you *have died* and your life is hidden with Christ in God" (v. 3); "you *have been raised up*" (v. 1); "you *laid aside* the old self [man]" (v. 9); and you "*have put on* the new self [man] who is being renewed to a true knowledge according to the image of the One who created him" (v. 10; emphasis added). All four verbs are in the aorist tense in the Greek, indicating that they refer back to already completed action and must therefore refer to the same past event of salvation. In the context, "laid aside" and "have put on" cannot be other than exact parallels to "have died" and "have been raised up," which are clearly salvific in content.

Affirming the truth of these four aspects of conversion is the basis for the exhortations in the Colossian passage. Paul is describing salvation to the Colossians exactly as he does to the Ephesians. Although in Ephesians he does not refer specifically to the believer's union in the death and resurrection of Christ, he does allude to that reality when saying that the one who believes is "in Him." His references to the **old self** and the **new self** in both passages are obviously parallel.

This perspective is further proved by Paul's teaching in Romans 6, where he describes the nature of salvation, with emphasis on verbs. " *re* .*i.* 1 t*n* sin" (v. 2); "all of us . . . *have been baptized* into Christ Jesus" (v. 3); "*have been buried* with Him . . . into death" (v. 4); "we *have become united* with Him in . . . His death" (v. 5); "our old self *was crucified* with Him" (v. 6); "our body of sin *might be done away* with" (v. 6); "he who *has died*" (v. 7); and "we *have died* with Christ" (v. 8; emphasis added). Eight of those nine verbs are aorist in the Greek, looking back at an already accomplished event. One is in the perfect tense (v. 5), seeing the result of that past event. Again, Paul gives his exhortation on the basis of this description of the complete transformation of the believer at conversion (cf. Rom. 6:12-23).

The inescapable conclusion from what Paul says in Romans and Colossians is that salvation is a spiritual union with Jesus Christ in His death and resurrection that can also be described as the death of the "old self" and the resurrection of the "new self," who now walks in "newness of life." This union and new identity clearly means that salvation is transformation. It is not the addition of a new self to an old self. In Christ, the old self no longer exists (cf. 2 Cor. 5:17). That is what the Ephesians heard and were taught according to the truth in Jesus (4:21). The **old self** is the unconverted nature, described as **being corrupted in accordance with the lusts of deceit**. The **old self** of the unbeliever not only is corrupt but is increasingly **being corrupted** (present passive), because it is the tool for evil desire which is controlled by **deceit** (cf. 2:1-3). The gospel invitation is to lay the **old self** aside in repentance from sin that includes not just sorrow about sin but a turning from sin to God.

BECOME THE NEW SELF

and that you be renewed in the spirit of your mind, and put on the new self, which in the likeness of God has been created in righteousness and holiness of the truth. (4:23-24)

In contrast to the depraved, reprobate mind of the unregenerate person (vv. 17-18), the Christian **is renewed** continually **in the spirit of** [his] **mind** (cf. Col. 3:10). *Ananeoō* (to be **renewed**) appears only here in the New Testament. The best rendering of this present passive infinitive is as a modifier of the main verb **put on**, so that it would read "and being renewed in the spirit of your mind, **put on the new self**." This makes clear that such renewal is the consequence of "laying aside the old self" and is the context in which one may **put on the new self**. Salvation relates to the mind, which is the center of thought, understanding, and belief, as well as of motive and action. The **spirit of your mind** is explained by one commentator as intending to show that it is not in the sphere of human thinking or human reason, but in the moral sphere, that this renewal occurs. John Eadie says:

> The change is not in the mind psychologically, either in its essence or in its operation; and neither is it in the mind as if it were a superficial change of opinion on points of doctrine or practice; but it is in the spirit of the mind; in that which gives mind both its bent and its material of thought. It is not simply in the spirit as if it lay there in dim and mystic quietude; but it is in the spirit of the mind; in the power which, when changed itself, radically alters the entire sphere and business of the inner mechanism.

When a person becomes a Christian, God initially renews his **mind**, giving it a completely new spiritual and moral capability—a capability that the most brilliant and educated mind apart from Christ can never achieve (cf. 1 Cor. 2:9-16).

This renewal continues through the believer's life as he is obedient to the Word and will of God (cf. Rom. 12:1-2). The process is not a one-time accomplishment but the continual work of the Spirit in the child of God (Titus 3:5). Our resources are God's Word and prayer. It is through these means that we gain the mind of Christ (cf. Phil. 2:5; Col. 3:16; 2 Tim. 1:7), and it is through that mind that we live the life of Christ.

The renewed **spirit of** the believer's **mind** is a corollary to putting on the **new self**, which is the new creation made in the very **likeness of God** and **has been created in righteousness and holiness of the truth.** That which was once darkened, ignorant, hardened, calloused, sensual, impure, and greedy is now enlightened, learned in the **truth**, sensitive to sin, pure, and generous. Whereas it was once characterized by wickedness and sin, it is now characterized by **righteousness and holiness.** In Colossians 3:12, Paul calls believers "the chosen of God, holy and beloved."

It is essential to expand the concept of the **new self** so that it may be understood more fully. The word **new** *(kainos)* does not mean renovated but entirely new—new in species or character. The **new self** is new because it **has been created in the likeness of God.** The Greek is literally, "according to what God is"— a staggering statement expressing the wondrous reality of salvation. Those who confess Jesus Christ as Lord are made like God! Peter says we become "partakers of the divine nature" (2 Pet. 1:4).

In Galatians 2:20, Paul declares, "It is no longer I who live, but Christ lives in me." The image of God, lost in Adam, is more gloriously restored in the second Adam, the One who is the image of the invisible God (cf. 2 Cor. 4:4-6), where Paul describes Christ as the image of God, the treasure that dwells in us.

If believers have received the divine nature—the life of Christ, the likeness of God in this new self by an act of divine creation (cf. Col. 3:10)—it obviously must have been **created in righteousness and holiness of the truth.** In the Greek, the word **truth** is placed last to contrast with deceit (v. 22), and the best rendering is that of the NIV: "true righteousness and holiness." God could create no less (see Luke 1:75).

Righteousness relates to our fellow men and reflects the second table of the law (Ex. 20:12-17). **Holiness** *(hosiotēs,* sacred observance of all duties to God) relates to God and reflects the first table (Ex. 20:3-11). The believer, then, possesses a new nature, a new self, a holy and righteous inner person fit for the presence of God. This is the believer's truest self.

So righteous and holy is this **new self** that Paul refuses to admit that any sin comes from that new creation in God's image. Thus his language in Romans 6-7 is explicit in placing the reality of sin other than in the new self. He says, "Do not let sin reign in your *mortal body*" (6:12) and, "Do not go on presenting the *members of your body* to sin" (6:13, emphasis added).

In those passages Paul places sin in the believer's life in the body. In chapter 7 he sees it in the flesh. He says, "No longer am I the one doing it, but sin which indwells me" (v. 17), "Nothing good dwells in me, that is, in my flesh" (v. 18), "I am no longer the one doing it, but sin which dwells in me" (v. 20), and ". . . the law of sin which is in my members" (v. 23).

In those texts Paul acknowledges that being a new self in the image of God does not eliminate sin. It is still present in the flesh, the body, the unredeemed humanness that includes the whole human person's thinking and behavior. But he will not allow that new inner man to be given responsibility for sin. The new "I" loves and longs for the holiness and righteousness for which it was created.

Paul summarizes the dichotomy with these words: "So then, on the one hand I myself with my mind [synonymous here with the new self] am serving the law of God, but on the other, with my flesh [synonymous here with unredeemed humanness contained in our sinful bodies] the law of sin" (Rom. 7:25). It is this struggle that prompts the anticipation for "the redemption of the body" described in Romans 8:23 (cf. Phil. 3:20-21).

We are new, but not yet *all new.* We are righteous and holy, but not yet *perfectly* righteous and holy. But understanding the genuine reality of our transforming salvation is essential if we are to know how to live as Christians in the Body of Christ to which we belong.

The remaining portions of the epistle contain exhortations to the believer to bring his body into obedience to the will of God.

Many rescue missions have a delousing room, where derelicts who have not had a bath in months discard all their old clothes and are thoroughly bathed and disinfected. The unsalvageable old clothes are burned and new clothes are issued. The clean man is provided clean clothes.

That is a picture of salvation, except that in salvation the new believer is not simply given a bath but a completely new nature. The continuing need of the Christian life is to keep discarding and burning the remnants of the old sinful clothing. "Do not go on presenting the members of your body to sin as instruments of unrighteousness," Paul pleads; "but present yourselves to God as those alive from the dead, and your members as instruments of righteousness to God" (Rom. 6:13).

The many therefores and wherefores in the New Testament usually introduce appeals for believers to live like the new creatures they are in Christ. Because of our new life, our new Lord, our new nature, and our new power, we are *therefore* called to live a correspondingly new life-style.

Principles of
New Life

14

Therefore, laying aside falsehood, speak truth, each one of you, with his neighbor, for we are members of one another. Be angry, and yet do not sin; do not let the sun go down on your anger, and do not give the devil an opportunity. Let him who steals steal no longer; but rather let him labor, performing with his own hands what is good, in order that he may have something to share with him who has need. Let no unwholesome word proceed from your mouth, but only such a word as is good for edification according to the need of the moment, that it may give grace to those who hear. And do not grieve the Holy Spirit of God, by whom you were sealed for the day of redemption. Let all bitterness and wrath and anger and clamor and slander be put away from you, along with all malice. And be kind to one another, tender-hearted, forgiving each other, just as God in Christ also has forgiven you. (4:25-32)

The only reliable evidence of a person's being saved is not a past experience of receiving Christ but a present life that reflects Christ. "The one who says, 'I have come to know Him' and does not keep His commandments, is a liar, and the truth is not in him" (1 John 2:4). New creatures act like new creatures. God is not progressively making new creations out of believers; believers are those whom He has already made new creations. "If any man is in Christ, he *is* a new creature; the old things passed away; behold, new things have come" (2 Cor. 5:17). This is Paul's primary concern in Romans 6, where he carefully describes the believer's "newness of life" (v. 4; cf. 7:6).

Paul has just demonstrated (vv. 17-24) that believers know salvation to be laying aside "the old self" and putting on "the new self" (Eph. 4:22, 24). Christians are not robots who simply react automatically to divine impulses. Although God sovereignly makes us new creatures, He also commands us in the strength of the Spirit to subdue our unredeemed humanness (1 Cor. 9:27), which still resides in us, and to live as new creatures in submission to Christ our new Master. The paradox of the Christian life is that both God's sovereignty and man's will are at work. The faithful believer responds positively to God's sovereign declarations and commands.

After showing what believers are and have positionally in Christ (chaps. 1-3), Paul first gives general basic instruction for the practicality of living the new life (4:1-24) and then continues throughout the rest of the letter to give specific commands for the conduct of that life. In 4:25-32 he gives commands reflecting several contrasts between the old life and the new. Based on their newness of life, believers are to change from lying to speaking the truth, from unrighteous anger to righteous anger, from stealing to sharing, from unwholesome words to edifying words, and from natural vices to supernatural virtues.

FROM LYING TO SPEAKING THE TRUTH

Therefore, laying aside falsehood, speak truth, each one of you, with his neighbor, for we are members of one another. (4:25)

This second **therefore** of the chapter (see v. 17) provides an anticipated response to the general description of the new life in Christ described in verses 20-24 and introduces the first specific command for the new walk.

Liars will not inherit the kingdom of God. "For the cowardly and unbelieving and abominable and murderers and immoral persons and sorcerers and idolaters and all liars, their part will be in the lake that burns with fire and brimstone, which is the second death" (Rev. 21:8; cf. 1 Cor. 6:9). A believer can fall into lying just as he can fall into any sin, but if his life is a habitual flow of lies that proceed from a heart that seeks to deceive, he has no biblical basis for believing he is a Christian. The person who continually lies as a regular part of his daily living shows himself to be a child of Satan not of God (John 8:44). Satan lies about God, Christ, life, death, heaven, hell, Scripture, good, evil, and everything else. Every religious system apart from Christianity is built around various deceptions of Satan. Even the few and limited truths that may be found in human religions are scheming parts of a greater network that seeks to deceive.

Ever since the Fall, lying has been a common characteristic of unregenerate mankind. Our society today is so dependent on lying that if it suddenly turned to telling the truth our way of life would collapse. If world leaders began speaking only the truth, World War III would certainly ensue. So many lies are piled on other lies, and so many organizations, businesses, economies, social orders, governments, and treaties are built on those lies that the world system would disintegrate if lying suddenly ceased. Resentment and animosity would know no bounds, and the confusion would be unimaginable.

Lying includes more than simply telling direct falsehoods. It also includes exaggeration, adding falsehood to that which begins as true. Some years ago a Christian man became widely known for his powerful and moving testimony. But after several years he stopped. When asked why, he replied with some degree of integrity, "Over the years I embellished the story so much that I no longer knew what was true and what was not."

Cheating in school and on income tax returns is a form of lying. Making foolish promises, betraying a confidence, flattery, and making excuses are all forms of lying.

The Christian should have no part of any kind of lying. He is to be characterized by **laying aside falsehood**, because **falsehood** is incompatible with his new nature and unacceptable to his new Lord. *Apotithēmi,* from which **laying aside** is derived, has to do with discarding, stripping off, casting away, and the like. It is the word Luke used of the Jewish leaders in Jerusalem who, as they were stoning Stephen, "*laid aside* their robes at the feet of a young man named Saul" (Acts 7:58). They laid aside their outer garments so they could more freely do their wicked work. The Christian lays **aside falsehood** so he can be free to do the righteous work of the Lord.

Quoting Zechariah 8:16, Paul goes from the negative prohibition on to the positive command, **speak truth, each one of you, with his neighbor.** Christ is Himself "the way, and the truth, and the life" (John 14:6); the Holy Spirit is "the Spirit of truth" (v. 17); and God's Word is truth (17:17). When a person becomes a believer he steps out of the domain of **falsehood** into the domain of **truth**, and every form of lying therefore is utterly inconsistent with his new self.

It should be said that telling the truth does not require telling everything we know. Truthfulness is not in conflict with keeping a confidence or other legitimate secrets. Everything we say should be unqualifiedly true, and to purposely withhold information in order to deceive and mislead is a form of lying. But truthfulness does not demand our telling everything we know with no regard for its impact. Nor does it demand that we unburden all our ill feelings, doubts, and hatreds on those whom we dislike—in the kind of pseudo-honesty promoted by Freudian psychology and other such philosophies. Our concern as Christians should be for God to deal with our wrong feelings and remove them, not to wantonly express them in some inept attempt at self-justification or in the misguided expectation that simply expressing them will somehow make them go away or will mend relationships they have caused to be broken. To readily admit as Paul did that we are not perfect or free of sin (Rom. 7:15-25; Phil. 4:12-14; etc.) is one thing; to broadcast detailed accounts of our sin is quite another.

God's economy is based on truth, and His people—either as individual believers or as the corporate church—cannot be fit instruments for His work unless they live in truthfulness. We are to **speak truth, each one of** [us], **with his neighbor, for we are members of one another.** The word **neighbor** is defined by the phrase **members of one another** and means fellow Christians. We are to **speak truth** to everyone and in every situation, but we have a special motive to be truthful with other believers, because we are fellow members of Christ's Body, the church, and therefore **members of one another.**

Our physical bodies cannot not function properly or safely if each member does not correctly communicate to the others. If our brain were suddenly to start giving false signals to our feet, we would stumble or walk in front of a moving truck instead of stopping on the curb. If it falsely reported hot and cold, we could freeze to death because we felt too warm or be scalded in a hot shower while feeling chilly. If our eyes decided to send false signals to the brain, a dangerous curve in the highway might appear straight and safe, and we would crash. If the nerves in our hands and feet failed to tell our brain that injury was occurring, our foot could be mangled or our fingers burned without our knowing it. That is precisely the great danger of leprosy—injuries, disease, and other afflictions devastate the body because nerves fail to send danger signals of pain.

The church cannot function properly if its **members** shade the truth with **one another** or fail to work together honestly and lovingly. We cannot effectively minister to each other or with each other if we do not speak "the truth in love" (Eph. 4:15), especially among our fellow believers.

From Unrighteous Anger to Righteous Anger

Be angry, and yet do not sin; do not let the sun go down on your anger, and do not give the devil an opportunity. (4:26-27)

Parorgismos (**anger**) is not momentary outward, boiling-over rage or inward, seething resentment, but rather a deep-seated, determined and settled conviction. As seen in this passage, its New Testament use can represent an emotion good or bad, depending on motive and purpose.

Paul's command is to **be angry** (from *orgizō*), with the qualification **and yet do not sin.** In this statement he may be legitimatizing righteous indignation, anger at evil, at that which is done against the Person of the Lord and against His will and purpose. It is the anger of the Lord's people who hate evil (Ps. 69:9). It is the anger that abhors injustice, immorality, and ungodliness of every sort. It is the anger of which the great English preacher F. W. Robertson wrote in one of his letters. When he once met a certain man who was trying to lure a young girl into prostitution, he became so angry that he bit his lip until it bled.

Jesus expressed righteous anger at the hard-heartedness of the Pharisees who resented His healing the man with the withered hand on the Sabbath (Mark

3:5). Although the word itself is not used in the gospel accounts of the events, it was no doubt that kind of anger that caused Jesus to drive the moneychangers out of the Temple (Matt. 21:12; John 2:15). Jesus was always angered when the Father was maligned or when others were mistreated, but He was never selfishly angry at what was done against Him. That is the measure of righteous anger.

Anger that is **sin**, on the other hand, is anger that is self-defensive and self-serving, that is resentful of what is done against oneself. It is the anger that leads to murder and to God's judgment (Matt. 5:21-22).

Anger that is selfish, undisciplined, and vindictive is sinful and has no place even temporarily in the Christian life. But anger that is unselfish and is based on love for God and concern for others not only is permissible but commanded. Genuine love cannot help being angered at that which injures the object of that love.

But even righteous anger can easily turn to bitterness, resentment, and self-righteousness. Consequently, Paul goes on to say, **do not let the sun go down on your anger, and do not give the devil an opportunity**. Even the best motivated anger can sour, and we are therefore to put it aside at the end of the day. Taken to bed, it is likely to **give the devil an opportunity** to use it for his purposes. If anger is prolonged, one may begin to seek vengeance and thereby violate the principle taught in Romans 12:17-21,

> Never pay back evil for evil to anyone. Respect what is right in the sight of all men. If possible, so far as it depends on you, be at peace with all men. Never take your own revenge, beloved, but leave room for the wrath of God, for it is written, "Vengeance is Mine, I will repay," says the Lord. "But if your enemy is hungry, feed him, and if he is thirsty, give him a drink; for in so doing you will heap burning coals upon his head. Do not be overcome by evil, but overcome evil with good."

It may also be that verses 26b-27 refer entirely to this unrighteous anger, in which case Paul uses the imperative in the sense of saying that, because anger may come in a moment and overtake a believer, and because it has such a strong tendency to grow and fester, it should be dealt with immediately—confessed, forsaken, and given to God for cleansing before we end the day.

In any case of anger, whether legitimate or not, if it is courted, "advantage [will] be taken of us by Satan" (2 Cor. 2:11), and he will feed our anger with self-pity, pride, self-righteousness, vengeance, defense of our rights, and every other sort of selfish sin and violation of God's holy will.

FROM STEALING TO SHARING

Let him who steals steal no longer; but rather let him labor, performing with his own hands what is good, in order that he may have something to share with him who has need. (4:28)

The third command Paul sets forth demands a change from stealing to sharing. No one is completely free from the temptation to steal. Many children go through a phase of thinking it is fun to steal, sometimes simply for the sake of stealing. There is a certain fleshly attraction in taking that which does not belong to us and trying to get by with it. The old self had a built-in inclination to steal, and that is one of the many characteristics of the old self that "the new self, which [is] in the likeness of God" (v. 24) puts away. The Christian is to **steal** [*kleptō,* from which comes kleptomaniac] **no longer.**

In the past several decades shoplifting has grown alarmingly, a large percentage of it being done by employees. In some large stores up to a third of the price of the merchandise is used to cover theft losses of various sorts. Intentional overestimating, falsified cost overruns, and outright embezzlement are rampant throughout business and industry. Padding expense accounts, reporting more hours than were worked, failing to report income to the IRS, and other such deceptions are accepted as normal by many people. To them, stealing is simply a game in which getting caught is the only cause for regret or shame.

Grand larceny, petty theft, taking some of your dad's money off the dresser, reneging on a debt, not paying fair wages, or pocketing what a clerk overpays in change are all stealing. There is simply no end to ways we can steal, and whatever the ways are and whatever the chances for being caught, stealing is sin and has no part in the new walk of the new man in Christ.

The alternative to stealing is to **labor . . . in order . . . to share with him who has need.** It is God's plan for everyone to work who is able to do so. "If anyone will not work, neither let him eat. For we hear that some among you are leading an undisciplined life, doing no work at all" (2 Thess. 3:10-11). The Christian who does not work and "provide for his own, and especially for those of his household, . . . has denied the faith, and is worse than an unbeliever" (1 Tim. 5:8).

Our **labor** should be in **what is good,** in work that is honest, honorable, and productive. The term *agathos* (**good**) connotes that which is good in quality, and here refers to God-honoring employment. A Christian should never be involved in a job, profession, work, or business that demands compromise of God's standards, that dishonors Him, violates His holy commands, or misleads or harms others in any way.

Performing with his own hands stresses the truth that the norm is for every person to be responsible for his own provision, and even more, to share with those who, in spite of hard work or because of devastation or incapacity, are in **need.**

Not only should our work harm no one, it should be for the specific purpose of helping them—**to share with him who has need.** A Christian's desire to earn more should be for the purpose of being able to give more and help more. Beyond providing for his own and his family's basic needs, he gains so he can give. Like the rest of his life, a Christian's occupation—directly or indirectly—should above all else be a means of service to God and to others.

"When you give a reception," Jesus said, "invite the poor, the crippled, the lame, the blind, and you will be blessed, since they do not have the means to repay you; for you will be repaid at the resurrection of the righteous" (Luke 14:13-14). As he visited them at Miletus on his way to Jerusalem, Paul's last words to the Ephesian elders were: "I have coveted no one's silver or gold or clothes. You yourselves know that these hands ministered to my own needs and to the men who were with me. In everything I showed you that by working hard in this manner you must help the weak and remember the words of the Lord Jesus, that He Himself said, 'It is more blessed to give than to receive'" (Acts 20:33-35).

FROM UNWHOLESOME WORDS TO WHOLESOME WORDS

Let no unwholesome word proceed from your mouth, but only such a word as is good for edification according to the need of the moment, that it may give grace to those who hear. And do not grieve the Holy Spirit of God, by whom you were sealed for the day of redemption. (4:29-30)

A fourth change in the Christian's life should be from speaking unwholesome words to speaking wholesome ones. His speech should be transformed along with everything else.

Sapros (**unwholesome**) refers to that which is corrupt or foul and was used of rotten fruit, vegetables, and other spoiled food. Foul language should never **proceed from** the **mouth** of a Christian, because it is totally out of character with his newness of life. **Unwholesome** language should be as repulsive to us as a rotten apple or a spoiled piece of meat. Off-color jokes, profanity, dirty stories, vulgarity, double entendre, and every other form of corrupt talk should never cross our lips. "But now you also," Paul wrote the Colossians, "put them all aside: anger, wrath, malice, slander, and abusive speech from your mouth" (Col. 3:8; cf. Eph. 5:4).

The tongue is exceedingly difficult to control. It is "a fire," James says, "the very world of iniquity; the tongue is set among our members as that which defiles the entire body, and sets on fire the course of our life, and is set on fire by hell. For every species of beasts and birds, of reptiles and creatures of the sea, is tamed, and has been tamed by the human race. But no one can tame the tongue; it is a restless evil and full of deadly poison" (James 3:6-8).

How much it must have grieved Peter to remember that he not only denied his Lord but that he even denied him with cursing and swearing (Matt. 26:74). Perhaps that memory caused Peter to pray with David, "Set a guard, O Lord, over my mouth; keep watch over the door of my lips" (Ps. 141:3). Only the Lord has sufficient power to control our lips and guard them from every **unwholesome word**. The tongue, of course, only speaks what the heart tells it to say. "The mouth speaks out of that which fills the heart," Jesus said (Matt. 12:34; cf. Mark 7:14-23). A foul mouth comes from a foul heart, and the only way for the Lord to cleanse our tongue is through His Word, which fills the heart with "whatever is true, whatever is honorable, whatever is right, whatever is pure, whatever is lovely, whatever is of good repute," and all that is excellent and "worthy of praise" (Phil. 4:8).

In addition to renouncing corrupt and harmful language we are to develop speech that is pure, helpful, and pleasing to God. Paul here mentions three specific characteristics of wholesome speaking: it is edifying, appropriate, and gracious.

First, the words of a Christian are to be **good for edification**. Our speech should build up by being helpful, constructive, encouraging, instructive, and uplifting. Sometimes, of course, it must be corrective; but that, too, is edifying when done in the right spirit. Proverbs 25:12 admonishes: "Like an earring of gold and an ornament of fine gold is a wise reprover to a listening ear." The preacher of Ecclesiastes "sought to find delightful words and to write words of truth correctly," and such words spoken by a wise man "are like goads . . . and well-driven nails" (Eccles. 12:10-11).

Second, everything we say should be appropriate, **according to the need of the moment**. It is not that every word we speak is to be freighted with great significance, but that what we say should always be fitting for the situation, so that it constructively contributes to all. Obviously, we should never unnecessarily mention things that might harm, discourage, or disappoint someone else. Some things—though they may be absolutely true and perfectly wholesome—are better left unsaid. Everyone admires the wisdom and virtue of those who speak less often but usually say something of benefit. Proverbs 25:11 teaches: "Like apples of gold in settings of silver is a word spoken in right circumstances." Proverbs 15:23 affirms that "a man has joy in an apt answer, and how delightful is a timely word!" In fact, "He kisses the lips who gives a right answer" (Prov. 24:26).

Third, what we say should be gracious, **that it may give grace to those who hear**. As Paul has already said, the mature Christian not only speaks the truth but speaks it in love (v. 15). Raw truth is seldom appropriate and is often destructive. We have been saved in grace and we are kept in grace; therefore we are to live and speak in grace. Just as grace supremely characterizes God it should also characterize His children.

Graciousness always characterized Jesus. Isaiah said of the loveliness of the speech of Christ: "The Lord God has given Me the tongue of disciples, that I may know how to sustain the weary one with a word" (Isa. 50:4). On one occasion Luke records the effect of the Savior's words: "And all were speaking well of Him, and wondering at the gracious words which were falling from His lips" (Luke 4:22). A few moments later, the ones who spoke those words became enraged, took Jesus to the edge of the city, and would have thrown Him over the cliff to His death had He not disappeared from their midst (vv. 28-30). But Jesus had not become ungracious. Had the people admitted the truth He reminded them of about the spiritual rebelliousness of Israel, confessed that they themselves were guilty of the same sin, and accepted the fact of God's offering His grace to Gentiles, they would indeed have been edified and built up. Even telling men of their sin is a gracious thing to do, if it is done for the right purpose and in the right spirit, because until a person faces up to and repents of his sin he cannot experience the grace of salvation.

"Let your speech always be with grace," Paul told the Colossians, "seasoned, as it were, with salt" (Col. 4:6). Salt is a preservative and helps retard spoilage. The gracious words of Christians help retard the moral and spiritual spoilage in the world around them. They also provide strength and comfort to those in need. Our graciousness reflects the grace of Christ, who uses our graciousness to draw others to His grace.

A powerful motivation for putting off unwholesome talk is that not to do so will **grieve the Holy Spirit of God.** All sin is painful to God, but sin in His children breaks His heart. When His children refuse to change the ways of the old life for the ways of the new, God grieves. **The Holy Spirit of God** weeps, as it were, when he sees Christians lying instead of speaking the truth, becoming unrighteously rather than righteously angry, stealing instead of sharing, and speaking corrupt instead of uplifting and gracious words.

Whatever violates the will of God and the holiness of the heart will **grieve** the third Person of the Trinity. Grieving can lead to quenching (1 Thess. 5:19) and to a forfeiture of power and blessing. It should be noted also that such responses by the **Holy Spirit** indicate His personhood, which is seen in the use of personal pronouns referring to Him (cf. John 14:17; 16:13; etc.). His identity as Comforter, or Helper (John 14:16, 26; 15:26; 16:7), indicates that He is like Christ, who is a person. The **Holy Spirit** has intellect (1 Cor. 2:11), feelings (Rom. 8:27; 15:30), and will (1 Cor. 12:11). He works (1 Cor. 12:11), searches (1 Cor. 2:10), speaks (Acts 13:2), testifies (John 15:26), teaches (John 14:26), convicts (John 16:8-11), regenerates (John 3:5), intercedes (Acts 8:26), guides (John 16:13), glorifies Christ (John 16:14), and directs service to God (Acts 16:6-7).

Specifically in light of this text in Ephesians, the personhood of the **Holy Spirit** is seen in the fact that He can be treated as a person. He can be tested (Acts 5:9), lied to (Acts 5:3), resisted (Acts 7:51), insulted (Heb. 10:29), and blasphemed (Matt. 12:31-32).

Paul asks, in effect, "How can we do that which is so displeasing to the One **by whom [we] have been sealed for the day of redemption?"** (see 1:13-14). **The Holy Spirit** is God's personal mark of authenticity on us, His stamp of divine approval. How can we **grieve** the One who is our Helper, Comforter, Teacher, Advocate, Divine Resident of our hearts, and guarantor of our eternal redemption? How can we ungraciously grieve God's infinitely gracious **Holy Spirit?** He has done so much for us that, out of gratitude, we ought not to **grieve** Him.

The command not to show ingratitude to the Divine Spirit is based on the fact that He has secured our salvation. Paul is not saying we should avoid sin in order to keep our salvation, but rather that we should be eternally grateful to the **Holy Spirit** for His making it impossible for us to lose it.

From Natural Vices to Supernatural Virtues

Let all bitterness and wrath and anger and clamor and slander be put away from you, along with all malice. And be kind to one another, tender-hearted, forgiving each other, just as God in Christ also has forgiven you. (4:31-32)

The final change Paul mentions is from natural vices to supernatural virtues and amounts to a summary of the other changes.

Man's natural tendency is to sin, and the natural tendency of sin is to grow into greater sin. And a Christian's sin will grow just like that of an unbeliever. If not checked, our inner sins of **bitterness and wrath and anger** will inevitably lead to the outward sins of **clamor, slander,** and other such manifestations of **malice.**

Bitterness (*pikria*) reflects a smoldering resentment, a brooding grudge-filled attitude (see Acts 8:23; Heb. 12:15). It is the spirit of irritability that keeps a person in perpetual animosity, making him sour and venemous. **Wrath** (*thumos*) has to do with wild rage, the passion of the moment. **Anger** (*orgē*) is a more internal smoldering, a subtle and deep feeling. **Clamor** (*kraugē*) is the shout or outcry of strife and reflects the public outburst that reveals loss of control. **Slander** (*blasphēmia*, from which we get blasphemy) is the ongoing defamation of someone that rises from a bitter heart. Paul then adds **malice** (*kakia*), the general term for evil that is the root of all vices. All of these, he says, must **be put away from you.**

These particular sins involve conflict between person and person—believer and unbeliever and, worse still, between believer and believer. These are the sins that break fellowship and destroy relationships, that weaken the church and mar its testimony before the world. When an unbeliever sees Christians acting just like the rest of society, the church is blemished in his eyes and he is confirmed still further in resisting the claims of the gospel.

In place of those vices we are rather to **be kind to one another, tender-hearted, forgiving each other, just as God in Christ also has forgiven** us. These are graces God has shown to us and they are the gracious virtues we are to show to others. God did not love us, choose us, and redeem us because we were deserving, but purely because He is gracious. "God demonstrates His own love toward us, in that while we were yet sinners, Christ died for us. . . . While we were enemies, we were reconciled to God through the death of His Son" (Rom. 5:8, 10). If God is so gracious to us, how much more, then, should we **be kind, . . . tender-hearted,** and **forgiving** to fellow sinners, especially **to one another.**

Being unconditionally **kind** characterizes the Lord, as Luke 6:35b shows: "For He Himself is kind to ungrateful and evil men." Paul speaks of "the riches of His kindness . . . that leads you to repentance" (Rom. 2:4). We are to be like our heavenly Father, says Christ, and are to "love [our] enemies, and do good, and lend, expecting nothing in return; and [our] reward will be great, and [we] will be sons of the Most High" (Luke 6:35a).

Tender-hearted has the idea of being compassionate, and reflects a feeling deep in the bowels, or stomach, a gnawing psychosomatic pain due to empathy for someone's need. **Forgiving each other** is so basic to reflecting Christlike character that it needs little comment. The most graphic illustration of forgiveness is in the parable of Matthew 18:21-35. When Peter asked about the limits of forgiveness, the Lord told him a story of a man with an unpayable debt who was forgiven by his creditor, the king. This was a picture of salvation—God forgiving a sinner the unpayable debt of unrighteous rebellion against Him.

The forgiven man then went to someone who owed him a small amount and had him imprisoned for nonpayment. He who eagerly accepted a massive, comprehensive forgiveness would not forgive a small, easily-payable debt of another person. The incongruity of his action shows the heinousness of a believer's unforgiving heart, and the man was severely chastened by the Lord for his wicked attitude.

Paul has this same relationship in mind as he calls for believers to forgive **just as God in Christ also has forgiven you.** Can we who have been forgiven so much not forgive the relatively small things done against us? We, of all people, should always be eager to forgive.

The parallel text to this passage, found in Colossians 3:1-17, forms a fitting summation to Paul's teaching here.

> If then you have been raised up with Christ, keep seeking the things above, where Christ is, seated at the right hand of God. Set your mind on the things above, not on the things that are on earth. For you have died and your life is hidden with Christ in God. When Christ, who is our life, is revealed, then you also will be revealed with Him in Glory.
>
> Therefore consider the members of your earthly body as dead to immorality, impurity, passion, evil desire, and greed, which amounts to idolatry. For it is on account of these things that the wrath of God will come, and in them you also once walked, when you were living in them. But now you also, put them all aside: anger, wrath, malice, slander, and abusive speech from your mouth. Do not lie to one another, since you laid aside the old self with its evil practices, and have put on the new self who is being renewed to a true knowledge according to the image of the One who created him—a renewal in which there is no distinction between Greek and Jew, circumcised and uncircumcised, barbarian, Scythian, slave and freeman, but Christ is all, and in all.
>
> And so, as those who have been chosen of God, holy and beloved, put on a heart of compassion, kindness, humility, gentleness and patience; bearing with one another, and forgiving each other, whoever has a complaint against anyone, just as the Lord forgave you, so also should you. And beyond all these things put on love, which is the perfect bond of unity. And let the peace of Christ rule in your hearts, to which indeed you were called in one body; and be thankful. Let the word of Christ richly dwell within you, with all wisdom teaching and admonishing one another with psalms and hymns and spiritual songs, singing with thankfulness in your hearts to God. And whatever you do in word or deed, do all in the name of the Lord Jesus, giving thanks through Him to God the Father.

Walking in Love

15

Therefore be imitators of God, as beloved children; and walk in love, just as Christ also loved you, and gave Himself up for us, an offering and a sacrifice to God as a fragrant aroma. But do not let immorality or any impurity or greed even be named among you, as is proper among saints; and there must be no filthiness and silly talk, or coarse jesting, which are not fitting, but rather giving of thanks. For this you know with certainty, that no immoral or impure person or covetous man, who is an idolater, has an inheritance in the kingdom of Christ and God. Let no one deceive you with empty words, for because of these things the wrath of God comes upon the sons of disobedience. Therefore do not be partakers with them; (5:1-7)

In this passage Paul first presents the positive truths about true godly love and then the negative truths about Satan's counterfeit love and its consequences.

THE PLEA

Therefore be imitators of God, as beloved children; and walk in love, (5:1-2a)

The **walk** of the believer is a key matter to Paul. He has introduced the fact that ours is to be a worthy walk (4:1) and a walk different from the world's (4:17). He will also call for a walk in light (5:8) and a walk in wisdom (5:15). In this verse the apostle pleads with believers to **walk** in such a way that daily life is characterized by **love**. Growing in love is a continuing need for every believer, since love fulfills all of God's law (Rom. 13:8-10). As we grow in love we also see the need to be even more loving. And since biblically defined love is so contrary to the flesh, we are always in need of reminders and encouragement to love.

Therefore refers back to the last part of chapter 4, especially verse 32. Kindness, tender-heartedness, and forgiveness are characteristics of God, who is love. God Himself is infinitely kind, tender-hearted, and forgiving, and we achieve those virtues by imitating their Source.

Mimētēs (**imitator**) is the term from which we get *mimic,* someone who copies specific characteristics of another person. As **imitators of God**, Christians are to imitate God's characteristics, and above all His **love**. The whole of the Christian life is the reproduction of godliness as seen in the person of Christ. God's purpose in salvation is to redeem men from sin and to conform them "to the image of His Son" (Rom. 8:29). To be conformed to Christ is to become perfect, just as God is perfect (Matt. 5:48). "As obedient children," Peter tells us, "do not be conformed to the former lusts which were yours in your ignorance, but like the Holy One who called you, be holy yourselves also in all your behavior; because it is written, 'You shall be holy, for I am holy'" (1 Pet. 1:14-16; cf. Lev. 11:44). The great hope of believers is, "We know that, when He appears, we shall be like Him, because we shall see Him just as He is" (1 John 3:2). Imitating His **love** is possible because "the love of God has been poured out within our hearts through the Holy Spirit who was given to us" (Rom. 5:5).

When Alexander the Great discovered a coward in his army who also was named Alexander, he told the soldier, "Renounce your cowardice or renounce your name." Those who carry God's name are to **be imitator's** of His character. By His grace it is possible to reflect Him even in our present limitations.

To know what God is like we must study His Word, His revelation of Himself, His great Self-disclosure. Yet the more we learn of God's character the more we learn how far above us He is and how impossible in ourselves it is fulfill the command to be like Him, to be absolutely perfect, just as He is. That is why we need "to be strengthened with power through His Spirit in the inner man" in order to "be filled up to all the fulness of God" (Eph. 3:16, 19). The only way we can become **imitators of God** is for the Lord Jesus Christ to live His perfect life through us. We are totally dependent on His Spirit to become like Him. If we are to obey Paul's admonition to the Corinthians, "let all that you do be done in love" (1 Cor. 16:14), we must submit to the controlling influence of the Spirit.

It is natural for **children** to be like their parents. They have their parents' nature and they instinctively imitate their parents' actions and behavior. Through Jesus Christ God has given us the right to become His children (John 1:12; Gal. 3:26). As Paul declared at the beginning of this letter, God "predestined us to adoption as sons through Jesus Christ to Himself, according to the kind intention of His will" (Eph. 1:5). Because our heavenly Father is holy, we are to be holy. Because He is kind, we are to be kind. Because He is forgiving, we are to be forgiving. Because God in Christ humbled Himself, we are to humble ourselves. Because God is love, as His **beloved children** we are to **walk in love**. This ability is not natural, however, but supernatural—requiring a new nature and the continuous power of the Holy Spirit flowing through us by obedience to God's Word.

The greatest evidence of love is undeserved forgiveness. The supreme act of God's love was to give "His only begotten Son, that whoever believes in Him should not perish, but have eternal life" (John 3:16). God's love brought man's forgiveness. God loved the world with such a great love that He offered forgiveness to sinful, rebellious, wretched, vile mankind, by sending His own Son to give His life on the cross that they might not suffer death. He offered the world the free gift of eternal fellowship with Him.

Because forgiveness is the supreme evidence of God's love, it will also be the most convincing proof of our love. Love will always lead us to forgive others just as love led God in Christ to forgive us (Eph. 4:32). Nothing more clearly discloses a hard, loveless heart than lack of forgiveness. Lack of forgiveness betrays lack of love (see 4:31). The presence of forgiveness always proves the presence of love, because only love has the motive and power to forgive. The extent of our love is the extent of our ability to forgive.

Whatever another believer may do against us, no matter how terrible or destructive or unjustified, Christ has paid the penalty for that sin. No matter how others may hurt, slander, persecute, or in any way harm us, Christ's sacrifice was sufficient to pay their penalty. When a Christian expresses, or even harbors, vengeance toward a brother, he not only sins by allowing selfish hatred to control him but he sins by profaning Christ's sacrifice—by seeking to mete out punishment for a sin whose penalty has already been paid by his Lord.

Because Christ has paid the penalty for every sin, we have no right to hold any sin against any person, even a nonbeliever. Peter thought that forgiving someone "up to seven times" was generous. But Jesus said, "I do not say to you, up to seven times, but up to seventy times seven" (Matt. 18:22). In Christ *all* our "sins are forgiven for His name's sake" (1 John 2:12); He has "forgiven us *all* our transgressions" (Col. 2:13, emphasis added). "In Him we have redemption through His blood, the forgiveness of our trespasses, according to the riches of His grace" (Eph. 1:7).

Just as the depth of God's love is shown by how much He has forgiven, the depth of our love is shown by how much we forgive. "Above all," Peter says, "keep fervent in your love for one another, because love covers a multitude of sins" (1 Pet. 4:8). The Greek word behind "fervent" refers to a muscle stretched to the limit. Our love is to stretch to the limit in order to cover "a multitude of sins." The greater our love the greater the multitude of sins it will cover in forgiveness.

The depth of our love is also shown by how much we know we have been forgiven. When Jesus was eating dinner with Simon the Pharisee, a prostitute came into the house and anointed Jesus' feet with her tears and with expensive perfume. Simon was incensed at what she did and was disappointed in Jesus for allowing such a woman to touch Him. Jesus responded by telling a parable: "'A certain moneylender had two debtors: one owed five hundred denarii, and the other fifty. When they were unable to repay, he graciously forgave them both. Which of them therefore will love him more?' Simon answered and said, 'I suppose the one whom he forgave more.' And He said to him, 'You have judged correctly.'" After comparing the ways that Simon and the woman had treated Him, Jesus said, "For this reason I say to you, her sins, which are many, have been forgiven, for she loved much; but he who is forgiven little, loves little" (Luke 7:36-47).

Because Simon had no real sense of the enormity of the sin in his own life, and therefore sensed no need for forgiveness, he was unforgiving of others—especially those whom he considered moral and social outcasts. Unforgiveness is the measure of self-righteousness just as forgiveness is the measure of love. Our ability to love, and therefore to forgive, depends on our sense of how much God has forgiven us. Unforgiveness is also a measure of unbelief, because the person who feels no need for forgiveness feels no need for God.

Robert Falconer tells the story of his witnessing among destitute people in a certain city and of reading them the story of the woman who wiped Jesus' feet with her tears. While he was reading he heard a loud sob and looked up at a young, thin girl whose face was disfigured by smallpox. After he spoke a few words of encouragement to her, she said, "Will He ever come again, the One who forgave the woman? I have heard that He will come again. Will it be soon?" "He could come any time. But why do you ask?" Falconer replied. After sobbing again uncontrollably, she said, "Sir, can't He wait a little while? My hair ain't long enough yet to wipe His feet."

The person who sees the greatness of his own forgiveness by God's love will himself in love be forgiving. He forgives in love because his heavenly Father has forgiven in love and he desires to be an imitator of His Father.

THE PATTERN

just as Christ also loved you, and gave Himself up for us, an offering and a sacrifice to God as a fragrant aroma. (5:2b)

A young child often learns to draw by tracing. The more carefully he traces, the truer the likeness of his copy is to the original.

The pattern for Christian living is **Christ** Himself, the one by whom every believer is to trace his life. The great difference between this tracing and that of a young child learning to draw is that we will never have a time when Christ will cease to be our pattern. And we will never be "on our own," sufficiently skilled in ourselves to live as He lived. In fact, our part is not so much to pattern our lives ourselves as to allow God's Spirit to pattern us after His Son. Second Corinthians 3:18 expresses this profound truth in magnificent terms: "But we all, with unveiled face beholding as in a mirror the glory of the Lord, are being transformed into the same image from glory to glory, just as from the Lord, the Spirit."

The summum bonum of **Christ** that we are to imitate is His love. He **loved us and gave Himself up for us.** Giving of oneself to others is the epitome of *agapē* love. Biblical love is not a pleasant emotion or good feeling about someone, but the giving of oneself for his welfare (cf. 1 John 3:16). Divine love is unconditional love, love that depends entirely on the one who loves and not on the merit, attractiveness, or response of the one loved. **Christ** did not simply have a deep feeling and emotional concern for mankind. Nor did He sacrifice Himself for us because we were deserving (cf. Rom. 5:8, 10). "While we were yet sinners," He **gave Himself us for us** purely out of sovereign, gracious love, taking our sin upon Himself and paying its penalty in our behalf.

God's love, and all love that is like His, loves for the sake of giving, not getting. With conditional love, if the conditions are not met there is no obligation to love. If we do not get, we do not give. But God's makes no conditions for His love to us and commands that we love others without conditions. There is no way to earn God's love or to deserve it by reason of human goodness.

Romantic, emotional love between husband and wife ebbs and flows, and sometimes disappears altogether. But loss of romantic love is never an appropriate excuse for dissolving a marriage, because the love that God specifically commands husbands to have for their wives is *agapē* love (Eph. 5:25; 3:19; cf. Titus 2:4; etc.)— love like His own undeserved love for us, love that is based on willful choice in behalf of the one loved, regardless of emotions, attraction, or deserving. Romantic love enhances and beautifies the relationship between husband and wife, but the binding force of a Christian marriage is God's own kind of love, the love that loves because it is the divine nature to love. It is the love of giving, not of getting; and even when it ceases to get, it continues to give. Where there is the sacrificial love of willful choice, there is also likely to be the love of intimacy, feeling, and friendship (*philia*).

God loved us while we were still sinners and enemies, and He continues to love us as believers, even though we continue to sin and fall short of His perfection and His glory. He loves us when we forget Him, when we disobey Him, when we deny Him, when we fail to return His love, and when we grieve His Holy Spirit. When Jude said, "Keep yourselves in the love of God" (Jude 21), he was indicating the responsibility to stay in the place where that divine love sheds its blessing.

Those who are given God's nature through Jesus Christ are commanded to love as God loves. In Christ, it is now *our* nature to love just as it is God's nature to love—because His nature is now our nature. For a Christian not to love is for him to live against his own nature as well as against God's.

Lovelessness is therefore more than a failure or shortcoming. It is sin, willful disobedience of God's command and disregard of His example. To love as

God loves is to love *because* God loves, because we are to "be imitators of God, as beloved children" and because **Christ also loved** [us], **and gave Himself up for us, an offering and a sacrifice to God.**

God's love not only is forgiving and unconditional but is also self-sacrificing. Therefore to love as God loves is to love sacrificially, to love by the giving of ourselves as He **gave Himself.**

The Christian's walk in love is to extend to every person, believer and unbeliever. If God's love can reach out even to His enemies, how can we refuse to love our enemies? If He loves His imperfect children with a perfect love, how can we not love fellow believers, whose imperfections we share? And if divine love led Christ to sacrifice Himself for unworthy and ungrateful sinners, how can we not give ourselves to fellow sinful people, unbelievers as well as believers, in His name?

Shortly before His betrayal and arrest, Jesus was having supper with His disciples. During the meal the disciples began arguing among themselves as to which was the greatest. Their Lord was facing His ultimate humiliation and affliction, and yet their only concern was for themselves, for their own prestige, rank, and glory. When the Lord most needed their comfort, encouragement, and support, they acted as if He were not with them. All their attention was focused selfishly on themselves (Luke 22:24).

It was then that Jesus picked up a basin of water and began washing their feet, a task usually reserved for the lowest of servants. Despite their callous lack of concern for His impending suffering and death, Jesus humbly, forgivingly, unconditionally, and self-sacrificially ministered to them. After He finished washing their feet and returned to the supper table, "He said to them, 'Do you know what I have done to you? You call Me Teacher and Lord; and you are right, for so I am. If I then, the Lord and the Teacher, washed your feet, you also ought to wash one another's feet. For I gave you an example that you also should do as I did to you. Truly, truly, I say to you, a slave is not greater than his master; neither is one who is sent greater than the one who sent him" (John 13:12-16). Later He commanded them to love in this same manner (John 13:34-35).

Christ's giving **Himself up for us, an offering and a sacrifice to God** was a **fragrant aroma** to His heavenly Father because that sacrifice demonstrated in the fullest and most ultimate way God's kind of love. The words for us indicate the personal expression of love directed at all who believe. (This does not limit the provision of the atonement only to believers, as other Scriptures make clear. See John 1:29; 3:15-16; Rom. 10:13; 2 Cor. 5:14; 1 Tim. 2:4, 6; 4:10; 2 Pet. 2:1; 1 John 2:2; 4:14.)

The first five chapters of Leviticus describe five offerings commanded by God of the Israelites. The first three were the burnt offering, the meal offering, and the peace offering. The burnt offering (Lev. 1:1-17) depicted Christ's total devotion to God in giving His very life to obey and please His Father; the meal (grain) offering (Lev. 2:1-16) depicted Christ's perfection, and the peace offering (Lev. 3:1-17; 4:27-31) depicted His making peace between God and man. All of those offerings obviously spoke of what was pleasing to God. Of each, the Scripture says it provided a "soothing aroma to the Lord" (Lev. 1:9, 13, 17; 2:2, 9, 12; 3:5, 16). Philippians 4:18 explains that the fragrant aroma meant the sacrifice was "acceptable, . . . well-pleasing to God." But the other two offerings—the sin (Lev. 4:1-26, 32-35) and the trespass (Lev. 5:1-19) offerings—were repulsive to God, because, though they depicted Christ, they depicted Him as bearing the sin of mankind. They depicted the Father's turning His back on the Son when "He made Him who knew no sin to be sin on our behalf" (2 Cor. 5:21), at which time Jesus exclaimed from the cross, "My God, My God, why hast Thou forsaken Me?" (Matt. 27:46).

While Christ was the sin-bearer, God could not look on Him or rejoice in Him or be pleased in Him. But when the Father raised Christ from the dead, the sacrifice that caused Him to become sin became the sacrifice that conquered sin. The sin that put Him to death was itself put to death, and that great act of love was **to God as a fragrant aroma.** That **fragrant aroma** spreads its fragrance to everyone on earth who will place himself under the grace of that sacrifice, and it will spread its fragrance throughout heaven for all eternity. In all aspects, our lives should please God (cf. 2 Cor. 2:14-16).

THE PERVERSION

But do not let immorality or any impurity or greed even be named among you, as is proper among saints; and there must be no filthiness and silly talk, or coarse jesting, which are not fitting, but rather giving of thanks. (5:3-4)

Whatever God establishes, Satan will counterfeit. Where God establishes true love, Satan produces counterfeit love. Counterfeit love characterizes Satan's children, those who are of the world, just as true love characterizes God's children, those who are citizens of heaven.

In contrast to godly, unselfish, forgiving love, the world's love is lustful and self-indulgent. It loves because the object of love is attractive, enjoyable, pleasant, satisfying, appreciative, loves in return, produces desired feelings, or is likely to repay in some way. It is always based on the other person's fulfilling one's own needs and desires and meeting one's own expectations. Worldly love is reciprocal, giving little in the expectation of getting much. Speaking of that kind of love, Jesus said, "For if you love those who love you, what reward have you? Do not even the tax-gatherers do the same?" (Matt. 5:46).

The world claims to want love, and love is advocated and praised from every corner. Romantic love especially is touted. Songs, novels, movies, and television serials continually exploit emotional, lustful desire as if it were genuine love. Questing for and fantasizing about the "perfect love" is portrayed as the ultimate human experience.

It should not be surprising that the misguided quest for that kind of love leads inevitably to **immorality** and **impurity,** because that kind of love is selfish and destructive, a deceptive counterfeit of God's love. It is always conditional and is always self-centered. It is not concerned about commitment but only satisfaction; it is not concerned about giving but only getting. It has no basis for permanence because its purpose is to use and to exploit rather than to serve and to help. It lasts until the one loved no longer satisfies or until he or she disappears for someone else.

Porneia (**immorality**) refers to all sexual sin, and all sexual sin is against God and against godly love. It is the antonym of *enkrateia,* which refers to self-control, especially in the area of sex. When Paul spoke before Felix and his wife Drusilla, "discussing righteousness, self-control and the judgment to come, Felix became frightened and said, 'Go away for the present, and when I find time, I will summon you'" (Acts 24:24-25). Felix had stolen Drusilla from her former husband and was therefore living with her in an adulterous relationship. The sexual self-control of which Paul spoke pertained to lustful passion, as Felix understood. The message to the governor was that he was living contrary to God's righteousness by refusing to discipline his sexual desire, and for that he was subject to God's judgment.

Loss of sexual self-control leads to its opposite, which is **immorality** and **impurity.** *Akatharsia* (**impurity**) is a more general term than *porneia,* referring to anything that is unclean and filthy. Jesus used the word to describe the rottenness of decaying bodies in a tomb (Matt. 23:27). The other ten times the word is used in the New Testament it is associated with sexual sin. It refers to immoral thoughts, passions, ideas, fantasies, and every other form of sexual corruption.

Contemporary sex madness has even found its way into the church. The influence of the lustful world has been so pervasive and the church so weak and undiscerning that many Christians have become convinced that all sorts of sexual excesses and impurities are covered by grace or can be rendered morally safe if engaged in with the right attitude—especially if some Scripture verse can be twisted to give seeming support. But **immorality** and **impurity** cannot be sanctified or modified into anything better than what they are, which is wickedness—a crime against the holy God and the loving Savior. In 1 Corinthians 5:1-5 and 6:13-20 Paul shows that there is no place for that in the Christian life.

As mentioned under the discussion of Ephesians 4:19, **greed** is inseparable from **impurity.** Every form of sexual immorality is an expression of the self-will, self-gratification, and self-centeredness of **greed.** It is by nature contrary to love, which is self-giving. **Immorality** and **impurity** are but forms of **greed** in the realm of sexual sin. They are manifestations of sexual covetousness and express counterfeit love (which is really hate, since love seeks the purity of others and is unselfish), masquerading as something beautiful, good, and rewarding. Because those sins seem so attractive and promising, spouses are forsaken, children are neglected, homes are destroyed, friends are disregarded, as no effort is spared to fulfill the desire to have the one who is lusted after—all of that in the name of love.

Because of the strong sexual nature of human beings, sexual sins are powerful and can become perverted in unimaginable ways. If given free rein, sexual sins lead to complete insensitivity to the feelings and welfare of others, to horrible brutality, and frequently to murder—as news stories testify daily.

That is why the sins of **immorality or any impurity or greed** should not **even be named among** Christians, **as is proper among saints.** Those sins cannot in any way be justified, and they should not in any way be tolerated. The meaning of **saints** is "holy ones," and those who are holy have nothing to do with that which is unholy.

Paul continues his warning against this perversion of love by mentioning an extensive list of related sins that is sure to cover every believer at one time or another. Not only should Christians never engage in sexual sins of any kind, but they should never be guilty of **filthiness and silly talk, or coarse jesting**.

Filthiness has to do with general obscenity, any talk that is degrading and disgraceful. It comes from the same Greek root as "disgraceful" in verse 12, where Paul says that such vile things should not even be mentioned, much less participated in, and is related to the term in Colossians 3:8, meaning "dirty speech."

Mōrologia (**silly talk**) used only here in the New Testament, is derived from *mōros* (which means dull, or stupid, and is the word from which we get moron) and *legō* (to speak). It is stupid talk, talk only befitting someone who is intellectually deficient. It is sometimes referred to as low obscenity, foolish talk that comes from the drunk or the gutter mouth. It has no point except to give an air of dirty worldliness.

Eutrapelia (**coarse jesting**), on the other hand, refers to talk that is more pointed and determined. It carries the idea of quickly turning something that is said or done—no matter how innocent—into that which is obscene or suggestive. It is the filthy talk of a person who uses every word and circumstance to display his immoral wit. It is the stock-in-trade of the clever talk-show host who is never at a loss for sexual innuendo. But the low obscenity of **silly talk** and the "high" obscenity of **coarse jesting** come from the same kind of heart, the heart given over to moral **filthiness**.

In light of such clear teaching of God's Word, it is strange that so many Christians not only discuss but laugh and joke with impunity about almost every form of sexual intimacy, corruption, and perversion. But God's standard is clear: **there must be no filthiness and silly talk, or coarse jesting, which are not fitting**.

Instead of being involved in immorality or filthy speaking, the believer's mouth should be involved in the **giving of thanks**. Thanksgiving is an expression of unselfishness. The selfish and unloving person does not give thanks because he thinks he deserves whatever good thing he receives. The unselfish and loving person, on the other hand, focuses his life and his concern on the needs of others. Whatever good thing he receives from God or from other people he counts as undeserved and gracious. He is always thankful because his spirit is one of loving and of giving. Instead of using others, he serves them. Instead of trying to turn the innocent into the immoral, he seeks to change the immoral into what is righteous and holy. He is thankful because the holy life is the satisfying life, and people see love for God in the thankful person.

If Christians are known for anything it should be for love expressed toward God and others by unceasing thankfulness (cf. 1 Thess. 5:18, where the injunction is clear: "In everything give thanks; for this is God's will for you in Christ Jesus").

THE PUNISHMENT

For this you know with certainty, that no immoral or impure person or covetous man, who is an idolater, has an inheritance in the kingdom of Christ and God. Let no one deceive you with empty words, for because of these things the wrath of God comes upon the sons of disobedience. Therefore do not be partakers with them; (5:5-7)

It is clear that Paul is restating a truth he had taught the Ephesians many times while he pastored among them and, no doubt, one that others had reinforced. **For this you know with certainty,** he said. There should have been no doubt or confusion in their minds about what he was about to say, because it was nothing new.

God does not tolerate sin, and perverted love leads to punishment. Sin has no place in His kingdom and no place in His family. **Immoral, impure,** and **covetous** are from the same basic Greek words as *immorality, impurity* and *greed* in verse 3. Covetousness is a form of idolatry. The **covetous man,** therefore, is more than simply selfish and immoral; he is **an idolater** (cf. Col. 3:5).

Persons who are characterized by the sins Paul has just condemned in verses 3 and 4 will have no **inheritance in the kingdom of Christ and God.** No person whose life pattern is one of habitual immorality, impurity, and greed can be a part of God's **kingdom,** because no such person can belong to Him. Such would contradict the truths of Romans 6 and 2 Corinthians 5:17, as well as the instruction of 1 John regarding the characteristics of believers. The life described here testifies to an unredeemed, sinful nature—no matter what relationship to Christ a person might claim to have. God's children have God's nature, and the habitually sinful person proves that he does not have a godly nature (1 John 3:9-10). **The kingdom of Christ and God** refers to the sphere of salvation, the community of the redeemed and the place of eternal glory. The **kingdom** is the rule **of Christ and God,** which includes the present church, the future Millennium, and the eternal state in glory.

"For the grace of God has appeared, bringing salvation to all men, instructing us to deny ungodliness and worldly desires and to live sensibly, righteously and godly in the present age" (Titus 2:11-12). Every person who is saved, and is therefore a part of that glorious rule of **Christ and God,** is instructed by the Holy Spirit and by the inclination of his new nature to forsake sin and to seek righteousness. The person whose basic life pattern does not reflect that orientation cannot claim God as his Father or **the kingdom of Christ and God** as his **inheritance.**

It is dangerously deceptive for Christians to try to give assurance of salvation to someone who has no biblical grounds for such assurance. In his first letter to the church at Corinth, Paul gives an even more detailed listing of sins whose habitual practice proves a person is not saved and has no claim on God. "Do you not know that the unrighteous shall not inherit the kingdom of God? Do not be deceived; neither fornicators, nor idolaters, nor adulterers, nor effeminate, nor homosexuals, nor thieves, nor the covetous, nor drunkards, nor revilers, nor swindlers, shall inherit the kingdom of God" (1 Cor. 6:9-10). Such things do not characterize the children of God (cf. Gal. 5:17-21 for a similar insight). The verdict of God is that, no matter what may be the claim, a life dominated by sin like this is damned to hell.

People will try to deny that, but Paul warns not to listen to them. **Let no one deceive you with empty words,** telling you that sin is tolerable and that God will not exclude unrepentant sinners from His kingdom. **Empty words** are full of error, devoid of truth, and therefore they **deceive.**

It is **because of these things,** that is, because of the sins listed here and the lies of **empty words,** that **the wrath of God comes upon the sons of disobedience.** Such people are called **sons of disobedience** (see also 2:2) because it is their nature is to disobey and they are "children of wrath" (2:3; cf. 2 Thess. 1:8-10), the targets for God's guns of judgment.

God's attitude toward perverted love and sexual sin is seen clearly in Numbers 25:1-9, where the Israelites had relations with Moabite women and God slaughtered 24,000 of them. His attitude toward sexual sin has not changed, and perverted love attracts God's wrath like a fully-lit city attracts enemy bombers.

In a final warning, Paul says, **Therefore do not be partakers with them.** "Don't join the world in its evil," he says. "Don't be partners with them in wickedness. Be partners with Christ in righteousness. Don't imitate the world, but rather be imitators of God, as beloved children" (v. 1).

Living in Light

16

for you were formerly darkness, but now you are light in the Lord; walk as children of light (for the fruit of the light consists in all goodness and righteousness and truth), trying to learn what is pleasing the Lord. And do not participate in the unfruitful deeds of darkness, but instead even expose them; for it is disgraceful even to speak of the things which are done by them in secret. But all things become visible when they are exposed by the light, for everything that becomes visible is light. For this reason it says, "Awake, sleeper, and arise from the dead, and Christ will shine on you." (5:8-14)

This passage continues the emphasis on believers' being "imitators of God, as beloved children" (5:1). The first way we are to imitate God is in His love, which Paul shows both in its true and in its counterfeit forms, with Christ Himself being our divine pattern (vv. 2-7). In verses 8-14 the focus is on our imitating God in relation to light.

Scripture speaks of God as our "light and . . . salvation" (Ps. 27:1) and as "an everlasting light" (Isa. 60:19). His Word is called "a lamp to [our] feet, and a light to [our] path" (Ps. 119:105; cf. v. 130). Christ is called "a light of the nations" (Isa. 49:6), "the true light which . . . enlightens every man" (John 1:9), and "the light of the world" (John 8:12). For a believer to imitate God, therefore, he obviously must share in and reflect God's light.

In Scripture the figurative use of light has two aspects, the intellectual and the moral. Intellectually it represents truth, whereas morally it represents holiness. To live in light therefore means to live in truth and in holiness. The figure of darkness has the same two aspects. Intellectually it represents ignorance and falsehood, whereas morally it connotes evil.

The intellectual aspect of both figures pertains to what a person knows and believes, and the moral aspect pertains to way he thinks and acts. In 2 Corinthians Paul speaks about the intellectual aspect when he says, "The god of this world has blinded the minds of the unbelieving, that they might not see the light of the gospel of the glory of Christ, who is the image of God" (4:4; cf. Rom. 1:21; Eph. 4:18). In Isaiah 5 the prophet speaks of both the intellectual and the moral aspects when he says, "Woe to those who call evil good, and good evil; who substitute darkness for light and light for darkness" (v. 20). Both the teaching and the practice of those people were corrupt. Paul speaks of the moral aspect when he pleads with believers to "lay aside the deeds of darkness and put on the armor of light" (Rom. 13:12), and in the following verse he specifies some of the deeds of darkness: carousing, drunkenness, sexual promiscuity, sensuality, strife, and jealousy.

But everyone who belongs to God walks in light, both intellectually and morally. "This is the message we have heard from Him and announce to you," John said unequivocally, "that God is light, and in Him there is no darkness at all. If we say that we have fellowship with Him and yet walk in the darkness, we lie and do not practice the truth; but if we walk in the light as He Himself is in the light, we have fellowship with one another, and the blood of Jesus His Son cleanses us from all sin" (1 John 1:5-7).

In verses 8-14 Paul mentions five practical features we should recognize in order to faithfully walk in God's light. He gives the contrasts, characteristics, command, commission, and call of Christians as God's own children of light.

THE CONTRAST

for you were formerly darkness, but now you are light in the Lord; walk as children of light (5:8)

Paul here contrasts what every believer's life was like before salvation with what God intends it to be like after salvation. In doing so he simply states what should be obvious: A person who has been saved from sin should be through with sin and should live as a redeemed and purified child of God. To illustrate that point the apostle uses the common biblical figures of **darkness** and **light**.

WHAT WE WERE

The verb form of **were** reveals two important realities. First, the past tense indicates a condition that no longer exists, and that truth is reinforced by **formerly**.

Earlier in the letter, Paul says that we *"were* dead in [our] trespasses and sins," that we *"formerly* walked according to the course of this world, according to the prince of the power of the air," and that "we too all *formerly* lived in the lusts of our flesh, indulging the desires of the flesh and of the mind, and *were* by nature children of wrath, even as the rest" (2:1-3, emphasis added). For Christians, both intellectual and moral **darkness** are a thing of the past (cf. 4:17-20).

Second, the verb is not modified by a pronoun, such as *in* or *of.* In other places Scripture speaks of a person's being in or of darkness, but here it says we *were . . . darkness.* Before we came to Christ our total existence—our being as well as our behavior—was characterized by darkness. Their was no other aspect to our spiritual life than that of darkness. We were children of darkness and "sons of disobedience" (Eph. 5:6). We were not simply victims of Satan's system but were contributors to it. We were not merely in sin; our very nature was characterized by sin.

Scripture gives four basic characteristics of that spiritual **darkness.** First, it is the work of Satan. Those who are not the children of God are the children of their "father the devil, and [they] want to do the desires of [their] father," who "was a murderer from the beginning, and does not stand in the truth, because there is no truth in him" (John 8:44; cf. vv. 38, 41).

It is difficult even for Christians to imagine that the law-abiding, decent, and pleasant unbelievers we run into every day are children of Satan. Yet every person is either a child of the devil or a child of God. There are no other kinds of spiritual childhood, although there obviously are degrees in both kinds as far as life-style is concerned. But the unbelieving, well-dressed, sophisticated philanthropist will spend eternity apart from God in the same hell as the demon-serving witch doctor.

Second, spiritual darkness not only is the work but the domain of Satan. The unbeliever does Satan's work because he is under Satan's control (in Luke 22:53 he is called "the power of darkness") as a citizen of his "dominion of darkness" (Col. 1:13; cf. Eph. 6:12; 1 John 5:19). That is why it is so foolish for people to reject the claims of the gospel because they imagine they would have to give up their freedom and come into a forced and unwanted obedience to God. One of Satan's most deceptive and destructive lies is the idea that a person apart from God is free. The unbeliever is totally bound and imprisoned by Satan through sin. He cannot do anything but sin and he cannot obey anyone but Satan. Fallen man thinks he is free only because what he wants so closely agrees with what Satan wants. But the believer's obedience is the deepest desire of his heart (cf. Rom. 6:17-18, 22; 7:22; Ps. 119).

Third, spiritual darkness brings God's penalty. As Paul has just declared, "the wrath of God comes upon the sons of disobedience" (Eph. 5:6), who are "by nature children of wrath" (2:3). In the book of Romans he says, "The wrath of God is revealed from heaven against all ungodliness and unrighteousness of men, who suppress the truth in unrighteousness" (1:18).

Fourth, spiritual darkness leads to the ultimate destiny of eternal darkness.

Those who do not believe in Jesus Christ as Lord and Savior, whether they are Jew or Gentile, "shall be cast out into the outer darkness; in that place there shall be weeping and gnashing of teeth" (Matt. 8:12; cf. 1 Sam. 2:9; 2 Pet. 2:17). Those who reject Christ do so because they are content with darkness. And because they *choose* darkness rather than light, they will forever *have* darkness rather than light. Eternity simply crystallizes the choice into permanence.

That the world is confused, unjust, wicked, corrupt, and hopeless is testified to by every sensible observer, believer and unbeliever alike. There is constant compulsion to deceive, lie, steal, commit immorality, kill, and to do every other kind of evil. Just as obvious as the world's propensity to sin is the inescapable reality that reality cannot be found where men keep looking for it. Yet when God's supreme reality is offered in Jesus Christ, men turn away because the reality of His righteousness and goodness also reveals the reality of their own sin and wickedness. Jesus said, "And this is the judgment, that the light is come into the world, and men loved the darkness rather than the light; for their deeds were evil. For everyone who does evil hates the light, and does not come to the light, lest his deeds should be exposed. But he who practices the truth comes to the light, that his deeds may be manifested as having been wrought by God" (John 3:19-21).

It is as if a person were lost in an abandoned mine. The more he tries to find his way out, the farther he goes into the mine. Every tunnel he takes leads either to a dead end or to another tunnel. He has no idea where he is or which way to go. His eyes are wide open but all he can see is oppressive blackness. After a week of groping about the cold, dirty tunnels and shafts he notices a faint light. With all his remaining energy he makes his way toward that light and eventually finds his way to the outside. But because the light is so bright and hurts his eyes, he begins to wonder if he is really better off. He remembers a few things in the mine that gave him temporary enjoyment by distracting his attention from his plight. And he goes back into the mine to live.

That story, strange and unlikely as it is, is repeated countless times every day in an infinitely more tragic way—as people see the gospel of light and life and turn back to the old way of darkness and death.

WHAT WE ARE

The second verb in verse 8 (**are**) also tells us two important things. The present tense indicates our new spiritual condition, in contrast to what we were before trusting Christ. **Now [we] are light in the Lord.** Christ "delivered us from the domain of darkness, and transferred us to the kingdom of His beloved Son" (Col. 1:13), and He has "called [us] out of darkness into His marvelous light" (1 Pet. 2:9).

Like **were**, the verb **are** is not modified. Scripture sometimes speaks of believers being in and of the light, but here we are said to *be* light. "You *are* the light of the world," Jesus said (Matt. 5:14). Because we now share Christ's own nature, we share in His light. Just as He is the "light of the world" (John 8:12), His people are also "the light of the world" (Matt. 5:14). Because we are *in the Lord,* we who were once children of darkness are now *children of light,* and it is as such children that we should *walk.*

THE CHARACTERISTICS

(for the fruit of the light consists in all goodness and righteousness and truth), trying to learn what is pleasing the Lord. (5:9-10)

In what appears to be a parenthetical statement, the manifest characteristics of the children of light are given in what Paul here calls **the fruit of the light**. (The better Greek manuscripts have "the fruit of the light," as here, rather than "the fruit of the Spirit," as in the Authorized Version.) The three supreme characteristics, or **fruit**, of our walk as children of light are **all goodness and righteousness and truth**.

These are the tests of true faith, of a true saving relationship to the Lord Jesus Christ. A "decision" for Christ, church membership, faithful attendance at worship services, being baptized, financial support of the Lord's work, and many other such things are often used as evidence of salvation. The faithful Christian should do all of those things, but they are behaviors that are easily done in the flesh and are therefore unreliable in themselves as evidence. On the other hand, the three characteristics Paul mentions here are spiritual works that cannot be achieved in the flesh. The **all** reflects the perfection of the divine standard.

The first characteristic is **all goodness** (cf. "all malice" in 4:31). A number of Greek words are translated "good" or "goodness" in the New Testament. *Kalos* denotes that which is intrinsically right, free from defects, beautiful, and honorable. Both John the Baptist and Jesus used the term for the "good fruit" without which a tree "is cut down and thrown into the fire" (Matt. 3:10; 7:19). Paul uses the term when he tells Timothy that "everything created by God is good" (1 Tim. 4:4). It is also used of that which is morally good (see Gal. 4:18; 1 Tim. 5:10, 25; Titus 2:7, 14). *Chrēstos,* also often translated "good," refers to that which is pleasant, useful, suitable, or worthy. Paul uses this word when he declares that "bad company corrupts good morals" (1 Cor. 15:33).

But in the present passage Paul uses *agathōsunē,* which refers to moral excellence, to being good in both nature and effectiveness. Like *agapē* love, *agathōsunē* **goodness** finds its fullest and highest expression in that which is willingly and sacrificially done for others. "Always seek after that which is *good* for one another and for all men," Paul told the Thessalonians (1 Thess. 5:15). In his next letter to that church the apostle prays "that our God may count you worthy of your calling, and fulfill every desire for *goodness* and the work of faith with power" (2 Thess. 1:11, emphasis added). This **goodness** that is a **fruit of light** is also a fruit of the Spirit (Gal. 5:22).

The second result, or **fruit**, of our walk as children of light is **righteousness** and has to do first of all with our relationship to God. "To the one who does not work, but believes in Him who justifies the ungodly, his faith is reckoned as righteousness" (Rom. 4:5; cf. Eph. 4:24; Phil. 3:9). But **righteousness** also has to do with how we live. Those who are made righteous are commanded to live righteously, to present themselves "to God as those alive from the dead, and [their] members as instruments of righteousness to God" (Rom. 6:13). Because Christ has given us His own righteous nature, we are to "pursue righteousness" (1 Tim. 6:11). Because we know that Christ is righteous, John says, we also "know that everyone also who practices righteousness is born of Him" (1 John 2:29).

The third **fruit of the light** is **truth. Truth** has to do with honesty, reliability, trustworthiness, and integrity—in contrast to the hypocritical, deceptive, and false ways of the old life of darkness.

We see therefore that **goodness** pertains primarily to our relationship with others, **righteousness** primarily to our relationship to God, and **truth** primarily to personal integrity. In those three things and in those three ways **the fruit of the light consists.**

Without that **fruit** there is no evidence of the life of God. "Beware of the false prophets, who come to you in sheep's clothing," Jesus warned, "but inwardly are ravenous wolves. You will know them by their fruits. Grapes are not gathered from thorn bushes, nor figs from thistles, are they?" (Matt. 7:15-16). Every person bears fruit of some kind. Those who are darkness bear bad fruit, and those who are light bear good fruit. The person, therefore, who does not bear some fruit of righteousness in his life has no claim on Christ. There is no such thing as a fruitless Christian. Where there is life, there is evidence of life, just as where there is death, there will be evidence of death. The child of light produces **the fruit of the light** and is called to increase in that production (Col. 1:10).

A Christian can fall into sin, and when he does the fruitfulness of his life suffers. Righteous fruit cannot flourish from sin. But the complete absence of *any* **fruit of goodness and righteousness and truth** proves the complete absence of salvation (cf. 2:10).

The Christian life, just as every other kind of life, is only healthy when it is growing. As far as the walk of the believer is concerned, the primary focus is to be a concern about continually *trying to learn what is pleasing to the Lord.* As we are obedient to what we know, our knowledge of the Lord and of His will increases and deepens. As we are faithful to the light, we are given more of this light.

Dokimazō (from which comes **trying to learn**) also carries the idea of proving or testing. As Christians **learn** and grow in **goodness and righteousness and truth**, they will give verification or evidence that they are who they claim to be, children of God and of light. The child of God will bear resemblance to the heavenly Father, who is his "light and . . . salvation" (Ps. 27:1).

Assurance of salvation cannot be reliably determined by what has happened in the past, no matter how dramatic or meaningful at the time. It can only be based with certainty on the evidence of present **fruit** being produced by a spiritual life (see 2 Pet. 1:5-11).

Because they are not carrying weapons, hand grenades, explosives, or other illegal items, most people have no fear of sending their luggage through an X-ray machine at the airport. In the same way, as Christians we should not be afraid to be scrutinized either under the light of God's Word or under the critical eye of a world that is constantly looking for inconsistencies between our profession and our lifestyle. We should have nothing to hide.

THE COMMAND

And do not participate in the unfruitful deeds of darkness, (5:11a)

Sunkoinōneō (to **participate in**) may also be translated "to become a partaker together with others." The child of light should not become involved in evil even by association. We cannot witness to the world if we do not go out into the world; and we cannot go far into the world before coming in contact with all sorts of wickedness. But we are never to identify with that wickedness or give it opportunity to take hold in our own life. To compromise God's standards is to weaken our witness as well as our character. No act of unrighteousness is permissible.

We are not even to have contact at all with a fellow believer who is openly sinning. "I wrote you in my letter not to associate with immoral people," Paul said to the Corinthians. "I did not at all mean with the immoral people of this world, or with the covetous and swindlers, or with idolaters; for then you would have to go out of the world. But actually, I wrote to you not to associate with any so-called brother if he should be an immoral person, or covetous, or an idolater, or a reviler, or a drunkard, or a swindler—not even to eat with such a one" (1 Cor. 5:9-11; cf. 2 Thess. 3:6, 14).

Paul's command is direct and simple: Christians who are to produce the righteous fruit of light are to have nothing at all to do with **the unfruitful deeds of darkness.** These unspecified **deeds of darkness** are typified by the specific sins he has already mentioned in chapters 4 and 5—lusts of deceit, falsehood, stealing, unwholesome speech, bitterness, wrath, anger, clamor, slander, malice, immorality, impurity, greed, filthiness, silly talk, coarse jesting, covetousness, and idolatry. Those and every other kind and degree of sin are to be avoided by the believer, because they bring no benefit to man or glory to God.

THE COMMISSION

but instead even expose them; for it is disgraceful even to speak of the things which are done by them in secret. But all things become visible when they are exposed by the light, for everything that becomes visible is light. (5:11b-13)

The Christian's responsibility goes further than not participating in the sinful ways of the world; he is **instead even** to **expose them.** To ignore evil is to encourage it; to keep quiet about it is to help promote it. The verb here translated **expose** (from *elegchō*) can also carry the idea of reproof, correction, punishment, or discipline. We are to confront sin with intolerance.

Sometimes such exposure and reproof will be direct and at other times indirect, but it should always be immediate in the face of anything that is sinful. When we are living in obedience to God, that fact in itself will be a testimony against wrong. When those around us see us helping rather than exploiting, hear us talking with purity instead of profanity, and observe us speaking truthfully rather than deceitfully, our example will itself be a rebuke of selfishness, unwholesome talk, and falsehood. Simply refusing to participate in a dishonest business or social practice will sometimes be such a strong rebuke that it costs us our job or a friendship. Dishonesty is terribly uncomfortable in the presence of honesty, even when there is no verbal or other direct opposition.

Often, of course, open rebuke is necessary. Silent testimony will only go so far. Failure to speak out against and to practically oppose evil things is a failure to obey God. Believers are to **expose them** in whatever legitimate, biblical ways are necessary. Love that does not openly **expose** and oppose sin is not biblical love. Love not only "does not act unbecomingly" itself but it "does not rejoice in unrighteousness" wherever it might be found (1 Cor. 13:5-6). Our Lord said, "If your brother sins, go and reprove him in private. . . . If he does not listen to you, take one or two more with you. . . . If he refuses to listen to them, tell it to the church" (Matt. 18:15-17). This is the responsibility of every Christian (cf. 1 Tim. 5:1, 20; 2 Tim. 4:2; Titus 1:13; 2:15).

Unfortunately, many Christians are so barely able to keep their own spiritual and moral houses in order that they do not have the discernment, inclination, or power to confront evil in the church or in society at large. We should be so mature in biblical truth, and in obedience, holiness, and love that part of the natural course of our life is to expose, rebuke, and offer the remedy for every kind of evil.

Many Christians do not expose and rebuke evil because they do not take it seriously. They laugh and joke about things that are unadulterated wickedness, that are immoral and ungodly in the extreme. They recognize the sinfulness of those things and would likely never participate in them; but they enjoy them vicariously from a distance. In so doing, they not only fail be an influence against the evil but are instead influenced by it—contaminated by it to the full extent that they think and talk about it without exposing and rebuking it.

Paul goes on to say that **it is disgraceful even to speak of the things which are done by them in secret.** Some things are so vile that they should be discussed in as little detail as possible, because even describing them is morally and spiritually dangerous.

Some diseases, chemicals, and nuclear by-products are so extremely deadly that even the most highly trained and best-protected technicians and scientists who work with them are in constant danger. No sensible person would work around such things carelessly or haphazardly.

In the same way, some things are so spiritually **disgraceful** and dangerous that they should be sealed off not only from direct contact but even from conversation. They should be exposed only to the extent necessary to be rid of them.

Some books and articles written by Christians on various moral issues are so explicit that they almost do as much to spread as to cure the problem. We can give God's diagnosis and solution for sins without portraying every sordid detail.

Our resource for exposing evil is Scripture, which is the light (Ps. 119:105, 130; Prov. 6:23; Heb. 4:13-13) and is "profitable for teaching, for reproof, for correction, for training in righteousness" (2 Tim. 3:16). **All things become visible when they are exposed by the light** of God's Word. Our commission as children of light is to hold everything up to the light of Scripture, to expose and seek to remedy whatever is evil.

Because they have no windows and are built side-by-side on narrow streets, most shops in Middle Eastern cities are quite dark inside. To get a good look at what he is buying a customer must take the merchandise out into the sunshine. In that bright light the article can be seen for what it really is, and any flaws and imperfections will be obvious.

The phrase **for everything that becomes visible is light** is a part of verse 14 in the best Greek manuscripts, and is better translated, "for it is light that makes everything visible" (NIV). **Light** is that which makes things manifest, that which shows them to be as they actually are. When sin is revealed, it loses its "hiddenness" and is seen for the ugliness it is.

THE CALL

For this reason it says, "Awake, sleeper, and arise from the dead, and Christ will shine on you." (5:14)

Paul here offers an invitation, a call for those who are not children of light to come to the light and be saved.

The words are adapted from Isaiah 60:1, which reads, "Arise, shine; for your light has come, and the glory of the Lord has risen upon you." Paul shows the prophetic meaning of those texts by declaring that "the glory of the Lord [that] has risen" is none other than Jesus **Christ**, the Messiah for whom and in whom Isaiah and every other godly Jew had so longed hoped.

Many commentators believe verse 14 is taken from an Easter hymn sung by the early church and used as an invitation to unbelievers who might have been in the congregation. The words are a capsule summary of the gospel. **Awake, sleeper** describes the sinner who is asleep in the darkness of sin and unaware of his lost condition and tragic destiny. Like a spiritual Rip Van Winkle, he will sleep through God's time of grace unless someone awakens him to his predicament and need.

Arise from the dead is a summons to repentance, an appeal to turn away from the dead ways of sin. **Christ will shine on you** is the good news that God has provided a remedy for every sinful person who will come to Him through His blessed Son, the Savior of mankind. (See Isa. 55:6-7 for a similar Old Testament invitation.)

The story is told of a great fire in Edinburgh, Scotland, in which people hurried to exit the building through a passage that led to the street. They were almost safe when a rush of smoke met them, blowing into the passage from the outside. Instead of running through the smoke, they entered a door into a room that seemed safe. But soon all the oxygen was exhausted and they all suffocated. If only they had seen the light they might have lived.

Horatius Bonar wrote:

> I heard the voice of Jesus say,
> "I am this dark world's light;
> Look unto Me, thy morn shall rise,
> And all thy day be bright."
> I looked to Jesus, and I found
> In Him my star, my sun;
> And in that light of life I'll walk,
> Till traveling days are done.

Proverbs 4:18 sums up the words of the apostle: "The path of the righteous is like the light of dawn, that shines brighter and brighter until the full day."

Walking in Wisdom

17

Therefore be careful how you walk, not as unwise men, but as wise, making the most of your time, because the days are evil. So then do not be foolish, but understand what the will of the Lord is. (5:15-17)

The word *fool* commonly refers to a person who acts unintelligently and irresponsibly. But Scripture defines a fool as a person who says "in his heart, 'There is no God'" and who is morally corrupt, doing "abominable deeds" (Ps. 14:1). The fool is the person who lives apart from God—either as a theological or practical atheist or as both, denying God by his actions as well as his words. The supreme fool is the person who has anti-God thinking and living patterns.

Because men are born separated from God and with hearts that are naturally against Him (Rom. 5:8, 10; Eph. 2:3; Col. 1:21), they are born spiritually foolish. "For even though they knew God, they did not honor Him as God, or give thanks; but they became futile in their speculations, and their foolish heart was darkened. Professing to be wise, they became fools" (Rom. 1:21-22). "A natural man does not accept the things of the Spirit of God; for they are foolishness to him, and he cannot understand them, because they are spiritually appraised" (1 Cor. 2:14). The natural man has the most important things in life exactly reversed. Consequently, he thinks foolishness is wisdom and wisdom is foolishness.

No man can live without a god of some sort, and the spiritual fool inevitably substitutes a false god for the true God. He creates gods of his own making (Rom. 1:21-23) and, in effect, becomes his own god, his own authority in all things. "The way of a fool is right in his own eyes" (Prov. 12:15), and therefore he determines right and wrong and truth and falsehood entirely by his own fallen thinking and sinful inclination.

When the fool sets himself up as his own god, he will naturally "mock at sin" (Prov. 14:9). Sin is that which is against God, and since the fool does not recognize God, he does not recognize sin. The spiritually self-sufficient fool makes his own rules and justifies his own behavior, and in doing so he refuses to acknowledge sin and its consequences.

The fool cannot help spreading his foolishness. The more he is convinced of the wisdom of his folly, the more he will seek to propagate it. By what he says and by what he does he gives continual testimony to his denial of God, to his becoming his own god, and to his mocking of sin. No matter what his intellectual level, academic achievements, talents, wealth, or reputation, the mouth of the natural man can spiritually do nothing but spout folly (Prov. 15:2).

The unregenerate person is a fool because he denies God by belief and by practice. He is a fool because he becomes his own god. He is a fool because he mocks sin. And he is a fool because he contaminates the rest of society with the ungodly foolishness that damns his own soul. He bequeaths his legacy of foolishness to his children, his friends, and his society—to everyone who falls under the influence of his folly.

"Because they hated knowledge, and did not choose the fear of the Lord," the writer of Proverbs says of fools, "they shall eat of the fruit of their own way, and be satiated with their own devices, for the waywardness of the naive shall kill them, and the complacency of fools shall destroy them" (Prov. 1:29-32).

The knowledge that the ungodly person hates is not practical, factual knowledge. On the contrary, he prides himself in how much he knows. Someone has estimated that, if all of man's accumulated knowledge from the beginning of recorded history to 1845 were represented by one inch, what he learned from 1845 until 1945 would amount to three inches and what he learned from 1945 until 1975 would represent the height of the Washington Monument! Since then it has probably doubled. Few people, however, would argue that the incredible leap in scientific, technological, and other such knowledge has been paralleled by a corresponding leap in common sense wisdom, not to mention spiritual and moral wisdom. If anything, man's understanding of what he is and doing and why he is doing it seems to decrease as his practical knowledge increases. The more learned he becomes in that superficial kind of knowledge, the less need he sees for the knowledge that comes only from God.

Therefore the ultimate destiny of fools is that they are "always learning and never able to come to the knowledge of the truth" (2 Tim. 3:7) and they "die for lack of understanding" (Prov. 10:21) even while accumulating great amounts of information. They become smarter and more foolish at the same time. Foolishness comes from trusting in purely human knowledge and excluding divine knowledge. Men's foolishness increases with their knowledge only when their self-reliance increases. The natural, unregenerate man suffers from his congenital and terminal foolishness because he will not submit to God. He accumulates vast knowledge apart from God, but spiritual understanding and divine wisdom elude him. He hates the truth about sin and salvation.

Wisdom begins with fear of the Lord (Prov. 1:7) and continues by acknowledging His truth and ways. "Righteous men, wise men, and their deeds are in the hand of God" (Eccles. 9:1). The way to wisdom and the way to life is the way of God. The only power that can overcome a man's foolishness and turn him to wisdom is salvation, turning to God through Jesus Christ. Turning from foolishness to wisdom is turning from self to God. And it is God's own Word that is "able to give [us] the wisdom that leads to salvation through faith which is in Christ Jesus" (2 Tim. 3:15).

The kind of wisdom the Bible praises is not that prized by the ancient Greeks who were Paul's contemporaries. Their wisdom was characterized by philosophy and sophistry, the endless spinning and discussion of theories that have no real relation to life, that have no bearing on God or on practical living. The Greeks could, and often did, go from philosophy to philosophy without changing their basic attitudes or their basic way of life. They were simply playing the game of philosophy, with the sort of wisdom that does not *want* to come to the knowledge of the truth, because—unlike hypotheses and speculations—truth demands recognition, acceptance, and change.

In Scripture, on the other hand, wisdom is centered in conviction and behavior, specifically in recognizing and obeying God. When a person is saved he is moved from the realm of foolishness into the realm of wisdom. Just as his being a Christian leads him to walk worthily (4:1), humbly (4:2), in unity (4:3-16), separated from the world's ways (4:17-32), in love (5:1-7), and in light (5:8-14), it also leads him to walk in wisdom (5:15-17).

In the present passage, Paul mentions three things that the Lord's wisdom teaches His child. The wise believer knows his life principles, his limited privileges, and his Lord's purposes.

THE BELIEVER'S LIFE PRINCIPLES

Therefore be careful how you walk, not as unwise men, but as wise, (5:15)

The literal meaning of the Greek term translated **be** is "look, or observe," and Paul's command for believers to see that they **walk** carefully is based on what he has just been teaching. **Therefore** refers immediately back to the apostle's call for believers to walk as those who have been raised from the dead and are living in Christ's light (v. 14). It also reaches even further back to build upon his call for believers to be imitators of their heavenly Father (5:1). Christians are to walk wisely

217

rather than unwisely because they are God's beloved children, saved through the sacrifice of His beloved Son (5:1-2). Only the wise walk befits the children of God.

Paul commands believers to **walk . . . as wise** men. Just as they are to walk in humility, unity, separation, love, and light (4:1-5:14), they are also to walk in wisdom. In other words, they are to live like the people they *are*. In Christ we *are* one, we *are* separated, we *are* love, we *are* light, and we *are* wise—and what we do should correspond to what we are.

At salvation every believer has been made wise. Paul wrote to Timothy: "You have known the sacred writings which are able to give you the wisdom that leads to salvation through faith which is in Christ Jesus" (2 Tim. 3:15). By God's grace, the saved "are in Christ Jesus, who became to us wisdom from God, and righteousness and sanctification, and redemption" (1 Cor. 1:30). Just as in Christ God miraculously makes us immediately righteous, sanctified, and redeemed, He also makes us immediately wise. The moment we were saved we became a repository of wisdom that henceforth renders us responsible for our behavior. Because we are in Christ, "the treasures of wisdom and knowledge" that are hidden in Him (Col. 2:3) are therefore also hidden in us. John wrote of the Holy Spirit, the resident truth teacher in the life of every saint: "But you have an anointing from the Holy One, and you all know. I have not written to you because you do not know the truth, but because you do know it" (1 John 2:20-21). Further, he said, "You have no need for anyone [any human teacher with simply human wisdom] to teach you," because "His anointing teaches you about all things, and is true" (v. 27). We cannot have salvation without God's wisdom any more than we can have salvation without his righteousness, sanctification, and redemption.

"Easy-believism" is a bane of the contemporary church because, among other things, it purports to offer salvation in segments. First it is claimed that men are born again by accepting Christ as Savior. Then, as they grow in grace, they may renounce sin; start pursuing righteousness, sanctification, and wisdom; and receive Him as Lord. But Paul said, "For the grace of God has appeared, bringing salvation to all men, instructing us to deny ungodliness and worldly desires and to live sensibly, righteously and godly in the present age" (Titus 2:11-12). The very first instruction of the gospel to the saved person is to renounce and forsake sin and to live a godly, righteous life. That instruction, or wisdom, is a part of the new birth, not something subsequent to it.

As Jesus made clear in the Beatitudes, among the first and most necessary marks of salvation are mourning over sin and hungering and thirsting for righteousness (Matt. 5:4, 6). As Paul made clear in the beginning of this letter, "In all wisdom and insight [God] made known to us the mystery of His will" (Eph. 1:8-9).

It is not that we do not grow in wisdom as we mature in the Christian life. We are specifically commanded to "grow in the grace and knowledge of our Lord and Savior Jesus Christ" (2 Pet. 3:18). As we become more and more conformed to our Lord and Savior, we will grow more and more in His love, joy, peace, and in every other fruit of the Spirit (Gal. 5:22-23). In another of God's divine paradoxes, we grow in what we have already been given in fullness. We grow practically in what we already possess positionally. Even Jesus "kept increasing in wisdom" (Luke 2:52), and some believers in the Jerusalem church were "full of . . . wisdom" (Acts 6:3).

Speaking to believers, James said, "If any of you lacks wisdom, let him ask of God, who gives to all men generously and without reproach, and it will be given to him" (James 1:5). Paul prayed that the Colossian believers would "be filled with the knowledge of His will in all spiritual wisdom and understanding" and that they would "let the word of Christ richly dwell within [them], with all wisdom teaching and admonishing one another" (Col. 1:9; 3:16). The believer begins his new life in Christ with all the wisdom necessary to live for His Lord, but he is also to continually grow in wisdom, that he can be even more mature, more faithful, and more productive in His service.

Akribōs (**careful**) has the basic meaning of accurate and exact, and carries the associated idea of looking, examining, and investigating something with great care. It also carries the idea of alertness. As believers walk through the spiritual mine field of the world, they are to be constantly alert to every danger that Satan puts in their way. That is why Jesus warned that "the gate is small, and the way is narrow that leads to life" (Matt. 7:14).

If it had not been written centuries before the time of Paul, Proverbs 2 would appear to be a commentary on Ephesians 5:15. Throughout the chapter the writer of Proverbs speaks of walking in the wise path and the wise way and of not going into the way of the wicked or straying into the company of evil people. Similarly, the first Psalm speaks of the blessed man as the one "who does not walk in the counsel of the wicked, nor stand in the path of sinners, nor sit in the seat of scoffers" (v. 1).

The idea of walking carefully and accurately in God's way is the theme of John Bunyan's *Pilgrim's Progress*. Every incident, conversation, and observation in that great classic of Christian literature focuses on obeying or disobeying, heeding or ignoring, following or departing from God's divine path for Christian living.

When I was a young boy I once walked across a narrow stream on a log that had numerous small branches sticking out of it. When a friend called to me I was momentarily distracted and tripped on one of the branches. I was already past the water and I fell into a bush of nettles on the shore. Because I had on only a swim suit, I was scratched rather painfully and the plant's microscopic needles were embedded over a large part of my body. That is a picture of what can happen to a believer when He is distracted from God's way.

When Christians sin and fall into Satan's traps, they do so because they live **as unwise men**, rather than **as wise**. They revert to following the wisdom of their old lives, which was really foolishness. "For we also once were foolish ourselves," Paul said, "disobedient, deceived, enslaved to various lusts and pleasures, spending our life in malice and envy, hateful, hating one another" (Titus 3:3). That is the kind of living from which God's wisdom is to separate us. "When the kindness of God our Savior and His love for mankind appeared, He saved us, not on the basis of deeds which we have done in righteousness, but according to His mercy, by the washing of regeneration and renewing by the Holy Spirit, whom He poured out upon us richly through Jesus Christ our Savior" (vv. 4-6). Our change in relationship to God is meant to bring a change in daily living, as Paul went on to explain to Titus: "Concerning these things I want you to speak confidently, so that those who have believed may be careful to engage in good deeds. These things are good and profitable for men" (v. 8).

After David had twice spared his life, the jealous and hypocritical Saul confessed that he had "played the fool and [had] committed a serious error" in seeking to take David's life (1 Sam. 26:21). Some years later, after David himself had become king, he proudly decided to take a census of his people. But "David's heart troubled him after he had numbered the people. So David said to the Lord, 'I have sinned greatly in what I have done. But now, O Lord, please take away the iniquity of Thy servant, for I have acted very foolishly.'" (2 Sam. 24:10).

As we learn from David and from many others in Scripture, believers are not immune from reverting to foolishness. The first way a believer plays the fool is by not believing God completely. He believes God for salvation but does not continue to believe Him in and for everything else. Jesus told the two disheartened disciples on the road to Emmaus, "O foolish men and slow of heart to believe in all that the prophets have spoken" (Luke 24:25). To the extent that we do not accept any part of God's Word, to that extent we are foolish.

A believer also plays the fool when he is disobedient. "You foolish Galatians," Paul said; "who has bewitched you, before whose eyes Jesus Christ was publicly portrayed as crucified? . . . Are you so foolish? Having begun by the Spirit, are you now being perfected by the flesh?" (Gal. 3:1, 3). By failing to hold firmly to the doctrine of salvation by faith alone, the Galatians fell prey to the heresy that a Gentile must become a ceremonial Jew before he could become a Christian.

Believers also play the fool when they put their hearts on the wrong things. Paul told Timothy, for example, that "those who want to get rich fall into temptation and a snare and many foolish and harmful desires which plunge men into ruin and destruction" (1 Tim. 6:9). It is tragic that so many Christians foolishly do not take God at His word in everything He says, do not obey Him in everything He commands, and desire so many things that He warns against. There is no excuse for Christians to live foolishly when God's wisdom belongs to them. "If any man is willing to do His will, he shall know of the teaching, whether it is of God," Jesus said to the Jews (John 7:17). The Christian who genuinely wants to know God's truth will never be in doubt, either. He has all the resources he needs "to be wise in what is good, and innocent in what is evil" (Rom. 16:19).

Many people in the world are fanatically dedicated to an ideology, a religion, or a fad. The devoted Communist sacrifices everything for the party. The cultist will give all his earnings to his guru. The physical fitness enthusiast will never miss an exercise class or eat an extra calorie. By means of incredible self-discipline, men seeking acceptance with their deities have trained themselves to walk on beds of coals and lie on beds of nails as evidence of their religious commitment.

Some years ago I met a recently converted young woman who was a nationally ranked distance runner. To keep in shape she ran fifteen miles a day. A month or so later she came up to me after a morning worship service and asked if I remembered her. She seemed familiar but had changed so much during that brief time that I did not recognize her. She told me who she was and explained that she had contracted a disease that the doctors had not yet been able to diagnose and that left her barely able to walk. Rather than being discouraged, however, she said that she was determined to channel the discipline that had made her such a fine athlete into discipline for the things of the Lord. That is the mark of a **wise** Christian.

THE BELIEVER'S LIMITED PRIVILEGES

making the most of your time, because the days are evil. (5:16)

It is common not to finish what we begin. Sometimes a symphony is unfinished, a painting uncompleted, or a project left half-done because the musician, painter, or worker dies. But usually it is simply the death of a person's commitment that causes the incompletion. Dreams never become reality and hopes never materialize because those working toward them never get beyond the first few steps. For many people, including many Christians, life can be a series of unfinished symphonies. Even in the familiar opportunities of everyday Christian living, those who are truly productive have mastered the use of the hours and days of their lives.

Whether in the artistic, business, personal, or spiritual realm, no one can turn a dream into reality or fully take advantage of opportunity apart from **making the most of** [his] **time**.

Paul did not here use *chronos*, the term for clock **time**, the continuous time that is measured in hours, minutes, and seconds. He rather used *kairos*, which denotes a measured, allocated, fixed season or epoch. The idea of a fixed period is also seen in the use of the definite article in the Greek text, which refers to *the* time, a concept often found in Scripture (cf. Ex. 9:5; 1 Pet. 1:17). God has set boundaries to our lives, and our opportunity for service exists only within those boundaries. It is significant that the Bible speaks of such times being shortened, but never of their being lengthened. A person may die or lose an opportunity before the end of God's time, but he has no reason to expect his life or his opportunity to continue after the end of his predetermined time.

Having sovereignly bounded our lives with eternity, God knows both the beginning and end of our time on earth. As believers we can achieve our potential in His service only as we maximize the time He has given us.

An ancient Greek statue depicted a man with wings on his feet, a large lock of hair on the front of his head, and no hair at all on the back. Beneath was the inscription: "Who made thee? Lysippus made me. What is thy name? My name is Opportunity. Why hast thou wings on thy feet? That I may fly away swiftly. Why hast thou a great forelock? That men may seize me when I come. Why art thou bald in back? That when I am gone by, none can lay hold of me."

Exagorazō (**making the most of**) has the basic meaning of buying, especially of buying back or buying out. It was used of buying a slave in order to set him free; thus the idea of redemption is implied in this verse. We are to redeem, buy up, all the time that we have and devote it to the Lord. The Greek is in the middle voice, indicating that we are to buy the time up for ourselves—for our own use but in the Lord's service.

Paul pleads for us to make **the most of** our **time** immediately after he pleads for us to walk wisely rather than foolishly. Outside of purposeful disobedience of God's Word, the most spiritually foolish thing a Christian can do is to waste time and opportunity, to fritter away his life in trivia and in half-hearted service of the Lord.

Shakespeare wrote,

> There is a tide in the affairs of men,
> Which, taken at the flood, leads on to
>   fortune;
> Omitted, all the voyage of their life
> Is bound in shallows and in miseries.
>   (*Julius Caesar,* 4.3.217)

Napoleon said, "There is in the midst of every great battle a ten to fifteen minute period that is the crucial point. Take that period and you win the battle; lose it and you will be defeated."

When we walk obediently in the narrow way of the gospel, we walk carefully, **making the most of** our **time.** We take full advantage of every opportunity to serve God, redeeming our time to use for His glory. We take every opportunity to shun sin and to follow righteousness. "So then," Paul said, "while we have opportunity, let us do good to all men, and especially to those who are of the household of the faith" (Gal. 6:10).

For His own reasons, God allows some of His children to live and serve far into old age. Others He grants only a few years or even a few weeks. But none of us knows how long or short his own allocation of **time** will be.

When I was a boy I had a friend who, like myself, planned to be a pastor. He often told me of his plans to finish high school, go to college and seminary, and enter the pastorate. But in the twelfth grade my friend was driving his canvas-top coupe down a street and the brakes suddenly locked, catapulting him through the car top and onto the street. He struck his head against the curb and was killed instantly.

The great sixteenth-century reformer Philipp Melanchthon kept a record of every wasted moment and took his list to God in confession at the end of each day. It is small wonder that God used him in such great ways.

Many biblical texts stand as warning beacons to those who think they will always have time to do what they should. When Noah and his family entered the ark and shut the door, the opportunity for any other person to be saved from the flood was gone. Because King Ahab disobeyed God by sparing the life of the wicked Ben-hadad, he was told by a prophet, "Thus says the Lord, 'Because you have let go out of your hand the man whom I had devoted to destruction, therefore your life shall go for his life, and your people for his people'" (1 Kings 20:42).

The five foolish virgins who let their oil run out before the bridegroom came were shut out from the wedding feast (Matt. 25:8-10). "We must work the works of Him who sent Me, as long as it is day," Jesus said; "night is coming, when no man can work" (John 9:4). To the unbelieving Pharisees He said, "I go away, and you shall seek Me, and shall die in your sin; where I am going, you cannot come" (John 8:21). After centuries of God's offering His grace to Israel, Jesus lamented, "O Jerusalem, Jerusalem, who kills the prophets and stones those who are sent to her! How often I wanted to gather your children together, the way a hen gathers her chicks under her wings, and you were unwilling" (Matt. 23:37). Judas, the most tragic example of wasted opportunity, spent three years in the very presence of the Son of God, as one of the inner circle of disciples, yet he betrayed His Lord and forfeited his soul for thirty pieces of silver.

Peter said, "If you address as Father the One who impartially judges according to each man's work, conduct yourselves in fear during the time of your stay upon earth" (1 Pet. 1:17). In his farewell remarks to the Ephesian elders at Miletus, Paul said, "I do not consider my life of any account as dear to myself, in order that I may finish my course, and the ministry which I received from the Lord Jesus" (Acts 20:24). Paul's course was prescribed by God, and within that course he would minister to the utmost until his last breath. He was determined to run with endurance the race that was set before him (see Heb. 12:1). At the end of his life he therefore could say, "I have fought the good fight, I have finished the course, I have kept the faith" (2 Tim. 4:7).

David had a great awareness of time. He prayed, "How long, O Lord? Wilt Thou hide Thyself forever? . . . Remember what my span of life is" (Ps. 89:46-47). In the midst of his distress, anxiety, and pain he felt diverted from what he ought to be doing and deserted by God. He therefore asked God how long he would be sidetracked. He knew that he would live for only so long and that whatever he did for the Lord would have to be done during that time. On another occasion he prayed, "Lord, make me to know my end, and what is the extent of my days, let me know how transient I am. Behold, Thou hast made my days as handbreadths, and my lifetime as nothing in Thy sight" (Ps. 39:4-5).

Paul spoke to the Corinthians about the time having been shortened (1 Cor. 7:29), and James warned, "Come now, you who say, 'Today or tomorrow, we shall go to such and such a city, and spend a year there and engage in business and

223

make a profit.' Yet you do not know what your life will be like tomorrow. You are just a vapor that appears for a little while and then vanishes away" (James 4:13-14).

Kefa Sempangi (whose story is told in the book *A Distant Grief,* Regal Books) was a national pastor in Africa and barely escaped with his family from brutal oppression and terror in his home country of Uganda. They made their way to Philadelphia, where a group of Christians began caring for them. One day his wife said, "Tomorrow I am going to go and buy some clothes for the children," and immediately she and her husband broke into tears. Because of the constant threat of death under which they had so long lived, that was the first time in many years they had dared even speak the word *tomorrow.*

Their terrifying experiences forced them to realize what is true of every person: there is no assurance of tomorrow. The only time we can be sure of having is what we have at the moment. To the self-satisfied farmer who had grandiose plans to build bigger and better barns to store his crops, the Lord said, "You fool! This very night your soul is required of you" (Luke 12:20). He had already lived his last tomorrow.

The experience of that African family also dramatically points up the truth that **the days are evil.** We are to make the most of our opportunities not only because our days are numbered but because the world continually opposes us and seeks to hinder our work for the Lord. We have little time and much opposition.

Because **the days are evil,** our opportunities for freely doing righteousness are often limited. When we have opportunity to do something for His name's sake and for His glory, we should do so with all that we have. How God's heart must be broken to see His children ignore or halfheartedly take up opportunity after opportunity that He sends to them. Every moment of every day should be filled with things good, things righteous, things glorifying to God.

By **the days are evil** Paul may have specifically had in mind the corrupt and debauched living that characterized the city of Ephesus. The Christians there were surrounded by paganism and infiltrated by heresy (see 4:14). Greediness, dishonesty, and immorality were a way of life in Ephesus, a way in which most of the believers had themselves once been involved and to which they were tempted to revert (4:19-32; 5:3-8).

Less than a hundred years after Paul wrote the Ephesian epistle Rome was persecuting Christians with growing intensity and cruelty. Believers were burned alive, thrown to wild beasts, and brutalized in countless other ways. For the Ephesian church the **evil** times were going to become more and more evil. Several decades after Paul wrote this epistle, the Lord commended the church at Ephesus for its good works, perseverance, and resistance to false teaching. "But I have this against you," He continued, "that you have left your first love" (Rev. 2:2, 4). Because the church continued to languish in its devotion to the Lord, its lampstand was removed, as He had warned it would be if the believers there failed to "repent and do the deeds [they] did at first" (v. 5). Sometime during the second century the church in Ephesus disappeared, and there has never been a congregation there since. Because the church at Ephesus did not heed Paul's advice and the Lord's own specific warning, it ceased to exist. Instead of helping redeem the **evil days** in which it existed, the church fell prey to them.

If a sense of urgency was necessary in the days of the apostles, how much more is it necessary today, when we are so much nearer the Lord's return and the end of opportunity (see Rom. 13:11-14)?

When pastor Kefa Sempangi, mentioned above, began ministering at his church in Uganda, growth was small but steady. Idi Amin had come into military and political power and the people expected conditions in their country to improve. But soon friends and neighbors, especially those who were Christians, began to disappear. One day pastor Sempangi visited the home of a family and found their young son standing just inside in the doorway with a glazed looked on his face and his arms transfixed in the air. They discovered he had been in that state of rigid shock for days, after being forced to witness the inexpressibly brutal murder and dismembering of everyone else in his family.

Faced with a totally unexpected and horrible danger, pastor Sempangi's church immediately realized that life as they had known it was at an end, and that the very existence of the Lord's people and the Lord's work in their land was threatened with extinction. They began continuous vigils of prayer, taking turns praying for long hours at a time. When they were not praying they were witnessing to their neighbors and friends, urging them to receive Christ and be saved. The church stands today and it has not died. In many ways it is stronger than ever. Its lampstand is still very much in place and shining brightly for the Lord, because His people made the most of the time, did not succumb to the evil days in which they lived, and would not leave their first love. It cost many of them dearly, but they proved again that the blood of the martyrs is the seed of the church.

THE LORD'S PURPOSES

So then do not be foolish, but understand what the will of the Lord is. (5:17)

Do not be foolish repeats and reinforces Paul's previous plea for believers not to be unwise, and **understand what the will of the Lord is** expands and makes more explicit his plea to walk wisely (v. 15).

In light of the urgency to make the most of our time, not being **foolish** includes, among other things, not becoming anxious or panicked. When we look around at the pervasiveness of evil and at the unending needs for evangelism and service to others in Christ's name, it is easy to be overwhelmed. We are tempted either to give up and withdraw or to become hyperactive, losing precision, purpose, and effectiveness in a frenzy of superficial activity.

The proper sense of urgency, however, drives the wise believer to want more than ever to **understand what the will of the Lord is**, because he knows that only in the Lord's will and power can anything good and lasting be accomplished. He will not **be foolish** by running frenetically in every direction trying to see how many programs and projects he can become involved in. Such activity easily becomes futile and leads to burnout and discouragement, because it works in the power of the flesh even when it is well-intentioned. Trying to run ahead of God only puts us further behind in His work.

The work of many churches would be greatly strengthened if the number of its superfluous programs and activities were cut back and the Lord's will were sought more carefully and the principles of His Word applied more faithfully. When our priorities are God's priorities, He is free to work in us and through us to accomplish great things; but when our priorities are not His priorities He can do little with us because He has little of us.

The unwise believer who behaves in a **foolish** manner tries to function apart from God's **will**, and is inevitably weak, frustrated, and ineffective, both in his personal life and in his work for God. The only cure for such foolishness is to find and to follow the **will of the Lord.**

God's basic **will** is, of course, found in Scripture. Here we find His perfect and sufficient guidelines for knowing and doing what is pleasing to him. But the **will** of which Paul seems to be speaking here is the Lord's specific leading of individual believers. Although His plans and directions for each believer are not found in Scripture, the general principles for understanding them are there. God does not promise to show us His will through visions, strange coincidences, or miracles. Nor does He play a divine guessing game with us, seeing if we can somehow stumble onto His will like a small child finds an egg at an Easter egg hunt. God's deepest desire for all of His children is that they know and obey His will, and He gives us every possible help both to know and to obey it.

God's will for our lives is first of all to belong to Him through Jesus Christ. His first and primary will for every person is that he be saved and brought into the family and kingdom of God (1 Tim. 2:3-4). God's will is also that we be Spirit-filled. As Paul went on to teach in the following verse, we are not to "get drunk with wine, for that is dissipation, but be filled with the Spirit" (Eph. 5:18).

We experience God's will by being sanctified. "This is the will of God, your sanctification" (1 Thess. 4:3), Paul said. And we enjoy His will through proper submission to other men. "Submit yourselves for the Lord's sake to every human institution, whether to a king as the one in authority, or to governors as sent by him for the punishment of evil-doers and the praise of those who do right. For such is the will of God that by doing right you may silence the ignorance of foolish men" (1 Pet. 2:13-15). Likewise we are to be submissive to leaders in the church: "Obey your leaders, and submit to them; for they keep watch over your souls, as those who will give an account" (Heb. 13:17).

God's will may include suffering. "If when you do what is right and suffer for it you patiently endure it, this finds favor with God" (1 Pet. 2:20; cf. 3:17; 5:10). God's will culminates in believers' giving thanks no matter what. "In everything give thanks; for this is God's will for you in Christ Jesus" (1 Thess. 5:18).

When a person is saved, sanctified, submissive, suffering, and thankful, he is already *in* God's will. "Delight yourself in the Lord; and He will give you the desires of your heart" (Ps. 37:4), David tells us. In other words, when we *are* what God wants us to be, He is in control and our will is merged with His will, and He therefore gives us the desires He has planted in our hearts.

Jesus is our supreme example for fulfilling the commands of Ephesians 5:15-17. He always functioned according to the divine principles established by His Father: "Truly, truly, I say to you, the Son can do nothing of Himself, unless it is something He sees the Father doing; for whatever the Father does, these things the Son also does in like manner" (John 5:19; cf. v. 30). Second, Jesus knew that His time of earthly ministry was short and would soon be cut off, as seen in frequent sayings such as "My time has not yet come" and "My time has come." He always functioned according to His limited privilege of time and opportunity, using every moment of His life in His Father's work. Third, Jesus always functioned according to the His Father's purposes. "My food is to do the will of Him who sent Me, and to accomplish His work" (John 4:34).

"Therefore," Peter said, "since Christ has suffered in the flesh, arm yourselves also with the same purpose, because he who has suffered in the flesh has ceased from sin, so as to live the rest of the time in the flesh no longer for the lusts of men, but for the will of God" (1 Pet. 4:1-2).

The words of David sum up the proper reaction to this teaching: "I will sing of mercy and judgment: unto thee, O Lord, will I sing. I will behave myself wisely in a perfect way" (Ps. 101:1-2, KJV).

Do Not Get Drunk with Wine

18

And do not get drunk with wine, for that is dissipation, (5:18*a*)

The verse which these words introduce is one of the most crucial texts relating to Christian living, to walking "in a manner worthy of the calling with which [we] have been called" (4:1). Being controlled by the Holy Spirit is absolutely essential for living the Christian life by God's standards. God's way cannot be properly understood or faithfully followed apart from the working of the Spirit in the life of a believer.

But before Paul commanded us to "be filled with the Spirit" and gave the characteristics of the Spirit-filled life (vv. 18*b*-21), he first gave a contrasting and negative command, **And do not get drunk with wine.** Getting drunk with wine not only is a hindrance to, but a counterfeit of, being filled with the Spirit. In light of the apostle's preceding contrasts between light and darkness (vv. 8-14) and between wisdom and foolishness (vv. 15-17), his point here is that getting drunk is a mark of darkness and foolishness and that being filled with the Spirit is the source of a believer's being able to walk in light and wisdom.

There have been few periods of church history in which the drinking of alcoholic beverages has not been an issue of disagreement and debate. Evangelical churches and groups in our own day have widely differing views on the subject.

Denominations and missions organizations sometimes have differing views even within their own constituencies from country to country.

We must be clear that drinking or not drinking is not in itself a mark, and certainly not a measure, of spirituality. Spirituality is determined by what we are inside, of which what we do on the outside is but a manifestation.

Many reasons are given for drinking, one of the most common of which is the desire to be happy, or at least to forget a sorrow or problem. The desire for genuine happiness is both God-given and God-fulfilled. In Ecclesiastes we are told there is "a time to laugh" (3:4) and in Proverbs that "a joyful heart is good medicine" (17:22). David proclaimed that in the Lord's "presence is fulness of joy" (Ps. 16:11). Jesus began each beatitude with the promise of blessedness, or happiness, for those who come to the Lord in the Lord's way (Matt. 5:3-11). The apostle John wrote his first letter not only to teach and admonish fellow believers but that his own joy might "be made complete" (1:4). Paul twice counselled the Philippian Christians to "rejoice in the Lord" (3:1; 4:4). At Jesus' birth the angel announced to the shepherds, "Do not be afraid; for behold I bring you good news of a great joy which shall be for all the people" (Luke 2:10). God wants all men to be happy and joyful, and one of the great blessings of the gospel is the unmatched joy that Christ brings to the heart of every person who trusts in Him.

The problem with drinking in order to be happy is not the motive but the means. It brings only artificial happiness at best and is counterproductive to spiritual sensitivity. It is a temporary escape that often leads to even worse problems than the ones that prompted the drinking in the first place. Intoxication is never a remedy for the cares of life, but it has few equals in its ability to multiply them.

SCRIPTURE ALWAYS CONDEMNS DRUNKENNESS

Drinking to the point of drunkenness, of course, has few sane defenders even in the secular world. It has caused the loss of too many battles, the downfall of too many governments, and the moral corruption of too many lives and whole societies to be considered anything less than the total evil that it is. The United States alone presently has over twenty million alcoholics, almost three and a half million of which are teenagers. And alcohol is a killer.

Drunkenness is the clouding or disruption by alcohol of any part of a person's mind so that it affects his faculties. A person is drunk to the extent that alcohol has restricted or modified any part of his thinking or acting. Drunkenness has many degrees, but it begins when it starts to interrupt the normal functions of the body and mind.

Both the Old and New Testaments unequivocally condemn drunkenness. Every picture of drunkenness in the Bible is a picture of sin and disaster. Shortly after the Flood, Noah became drunk and acted shamelessly. Lot's daughters caused him to become drunk and to commit incest with them, as a foolish and perverted means of having children. Ben-hadad and his allied kings became drunk and were all slaughtered except Ben-hadad, who was spared only by the disobedience of Israel's King Ahab (1 Kings 20:16-34). Belshazzar held a drunken feast in which he and his guests praised the gods of gold, silver, bronze, iron, wood, and stone. And during the very midst of the drunken brawl the kingdom was taken from Belshazzar (Dan. 5). Some of the Corinthian Christians became drunk while at the Lord's table, and God caused some of them to become weak and sick and others to die because of their wicked desecration (1 Cor. 11:27-30).

The book of Proverbs has many warnings about drinking. Speaking as a father, the writer said, "Listen, my son, and be wise, and direct your heart in the way. Do not be with heavy drinkers of wine, or with gluttonous eaters of meat; for the heavy drinker and the glutton will come to poverty, and drowsiness will clothe a man with rags" (Prov. 23:19-21). Our skid rows today are filled with more men clothed in rags because of drunkenness than the ancient writer of Proverbs could ever have imagined. A few verses later he asked, "Who has woe? Who has sorrow? Who has contentions? Who has complaining? Who has wounds without cause? Who has redness of eyes? Those who linger long over wine, those who go to taste mixed wine. Do not look on the wine when it is red, when it sparkles in the cup, when it goes down smoothly" (vv. 29-31). Wine is enticing to look at, with its bright color, sparkling bubbles, and smooth taste—just as modern commercials vividly portray it. What the commercials are careful not to say is that "at last it bites like a serpent, and stings like a viper. Your eyes will see strange things, and your mind will utter perverse things" (vv. 32-33).

We also read in Proverbs that "wine is a mocker, strong drink a brawler, and whoever is intoxicated by it is not wise" (20:1). Drunkenness mocks a person by making him think he is better off instead of worse off, smarter instead of more foolish, and happier instead of simply dazed. It is a favorite tool of Satan for the very reason that it deceives while it destroys. Surely it presents vulnerability to demons. The drunk does not learn his lesson and is deceived over and over again. Even when he is waylaid, beaten, and finally awakens from his drunken stupor he "will seek another drink" (23:35).

Between those two warnings about drunkenness we are told, "A harlot is a deep pit, and an adulterous woman is a narrow well. Surely she lurks as a robber, and increases the faithless among men" (vv. 27-28). The revered Old Testament scholar Franz Delitzsch commented, "The author passes from the sin of uncleanness to that of drunkenness; they are nearly related, for drunkenness excites fleshly lust; and to wallow with delight in the mire of sensuality, a man created in the image of God must first brutalize himself by intoxication." (Johann K. F. Keil and Franz Julius Delitzsch, vol. 4 of *Old Testament Commentaries* [Grand Rapids: Associated Publishers and authors, n. d.], 750.)

Isaiah warned, "Woe to those who rise early in the morning that they may pursue strong drink; who stay up late in the evening that wine may inflame them!" (Isa. 5:11). An alcoholic characteristically begins drinking in the morning and continues through the day and evening. Again the prophet portrayed a vivid scene when he said, "And these also reel with wine and stagger from strong drink: the priest and the prophet reel with strong drink, they are confused by wine, they stagger from strong drink; they reel while having visions, they totter when rendering judgment. For all the tables are full of filthy vomit, without a single clean place" (28:7-8).

Scripture shows drunkenness in its full ugliness and tragedy, as always associated with immorality, dissolution, unrestrained behavior, wild, reckless behavior, and every other form of corrupt living. It is one of the sinful deeds of the flesh that are in opposition to the righteous fruit of the Spirit (Gal. 5:19-23). Drunkenness is first of all a sin. It develops attendant disease as it ravages the mind and body, but it is basically a sin, a manifestation of depravity. It must therefore be confessed and dealt with as sin.

Peter told believers to forsake the way of the Gentiles, who pursued "a course of sensuality, lusts, drunkenness, carousals, drinking parties and abominable idolatries" (1 Pet. 4:3). Paul admonished the Thessalonians, "Let us not sleep as others do, but let us be alert and sober. For those who sleep do their sleeping at night, and those who get drunk at night. But since we are of the day, let us be sober, having put on the breastplate of faith and love, and as a helmet, the hope of salvation" (1 Thess. 5:6-8; cf. Rom. 13:13). He warned the Corinthian believers that they were not even "to associate with any so-called brother if he should be an immoral person, or covetous, or an idolater, or a reviler, or a drunkard, or a swindler—not even to eat with such a one" (1 Cor. 5:11). In the next chapter he went on to say, "Do not be deceived; neither fornicators, nor idolaters, nor adulterers, nor effeminate, nor homosexuals, nor thieves, nor the covetous, nor drunkards, nor revilers, nor swindlers, shall inherit the kingdom of God" (6:9-10).

It is possible for a Christian to become drunk, just as it is possible for him to fall into other sins. But his life will not be continually characterized by drunkenness or any of the other sins mentioned by Peter and Paul.

In light of the Ephesian situation, however, it must be recognized that Paul's primary concern in the present passage is religious, not moral. To the Ephesians, as to most pagans and former pagans of that day, drunkenness was closely associated with the idolatrous rites and practices that were an integral part of temple worship. In the mystery religions, which began in ancient Babylon and were copied and modified throughout the Near East and in Greek and Roman cultures, the height of religious experience was communion with the gods through various forms of ecstasy. To achieve an ecstatic experience the participants would use self-hypnosis and frenzied dances designed to work themselves up to a high emotional pitch. Heavy drinking and sexual orgies contributed still further to the sensual stupor that their perverted minds led them to think was creating communion with the gods.

The modern drug and hard rock culture is little different from those pagan rites. Drugs, psychedelic lighting, ear-pounding music, and suggestive lyrics and antics all combine to produce near-hysteria in many of the performers and spectators. It is significant that much of this subculture is directly involved in one or more of the Eastern, mystical religions that teach greater spiritual awareness through escape into supposed higher levels of consciousness induced by drugs, repetition of prescribed names or words, and other such superstitious and demonic means.

The greatest god of ancient mythology was known as Zeus (Greek), Jupiter (Roman), and by other names in various regions and times. In what we can now see as a Satanic counterfeit of Jesus' conception by the Holy Spirit, myth claimed that Zeus somehow caused the goddess Semele to become pregnant without having contact with her. Semele decided that she had a right to see the father of her child, and while it was still in her womb she approached Zeus, only to be instantly incinerated by his glory. Before it could be destroyed, Zeus snatched the unborn child from her womb and sewed it into his thigh, where it continued to develop until birth. The infant god was named Dionysius and was destined by Zeus to become ruler of the earth.

The legend further told that when the Titans, who then inhabited the earth, heard of Zeus's plan they stole the baby Dionysius and tore him limb from limb. Again the child was rescued by his father Zeus, who swallowed Dionysius's heart and miraculously recreated him. Zeus then struck the Titans with lightning, reducing them to ashes from which was raised the human race. As ruler of this new race, Dionysius developed a religion of ascendancy, whereby human beings could rise to a level of divine consciousness. The mystical system he devised was comprised of wild music, frenzied dancing, sexual perversion, bodily mutilation, eating of the raw flesh of sacrificial bulls, and drunkenness. Dionysius became known as the god of wine, the intoxicating drink that was integral to the debauched religion that centered around him. His Roman counterpart was Bacchus, from whose name we get *bacchanalia,* the Roman festival celebrated with wild dancing, singing, drinking, and revelry that has for over two thousand years been synonymous with drunken debauchery and sexual orgy.

The city of Baalbek, in eastern Lebanon, contains some of the most fascinating ruins of the ancient world. It is the site of pagan temples first erected in the name of various Canaanite gods, and later rededicated in the names of corresponding Greek and then Roman deities when it was conquered by those empires. The central temple was that of Bacchus, the columns and parapets of which are intricately and profusely decorated with carvings of grapevines— symbolic of the excessive use of wine that characterized their orgiastic worship.

That is precisely the type of pagan worship with which the Ephesians were well acquainted and in which many believers had once been involved. It was also the type of worship and associated immorality and carnality from which many of the Corinthian believers had such a difficult time divorcing themselves and for which Paul rebuked them strongly. "Is not the cup of blessing which we bless a sharing in the blood of Christ? Is not the bread which we break a sharing in the body of Christ? . . . I say that the things which the Gentiles sacrifice, they sacrifice to demons, and not to God; and I do not want you to become sharers in demons. You cannot drink the cup of the Lord and the cup of demons; you cannot partake of the table of the Lord and the table of demons" (1 Cor. 10:16, 20-21). Later in the letter he gave a similar rebuke: "Therefore when you meet together, it is not to eat the Lord's Supper, for in your eating each one takes his own supper first; and one is hungry and another is drunk" (11:20-21). Satan is a thief and a liar, and he revels in stealing the most beautiful and sacred things of the Lord and counterfeiting them in sensually attractive perversions that entice men into sin and deceive them about the truth.

In Ephesians 5:18, Paul was therefore not simply making a moral but also a theological contrast. He was not only speaking of the moral and social evils of drunkenness, but of the spiritually perverted use of drunkenness as a means of worship. Christians are not to seek religious fulfillment through such pagan means as getting *drunk with wine,* but are to find their spiritual fulfillment and enjoyment by being "filled with the Spirit." The believer has no need for the artificial, counterfeit, degrading, destructive, and idolatrous ways of the world. He has God's own Spirit indwelling him, the Spirit whose great desire is to give believers the fullest benefits and enjoyment of their high position as children of God.

The context of this passage further indicates that Paul was speaking primarily about the religious implications of drunkenness. The frenzied, immoral, and drunken orgies of pagan ceremonies were accompanied by correspondingly corrupt liturgies. In verses 19-20 Paul showed the kind of liturgy that pleases God: Spirit-filled believers "speaking to one another in psalms and hymns and spiritual songs, singing and making melody with your heart to the Lord; always giving thanks for all things in the name of our Lord Jesus Christ to God, even the Father."

SCRIPTURE SOMETIMES COMMENDS WINE

Despite its many warnings about the dangers of wine, the drinking of it is not totally forbidden in Scripture and is, in fact, sometimes even commended. Drink offerings of wine accompanied many of the Old Testament sacrifices (Ex. 29:40; Num. 15:5; cf. 28:7). It is likely that a supply of wine was kept in the Temple for that purpose. The psalmist spoke of "wine which makes man's heart glad" (Ps. 104:15), and the writer of Proverbs advised giving "strong drink to him who is perishing, and wine to him whose life is bitter" (31:6). In speaking of God's gracious invitation to salvation, Isaiah declared, "Ho! Every one who thirsts, come to the waters; and you who have no money come, buy and eat. Come, buy wine and milk without money and without cost" (Isa. 55:1).

Paul advised Timothy, "No longer drink water exclusively, but use a little wine for the sake of your stomach and your frequent ailments" (1 Tim. 5:23). Jesus' first miracle was turning water into wine at the wedding feast at Cana (John 2:6-10). He also spoke favorably of wine in the parable of the Good Samaritan, who poured oil and wine on the wounds of the man he found beaten by the roadside (Luke 10:34).

Like many other things, the kind of wine of which Scripture speaks (discussed below) has the potential either for evil or good. I believe there was a time when the juice of the grape, like every other thing God created, was only good and did not have even the potential for evil. Fermentation, a form of decay, likely was made possible by the corruption of nature at the Fall and actually began with the vast environmental change caused by the Flood and the accompanying removal of the vapor canopy over the earth that had protected it from direct sunlight. It is not unreasonable to believe that in the millennial kingdom the process will again be reversed, when the curse is removed and nature is restored to its original state of perfect goodness.

Guidelines for Christians

In light of the fact that Scripture gives many warnings about drinking wine, yet does not forbid it and even commends it in certain circumstances, how can a believer know what to do? Following are eight suggestions, given in the form of questions, which if answered honestly in light of Scripture will serve as helpful guidelines.

IS TODAY'S WINE THE SAME AS THAT IN BIBLE TIMES?

Our first task in answering this question is to determine exactly what kind of wine is referred to in the Bible, and the second is to determine how that wine compares to what is produced and drunk today. Many sincere, Bible-honoring Christians justify their drinking wine on the basis of its being an acceptable practice both in the Old and New Testaments. But if the kind of wine used then was different from that used today, then application of the biblical teaching concerning wine will also be different.

One kind of wine, called *sikera* in Greek (see Luke 1:15) and *shēkār* in Hebrew (see Prov. 20:1; Isa. 5:1), is usually translated "strong drink" because of its high alcohol content and consequent rapid intoxication of those who drank it.

A second kind of wine was called *gleukos* (from which we get our English term *glucose*) and referred to new wine, which was especially sweet. Some of the onlookers at Pentecost accused the apostles of being drunk on this kind of wine (Acts 2:13). The corresponding Hebrew word is *tîrôsh* (see Prov. 3:10; Hos. 9:2; Joel 1:10). Because freshly-squeezed juice would ferment rapidly and could cause intoxication even when not fully aged, it was generally mixed with water before drinking.

A third kind of wine, however, is the one most often referred to in both the Old and New Testaments. The Hebrew word for that wine is *yayin*, which has the root meaning of bubbling or boiling up. The figure of bubbling did not come from the pouring of the wine but from the boiling of the fresh grape juice to reduce it to a heavy syrup, sometimes even a thick paste, that made it suitable for storage without spoiling. Because boiling removes most of the water and kills all the bacteria, the concentrated state of the juice does not ferment. *Yayin* most often referred to the syrup or paste mixed with water and used as a drink (cf. Ps. 75:8; Prov. 23:30). Even when the reconstituted mixture was allowed to ferment, its alcohol content was quite low.

The most common New Testament Greek word for this third kind of wine is *oinos,* and in its most general sense simply refers to the juice of grapes. Any accurate Jewish source will point out that *yayin,* mixed wine, or *oinos,* does not refer only to intoxicating liquor made by fermentation, but more often refers to a thick nonintoxicating syrup or jam produced by boiling to make it storable. In Jesus' illustration of putting new wine (*oinos,* not *gleukos*) only into new wineskins, He was possibly saying that it was thereby "preserved" from fermentation as well as from spillage (Matt. 9:17).

The practice of reducing fresh grape juice to a syrup by boiling or evaporation was widespread in the biblical Near East as well as in the Greek and Roman cultures of that day—and is not uncommon in Palestine, Syria, Jordan, and Lebanon in our own day. In addition to being diluted for use as a beverage, the heavy syrup was used as a flavoring and as a jam-like spread on bread and pastries. Both the syrup and most of the drink made from it were completely nonintoxicating.

The Jewish Mishnah—the ancient oral and later written interpretations of the Mosaic law that preceded the Talmud—states that the Jews regularly used boiled wine, that is, grape juice reduced to a thick consistency by heating. Aristotle described the wine of Arcadia as being so thick that it had to be scraped from the skin bottles in which it was stored and the scrapings diluted with water in order to make a drink. The Roman historian Pliny often referred to nonintoxicating wine. The Roman poet Horace wrote in 35 b.c., "Here you quaff under a shade, cups of unintoxicating wine." In the ninth book of his *Odyssey* Homer told of Ullyses putting in his boat a goatskin of sweet black wine that was diluted with twenty parts of water before being drunk. In A.D. 60 the Greek biographer Plutarch commented that "filtered wine neither inflames the brain nor infects the mind and the passions, and is much more pleasant to drink."

Writing in *Christianity Today* magazine (June 20, 1975), Robert Stein explains that the ancient Greeks kept their unboiled, unmixed, and therefore highly-alcoholic wine in large jugs called amphorae. Before drinking they would pour it into smaller vessels called kraters and dilute it with water as much as twenty to one. Only then would the wine be poured into killits, the cups from which it was drunk. It was this diluted form that was commonly referred to simply as wine (*oinos*). The undiluted liquid was called *akratesteron,* or "unmixed wine," wine that had not been diluted in a krater. Even among the civilized pagans, drinking unmixed wine was considered stupid and barbaric. Mr. Stein quotes Mnesitheus of Athens:

> The gods have revealed wine to mortals, to be the greatest blessing for those who use it aright, but for those who use it without measure, the reverse. For it gives food to them that take it and strength in mind and body. In medicine it is most

beneficial; it can be mixed with liquid and drugs and it brings aid to the wounded. In daily intercourse, to those who mix and drink it moderately, it gives good cheer; but if you overstep the bounds, it brings violence. Mix it half and half, and you get madness; unmixed, bodily collapse.

From an early Christian volume called *The Apostolic Tradition* we learn that the early church followed the custom of using only such mixed wine, whether made from a syrup or from the unmixed liquid.

Naturally fermented wine has an alcoholic content of from nine to eleven percent. For an alcoholic beverage such as brandy to have a higher content, it must be artificially fortified by distilling already-fermented wine. The unmixed wine of the ancients therefore had a maximum alcohol content of eleven percent. Even mixed half and half (a mixture which Mnesitheus said would bring madness), the wine would have had less than five percent alcohol. Since the strongest wine normally drunk was mixed at least with three parts water to one of wine, its alcohol content would have been in a range no higher than 2.25-2.75 percent—well below the 3.2 percent that today is generally considered necessary to classify a beverage as alcoholic.

It is clear, therefore, that whether the *yayin* or *oinos* mentioned in Scripture refers to the thick syrup itself, to a mixture of water and syrup, or to a mixture of water and pure wine, the wine was either nonalcoholic or only slightly alcoholic. To **get drunk with** mixed **wine** (*oinos*) would have required consuming a large quantity—as is suggested in other New Testament passages. "Addicted to wine" (1 Tim. 3:3; Titus 1:7) translates one Greek word (*paroinos*) and literally means "at, or beside, wine," and carries the idea of sitting beside the wine cup for an extended period of time.

The answer to the first question is clearly no. The wine of Bible times was not the same as the unmixed wine of our own day. Even the more civilized pagans of Bible times would have considered the drinking of modern wines to be barbaric and irresponsible.

IS IT NECESSARY?

The second question that helps us determine whether or not a believer today should drink wine is, "Is drinking wine necessary for me?" In Bible times, as in many parts of the world today, good drinking water either did not exist or was scarce. The safest drink was wine, and wine that had alcoholic content was especially safe because of the antiseptic effect of the alcohol. It actually purified the water.

Yet it seems hard to believe that the wine Jesus miraculously made at the wedding feast in Cana or that He served at the Lord's Supper and on other occasions was fermented. How could He have made or served that which had even the potential for making a person drunk? When He made the wine at Cana, He first instructed the servants to fill the jars with water, as if to testify that the wine He was about to create was obviously mixed. The wedding guests commented on the high quality of the wine (John 2:10), and because they called it *oinos*, it obviously was like the mild drink they were accustomed to making by adding water to boiled-down syrup.

Even though circumstances often required or made advisable the drinking of wine that contained alcohol, the preferred wine even in Bible times had little or none. Modern believers therefore cannot appeal to the biblical practice to justify their own drinking, because so many alternatives are now readily and cheaply available. Drinking alcoholic beverages today is an extremely rare necessity; most often it is simply a matter of preference.

Nor is drinking necessary in order to prevent embarrassing or offending friends, acquaintances, or business associates. A Christian's witness is sometimes resented and costly, but most people are inclined to respect our abstinence when it is done out of honest conviction and is not flaunted self-righteously or judgmentally. The argument of not wanting to offend others is more likely to be based on concern for our own image and popularity than on genuine concern for their feelings and welfare. Some feel that drinking is sometimes necessary for the sake of establishing a relationship with an unsaved person with a view to bringing him to saving faith. But such a view of evangelism fails miserably in understanding the sovereign work of God and the power of the gospel apart from human devices.

IS IT THE BEST CHOICE?

Because drinking of wine is not specifically and totally forbidden in Scripture and because it is not a necessity for believers in most parts of the world today, the drinking of it is a matter of choice. The next question is therefore, Is it the best choice?

Throughout the history of God's people He has given higher standards for those in positions of greater responsibility. Under the sacrificial system instituted under Moses and described in Leviticus 4-5, the ordinary person was required to give a female goat or a lamb as a sin offering—or two pigeons or two doves (5:7), or even a meal (grain) offering (5:11), if he was very poor. But a ruler had to offer a male goat, and the congregation as a whole or the high priest had to offer a bull.

Aaron and all succeeding high priests were also given higher personal standards by which to live. They were commanded, "Do not drink wine or strong drink, neither you nor your sons with you, when you come into the tent of meeting, so that you may not die—it is a perpetual statute throughout your generations" (Lev. 10:9). Because the high priest was called apart to a higher office, he was also called to a higher commitment to God and to a higher quality of living. Whether their drink restriction pertained to their total living or only to the time while they were actually serving in the Tabernacle or Temple, their ministry for the Lord was to be marked by total abstinence from all alcoholic beverage. Their minds and bodies were to be clear, pure, and fully functional when they ministered in the

Lord's name. There was to be no risk of moral or spiritual compromise in sacred ministry.

The same high standard applied to rulers in Israel. "It is not for kings, O Lemuel, it is not for kings to drink wine, or for rulers to desire strong drink, lest they drink and forget what is ordered, and pervert the rights of all the afflicted" (Prov. 31:4-5). Their judgment was not to be clouded even by the amount of alcohol found in wine (*yayin*), much less by the much higher amount in strong drink (*shēkār*). Strong drink was to be given only "to him who is perishing," as a sedative to ease his pain (v. 6). Any other use of it was not condoned. Normal mixed wine could be given for enjoyment "to him whose life is bitter. Let him drink and forget his poverty, and remember his trouble no more" (vv. 6-7). But the high priests and the rulers of the people were to drink neither *yayin* nor *shekar*.

Any person in Israel could choose to set himself apart for God in a special way by taking the Nazirite vow. "When a man or woman makes a special vow, the vow of a Nazirite, to dedicate himself to the Lord, he shall abstain from wine and strong drink; he shall drink no vinegar, whether made from wine or strong drink, neither shall he drink any grape juice, nor eat fresh or dried grapes. All the days of his separation he shall not eat anything that is produced by the grape vine, from the seeds even to the skin" (Num. 6:2-4). A Nazirite also vowed not to shave his head or to ceremonially contaminate himself by touching a dead body as long as his vow was in effect (vv. 5-7).

The name Nazirite comes from the Hebrew *nāzîr*, which means "separated, or consecrated." Such separation was voluntary and could last from 30 days to a lifetime. But while the person, man or woman, was set apart in that way for special service to the Lord, his life was to be marked by special purity, including abstention from anything even associated with alcoholic drink. The Nazirite was, in a sense, stepping up to the level of a ruler or high priest by his act of special consecration and separation.

Scripture names only three men who were Nazirites for life—Samson, Samuel, and John the Baptist. All three were set apart as Nazirites before they were born, Samuel by his mother (1 Sam. 1:11) and Samson and John the Baptist by the Lord Himself (Judg. 13:3-5; Luke 1:15). The mothers of both Samson and Samuel also abstained from wine and strong drink (Judg. 13:4; 1 Sam. 1:15), Samson's mother by the direct command of the angel.

Though we do not know their identities, many other Nazirites lived in Israel and served the Lord through their specially consecrated lives (see Lam. 4:7, AV, but see also NASB; Amos 2:11). Unfortunately, many of them were forcibly corrupted by their fellow Israelites, who "made the Nazirites drink wine" (Amos 2:12; cf. Lam. 4:8). The world resents those whose high standards are a rebuke to low living. Instead of trying to attain a higher level for themselves, people who are worldly and fleshly—including worldly and carnal Christians—seek to bring those who live purely down to their own corrupt level.

In Jeremiah's day the entire clan of the Rechabites had taken a vow not to drink wine, and had remained faithful to that vow. Because of their faithfulness, the Lord had Jeremiah set them up as a standard of righteous living, in contrast to the corrupt unfaithfulness of Judah, on whom He was about to bring judgment (Jer. 35:1-19).

The most outstanding Nazirite was John the Baptist, of whom Jesus said, "Truly, I say to you, among those born of women there has not arisen anyone greater" (Matt. 11:11). Before John was born, the angel said of him, "He will be great in the sight of the Lord, and he will drink no wine (*oinos*) or liquor (*sikera*); and he will be filled with the Holy Spirit, while yet in his mother's womb" (Luke 1:15).

Yet Jesus went on to say in regard to John the Baptist that "he who is least in the kingdom of heaven is greater than he" (Matt. 11:11). In Jesus Christ, every believer is on the spiritual level of a high priest, a ruler, and a Nazirite. Christ loves us and has "released us from our sins by His blood, and He has made us to be a kingdom, priests to His God and Father" (Rev. 1:5-6). Christians are a "chosen race, a royal priesthood, a holy nation, a people for God's own possession" (1 Pet. 2:9; cf. v. 5). Every Christian is specially set apart for God, and every Christian is to be separated from everything that is unclean (2 Cor. 6:17). "Therefore, having these promises, beloved," Paul continued, "let us cleanse ourselves from all defilement of flesh and spirit, perfecting holiness in the fear of God" (7:1).

God did not lower His standards for New Testament saints, who are greater, Jesus said, even than John the Baptist. In both the Old and New Testaments drinking wine or strong drink disqualified a person from the leadership of God's people. Christian leaders, like those of the Old Testament, are held to specially high standards. Overseers, or bishops, who are the same as elders and pastors, must not be "addicted to wine," which, as mentioned above, translates one word (*paroinos*) and literally means "at, or by, wine." A leader in the church is not even to be beside wine. "Must" (1 Tim. 3:2) is from the Greek particle *dei*, and carries the meaning of logical necessity rather than moral ought. Paul is therefore saying that leaders in the church of Jesus Christ not only ought but "must be . . . not addicted to wine" (vv. 2-3).

James said, "Let not many of you become teachers, my brethren, knowing that as such we shall incur a stricter judgment" (James 3:1), and Jesus said, "From everyone who has been given much shall much be required" (Luke 12:48). If Old Testament high priests, Nazirites, kings, judges, and other rulers of the people were to be clear-minded at all times, the Lord surely does not have lower standards for leaders in the church, which is the present incarnate Body of His own Son, Jesus Christ. For deacons, whose responsibility is to serve rather than to give leadership, the standard is less stringent. They are allowed to drink wine but are not to be "addicted," which is from a different Greek word (*prosechontas*), meaning "to be occupied with." Such allowance still forbids drunkenness, and it reflects the distinct place of the elder, pastor, bishop, who should totally avoid any possibility of having his thinking clouded. The thrust of Paul's message here seems to be that, because of the need for clear minds and pure example, the decision-making leaders of the church, are to be held to the highest possible standards of conduct, including abstinence from all alcoholic beverages, and that deacons, who are not in such critical roles, are allowed to drink wine in moderation.

That Paul advised Timothy to "no longer drink water exclusively, but use a little wine for the sake of your stomach and your frequent ailments" (1 Tim. 5:23) indicates that, consistent with his leadership abstinence, Timothy previously had drunk no wine at all and that Paul's recommendation to start drinking "a little wine" was purely for medicinal purposes. Every believer is to present his body "a living and holy sacrifice, acceptable to God" (Rom. 12:1), in total consecration to Him.

IS IT HABIT FORMING?

A fourth area of concern for believers should be the matter of addiction. Many things become habitual, and many of the habits we form are beneficial. On the other hand, many other habits are harmful and are difficult to break.

Paul's principle that though all things for him were lawful, he would "not be mastered by anything" (1 Cor. 6:12) clearly applies to the danger of alcohol addiction. Alcohol easily produces overpowering dependency. In addition to the alcohol's direct clouding of the brain and disruption of bodily functions, the dependency itself distracts the attention and interferes with the judgment of the one who is addicted.

A Christian not only must avoid sin but must avoid the potential for sin. We should not allow ourselves to get under the influence or control of anyone or anything that leads us away from the things of God even to a small extent. The safest and wisest choice for a Christian is to avoid even the potential for wrong influence.

Even when something is not habit-forming for us, it may be for someone who is looking at and following our example. Because alcohol is universally acknowledged to be highly addictive, a Christian's drinking unnecessarily creates the potential for the alcohol addiction of someone else.

IS IT POTENTIALLY DESTRUCTIVE?

A fifth concern should be for alcohol's potential destructiveness. The pagan writer Mnesitheus, already quoted, spoke of wine mixed with half water as causing madness and of unmixed wine's bringing bodily collapse. The mental, physical, and social destructiveness of alcohol is too evident to need much documentation.

Over 40 percent of all violent deaths are alcohol related, and at least 50 percent of all traffic fatalities involve drinking drivers. It is estimated that at least one fourth of all hospitalized psychiatric patients have a problem with alcohol. Heavy consumption of alcohol causes cirrhosis of the liver and countless other physical disorders. Alcohol-related problems cost billions of dollars each year in lost income to employers and employees, in settlements by insurance companies and in higher premiums for their customers, and in many other less direct ways.

Dissipation, to which drunkenness inevitably leads, is from *asōtia,* which literally means "that which is unable to be saved." It was used of a person who was hopelessly and incurably sick and also was used of loose, profligate living, as in that of the prodigal son (Luke 15:13). **Dissipation** is therefore a form of self-destruction.

As mentioned earlier in the chapter, the Old Testament gives many vivid accounts of the close association of heavy drinking with immorality, rebellion, incest, disobedience to parents, and corrupt living of every sort. Violence is a natural companion of strong drink (Prov. 4:17), and "wine is a mocker, strong drink a brawler" (20:1).

The prophet Joel cried, "Awake, drunkards, and weep; and wail, all you wine drinkers, on account of the sweet wine that is cut off from your mouth" (Joel 1:5). Later in his message he said, "They have also cast lots for My people, traded a boy for a harlot, and sold a girl for wine that they may drink" (3:3). Habakkuk warned, "Woe to you who make your neighbors drink, who mix in your venom even to make them drunk so as to look on their nakedness! You will be filled with disgrace rather than honor. Now you yourself drink and expose your own nakedness. The cup in the Lord's right hand will come around to you, and utter disgrace will come upon your glory" (Hab. 2:15-16).

The Christian must ask himself if it is wise for him to have any part of something that has such great potential for destruction and sin.

WILL IT OFFEND OTHER CHRISTIANS?

In speaking of food sacrificed to idols, Paul said, "We know that there is no such thing as an idol in the world, and that there is no God but one. . . . However not all men have this knowledge; but some, being accustomed to the idol until now, eat food as if it were sacrificed to an idol; and their conscience being weak is defiled. But food will not commend us to God; we are neither the worse if we do not eat, nor the better if we do eat. But take care lest this liberty of yours somehow become a stumbling block to the weak. . . . For through your knowledge he who is weak is ruined, the brother for whose sake Christ died" (1 Cor. 8:4, 7-9, 11).

A Christian who himself is perfectly able to drink in moderation is not able to guarantee that his example will not cause a weaker fellow Christian to try drinking and become addicted. Not only that, but just as in Paul's day, a former drunk who becomes a Christian will often associate many immoral and corrupt activities with drinking, and to see a fellow Christian drink is likely to offend his conscience. Our freedom in Christ stops where it begins to harm others, especially fellow believers. We have no right to "destroy with [our] food [or drink] him for whom Christ died" (Rom. 14:15). We cannot be absolutely certain even of our own ability to always drink in moderation, and even less certain that our example will not cause others—including our children—to drink beyond moderation. "Do not tear down the work of God for the sake of food," Paul continued. "All things indeed are clean, but they are evil for the man who eats and gives offense. It is good not to eat meat or to drink wine, or to do anything by which your brother stumbles" (vv.

20-21). Our own freedom in Christ should not be cherished above the welfare of even one other believer. We are to do those things "which make for peace and the building up of one another" (v. 19).

WILL IT HARM MY CHRISTIAN TESTIMONY?

To exercise our liberty in a way that might harm a brother in Christ cannot possibly enhance our testimony to unbelievers. Drinking might make us more acceptable in some circles, but our lack of concern for fellow Christians would work against any positive witness we might give. It would also hinder our testimony before many other Christians, who, though they might not be concerned about our influence hindering their own living for the Lord, would nevertheless be concerned about how it might harmfully influence other Christians.

Paul's standard given to the Corinthians indicates that the best testimony is to refuse a pagan host so as not to offend a brother: "If one of the unbelievers invites you, and you wish to go, eat anything that is set before you, without asking questions for conscience' sake. But if anyone should say to you, 'This is meat sacrificed to idols,' do not eat it, for the sake of the one who informed you, and for conscience' sake; I mean not your own conscience, but the other man's; for why is my freedom judged by another's conscience?" (1 Cor. 10:27-29). The witness is most effective if the pagan host can see how much you love and care for your Christian brother.

"Not one of us lives for himself, and not one dies for himself; for if we live, we live for the Lord, or if we die, we die for the Lord; therefore whether we live or die, we are the Lord's" (Rom. 14:7-8). Because everything a Christian is and has is the Lord's, the apostle also said, "Whether, then, you eat or drink or whatever you do, do all to the glory of God. Give no offense either to Jews or to Greeks or to the church of God; just as I also please all men in all things, not seeking my own profit, but the profit of the many, that they may be saved" (1 Cor. 10:31-33).

If we want to reach people who are not saved, as well as give an encouraging example to those who are, we will not exercise our liberty to drink or to do anything else that would cause them to be spiritually offended or misled.

IS IT RIGHT?

In light of all the above questions, the Christian should finally ask, Is it right for me to drink at all? We have seen that the answer to the first question is clearly no—the wine drunk in Bible times is not the same as contemporary wine. The answers to the second and third questions are also no for the majority of believers today—it is generally unnecessary to drink wine and is seldom the best choice. The answer to the next four questions is yes in at least some degree. Drinking is clearly habit forming and potentially destructive, and it is likely to offend other Christians and could harm our testimony before unbelievers.

A man once said to me, "I have a beer with the boys sometimes. Is that wrong?" I replied, "What do *you* think about it?" "Well, I don't think it's wrong; but it bothers me." "Do you like being bothered?" I asked. "No, I don't," he said. "You know how to stop being bothered don't you?" I continued, to which he gave the obvious answer, "Yes. Stop drinking."

Paul explicitly said, "He who doubts is condemned if he eats, because his eating is not from faith; and whatever is not from faith is sin" (Rom. 14:23). Even if we believe that something is not sinful in itself, if we cannot do it with a completely free conscience, we sin because we do it against our conscience. Going against our conscience will push us into self-condemnation and self-imposed guilt. Conscience is a God-given alarm to guard against sin, and whenever we go against it we weaken it and make it less sensitive and less reliable, thereby training ourselves to reject it. To continually go against conscience is to cause it to become "seared . . . as with a branding iron" (1 Tim. 4:2) and to become silent. When that happens, we lose a very powerful agent God has given to lead us (cf. 1 Tim. 1:5, 19).

As we ask ourselves questions about drinking, the final one is the most important: Can I do it before others and before God in total faith and confidence that it is right?

Be Filled with the Spirit—part 1

19

but be filled with the Spirit, speaking to one another in psalms and hymns and spiritual songs, singing and making melody with your heart to the Lord; always giving thanks for all things in the name of our Lord Jesus Christ to God, even the Father; and be subject to one another in the fear of Christ. (5:18*b*-21)

Apart from the truth in verse 18, which is the heart of Paul's message, the book of Ephesians would appear to be legalistic. Every exhortation he gives would have to be fulfilled through the power of the flesh. Believers would need to rely on their own resources and strength to follow the great road map of the Christian life that the apostle presents in chapters 4-6—and would, of course, find themselves completely deficient. Christians cannot walk in humility, unity, separation, light, love, and wisdom apart from the energizing of the Holy Spirit. To walk without the Spirit is to walk unwisely and foolishly (see vv. 15-17). We can "be imitators of God, as beloved children" (5:1) only as we are **filled with the Spirit** (cf. John 15:5).

In 5:18-21 Paul first presents the contrast of the way of the flesh with the way of the Spirit. As seen in the preceding discussion of v. 18*a*, the way of the flesh is characterized by the pagan religion out of which many of the Ephesian believers had come, a religion that centered around drunken, immoral orgies of supposed ecstasy, in which a person tried to progressively elevate himself into communion with the gods. It is the way of self, pride, immorality, greed, idolatry, confusion, deception, fantasy, falsehood, and even demonism. It is the way of darkness and foolishness (see 5:3-17).

In vv. 18b-21 the apostle gives the other side of the contrast—the godly walk of God's children that expresses itself in the Spirit-controlled life and worship of beauty and holiness. He first gives the central command of the epistle (which is the focal point of the New Testament for believers) and follows it with an outline of the consequences of obedience to that command.

The Command

but be filled with the Spirit, (5:18b)

Although Paul was not present when the Holy Spirit manifested Himself so powerfully at Pentecost, he must have had that event in mind as he wrote **be filled with the Spirit**. Pentecost obviously occurred while he was still an unbeliever and before he began persecuting the church. But without Pentecost he and other unbelievers would have had no reason to persecute the church, because it would have been too weak and powerless to threaten Satan's domain. It was there that the other apostles heard the heavenly "noise like a violent, rushing wind," saw "tongues as of fire distributing themselves" and resting "on each one of them," and were "filled with the Holy Spirit and began to speak with other tongues, as the Spirit was giving them utterance" (Acts 2:2-4). It was also there that some of the crowd accused the apostles of being "full of sweet wine" (v. 13), probably expecting them to break out into the typical frenzied antics of mystical pagan worship.

Though others (such as Moses, Ex. 31:3; 35:31) had been filled with the Spirit for special purposes, it was at Pentecost that all believers in the church were first filled with the Holy Spirit. Every promise that Jesus gave to His disciples on the last night He was with them was fulfilled in some sense by the coming the Holy Spirit on that day. In fact, it was the coming of the Holy Spirit that made real all the promises of Jesus Christ.

Jesus said, "And I will ask the Father, and He will give you another Helper, that He may be with you forever; that is the Spirit of truth, whom the world cannot receive, because it does not behold Him or know Him, but you know Him because He abides with you, and will be in you" (John 14:16-17). The Holy Spirit's permanently indwelling all believers—rather than only being with some of them, as was true before Pentecost—is one of the great dispensational truths of the New Testament. In the new age, the church age, the Spirit of God would not be just be alongside His people but in them all (cf. 1 Cor. 3:16; 6:19). It is this residence of the Holy Spirit in believers that makes possible the fulfillment of all Jesus' other promises to His people, and in Ephesians 1:13 He is called "the Holy Spirit of promise."

The Holy Spirit is our divine pledge and security that Jesus' promises are fulfilled (2 Cor. 5:5). Among many other things, He guarantees and gives assurance that we will have a heavenly dwelling place in the Father's house (John 14:2-3); that we will do greater works, not in kind but in extent, even than He did (14:12; cf. Matt. 28:18-20; Acts 1:8); that whatever we ask in His name he will do (John 14:13-14); that we will have Christ's own peace (14:27); that the fullness of His joy will be in us (15:11). The Holy Spirit assures us that Jesus Christ and the Father are one (14:20); that we are indeed God's children (Rom. 8:16); that he will intercede for us, making our prayers effective (Rom. 8:26); and that He will bear fruit in our lives (Gal. 5:22-23).

But the work of the Holy Spirit in us and on our behalf can be appropriated only as He fills us. Every Christian is indwelt by the Holy Spirit and has the potential of receiving the fulfillment of all Christ's promises to those who belong to Him. But no Christian will have those promises fulfilled who is not under the full control of the Holy Spirit. We have just claim to all Christ's promises the moment we believe in Him, but we cannot have their fulfillment until we allow His Spirit to fill us and control us. Unless we know what it is to be directed by the Holy Spirit, we will never know the bliss of the assurance of heaven, or the joy of effective work for the Lord, of having our prayers answered constantly, or of indulging in the fullness of God's own love, joy, and peace within us.

THE MEANING OF BEING FILLED

Before we look specifically at what the filling of the Spirit is, we should clarify some of the things it is not. First, being filled with the Holy Spirit is not a dramatic, esoteric experience of suddenly being energized and spiritualized into a permanent state of advanced spirituality by a second act of blessing subsequent to salvation. Nor is it some temporary "zap" that results in ecstatic speech or unearthly visions.

Second, being filled with the Spirit is not the notion at the other extreme— simply stoically trying to do what God wants us to do, with the Holy Spirit's blessing but basically in our own power. It is not an act of the flesh which has God's approval.

Third, being filled is not the same as possessing, or being indwelt by, the Holy Spirit, because He indwells every believer at the moment of salvation. As Paul plainly states in the book of Romans, "If anyone does not have the Spirit of Christ, he does not belong to Him" (8:9; cf. John 7:38-39). A person who does not have the Holy Spirit does not have Christ. Even to the immature, worldly Corinthian believers, Paul said, "For by one Spirit we were all baptized into one body, . . . and we were all made to drink of one Spirit" (1 Cor. 12:13). Unlike believers before Pentecost, on whom the Holy Spirit would come temporarily (Judg. 13:25; 16:20; 1 Sam. 16:14; Ps. 51:11), all Christians are permanently indwelt by the Spirit.

Fourth, being filled with the Spirit does not describe a process of progressively receiving Him by degrees or in doses. Every Christian not only possesses the Holy Spirit but possesses Him in His fullness. God does not parcel out the Spirit, as if He could somehow be divided into various segments or parts. "He gives the Spirit without measure," Jesus said (John 3:34).

Fifth, it is also clear from 1 Corinthians 12:13 that the filling with the Spirit is not the same as the baptism of the Spirit, because every believer has been baptized with and received the Spirit. Although its results are experienced and enjoyed, baptism by and reception of the Spirit are not realities we can feel, and are certainly not experiences reserved only for specially-blessed believers. This miracle is a spiritual reality—whether realized or not—that occurs in every believer the moment he becomes a Christian and is placed by Christ into His Body by the Holy Spirit, who then takes up residence in that life.

Paul did not accuse the Corinthians of being immature and sinful because they did not yet have the Holy Spirit or the baptism in the Body and then exhort them to seek the Spirit in order to remedy the situation. Rather he reminded them that each one of them already possessed the Holy Spirit. Earlier in the letter he had pleaded with them to "flee immorality. Every other sin that a man commits is outside the body, but the immoral man sins against his own body. Or do you not know that your body is a temple of the Holy Spirit who is in you, whom you have from God, and that you are not your own?" (6:18-19). They were not sinning because of the Holy Spirit's absence but in spite of the Holy Spirit's presence. Even when a Christian sins he is still indwelt by the Holy Spirit, and it is that very fact that makes his sin even worse. When a Christian grieves the Spirit (Eph. 4:30) or quenches the Spirit (1 Thess. 5:19), he grieves or quenches the Spirit who resides within himself.

Finally, the filling with Spirit is not the same as being sealed, or secured, by Him. That is an accomplished fact (see on 1:13). Nowhere are believers commanded or exhorted to be indwelt, baptized, or sealed by the Holy Spirit. The *only* command is to be filled.

Be filled translates the present passive imperative of *plēroō,* and is more literally rendered as "be being kept filled." It is a command that includes the idea of conscious continuation. Being filled with the Holy Spirit is not an option for believers but a mandate. No Christian can fulfill God's will for his life apart from being filled with His Spirit. If we do not obey this command, we cannot obey any other—simply because we cannot do any of God's will apart from God's Spirit. Outside of the command for unbelievers to trust in Christ for salvation, there is no more practical and necessary command in Scripture than the one for believers to be filled with the Spirit.

Commands such as this one remind us of the fact that believers are subject to divine authority and are called to obedience as the most basic element of Christian living. In some Christian circles, the manner of living, and even the actual teaching, reflects the notion that just being in the kingdom is all that really matters. Anything one might do in obedience to the Lord after that is considered to be simply a kind of spiritual "extra credit." Some would say that in Christ there is safety from hell, and that even if all works are burned up and no rewards are given, one will still go to heaven. Even the most obscure corner of heaven will still be heaven, it is argued, and all believers will live there in eternal bliss.

That sort of thinking is totally out of harmony with the teaching of the New Testament. It comes from spiritual hardness of heart and tends to produce a life that is careless and indifferent, and often immoral and idolatrous. The person with such an unscriptural attitude toward the things of God is either walking in direct opposition to the Spirit or else does not possess the Spirit at all—in which case he is not a Christian. Submission to the will of God, to Christ's lordship, and to the guiding of the Spirit is an essential, not an optional, part of saving faith. A new, untaught believer will understand little of the full implications of such obedience, but the spiritual orientation of his new nature in Christ will bring the desire for submission to God's Word and God's Spirit. A person who does not have that desire has no legitimate claim on salvation.

To resist the filling and control of the Holy Spirit is flagrant disobedience, and to deny or minimize its importance is to stand rebelliously against the clear teaching of God's own Word. Every Christian falls short of God's standards and will sometimes fall into sin and indifference. But he cannot be continually content in such a state, because the experience of sin and indifference will be in a constant struggle with his new nature (see Rom. 7:14-25). He knows they cannot be justified or in any way reconciled with God's will.

As we learn from Paul's dealing with the Christians at Corinth, it is possible that for a time a believer may become and even remain carnal, or fleshly, to some extent (1 Cor. 3:1), but that will never be a true believer's basic orientation. The terms *carnal* or *fleshly* are most often used in the New Testament of unbelievers. "The mind set on the flesh is death," Paul said, "but the mind set on the Spirit is life and peace, because the mind set on the flesh is hostile toward God; for it does not subject itself to the law of God, for it is not even able to do so" (Rom. 8:6-7). A person whose mind is regularly set on the things of the flesh cannot be a Christian, because a Christian is "not in the flesh but in the Spirit, if indeed the Spirit of God dwells in [him]" (v. 9). A professed Christian who continually longs for the things of the world and the flesh needs to examine his heart carefully to see whether his carnality is that described in 1 Corinthians 3:1-3 or in Romans 8:6-8 (cf. 1 John 2:15-17; James 4:4).

Although every Christian is indwelt, baptized, and sealed by the Spirit, unless he is also **filled with the Spirit**, he will live in spiritual weakness, retardation, frustration and defeat.

The continuous aspect of being *filled* ("be being kept filled") involves day-by-day, moment-by-moment submission to the Spirit's control. The passive aspect indicates that it is not something we do but that we allow to be done in us. The filling is entirely the work of the Spirit Himself, but He works only through our willing submission. The present aspect of the command indicates that we cannot rely on a past filling nor live in expectation of future filling. We can rejoice in past fillings and hope for future fillings, but we can live only in present filling.

The mark of a good marriage relationship is not the love and devotion the husband and wife have had in the past—as meaningful and lovely as that may have been—nor is it the love and devotion they hope to have in the future. The strength of their marriage is in the love and devotion they have for each other in the present.

Plēroō connotes more than filling something up, as when someone pours water in a glass up the rim. The term was used in three additional senses that have great significance for Paul's use of it here. First, it was often used of the wind filling a sail and thereby carrying the ship along. To be filled with the Spirit is to be moved along in our Christian life by God Himself, by the same dynamic by which the writers of Scripture were "moved by the Holy Spirit" (2 Pet. 1:21).

Second, *plēroō* carries the idea of permeation, and was used of salt's permeating meat in order to flavor and preserve it. God wants His Holy Spirit to so permeate the lives of His children that everything they think, say, and do will reflect His divine presence.

Third, *plēroō* has the connotation of total control. The person who is filled with sorrow (see John 16:6) is no longer under his own control but is totally under the control of that emotion. In the same way, someone who is filled with fear (Luke 5:26), anger (Luke 6:11), faith (Acts 6:5), or even Satan (Acts 5:3) is no longer under his own control but under the total control of that which dominates him. To be filled in this sense is to be totally dominated and controlled, and it is the most important sense for believers. As we have already seen, to **be filled with the Spirit** is not to have Him somehow progressively added to our life until we are full of Him. It is to be under His total domination and control. This is in direct contrast to the uncontrolled drunkenness and dissipation in the worship of Dionysius that was alluded to in the first half of the verse.

We see the controlling work of the Holy Spirit even in Jesus' life while He ministered in the flesh. The Holy Spirit led Him "into the wilderness to be tempted by the devil" (Matt. 4:1). We learn from the parallel passage in Luke that it was Jesus' being "full of the Holy Spirit" that prepared Him to be "led about by the Spirit in the wilderness" (4:1). The account in Mark uses an even stronger term, saying that "the Spirit impelled Him to go out into the wilderness" (1:12). It was not that Jesus resisted or had to be coerced, because His greatest joy was to do His Father's will (John 4:34), but that He submitted Himself entirely to the Spirit's control. Because He was full of the Spirit He was controlled by the Spirit.

The Christian who is filled with the Holy Spirit can be compared to a glove. Until it is filled by a hand, a glove is powerless and useless. It is designed to do work, but it can do no work by itself. It works only as the hand controls and uses it. The glove's only work is the hand's work. It does not ask the hand to give it an assignment and then try to complete the assignment without the hand. Nor does it gloat or brag about what it is used to do, because it knows the hand deserves all the credit. A Christian can accomplish no more without being filled with the Holy Spirit than a glove can accomplish without being filled with a hand. Anything he manages to do is but wood, hay, and straw that amounts to nothing and will eventually be burned up (1 Cor. 3:12-15). Functioning in the flesh produces absolutely nothing of spiritual value.

When the church at Jerusalem wanted men to free the apostles for the more important work of prayer and ministering the Word, they chose men such as Stephen, who was "full of faith and of the Holy Spirit" (Acts 6:4-5). Because Stephen continued in the fullness of the Spirit, "he gazed intently into heaven and saw the glory of God, and Jesus standing at the right hand of God," even as he was about to be stoned to death (Acts 7:55). Being filled with the Spirit detaches us from the desires, the standards, the objectives, the fears, and the very system of this world and gives us a vision of God that comes in no other way. Being filled with the Spirit makes everything else of secondary importance, and often of no importance at all.

Although Peter was first filled with the Holy Spirit at Pentecost along with all the other disciples, some while later he spoke to the assembled Jewish leaders in Jerusalem and it is again said that he was "filled with the Holy Spirit" (Acts 4:8).

Before God could use Saul, who later became Paul, as apostle to the Gentiles, He had Ananias lay his hands on Saul's head and tell him, "Brother Saul, the Lord Jesus, who appeared to you on the road by which you were coming, has sent me so that you may regain your sight, and be filled with the Holy Spirit" (Acts 9:17). Without the yieldedness that allowed the filling of the Spirit, Paul would have been of no more use to the Lord than were the worldly members at Corinth among whom he would later minister.

When the church at Jerusalem needed a man to help with the ministry to Gentiles in Antioch, "they sent Barnabas . . . for he was a good man, and full of the Holy Spirit" (Acts 11:22, 24). We read that Paul was "filled with the Holy Spirit" as he confronted the deceitful magician named Elymas (Acts 13:9), and that "the disciples were continually filled with joy and with the Holy Spirit" while being ridiculed and persecuted (13:52).

The concern we often hear about recapturing the dedication, zeal, love, and power of the early church is commendable. But we cannot have the early church's spiritual power simply by trying to copy its methods of operation. We can experience those believers' spiritual power only when we are surrendered to the Holy Spirit's control as they were. It was not their methodology but their Spirit-filled lives that empowered believers to turn the world upside down in the first century (Acts 17:6).

THE MEANS OF BEING FILLED

God commands nothing for which He does not provide the means to obey. And if God commands something of us, we do not need to pray for it, because it is obviously His will and intent for us to do it. It is God's deepest desire that each of His children be filled with His Spirit. We only need to discover the resources He has provided to carry out that obedience.

To **be filled with the Spirit** involves confession of sin, surrender of will, intellect, body, time, talent, possessions, and desires. It requires the death of selfishness and the slaying of self-will. When we die to self, the Lord fills with His

Spirit. The principle stated by John the Baptist applies to the Spirit as well as to Christ: "He must increase, but I must decrease" (John 3:30).

Paul's command to the Colossians, "Let the word of Christ richly dwell within you," was followed by a series of subsequent and dependent commands (Col. 3:16-25) that exactly paralleled those Paul gave in Ephesians 5:19-33 as being results of the filling of the Spirit. In both cases we see that singing, giving thanks, and submissiveness follow being filled with the Spirit and letting the word of Christ dwell in us. It is therefore easy to conclude that the filling of the Spirit is not an esoteric, mystical experience bestowed on the spiritual elite through some secret formula or other such means. It is simply taking the Word of Christ (Scripture) and letting it indwell and infuse every part of our being. To be filled with God's Spirit is to be filled with His Word. And as we are filled with God's Word, it controls our thinking and action, and we thereby come more and more under the Spirit's control. As Charles Spurgeon said, the Christian's blood should be "bibline," bleeding Scripture wherever he may be pricked or cut.

Peter's strength lay in his always seeking to be near Jesus. When Jesus walked down a road, Peter was with Him. When He went up to the mountain or out in a boat, Peter went with Him. Peter got into trouble only when he got away from His Lord. When he stayed near the Lord, he did the miraculous, said the miraculous, and had miraculous courage.

When Peter saw Jesus standing on the water some distance from the boat, he stepped out on the water himself when Jesus said, "Come!" and found himself walking on the water just like the Lord—until his attention turned from Jesus to himself and his circumstances (Matt. 14:27-31). On another occasion, when Jesus asked His disciples, "But who do you say that I am?" Peter immediately "answered and said, 'Thou art the Christ, the Son of the living God.' And Jesus answered and said to him, 'Blessed are you, Simon Barjona, because flesh and blood did not reveal this to you, but My Father who is in heaven'" (Matt. 16:15-17). Because his mind and spirit were centered on Christ, Peter was used by God to make that great testimony to Jesus' messiahship and divine sonship. A short while later, however, Peter pitted his own understanding against the Lord's, and discovered that he then spoke for Satan rather than for God (16:22-23).

When the soldiers came to arrest Jesus in the Garden of Gethsemane, they drew back and fell to the ground when Jesus identified Himself as the One they were seeking. Perhaps taking courage from that reaction, Peter took out his sword and cut off the right ear of Malchus, a slave of the high priest, and probably would have continued fighting to the death had not Jesus restrained him (John 18:3-11; cf. Luke 22:47-51). When he was near the Lord, he feared no one. But when a short while later he found himself separated from the Lord, he did not have the courage even to admit knowing Jesus (John 18:15-27).

After the ascended Lord sent His Holy Spirit to indwell and fill His disciples as He had promised, Peter found himself again able to say and do the miraculous and to have miraculous courage. He had the courage to fearlessly proclaim His risen Lord in the place where, a few months earlier, He had been arrested, beaten, and crucified—and found his message miraculously empowered and blessed, with some three thousand coming to salvation from that one sermon (Acts 2:14-41). When the lame man near the Temple asked Peter and John for alms, Peter replied, "'I do not possess silver and gold, but what I do have I give to you: In the name of Jesus Christ the Nazarene—walk!' And seizing him by the right hand, he raised him up; and immediately his feet and his ankles were strengthened" (Acts 3:1-7). When he was arrested by the Sanhedrin and questioned about the healing, Peter was "filled with the Holy Spirit" and proclaimed that he had healed by the power of Jesus Christ, whom they had crucified. Because they could not deny the miracle and were afraid of the many people who glorified God because of it, the Jewish leaders simply commanded Peter and John to no longer preach in Jesus' name. Peter responded, "Whether it is right in the sight of God to give heed to you rather than to God, you be the judge; for we cannot stop speaking what we have seen and heard" (Acts 4:1-22).

To **be filled with the Spirit** is to live in the consciousness of the personal presence of the Lord Jesus Christ, as if we were standing next to Him, and to let His mind dominate our life. It is to fill ourselves with God's Word, so that His thoughts will be our thoughts, His standards our standards, His work our work, and His will our will. As we yield to the truth of Christ, the Holy Spirit will lead us to say, do, and be what God wants us to say, do, and be. "We all, with unveiled face beholding as in a mirror the glory of the Lord, are being transformed into the same image from glory to glory, just as from the Lord, the Spirit" (2 Cor. 3:18). Christ consciousness leads to Christ likeness.

Perhaps the best analogy of moment-by-moment yielding to the Holy Spirit's control is the figure of walking, the figure Paul introduced in Ephesians 4:1. Walking involves moving one step at a time, and can be done in no other way. Being **filled with the Spirit** is walking thought by thought, decision by decision, act by act under the Spirit's control. The Spirit-filled life yields every step to the Spirit of God. "Walk by the Spirit, and you will not carry out the desire of the flesh. For the flesh sets its desire against the Spirit, and the Spirit against the flesh; for these are in opposition to one another, so that you may not do the things that you please" (Gal. 5:16-17). Our flesh is the beachhead of sin, the yet unredeemed part of our humanness that is exposed to and inclined toward sin. Even as Christians, as new creatures in Christ, our spiritual and moral Achilles' heel is the flesh, the remnant of the old self that seeks to drag us down from behavior consistent with our heavenly citizenship. Paul spoke of it as "a different law in the members of my body, waging war against the law of my mind, and making me a prisoner of the law of sin which is in my members" (Rom. 7:23). The only way to override that residual sinfulness, our evil desires, and the temptations of Satan is to function in the Spirit.

Not to be filled with the Spirit is to fall back into "the deeds of the flesh . . . which are: immorality, impurity, sensuality, idolatry, sorcery, enmities, strife, jealousy, outbursts of anger, disputes, dissensions, factions, envyings, drunken- ness, carousings, and things like these" (Gal. 5:19-21). We do not have to consciously choose to do the deeds of the flesh. If we are not living under the control of God's Word and Spirit, the deeds of the flesh are the only things we *can* do, because the flesh is the only resource we have in ourselves.

The sole defense against the negative power of temptation, sin, and Satan is the positive power of the Holy Spirit. We have no power over those evils, and to try to combat them in our own strength is to try to walk on water by our own power. We win spiritual victories only when God's Holy Spirit does battle for us.

But when we surrender to the control of God's Spirit, we find Him producing amazing things in us, things which are entirely of His doing. Paul calls these marvelous blessings the fruit of the Spirit, and they are: "love, joy, peace, patience, kindness, goodness, faithfulness, gentleness, self-control" (Gal. 5:22-23). The person who is Spirit-controlled and who bears the Spirit's fruit is the person who belongs to Christ and who has "crucified the flesh with its passions and desires. If we live by the Spirit," Paul continued, "let us also walk by the Spirit" (Gal. 5:24-25). To walk in the Spirit is to fulfill the ultimate potential and capacity of our life on earth as God's children.

Be Filled with the Spirit—part 2

20

but be filled with the Spirit, speaking to one another in psalms and hymns and spiritual songs, singing and making melody with your heart to the Lord; always giving thanks for all things in the name of our Lord Jesus Christ to God, even the Father; and be subject to one another in the fear of Christ. (5:18*b*-21)

Following His command to **be filled with the Spirit**, Paul gave a summary of the consequences of obedience to that command.

THE CONSEQUENCES

speaking to one another in psalms and hymns and spiritual songs, singing and making melody with your heart to the Lord; always giving thanks for all things in the name of our Lord Jesus Christ to God, even the Father; and be subject to one another in the fear of Christ. (5:19-21)

Consequences of the Spirit-filled life (which greatly enrich our understanding of its nature) are mentioned throughout the remainder of the epistle, and in these verses we are given three of the most significant ones: singing, giving thanks, and submission. When God's Spirit controls us he will put a song in our own hearts and on our lips, give us thankfulness to God, and make us submissive to others. The first is initially inward, the second upward, and the third outward. The filling of the Holy Spirit makes us rightly related to ourselves, to God, and to others.

THE CONSEQUENCE WITH OURSELVES: SINGING

speaking to one another in psalms and hymns and spiritual songs, singing and making melody with your heart to the Lord; (5:19)

The Spirit-filled life produces music. Whether he has a good voice or cannot carry a tune, the Spirit-filled Christian is a singing Christian. Nothing is more indicative of a fulfilled life, a contented soul, and a happy heart than the expression of song.

The first consequence of the Spirit-filled life that Paul mentioned was not mountain-moving faith, an ecstatic spiritual experience, dynamic speaking ability, or any other such thing. It was simply a heart that sings. When the believer walks in the Spirit, he has an inside joy that manifests itself in music. God puts music in the souls and then on the lips of His children who walk in obedience.

When missionaries began evangelistic work among an Indian tribe I visited high in the Andes of Ecuador, they were frustrated for many years by lack of results. Suddenly the Spirit of God began to move and a large number of Indians were converted within a short time. In addition to a hunger for God's Word, one of the first evidences of their new life in Christ was a great desire to sing His praises. I listened as they stood for hours in their thatched-roof church and sang hymn after hymn. The song from their hearts was the most inescapable characteristic that set those believers apart from everyone else in their pagan village.

The Spirit's music is not hindered by a monotone or enhanced by a musical degree or magnificent voice. Spiritual joy will shine through a song sung with the raspy, off-pitch voice of a saint who is rejoicing in the Lord, and it will be absent from the song sung with technical skill and accuracy, but with a voice that rejoices only in self.

One of the greatest distinctions of Christianity should be in its music, because the music God gives is not the music the world gives. In Scripture, the word *new* is used more frequently in relation to song than to any other feature of salvation. God gives His new creatures a new song, a different song, a distinctive song, a purer song, and a more beautiful song than anything the world can produce.

"Sing for joy in the Lord, O you righteous ones," says the psalmist; "praise is becoming to the upright" (Ps. 33:1). It is because we have been made righteous, purified from sin, and have become partakers of God's own holiness that we sing. No one but a Christian has any legitimate reason to sing. God Himself puts a song in our mouths, "a song of praise to our God" (Ps. 40:3). Because we have salvation we sing songs of salvation. "Sing to the Lord a new song; sing to the Lord, all the earth. Sing to the Lord, bless His name; proclaim good tidings of His salvation from day to day" (Ps. 96:1-2; cf. 149:1).

One day the four living creatures and the twenty-four elders will fall down before Jesus Christ, the Lamb, and sing "a new song, saying, 'Worthy art Thou to take the book, and to break its seals; for Thou wast slain, and didst purchase for God with Thy blood men from every tribe and tongue and people and nation" (Rev. 5:8-9). God's new song is the song of redemption.

When God delivered Israel out of Egypt, all the people came together and sang a song to the Lord (Ex. 15:1-18). After they finished, Moses' sister, Miriam, led the women in further singing and dancing (vv. 20-21). After Deborah and Barak delivered Israel from the Canaanites, they "sang on that day" (Judg. 5:1). Of the 38,000 people who ministered at the Temple in Jerusalem, 4,000 were musicians; and in Nehemiah we read of antiphonal choirs (Neh. 12:31, 38). Throughout the Old Testament, and particularly in the Psalms, we read of many kinds of musical instruments that God's people used to praise Him.

The last thing Jesus and His disciples did after the Last Supper was to sing a hymn before they went out to the Garden of Gethsemane, where Jesus was arrested (Matt. 26:30). While they were imprisoned in Philippi, "about midnight Paul and Silas were praying and singing hymns of praise to God, and the prisoners were listening to them" (Acts 16:25). On the heavenly Mount Zion the 144,000 who will have been purchased from the earth will sing "a new song before the throne" of Christ (Rev. 14:3).

In Ephesians 5:19 Paul explains among whom, from where, with what, to whom, and how Spirit-filled believers are to sing.

Among whom do believers sing? The primary audience for our singing is to be fellow believers, **one another.** Throughout Scripture the singing of God's people is shown to be within the fellowship of believers. No music in the Bible is ever characterized as being or intended to be evangelistic. God may use the gospel content set to music to bring the truth to the lost and thus lead them to Himself. Since the message is so powerful, the open heart may receive it even though it comes with a melody. But that is not the intent for music, and when emotions are played on without a clear or complete presentation of God's truth to the mind, such music can be counterproductive by producing a feeling of well-being and contentment that is a counterfeit of God's peace and that serves to further insulate an unbeliever from the saving gospel.

It should be noted that the many contemporary entertainers who think they are using their rock-style music to evangelize the lost are often doing nothing more than contributing to the weakening of the church. Evangelizing with contemporary music has many serious flaws. It tends to create pride in the musicians rather than humility. It makes the gospel a matter of entertainment when there is not one thing in it that is at all entertaining. It makes the public proclaimers of Christianity those who are popular and talented in the world's eyes, rather than those who are godly and gifted teachers of God's truth. In using the world's genres of music, it blurs the gap between worldly Satanic values and divine ones. It tends to deny the power of the simple gospel and the sovereign saving work of the Holy Spirit. It creates a wide generation gap in the church, thus contributing to the disunity and lack of intimacy in the fellowship of all believers. It leads to the propagation of bad or weak theology and drags the name of the Lord down to the level of the world. The music of the gospel is certainly not a legitimate means for making money or seeking fame, and it must never be allowed to cheapen what is priceless, or trivialize what is profound.

The songs of faith are not for the world to sing or really even to hear. The unsaved person has no comprehension of the praises we sing, because he has no presence of God's Spirit within him. He cannot sing the song of redemption because he is not redeemed. Christian singing is an expression of individual and corporate worship, of celebrating life together in Jesus Christ.

For over a thousand dark years of its history (c. 500-1500) the church in general did not sing. From shortly after New Testament times until the Reformation, what music the church had was usually performed by professional musicians. The music they presented could not be understood or appreciated by the average church member. In any case, they could only sit and listen, unable to participate. But when the Bible came back into the church during the Reformation, singing came with it. Martin Luther and some of the other Reformation leaders are among the greatest hymn writers of church history. Where the true gospel is known and believed, music is loved and sung. God's Spirit in the heart puts music in the heart.

How do believers sing? When they are filled with the Spirit, they are to be **speaking . . . in psalms and hymns and spiritual songs, singing and making melody. Speaking** comes from *laleō,* is an onomatopoeic word that originated from chatter or babble, probably of little children first learning to talk, saying sounds such as "la, la, la." It was also used of the chirp of birds or the grunts and other noises of animals. In its most basic sense, the term simply meant to make a sound.

Trumpets (Rev. 4:1) and even peals of thunder (10:4) are said to be speaking. The psalmist called God's people to join all the earth in shouting "joyfully to God" (Ps. 66:1). **Speaking** here includes any sound offered to God from a Spirit-filled heart. The music from an organ or choir is no more acceptable to God than the sounds of a guitar or home-made flute. The sound that pleases Him is the sound that comes as a result of a heart submissive to His Spirit and that sings or plays to His glory.

Psalms refers primarily to the Old Testament psalms put to music, but the term was also used of vocal music of any sort, such as solos and anthems. The early church did most of its singing directly from the psaltery, using various tunes familiar to the congregation—a pattern followed for hundreds of years by many European and American churches, and still used in some congregations today. The **psalms** primarily speak about the nature and work of God, especially in the lives of believers. Above everything else, they magnify and glorify God.

Hymns refers primarily to songs of praise, which in the early church were probably distinguished from the **psalms**, which exalted God, in that they specifically praised the Lord Jesus Christ. Many biblical scholars believe that various New Testament passages (such as Col. 1:12-16) were used as hymns in the early church. **Spiritual songs** were probably songs of testimony that covered a broad category that included any music expressing spiritual truth.

In the church today we could classify renditions of Psalms 23 and 84 as **psalms**, "A Mighty Fortress is Our God" and "The Old Rugged Cross" as **hymns**, and "O How He Loves You and Me" and "I'd Rather Have Jesus" as **spiritual songs**. The intent of the writer here, however, is simply to give latitude for all kinds of musical expression to exalt the Lord.

Singing is from *adō*, which simply means to sing with the voice. But in the New Testament it is always used in relation to praising God (see also Col. 3:16; Rev. 5:9; 14:3; 15:3).

The human voice is the most beautiful of all instruments. Its various tones, inflections, and moods seem almost limitless. Because it is itself human, it can speak to us as no other form of music.

Yet the sound God is looking for in His children is the sound made out of a Spirit-filled heart—whether the voice that makes the sound is rough and unpolished or smooth and highly trained. That is why every believer is just as capable as any other believer of **singing** the praises that God puts in his heart.

The gift of a good voice or of other musical talent does not demand, as many argue, that it should necessarily be used for performing special music in the church. The gift of music no more demands public display than does the gift of carpentry, cooking, medicine, or any other. That which is done to glorify God is done for that purpose alone, and its being noticed or unnoticed is secondary and incidental. Whether we sing alone in our home or car, sing with a few friends around the piano or with guitars, or sing in a large choir leading hundreds of people in worship, we should do it from a Spirit-filled heart that seeks no glory but God's.

Psalto (**making melody**) is related to the term from which we get *psalm* and literally means to pluck on a stringed instrument, particularly a harp, with the fingers. The word, however, came to represent the making of any instrumental music. The Spirit-filled heart expresses itself in any sort of vocal or instrumental music, in both **singing and making melody**.

Much music in the church today truly honors God and blesses those who hear it. And whether given as **psalms** about God's greatness, as **hymns** of Christ's redemption, or as **spiritual songs** of testimony of God's power, help, or comfort, such music is to be an expression of the Spirit-filled church. Whether given through the voice in **singing** or through instruments in **making melody**, that is the music that honors, glorifies, and pleases God.

Our Lord Himself will sing one day, and in our very midst. He said to His Father, "I will proclaim Thy name to My brethren, in the midst of the congregation I will sing Thy praise" (Heb. 2:12). But even now, when our hearts are filled with the Holy Spirit, Jesus sings songs of praise to the Father through us. Therefore when we quench the Spirit, we quench the song of Christ to the Father in our life.

From where do believers sing? The songs of salvation originate **with your heart**. The Greek form of this phrase allows for several meanings. There is no preposition here in the Greek, and in such cases the preposition is determined by the case of the noun—which here has several possibilities, all of which seem appropriate to the context. If the case of **heart** is taken as an instrumental of cause, the idea is that our hearts cause us to sing and make melody to God. As an instrumental of means, the idea is that our hearts are the channels through which we sing praises. As a locative, the idea is that the singing is centered in our hearts.

A person who does not have a song in his heart cannot sing from his heart or with his heart. He can only sing with his lips, and neither his music nor his message will have the power of the Spirit to bless others in Christ's name.

Even as Christians we will not have a true song in our hearts unless we are under the Spirit's control. It is possible to sing for pride, to sing for acclaim and fame, and to sing for money—but such singing is Spiritless singing. A person who comes to worship while bitter toward God, angry with a loved one or friend, or in any other way is out of harmony with God's Spirit should not participate in singing God's praises. Hypocrisy can neither praise nor please the Lord. When peoples' hearts are not right with God, He has a way of turning their "festivals into mourning" and their "songs into lamentation" (Amos 8:10). Through the same prophet God said, "Take away from Me the noise of your songs; I will not even listen to the sound of your harps. But let justice roll down like waters and righteousness like an everflowing stream" (5:23-24). "Stop your songs until your hearts are right," he was saying.

Our music cannot be like the music of the world, because our God is not like their gods. Most of the world's music reflects the world's ways, the world's standards, the world's attitudes, the world's gods. To attempt to use such music to reach the world is to lower the gospel in order to spread the gospel. If the world hears that our music is not much different from theirs, it will also be inclined to believe that the Christian way of life is not much different from theirs. Christians cannot honestly sing the world's philosophies nor can the world honestly sing the Christian's message, because they sing from utterly different hearts. The Christian's heart and music belong to God and His righteousness, while the world's heart and music belong to Satan and his unrighteousness.

Because the Christian's music is God's music, it will be sung in heaven throughout all the ages to come. And because the world's music is Satan's music, it will one day cease, never to be heard again. The sounds of the world's "harpists and musicians and flute-players and trumpeters will not be heard . . . any longer" (Rev. 18:22). To those who make music that is not His, God declares, "I will silence the sound of your songs, and the sound of your harps will be heard no more" (Ezek. 26:13). In hell, the ungodly will not even have their own music.

The pulsating rhythms of native African music mimics the restless, superstitious passions of their culture and religion. The music of the Orient is dissonant and unresolved, going from nowhere to nowhere, with no beginning and no end—just as their religions go from cycle to cycle in endless repetitions of meaningless existence. Their music, like their destiny, is without resolution. The music of much of the Western world is the music of seduction and suggestiveness, a musical counterpart of the immoral, lustful society that produces, sings, and enjoys it.

Rock music, with its bombastic atonality and dissonance, is the musical mirror of the hopeless, standardless, purposeless philosophy that rejects both God and reason and floats without orientation in a sea of relativity and unrestrained self-expression. The music has no logical progression because it comes from a philosophy that renounces logic. It violates the brain because its philosophy violates reason. It violates the spirit, because its philosophy violates truth and goodness. And it violates God, because its philosophy violates all authority outside of self.

Not only the titles and lyrics of many rock songs but the names of many rock groups shamelessly flaunt a godless, immoral, and often demonic orientation. The association of hard rock with violence, blasphemy, sadomasochism, sexual immorality and perversion, alcohol and drugs, and Eastern mysticism and the occult are not accidental. They are fed from the same ungodly stream. A leading rock singer once said, "Rock has always been the devil's music. It lets in the baser elements." Another testified, "I find myself evil. I believe in the devil as much as God. You can use either to get things done." Putting a Christian message in such musical form does not elevate the form but degrades the message to the level already established in the culture by that form.

A great majority of young people in modern Western society are continually assaulted with a philosophy set to music that simultaneously destroys their bodies, short-circuits their minds, and perverts their spirits. A young man who was converted out of that involvement once said to me, "Whenever I hear rock music, I feel a tremendous urge to get drunk or go back on drugs." The association was so strong that simply hearing the music triggered his old addictions.

Many of the physical and emotional effects of rock music can be demonstrated scientifically. Howard Hansen of the Eastman School of Music once wrote, "First, everything else being equal, the further the tempo is accelerated in music from the pulse rate toward the upper limit of practical tempo, the greater becomes the emotional tension." He says further that "as long as the subdivisions of the metric units are regular and the accents remain strictly in conformity with the basic patterns, the effect may be accelerated but will not be disturbing. Rhythmic tension is heightened by increase in dynamic power."

Several years ago a college in Colorado made a study of the effects of music on plants. Plants exposed to beautiful, soothing music thrived and turned toward the speaker. In an otherwise identical environment, another group of the same type of plant was exposed to acid rock. Those plants turned away from the speaker and within three days had shriveled and died. Further experimentation proved that the sound waves of the rock music had actually destroyed the plants' cells.

Whether or not human cells are destroyed by rock music, things of even greater value are destroyed. When fast tempo, unrhythmical beat, high volume, and dissonance are coupled with wild shrieks, blasphemous and lewd lyrics, and suggestive body movements, the brain is bypassed, the emotions are mangled, the conscience is hardened, and Satan has an open door. Even the ancient pagan Aristotle wisely observed: "Music represents the passions of the soul, and if one listens to the wrong music he will become the wrong kind of person."

Scripture's admonition that "all things be done properly and in an orderly manner" (1 Cor. 14:40) applies to music as well as to everything else. God created an orderly universe, and anything that is confused and disorderly is out of harmony with the universe and with its Maker. "Watch over your heart with diligence, for from it flow the springs of life" (Prov. 4:23). Paul commanded believers: "Whatever is true, whatever is honorable, whatever is right, whatever is pure, whatever is lovely, whatever is of good repute, if there is any excellence and if anything worthy of praise, let your mind dwell on these things" (Phil. 4:8).

The Spirit-filled Christian is happy, peaceful, assured, and productive regardless of the circumstances. Whether he is freely worshiping among fellow believers on Sunday morning or sitting in painful stocks in a dungeon at midnight like Paul and Silas (Acts 16:24-25), his heart will always be **singing and making melody**.

In his great allegory *Pilgrim's Progress,* John Bunyan pictured the pilgrim, Christian, falling into the slough of despond, straying into doubting castle, and enduring many other hardships, frustrations, and failures. And though the expression "filled with the Spirit" is not used in the story, each time Christian is delivered we see him going on his way singing. Every time he came back under the Spirit's control he had a song in his heart.

To whom do believers sing? Although believers sing among themselves, their songs are to be directed **to the Lord**. Our singing and making melody is not for the purpose of drawing attention to ourselves or of entertaining others but of rejoicing in and praising God. Whether we are singing a solo, singing with a choir, or singing with the congregation, our focus should be on the Lord, not on ourselves or other people. He is the audience to whom we sing.

At the dedication of the first Temple, "all the Levitical singers, Asaph, Heman, Jeduthun, and their sons and kinsmen, clothed in fine linen, with cymbals, harps, and lyres, standing east of the altar, and with them one hundred and twenty priests blowing trumpets in unison when the trumpeters and the singers were to make themselves heard with one voice to praise and to glorify the Lord" (2 Chron. 5:12-13). Because the Lord was pleased with their heart-felt and harmonious worship, "the house of the Lord was filled with a cloud, so that the priests could not stand to minister because of the cloud, for the glory of the Lord filled the house of God" (vv. 13-14). It should be the heart desire of all Christians that their praise of God in music, and in every other way, be "in unison" and that they "make themselves heard with one voice to praise and glorify the Lord"—because that is the only way God's people *can* acceptably praise and glorify Him.

Johann Sebastian Bach, probably the greatest musician of all time, said,

"The aim of all music is the glory of God." In his own life and work the great composer and organist sought to live out that aim, and through the music he dedicated solely to God countless generations of believers have been blessed.

The words of every Christian song should be biblical—distinctly, clearly, and accurately reflecting the teaching of God's Word. It is tragic that much music that goes under the name of Christian is a theological mishmash, often reflecting as much of the world's philosophy as of God's truth. Much is little more than personal sentimentality colored with Christian words.

Music that honors the Lord also blesses his people. A beautiful, soothing piece of music can calm nerves, remove fear and anxiety, reduce bitterness and anger, and help turn our attention from ourselves and the cares and problems of the world to God.

David not only was a man of God but a skillful musician. We are told that "whenever the evil spirit from God came to Saul, David would take the harp and play it with his hand; and Saul would be refreshed and be well, and the evil spirit would depart from him" (1 Sam. 16:23). The music blessed Saul emotionally (he was "refreshed"), physically (he was made "well"), and spiritually ("the evil spirit would depart from him").

Seventeenth- and eighteenth-century physicians often prescribed music for mentally disturbed patients. They even recommended certain types of music to treat certain types of disorders. Music does have "charms to soothe a savage breast." Working from a more scientific basis, modern behaviorists have proved those ideas to be sound. They have determined what kind of music makes a person more relaxed in a dentist's chair, what kind helps production in an office or assembly plant, what kind helps reduce impatience in an elevator, and so on. Music has been found to affect the muscles, nerves, and the flow of body fluids, including blood, saliva, and lymph. It can influence metabolism, heart rate, and pulse for either benefit or harm.

It is not possible to submit the spiritual effects of music to scientific testing, but it is beyond question that music that focuses the heart on praising God can help heal the spiritual ills of His people.

THE CONSEQUENCE TOWARD GOD: GIVING THANKS

always giving thanks for all things in the name of our Lord Jesus Christ to God, even the Father; (5:20)

People may have one of three possible attitudes about thanksgiving. The first is that it is unnecessary. Some people are not thankful simply because they think they deserve every good thing they have—and more. The rich farmer of Jesus' parable who was presumptuous about his future prosperity was also ungrateful for his past prosperity. As he looked around and realized his land was so productive that he did not have enough room to store all his crops, he decided to build bigger and better barns. After that he would say to his soul, "Soul, you have many goods laid up for many years to come; take your ease, eat, drink, and be merry" (Luke 12:19). He did not take God into consideration. Because he gave God no credit for his blessings, he saw no reason to give Him thanks. And because of his thankless presumption, God said to him, "You fool! This very night your soul is required of you; and now who will own what you have prepared?" (v. 20). Within that judgment lay the truth that the farmer could no more protect his possessions by his own power than he had produced them by his own power. The Lord gave, and the Lord took away. Not feeling the need to thank God is much worse than ingratitude; it is rank unbelief. This attitude is a form of practical atheism that fails to acknowledge God.

A second attitude about thanksgiving is that of the hypocrite. In another parable Jesus told of a self-righteous Pharisee who stood in the Temple and "was praying thus to himself, 'God, I thank Thee that I am not like other people: swindlers, unjust, adulterers, or even like this tax-gatherer. I fast twice a week; I pay tithes of all that I get'" (Luke 18:11-12). As Jesus made clear in the words "praying thus to himself," although the man used God's name, his thankfulness was to himself and for himself. The Pharisee used God's name only to call further attention to his false piety. And because God had no part in that prayer it was totally worthless. The humble, penitent tax-collector "went down to his house justified," whereas the proud, self-righteous Pharisee did not (v. 14). Like the rest of his life, the Pharisee's prayer of thanksgiving was hypocritical sham and pretense.

The third attitude about thanksgiving is that of the truly thankful person. Of the ten lepers Jesus healed on His way to Jerusalem, the only one who returned to thank Him was a Samaritan. But his thankfulness was genuine, and Jesus said to him, "Rise, and go your way; your faith has made you well" (Luke 17:19). The other nine lepers had sought Jesus' healing only for their own benefit. The Samaritan also sought it for God's glory (v. 18). His thankfulness was an expression of his trust in Jesus, his recognition that he was helpless in Himself and that his healing was undeserved and entirely by the Lord's grace. As a result, he received salvation. That is the thankfulness, the only thankfulness, that pleases God and that the Spirit-filled saint will offer.

A medieval legend tells of two angels sent to earth by the Lord to gather the prayers of the saints. One was to gather the petitions and the other the thanksgivings. The angel responsible for petitions was not able to carry them back to heaven in one load, while the angel responsible for thanksgivings carried his back in one hand.

That legend developed from the sad fact that God's children are more prone to ask than to thank. The Psalms are instructive in this regard, in that they contain more praise than petition. Believers come into their Father's presence through thanksgiving. We "enter His gates with thanksgiving, and His courts with praise" (Ps. 100:4). William Hendriksen picturesquely commented that "when a person prays without thanksgiving he has clipped the wings of prayer so that it cannot rise." In Ephesians 5:20 Paul tells when, for what, how, and to whom the Spirit-filled believer is to be thankful.

When are we to be thankful?—*always.* To be thankful **always** is to recognize God's control of our lives in every detail as He seeks to conform us to the image of His Son. To be thankless is to disregard God's control, Christ's lordship, and the Holy Spirit's filling. Nothing must grieve the Holy Spirit so much as the believer who does not give thanks. In *King Lear* (I.ii.283, 312) Shakespeare wrote, "Ingratitude, thou marble-hearted fiend! . . . How sharper than a serpent's tooth it is to have a thankless child!" When God brings trials and difficulties into our lives and we complain and grumble, we question His wisdom and love as well as His sovereignty.

Just as there are three attitudes toward thanksgiving there are also three levels of thankfulness. The first is to be thankful when we are blessed. When things are going well or God grants an especially welcome benefit, we are happy and grateful. When getting a job, being delivered from sickness, being reconciled with our spouse, or experiencing other such pleasant things, it is easy to be grateful to the Lord.

It is right to be thankful for blessings, as the Bible continually commands us to be. The song that Moses and the children of Israel sang after being delivered from Egypt (Ex. 15:1-21) was a beautiful and genuine expression of gratitude that pleased the Lord. That song will one day be partly repeated in heaven as a testimony of thanksgiving to Jesus Christ, the Lamb, for delivering His people from the beast (Rev. 15:1-4). But thankfulness for blessing is easy and requires little maturity.

The second level of thankfulness is that of being grateful for the hope of blessing and victory yet to come. The first level is after the fact, the second is in anticipation of the fact. Thanking God before a blessing is more difficult than thanking Him afterward, and requires more faith and spiritual maturity. This second level is where faith and hope begin, because it involves the unseen and the yet unexperienced. As He stood over the tomb of Lazarus, Jesus prayed, "Father, I thank Thee that Thou heardest Me. And I knew that Thou hearest Me always; but because of the people standing around I said it, that they may believe that Thou didst send Me" (John 11:41-42). Because He knew His heavenly Father always heard and answered His prayers, in total confidence He thanked Him in advance for what He knew would be done.

The believer at this level of thankfulness looks forward to victory before it is achieved, knowing that he will "overwhelmingly conquer through Him who loved us" (Rom. 8:37). He looks forward even to his own death or the death of a loved one and gives thanks to God, knowing that His grace is sufficient for every sorrow and every testing (2 Cor. 12:9) and that glorious resurrection awaits those who die in the Lord. He lives in hope.

As Judah was about to be attacked by the more powerful Moabites and Ammonites, King Jehoshaphat proclaimed a fast and prayed before all the people, earnestly proclaiming the Lord's power and goodness. He acknowledged Judah's weakness and their sure defeat if the Lord did not help them. "O our God, wilt Thou not judge them? For we are powerless before this great multitude who are coming against us; nor do we know what to do, but our eyes are on Thee" (2 Chron. 20:1-12). Then the king led his people out into the wilderness of Tekoa and instructed them to put their trust in the Lord and His prophets. At that point he commanded the Levitical singers to go out before the army and "'give thanks to the Lord, for His lovingkindness is everlasting.' And when they began singing and praising, the Lord set ambushes against the sons of Ammon, Moab, and Mt. Seir, who had come against Judah; so they were routed" (vv. 20-22). Judah thanked God for victory before the battle was even begun.

The third level of thankfulness is thanking God in the midst of the battle, while we are still undergoing trouble or testing—and even when it looks like we are failing or being overwhelmed.

When Daniel heard that King Darius had signed the decree forbidding the worship of any god or man but the king himself, he immediately "entered his house (now in his roof chamber he had windows open toward Jerusalem); and he continued kneeling on his knees three times a day, praying and giving thanks before his God, as he had been doing previously" (Dan. 6:10). Though his life was at risk, Daniel thanked God because God deserved his thanks, regardless of his threatening circumstances.

Even the prejudiced and disobedient Jonah ended his prayer from the stomach of the fish with these words: "But I will sacrifice to Thee with the voice of thanksgiving. That which I have vowed I will pay. Salvation is from the Lord" (Jonah 2:9). Nowhere in the prayer does the prophet ask for deliverance. Instead he praises God for past deliverance, acknowledges his own sinfulness and unfaithfulness, and closes with a declaration of thanks for the Lord's goodness.

After Peter and some of the other apostles in Jerusalem had been flogged and ordered not to speak again in the name of Jesus, "they went on their way from the presence of the Council, rejoicing that they had been considered worthy to suffer shame for His name" (Acts 5:41). In his prison cell, probably in Rome, Paul awaited trial and possible execution. While there he wrote his letter to the Philippian church, in which he gave thanks for their faithfulness and for the work God was continuing to do in them (1:3-6).

If we can only thank God when things are going well, our thankfulness is on the bottom rung of faithfulness. If we can thank Him in anticipation of what He will do in the future, we show more spiritual maturity. But to thank God while we are in the midst of pain, trials, or persecution shows a level of maturity that few Christians seem to know but that our heavenly Father wants all His children to have.

Being thankful is not a Christian option, a high order of living that we are free to choose or disregard. As Joni Eareckson Tada, a quadriplegic author, has observed, "Giving thanks is not a matter of feeling thankful, it is a matter of obedience."

For what are we to give thanks?—for all things. The greatest gift we can give to God is a thankful heart, because all we can give to Him is simply grateful recognition that all we have is from Him. We give Him **thanks for all things** because He has *given* us all things and because giving thanks in everything "is God's will . . . in Christ Jesus" (1 Thess. 5:18). Understanding "what the will of the Lord is" (Eph. 5:17) includes understanding that He wants His children to be thankful. The Spirit-filled heart sees God's gracious hand in every circumstance and knows "that God causes all things to work together for good to those who love God, to those who are called according to His purpose" (Rom. 8:28). The spiritual believer sees God's wise and loving care in the difficulties and trials as well as in blessing and prosperity. He thanks God for a job even if it is demanding and unfulfilling. He thanks God for his health, even if it is far from being what he would like it to be. He thanks God even when his dearest loved ones die, saying with Job, "The Lord gave and the Lord has taken away. Blessed be the name of the Lord" (Job 1:21).

In Christ, all things are for our sakes, in order "that the grace which is spreading to more and more people may cause the giving of thanks to abound to the glory of God" (2 Cor. 4:15). The ultimate goal is the glory of God, the means of giving Him glory is thanksgiving, and the reasons for thanksgiving are all the things He has done in the believer's life. To glorify God is to thank Him no matter how much we may hurt or be disappointed or fail to understand. The Spirit-filled Christian is "overflowing through many thanksgivings to God" and continually gives thanks to Him "for His indescribable gift" (2 Cor. 9:12, 15).

As God's children we are to be thankful first of all for the Lord Himself, for His goodness, love, grace, salvation, and every other blessing He gives. We are to be thankful for all men, for blessings and difficulties, for victories and defeats.

The only person who can genuinely give **thanks for all things** is the humble person, the person who knows he deserves nothing and who therefore gives thanks even for the smallest things. Lack of thankfulness comes from pride, from the conviction that we deserve something better than we have. Pride tries to convince us that our job, our health, our spouse, and most of what we have is not as good as we deserve. Pride was the root of the first sin and remains the root of all sin. Satan's pride led him to rebel against God and try to usurp God's throne. The pride of Adam and Eve led them to believe Satan's lie that they deserved more than they had and that they even had a right to be like God.

Believers are still subject to the temptations of pride. The only cure is humility, which comes with being filled with the Spirit, since being filled with the Spirit is to die to self. When we cease with selfishness, the consequence is to put Christ and His will above all else. Humility dethrones self and enthrones Christ, and in doing that it thankfully acknowledges that every good thing—including many things that do not at the time seem to be good—are from His gracious hand.

How are we to be thankful?—in the name of Jesus Christ. To give thanks in **the name of our Lord Jesus Christ** is to give thanks consistent with who He is and what He has done. We can give thanks always and for all things because no matter what happens to us it will turn out not only for our ultimate blessing but, more importantly, for His ultimate glory. When we sing, it is Christ singing through us, and when we give thanks, it is Christ giving thanks to the Father through us.

Were it not for Christ, it would be foolish to be thankful for everything, because apart from Him all things do *not* turn out for good. But because we are in Christ, the good things and the bad things all have a part in God's conforming us to the image of His Son. A person who is not a Christian does not have Christ interceding on his behalf at the right hand of God or indwelling his life. He does not have the promise of heirship in God's family and citizenship in God's kingdom—or any other of the wonderful promises of Christ. He does not have the indwelling of the Holy Spirit and cannot have His filling. He cannot be thankful for everything because for him everything does not give a reason for thanks. He sees only the present, not eternal glory.

But the child of God *is* indwelt by Christ, *is* a joint heir with Him, and *does* have the Son interceding for him at the Father's right hand. He has all of Christ's promises made certain through the Holy Spirit who indwells him. And as the Spirit fills him, he is cleansed from sin and made more and more into conformity to Christ.

The mature Christian, the Christian who is filled with the Spirit, becomes thankful as Christ Himself was thankful. Jesus was continually saying thanks to His Father. Before He multiplied the loaves and fish to feed the four thousand, "He gave thanks and broke them, and started giving them to His disciples to serve to them" (Mark 8:6; cf. Matt. 15:36). As mentioned above, He gave thanks before He called Lazarus from the grave (John 11:41). Even as He instituted the Lord's Supper, in anticipation of His soon-coming crucifixion, He thanked His Father for the bread that would become a memorial of His sacrificed body (Luke 22:19).

Jesus was ridiculed, despised, scorned, rejected, spat upon, blasphemed, beaten, and finally crucified. Yet because of His great humility He always gave thanks in all things. He deserved glory but received humiliation, deserved love but received hate, and deserved honor but received dishonor. He deserved praise but received scorn, deserved riches but received poverty, and deserved holiness but was made sin on our behalf. Yet He never lost His thankfulness to His heavenly Father, because He "emptied Himself, taking the form of a bond-servant, and being made in the likeness of men. And being found in appearance as a man, He humbled Himself by becoming obedient to the point of death, even death on a cross" (Phil. 2:7-8).

Because Jesus emptied Himself to the point of giving His own life, He is able to fill us with everything of which He emptied Himself, including life. We deserve humiliation, but in Christ we receive glory. We deserve to be hated but instead are loved, and deserve dishonor but receive honor. We deserve scorn but are given praise, deserve poverty but are given riches, and deserve sin's curse of death but are given righteousness and eternal life. For what can we not give thanks?

To whom are we to be thankful?—*God the Father*. The thanks that we give always, for all things, and in the name of the Lord Jesus Christ are given **to God, even the Father**. We thank our heavenly Father just as our Lord Himself did on earth. The giver of "every good thing bestowed and every perfect gift" (James 1:17) is the Receiver of every genuine and heartfelt thanksgiving. The beneficent Father is to be thanked for all things because He has given all things (see on 1:3).

Even those things that come through others come from God. We should be grateful for what anyone does for us, and we should thank them for it. But thankfulness to others will likely be little more than flattery if we do not acknowledge that the true source of the gift is God.

A mark of the unsaved person is thanklessness to God (Rom. 1:21), but a mark of the Spirit-filled believer is **always giving thanks for all things in the name of our Lord Jesus Christ to God, even the Father.** He is "anxious for nothing, but in everything by prayer and supplication with thanksgiving [lets his] requests be made known to God" (Phil. 4:6). He is "overflowing with gratitude" (Col. 2:7) and he continually offers "up a sacrifice of praise to God, that is, the fruit of lips that give thanks to His name" (Heb. 13:15).

A city missionary in London was called to an old tenement building where a woman lay dying in the last stages of a terrible disease. The room was cold and she had nowhere to lie but on the floor. When the missionary asked if there was anything he could do, she replied, "I have all I really need; I have Jesus Christ." Deeply moved, the missionary went home and penned these words:

> In the heart of London City,
>   Mid the dwellings of the poor,
> These bright and golden words were uttered,
>   "I have Christ. What want I more?"
> Spoken by a lonely woman dying on a garret floor,
>   Having not one earthly comfort,
> "I have Christ. What want I more?"

THE CONSEQUENCE TOWARD FELLOW BELIEVERS: SUBMISSION

and be subject to one another in the fear of Christ. (5:21)

The filling and control of the Holy Spirit will lead us to a spirit of humility, to the spirit that gives us the desire to seek the welfare of others before our own and to be mutually submissive. The rich details of this verse will be discussed in the next chapter, since the verse provides a transition to the coming section.

In the rest of chapter 5 and through 6:9, Paul expands on the principle of believers' submission as it controls the relationship of husbands and wives, children and parents, and slaves and masters.

The Necessary Foundation

And be subject to one another in the fear of Christ. (5:21)

This verse is a transition to Paul's extensive discussion of relationships that continues through 6:9. The general principle of mutual submission, **be subject to one another**, not only is a product of the filling of the Spirit (as indicated in the precious chapter) but is also the foundation of the more specific principles of authority and submission—in relation to husbands and wives, parents and children, and masters and slaves—with which the larger passage deals.

Among the worst tragedies of our day is the progressive death of the family as it has been traditionally known. Marital infidelity, exaltation of sexual sin, homosexuality, abortion, women's liberation, delinquency, and the sexual revolution in general have all contributed to the family's demise. Each one is a strand in the cord that is rapidly strangling marriage and the family.

Gays and lesbians are demanding the right to be married to each other, and many states as well as a growing number of church groups are recognizing that as a right. Lesbian couples, and even some gay couples, are bringing together the children they have had by various lovers of the opposite sex and calling the resulting group a family. Many unmarried women elect to keep and raise children to whom they have given birth. In such situations single-parent families are becoming as much a matter of choice as of necessity.

The new mentality about marriage is reflected in the belief of some sociologists and psychologists that marriage ought to radically change or be eliminated altogether—based on the argument that it is but a vestige of man's primitive understanding of himself and of society. Man "come of age" is presumed not to need the restrictions and boundaries that once seemed essential for productive, satisfying life.

Without a proper basis of authority for relationships, people grope for meaningful, harmonious, fulfilling relationships by whatever means and arrangements they can find or devise. Experimentation is their only resource, and disintegration of the family—and ultimately of society in general—is being disclosed as the inevitable consequence.

It is time for Christians to declare and live what the Bible has always declared and what the church has always taught until recent years: "God's standard for marriage and the family produces meaning, happiness, blessedness, reward, and fulfillment—and it is the *only* standard that can produce those results."

Yet confusion about God's standard for marriage and the family has found its way even into the church. A generation ago only one in every five hundred couples in the church got a divorce. Today the divorce rate in the church is many times that figure and becoming worse, and the church must deal with the problem in its own midst before it can give effective counsel to the world.

Divorce within the church has become so common that one Virginia pastor devised a special service in which, after the husband and wife state vows of mutual respect, God's blessing is invoked on the dissolution of their marriage. Partly because of the tragedies they have seen in marriages, especially that of their own parents, many young adults opt for simply living together. When one or the other becomes tired of the arrangement, they break up and look for someone else. Whatever minimal commitment may be involved is superficial and temporary. Lust has replaced love, and selfishness rules instead of sacrifice.

Many marriages that manage to avoid divorce are nevertheless characterized by unfaithfulness, deceit, disrespect, distrust, self-centeredness, materialism, and a host of other sins that shatter harmony, prevent happiness, and devastate the children.

With increased divorce comes decreased interest in having children. Some authorities estimate that in perhaps a third of the couples of child-bearing age, one or both of the partners have been sterilized. A growing percentage of babies conceived even within marriage are aborted because they are unwanted. And many who are allowed to be born are neglected, resented, and abused by their parents. Couples who do have children are having them later in life, so that the children do not inhibit the parents' plans for fun and fulfillment.

The pastor of a large evangelical church reported that, although most of them claimed to be Christians, at least seventy percent of the couples who came to him to be married were already living together. Many of them claimed that it was God's will for them to be married; but by living in such flagrant disobedience of His moral standards they had no basis for knowing His will about their marriage. Other couples who claim to be Christian come to be married for the second, third, or fourth time—and often maintain that the Lord has guided them each time.

God will forgive, cleanse, and restore the repentant believer, but He does not change His standards of righteousness and purity and does not promise to remove the often tragic consequences of disobedience. If the church seeks to accommodate those divine standards to the foolishness and sinfulness of its own members, it not only offends and grieves God but undercuts its testimony to the world. If marriage cannot be right in the church it can hardly be right in the world, any more than it was in Paul's day.

In New Testament times women were considered to be little more than servants. Many Jewish men prayed each morning: "God, I thank you that I am not a Gentile, a slave, or a woman." The provision related to divorce and remarriage in Deuteronomy 24 had been distorted to include virtually any offense or disfavor in the eyes of the husband. In Greek society the women's situation was even worse. Because concubines were common and a wife's role was simply to bear legitimate children and to keep house, Greek men had little reason to divorce their wives, and their wives had no recourse against them. Because divorce was so rare, there was not even a legal procedure for it. Demosthenes wrote, "We have courtesans for the sake of pleasure, we have concubines for the sake of daily cohabitation, and we have wives for the purpose of having children legitimately and being faithful guardians for our household affairs." Both male and female prostitution were indescribably rampant, and it is from the Greek term for prostitution and general unchastity (*porneia*) that we get our word *pornography*. Husbands typically found their sexual gratification with concubines and prostitutes, whereas wives, often with the encouragement of their husbands, found sexual gratification with their slaves, both male and female. Prostitution, homosexuality, and the many other forms of sexual promiscuity and perversion inevitably resulted in widespread sexual abuse of children—just as we see in our own day.

In Roman society things were worse still. Marriage was little more than legalized prostitution, with divorce being an easy legal formality that could be taken advantage of as often as desired. Many women did not want to have children because it ruined the looks of their bodies, and feminism became common. Desiring to do everything men did, some women went into wrestling, sword fighting, and various other pursuits traditionally considered to be uniquely masculine. Some liked to run bare-breasted while hunting wild pigs. Women began to lord it over men and increasingly took the initiative in getting a divorce.

Paul admonished believers in Ephesus to live in total contrast to the corrupt, vile, self-centered, and immoral standards of those around them. The relationship between husband and wife was to be modeled on that between Christ and His church. "For the husband is the head of the wife, as Christ also is the head of the church, He Himself being the Savior of the body. But as the church is subject to Christ, so also the wives ought to be to their husbands in everything. Husbands, love your wives, just as Christ also loved the church and gave Himself up for her" (5:23-25). The relationship between Christian husbands and wives is to be holy and indissoluble, just as that between Christ and His church is holy and indissoluble.

Christian marriages and families are to be radically different from those of the world. The relationships between husbands and wives and parents and children is to be so bathed in humility, love, and mutual submission that the authority of husbands and parents, though exercised when necessary, becomes almost invisible and the submission of wives and children is no more than acting in the spririt of gracious love.

In the Song of Solomon we see a beautiful model for marriage. Although the husband was a king, the dominate relationship with his wife was that of love rather than authority. The wife clearly recognized her husband's headship, but it was a headship clothed in love and mutual respect. "Like an apple tree among the trees of the forest, so is my beloved among the young men," she said. "In his shade I took great delight and sat down, and his fruit was sweet to my taste. He has brought me to his banquet hall, and his banner over me is love" (2:3-4). A banner was a public announcement, in this case an announcement of the king's love for his wife which he wanted to proclaim to the world. She not only had the security of hearing him tell her of his love but of hearing him tell the world of that love. "Sustain me with raisin cakes, refresh me with apples, because I am lovesick," she continued. "Let his left hand be under my head and his right hand embrace me" (vv. 5-6). Her husband was her willing and eager protector, provider, and lover.

Solomon responded by saying to her, "Arise, my darling, my beautiful one, and come along. For behold, the winter is past, the rain is over and gone" (vv. 10-11). Spring had come and his only thoughts were of his beloved. There was no hint of authoritativeness or superiority, but only love, respect, and concern for the welfare, joy, and fulfillment of his wife. She expressed the deep mutuality of their relationship in the expression "My beloved is mine, and I am his" (v. 16) and later, "This is my beloved and this is my friend" (5:16).

Families are the building blocks of human society, and a society that does not protect the family undermines its very existence. When the family goes, everything else of value soon goes with it. When the cohesiveness, meaningfulness, and discipline of the family are lost, anarchy will flourish. And where anarchy flourishes, law, justice, and safety cannot. The family nourishes and binds society together, whereas the anarchy that results from its absence only depletes, disrupts, and destroys.

The unredeemed can benefit greatly from following God's basic principles for the family, but the full power and potential of those principles can be understood and practiced by those who belong to Him by faith in His Son. Paul speaks to the Ephesians as fellow Christians, and apart from the divine life and resources that only Christians possess, the principles for marriage and the family that he gives in this letter are out of context and thus of limited benefit. The basic principle of being **subject to one another** finds its power and effectiveness only in **the fear of Christ.** The family can only be what God has designed it to be when the members of the family are what God has designed them to be—"conformed to the image of His Son" (Rom. 8:29). Just as an individual can find fulfillment only in a right relationship with God, so the family can find complete fulfillment only as believing parents and children follow His design for the family in the control and power of the Holy Spirit (Eph. 5:18b).

Persons who do not know or even recognize the existence and authority of God are not motivated to accept God's standard for marriage and the family or for anything else. They do not have the new nature or inner resources to fully follow those standards even if they wanted to.

Some years ago I was asked to speak on the Christian sex ethic to a philosophy class at a large secular university. Knowing the futility of trying to explain biblical sexual standards to those who question or openly reject the authority of Scripture, I began my presentation by saying words to this effect: "Christ's standards of ethics cannot be understood or appreciated by anyone who does not know Him as Savior and Lord. I do not expect most of you to agree with what Scripture says about sex ethics because most of you do not agree with what Scripture says about Jesus Christ. The presupposition of scriptural standards for *anything* is that a person have a right relationship to the One whose Word Scripture is. Only when you know and love the Lord Jesus Christ can you understand and desire to fulfill His standards for sex." One student raised his hand and said, "Well then, maybe you had better tell us how to know and love Jesus Christ." Gladly following that suggestion, I spent most of the hour showing the necessity and means for believing in Christ and devoted the last few minutes to explaining what commitment to Him means specifically in relation to sexual standards.

Only those who have died to sin and are alive to God (Rom. 6:4-6), those who are servants of righteousness (Rom. 6:16-22), those who are spiritually minded (Rom. 8:5-8), those who are empowered by the Spirit (Rom. 8:13) will rejoice for the privilege of living in the Lord's standard. Reverencing and adoring Christ is the basis of such a spirit of submission.

Unfortunately, many persons who know Jesus Christ as Savior and Lord do not maintain their living according to His moral, marital, and family laws. Because they are not at all times filled with His Spirit and fall to the level of the society around them, they are not sufficiently motivated or empowered to be obedient to their Lord in all things. They possess the Holy Spirit, but the Holy Spirit does not possess them. Consequently, many Christian couples argue and fight worse than many unbelievers. Many families in false religions, for example, and even some unreligious families, are more disciplined and harmonious on the surface than some Christian families. A carnal believer will have discord in his family just as he has discord in his own heart and in his relation to God.

We are drowning in a sea of marriage information today. A book on sex and marriage, whether from a secular or Christian viewpoint, is sure to sell. Many purportedly Christian books are as preoccupied with and indelicate about sex as their secular counterparts. Marriage conferences, seminars, and counselors abound—some of which may be solidly scriptural and well presented. But apart from a believer's being filled with the Holy Spirit and applying the ever-sufficient Word of God, even the best advice will produce only superficial and temporary benefit, because the heart will not be rightly motivated or empowered. On the other hand, when we are filled with the Spirit and thus are controlled in divine truth, we are divinely directed to do what is pleasing to God, because His Spirit controls our attitudes and relationships.

James said, "What is the source of quarrels and conflicts among you? Is not the source your pleasures that wage war in your members?" (James 4:1). Conflicts in the church, in the home, and in marriage always result from hearts that are directed by the self rather than by the Spirit of God. When self insists on its own rights, opinions, and goals, harmony and peace are precluded. The self-centered life is always in a battle for the top, and pushes others down as it climbs up in pride. The Spirit-centered life, on the other hand, is directed toward lowliness, toward subservience, and it lifts others up as it descends in humility. The Spirit-filled believer does "not merely look out for [his] own personal interests, but also for the interests of others" (Phil. 2:4).

Be subject is from *hupotassō,* originally a military term meaning to arrange or rank under. Spirit-filled Christians rank themselves under **one another**. The main idea is that of relinquishing one's rights to another person. Paul counseled the Corinthian believers to be in subjection to their faithful ministers "and to everyone who helps in the work and labors" (1 Cor. 16:16). Peter commands us to "submit [ourselves] for the Lord's sake to every human institution, whether to a king as the one in authority, or to governors as sent by him for the punishment of evildoers and the praise of those who do right. For such is the will of God" (1 Pet. 2:13-15; cf. Rom. 13:1-7). A nation cannot function without the authority of its rulers, soldiers, police, judges, and so on. Such people do not hold their authority because they are inherently better than everyone else but because without the appointment and exercise of orderly authority the nation would disintegrate in anarchy.

Likewise within the church we are to "obey [our] leaders, and submit to them; for they keep watch over [our] souls, as those who will give an account" (Heb. 13:17). God ordains that pastors and elders in the church be men. "Let a woman quietly receive instruction with entire submissiveness," Paul said. "But I do not allow a woman to teach or exercise authority over a man, but to remain quiet" (1 Tim. 2:11-12). Paul was not teaching from a personal bias of male chauvinism, as some claim, but was reinforcing God's original plan of man's headship. "For it was Adam who was first created, and then Eve," he explained. "And it was not Adam who was deceived, but the woman being quite deceived, fell into transgression. But women shall be preserved through the bearing of children if they continue in faith and love and sanctity with self-restraint" (vv. 13-15).

The submissive role of the woman was designed by God in creation and affirmed by His judicial act in response to the Fall. Yet the balance of responsibility and blessing is found in the woman's bearing of children. She is saved from seeking the role of a man and from identification as a second-class person by giving birth to children and being occupied with them, as well as by having the major influence on their early training and development. Women who have children and pursue a life of faith, love, holiness, and self-control give their best to their family, and thus to society. God has designed and called women to give birth to children, to nurse, caress, teach, comfort, and encourage them in their most formative years—in a way that fathers can never do. That should occupy their time and energy and preclude their seeking a place of leadership in the church.

When the church tries to operate apart from God's system of authority it creates confusion and frequently heresy. When Mary Baker Eddy took to herself the role of church leader and preacher, Christian Science was born. When Madam Elena Petrovna Blavatsky assumed the role of theologian and spiritual teacher, Theosophy was born. When Mrs. Charles Fillmore took to herself the same prerogatives, Unity was born. When Aimee Semple McPherson began preaching, Foursquare pentecostalism was born.

As with leaders in government, it is not that church leaders are inherently superior to other Christians or that men are inherently superior to women, but that no institution—including the church—can function without a system of authority and submission.

In the home, the smallest unit of human society, the same principle applies. Even a small household cannot function if each member fully demands and expresses his own will and goes his own way. The system of authority God has ordained for the family is the headship of husbands over wives and of parents over children.

But in addition to those necessary social functional relationships of authority and submission, God commands *all* Christians—leaders as well as followers, husbands as well as wives, parents as well as children—to "have this attitude in yourselves which was also in Christ Jesus, who, although He existed in the form of God, did not regard equality with God a thing to be grasped, but emptied Himself, taking the form of a bond-servant, and . . . humbled Himself by becoming obedient to the point of death, even death on a cross" (Phil. 2:5-8).

As Paul went on to explain (Eph. 5:22-6:9), the structural function of the family, like that of the church and of government, requires both authority and submission. But in all interpersonal relationships there is only to be mutual submission. Submission is a general spiritual attitude that is to be true of every believer in all relationships.

Even the authority-subject relationships in the church and home are to be controlled by love and modified by mutual submission. Wives have traditionally received the brunt of Ephesians 5:22-33, although the greater part of the passage deals with the husband's attitude toward and responsibilities for his wife. Paul devoted twice as much space to the husband's obligations as to the wife's. The husband not only is "head of the wife, as Christ also is the head of the church" (v. 23) but husbands are commanded to "love [their] wives, just as Christ also loved the church and gave Himself up for her" (v. 25). "Husbands ought also to love their own wives as their own bodies, . . . even as [themselves]" (vv. 28, 33). Christ's giving His life for the church was an act of divine submission of the Lord to His bride, that He might cleanse, glorify, and purify her "that she should be holy and blameless" (v. 27).

Likewise in the home, not only are children to "obey [their] parents in the

Lord," but fathers are not to "provoke [their] children to anger; but bring them up in the discipline and instruction of the Lord" (6:1, 4). Even while exercising authority over their children, parents are to submit to the children's moral and spiritual welfare. In love, husbands are to submit themselves to meeting the needs of their wives, and together they both are called to give themselves in love to their children.

In New Testament times, slaves were often an integral part of the household, and Paul's admonition to masters and slaves essentially dealt with family relationships. The husband and wife were masters of the household, of which the slaves and hired servants were an integral part. Here, too, Paul made clear not only that Christian slaves were to "be obedient to those who are [their] masters according to the flesh" and do good things for them (6:5, 8), but that masters were likewise to do good things for their slaves "and give up threatening, knowing that both [the slave's] Master and [their own] is in heaven, and there is no partiality with Him" (v. 9).

Every obedient, Spirit-filled Christian is a submitting Christian. The husband who demands his wife's submission to him but does not recognize his own obligation to submit to her distorts God's standard for the marriage relationship and cannot rightly function as a godly husband. Parents who demand obedience from their children but do not recognize their own obligation to submit in loving sacrifice to meet their children's needs are themselves disobedient to their heavenly Father and cannot rightly function as godly parents.

In 1 Corinthians 7 Paul made clear that the physical relationships and obligations of marriage are not one-sided. "Let the husband fulfill his duty to his wife," he says, "and likewise also the wife to her husband. The wife does not have authority over her own body, but the husband does; and likewise also the husband does not have authority over his own body, but the wife does" (vv. 3-4). Although God ordains husbands as heads over their wives, and parents as heads over their children, He also ordains a mutuality of submission and responsibility among *all* members of the family.

Although Christ was in the beginning with God and was God (John 1:1), was one with the Father (10:30), and was in the Father as the Father was in Him (14:11), He was nevertheless subject to the Father. From childhood Jesus devoted Himself to His Father's work (Luke 2:49), submitted Himself to His Father's will (John 5:30; 15:10; 20:21), and could do nothing apart from His Father (John 5:19). In explaining God's order of relationships, Paul says, "Christ is the head of every man, and the man is the head of a woman, and God is the head of Christ" (1 Cor. 11:3). Just as the Son is submissive to the Father in function but equal to Him in nature and essence, wives are to be submissive to their husbands, while being completely equal to them in moral and spiritual nature.

All believers are spiritual equals in every sense. "There is neither Jew nor Greek, there is neither slave nor free man, there is neither male nor female; for you are all one in Christ Jesus" (Gal. 3:28). We submit to one another as the Holy Spirit influences us to do so.

The Role and Priorities of the Wife

22

Wives, be subject to your own husbands, as to the Lord. For the husband is the head of the wife, as Christ also is the head of the church, He Himself being the Savior of the body. But as the church is subject to Christ, so also the wives ought to be to their husbands in everything. (5:22-24)

Because so much of the church has long disregarded the full teaching of Scripture, many believers find some of its truths to be unfamiliar and even hard to accept. And because the church has been so engulfed in, identified with, and victimized by worldly standards, God's standards seem out-of-date, irrelevant, and offensive to modern mentalities. His way is so high and so contrary to the way of the world that it is incomprehensible to many in and out of the church.

Over and over the New Testament calls us to another dimension of existence, a new way of thinking, acting, and living. To "walk in a manner worthy of the calling with which [we] have been called . . . and [to] put on the new self, which in the likeness of God has been created in righteousness and holiness of the truth" (Eph. 4:1, 24) is to fulfill the high calling to which we are called in a completely new life in a completely new, Spirit-filled way.

As was mentioned in the previous chapter, few areas of modern living have been so distorted and corrupted by the devil and the world and caused the church so much confusion as those of marriage and the family. It is these issues that Paul confronts in Ephesians 5:22—6:9. He expands and clarifies the general principle of mutual submission ("be subject to one another in the fear of Christ," v. 21) by giving several illustrations from the family, beginning with the relationship of husbands and wives. As pointed out at the end of our discussion of verse 21, Scripture makes clear that there are no spiritual or moral distinctions among Christians. "There is neither Jew nor Greek, there is neither slave nor free man, there is neither male nor female; for you are all one in Christ Jesus" (Gal. 3:28). There are no classifications of Christians. Every believer in Jesus Christ has exactly the same salvation, the same standing before God, the same divine nature and resources, and the same divine promises and inheritance (cf. Acts 10:34; Rom. 2:11; James 1:1-9).

But in matters of role and function God has made distinctions. Although there are no differences in intrinsic worth or basic spiritual privilege and rights among His people, the Lord has given rulers in government certain authority over the people they rule, to church leaders He has delegated authority over their congregations, to husbands He has given authority over their wives, to parents He has given authority over their children, and to employers He has given authority over employees.

In Ephesians 5:22-24 Paul begins this list by outlining the role, duties, and priorities of the wife in relation to her husband's authority. First he deals with the basic matter of the submission, then with its manner, motive, and model.

THE MATTER OF SUBMISSION

Wives, be subject to your own husbands, (5:22a)

Wives is not qualified, and therefore applies to every Christian wife, regardless of her social standing, education, intelligence, spiritual maturity or giftedness, age, experience, or any other consideration. Nor is it qualified by her husband's intelligence, character, attitude, spiritual condition, or any other consideration. Paul says categorically to *all* believing wives: **be subject to your own husbands.**

As indicated by italics in most translations, **be subject** is not in the original text, but the meaning is carried over from verse 21. The idea is: "Be subject to one another in the fear of Christ [and, as a first example,] **wives, . . . to your own husbands.**" As explained in the previous chapter, *hupotassō* means to relinquish one's rights, and the Greek middle voice (used in v. 21 and carried over by implication into v. 22) emphasizes the willing submitting of *oneself.* God's command is to those who are to submit. That is, the submission is to be a voluntary response to God's will in giving up one's independent rights to other believers in general and to ordained authority in particular—in this case the wife's **own husband.**

The wife is not commanded to obey (*hupakouō*) her husband, as children are to obey their parents and slaves their masters (6:1, 5). A husband is not to treat his wife as a servant or as a child, but as an equal for whom God has given him care and responsibility for provision and protection, to be exercised in love. She is not his to order about, responding to his every wish and command. As Paul proceeds to explain in considerable detail (vv. 25-33), the husband's primary responsibility as head of the household is to love, provide, protect, and serve his wife and family— not to lord it over them according to his personal whims and desires.

Your own husband suggests the intimacy and mutuality of the wife's submission. She willingly makes herself **subject to** the one she possesses as her **own husband** (cf. 1 Cor. 7:3-4). Husbands and wives are to have a mutual possessiveness as well as a mutual submissiveness. They belong to each other in an absolute equality. The husband no more possesses his wife than she possesses him. He has no superiority and she no inferiority, any more than one who has the gift of teaching is superior to one with the gift of helps. A careful reading of 1 Corinthians 12:12-31 will show that God has designed every person for a unique role in the Body of Christ, and the pervasive attitude governing all those roles and blending them together is "the more excellent way" of love (ch. 13).

As with spiritual gifts, the distinctions of headship and submission are entirely functional and were ordained by God. As a consequence of Eve's disobedience of God's command and her failure to consult with Adam about the serpent's temptation, God told her, "Your desire shall be for your husband, and he shall rule over you" (Gen. 3:16). The desire spoken of here is not sexual or psychological, both of which Eve had for Adam before the Fall as his specially created helper. It is the same desire spoken of in the next chapter, where the identical Hebrew word (*t'shûqâ*) is used. The term comes from an Arabic root that means to compel, impel, urge, or seek control over. The Lord warned Cain, "Sin is crouching at your door; it *desires* to have you [that is, control you], but you must master it" (4:7, NIV; emphasis added). Sin wanted to master Cain, but God commanded Cain to master sin. In light of this close context meaning of *t'shûqâ*, therefore, the curse on Eve was that woman's desire would henceforth be to usurp the place of man's headship and that he would resist that desire and would rule over her. The Hebrew word here for "rule" is not the same as that used in 1:28. Rather it represented a new, despotic kind of authoritarianism that was not in God's original plan for man's headship.

With the Fall and its curse came the distortion of woman's proper submissiveness and of man's proper authority. That is where the battle of the sexes began, where women's liberation and male chauvinism came into existence. Women have a sinful inclination to usurp man's authority and men have a sinful inclination to put women under their feet. The divine decree that man would rule over woman in this way was part of God's curse on humanity, and it takes a manifestation of grace in Christ by the filling of the Holy Spirit to restore the created order and harmony of proper submission in a relationship that has become corrupted and disordered by sin.

Eve was created from Adam's rib and ordained to be his companion, to be, as Adam himself beautifully testified, "bone of my bones, and flesh of my flesh" (Gen. 2:22-23). God's curse did not change His basic plan for mutuality in the marriage relationship or for the functional authority of the husband over the wife. Man was created first and was created generally to be physically, constitutionally, and emotionally stronger than woman, who is "a weaker vessel" (1 Pet. 3:7). Both before and after the Fall and the consequent curse, man was called to be the provider, protector, guide, and shepherd of the family, and woman called to be supportive and submissive.

In a parallel passage to Ephesians 5:22, Paul said, "Wives, be subject to your husbands, as is fitting in the Lord" (Col. 3:18). *Anēkō* (to be fitting) was sometimes used of that which was legally binding, as in Philemon 8, where Paul uses it in reference to legal propriety. The word refers to that which is the accepted standard of human society.

Any society that has taken either the obvious nature of women or the Word of God into consideration has fashioned its best laws in line with His. Laws against murder find their source in the Ten Commandments—just as do laws against stealing, adultery, perjury, and so on. The wife's submission to her husband is a divine principle that has been reflected to some degree in the legal codes of most societies.

For the past several hundred years western society has been bombarded with the humanistic, egalitarian, sexless, classless philosophy that was the dominant force behind the French Revolution. The blurring and even total removal of all human distinctions continues to be masterminded by Satan so as to undermine legitimate, God-ordained authority in every realm of human activity—in government, the family, the school, and even in the church. We find ourselves victimized by the godless, atheistic concepts of man's supreme independence from every external law and authority. The philosophy is self-destructive, because no group of people can live in orderliness and productivity if each person is bent on doing his own will.

Sadly, much of the church has fallen prey to this humanistic philosophy and is now willing to recognize the ordination of homosexuals, women, and others whose God Word specifically disqualifies from church leadership. It is usually argued that biblical teaching contrary to egalitarianism was inserted by biased editors, scribes, prophets, or apostles. And the church is reaping the whirlwind of confusion, disorder, immorality, and apostasy that such qualification of God's Word always spawns. Many Bible interpreters function on the basis of a hermeneutic that is guided by contemporary humanistic philosophy rather than the absolute authority of Scripture as God's inerrant Word.

Peter taught exactly the same truth as Paul in regard to the relationship of husbands and wives. "You wives, be submissive [also from *hupotassō*] to your own husbands" (1 Pet. 3:1a). The idea is not that of subservience or servility, but of willingly functioning under the husband's leadership. Peter also emphasized the mutual possessiveness of husbands and wives, using the same words as Paul—"your own husbands." Wives are to submit even when their husbands "are disobedient to the word, [that] they may be won without a word by the behavior of their wives, as they observe your chaste and respectful behavior" (vv. 1b-2). Instead of nagging, criticizing, and preaching to her husband, a wife should simply set a godly example before him—showing him the power and beauty of the gospel through its effect in her own life. Humility, love, moral purity, kindness, and respect are the most powerful means a woman has for winning her husband to the Lord.

When the wife's primary concern is for those inward virtues, she will not be preoccupied with "adornment [that is] merely external—braiding the hair, and wearing gold jewelry, or putting on dresses." Rather her concentration will be on "the hidden person of the heart, with the imperishable quality of a gentle and quiet spirit, which is precious in the sight of God" (1 Pet. 3:3-4; cf. 1 Tim. 2:9-10).

Modern society has elevated fashion almost to the point of idolatry. Clothing stores, newspaper and magazine advertising, and television commercials are like giant billboards that continually proclaim, "We covet clothes." Expensive, often ostentatious, jewelry for both men and women is becoming more and more prevalent as a means to flaunt material prosperity and glorify self. We are continually goaded to put our bodies and apparel on parade.

Scripture does not forbid careful grooming and attractive attire. Being sloppy and unkempt is not a virtue. Proverbs 31 commends the "excellent wife" who works diligently and whose "clothing is fine linen and purple" (vv. 10, 22). But inordinate attire worn for the purpose of flaunting wealth or attracting attention to ourselves is an expression of pride, the root of all other sins. It is contrary to and destructive of the humble and self-giving submissiveness that should characterize every Christian.

The preoccupation of believers should be with the spiritual adornment of the inside, "the hidden person of the heart," not the physical adornment of the outside. The wife's "gentle and quiet spirit" that comes from obedience to the Spirit's control is "imperishable" and is "precious in the sight of God" (1 Pet. 3:4). The Greek word for "precious" is *poluteles* and pertains to that which is of extraordinary value. It is the term used of "the alabaster vial of very costly perfume of pure nard" with which the woman at Bethany anointed Jesus' feet (Mark 14:3). God is not impressed with gold, expensive gems, and fashionable clothing, but with the woman who is genuinely humble, submissive, gentle, and quiet.

In the feminist movement, as well as in less extreme groups, we see women loudly and vociferously proclaiming their ideas, opinions, and rights in regard to virtually every issue—many times in the name of Christianity. Even when their basic position is biblical, their manner of advocating it often is not. God specifically excludes women from dominant leadership over men in the church and in the home, and whatever direct influence they have—which can be highly significant and powerful—should be by way of encouragement and support.

Holiness has always been the foremost concern of godly women. "For in this way in former times," Peter goes on the explain, "the holy women also, who hoped in God, used to adorn themselves, being submissive to their own husbands.

Thus Sarah obeyed Abraham, calling him lord, and you have become her children if you do what is right without being frightened by any fear" (1 Pet. 3:5-6). Just as Abraham was the symbolic father of the faithful (Rom. 4:11, 16), his wife, Sarah, was the symbolic mother of the submissive. Because Sarah had no fear of obeying God, she had no fear of what her husband, or any other person or circumstance, might do to her. God will take care of the consequences when His children are obedient to Him.

The Mishnah, an ancient codification of Jewish law and tradition, reflects the prevailing Jewish beliefs and standards that were accepted in Jesus' day. It describes the wife's duties as those of grinding flour, baking, cooking, nursing her children, spinning wool, laundering, and other such typical household chores. The husband's responsibility was to provide food, clothing, shoes, and such things. He often gave his wife a certain amount of money each week for her personal expenses. Many women worked with their husbands in the fields or in a trade—as did Aquila and Priscilla (Acts 18:2-3). A wife was allowed to work at crafts or horticulture at home and to sell the fruits of her labor. Profits were used either to supplement family income or to provide her with her own spending money. But if she worked apart from her husband in the marketplace or at a trade she was considered a disgrace. Apart from her household chores and possible work with her husband, a wife was also responsible for getting her sons ready for school (often taking them personally to prevent truancy), caring for guests, and doing charitable work. At all times she was to adorn herself properly, for the sake of modesty as well as nice appearance. The wife who faithfully carried her responsibilities was held in high regard in her family, in the synagogue, and in the community.

We learn from Paul that some of the women in the Corinthian church probably had become misled by the vocal and influential feminists of the city and began going out in public without a veil. The New Testament does not prescribe the wearing of veils for all women. Though it appears to have been the norm in in Corinth (cf. 1 Cor. 11:4-6), there is no reason to assume that Christian women in all the rest of the early churches wore veils. Apparently in Corinth the only women who traditionally did not wear veils were prostitutes or feminists, both of which groups had no regard for God or for the home. In that culture veils were a sign of moral propriety and submission, and failure to wear them a sign of immorality and rebelliousness. In that cultural circumstance Paul advised women to cover their heads "while praying or prophesying" (1 Cor. 11:5), lest they be considered to be rebelling against God's ordained principle of submissiveness. Paul did not here establish a permanent or universal mode of dress for Christian women, but reinforced the principle that they should never give to their society even the suggestion of rebelliousness or immorality. (For a more complete discussion of this vital passage, see the author's commentary 1 *Corinthians* [Chicago: Moody, 1984], pp. 251-63).

In his letter to Titus, Paul teaches that "older women likewise are to be reverent in their behavior, not malicious gossips, nor enslaved to much wine, teaching what is good, that they may encourage the young women to love their husbands, to love their children, to be sensible, pure, workers at home, kind, being subject [*hupotassō*] to their own husbands, that the word of God may not be dishonored" (2:3-5). Not only are older Christian women to be reverent and to avoid gossiping and excessive drinking, but they are to be engaged in teaching younger women. Older women are to teach younger women the requirements and priorities of Christian womanhood—especially in regard to their husbands and children. Husbands and wives alike are commanded to love each other and to love their children. Not to obey those clear commands is to dishonor God's Word.

For younger wives, to be "workers at home" is an especially great need in our day. One of the tragedies of the modern family is that often no one is home. There are in excess of fifty million working mothers (and the number constantly rises) in the United States, of whom at least two-thirds have school-age children.

The term "workers at home" in Titus 2:5 is from the compound Greek word *oikourgos,* which is derived from *oikos* (house) and a form of *ergon* (work). *Ergon,* however, does not simply refer to labor in general but often connotes the idea of a particular job or employment. It is the word Jesus used when He said, "My food is to do the will of Him who sent Me, and to accomplish His *work*" (John 4:34, emphasis added) and, on another occasion, "I glorified Thee on the earth, having accomplished the *work* which Thou hast given Me to do" (17:4, emphasis added). It is the word the Holy Spirit used in commanding the church at Antioch to "set apart for Me Barnabas and Saul for the *work* to which I have called them" (Acts 13:2, emphasis added). Paul used the word in relation to Epaphroditus, who "came close to death for the *work* of Christ" (Phil. 2:30, emphasis added) and in relation to the work of faithful Christian leaders in Thessalonica (1 Thess. 5:13). In other words, it is not that a woman is simply to keep busy in the home but that the home is the basic place of her employment, her divinely assigned job.

In his first letter to Timothy, Paul commands "younger widows to get married, bear children, keep house, and give the enemy no occasion for reproach" (5:14). A woman is to be the homekeeper, the one whose divinely assigned job is to take care of her husband and children. God's standard is for the wife and mother to work inside, not outside, the home. For a mother to get a job outside the home in order to send the children to a Christian school is to misunderstand her husband's role as provider as well as her own duty to the family. The good training her children receive in the Christian school may be counteracted by her lack of full commitment to the biblical standards for motherhood.

In addition to having less time to work at home and to teach and care for her children, a wife working outside the home often has a boss to whom she is responsible for pleasing in dress and other matters, complicating the headship of her husband. She is forced to submit to men other than her own husband and also is likely to become more independent in many ways, including financially, thereby fragmenting the unity of the family. She is also in danger of becoming enamored of the business world and of finding less and less satisfaction in her home responsibilities.

One of the great attractions of many cults for young people is the prospect of a family-like group in which they feel the acceptance and love they never received at home—frequently due to the mother's absence. Many studies have shown that most children who grow up in homes where the mother works are less secure than those whose mothers are always home. Her presence there, even when the child is in school, is an emotional anchor. Working mothers contribute to delinquency and a host of other problems that lead to the decline of the family and of the next generation. It is not that mothers who stay at home are automatically or categorically more responsible or spiritual than those who work. Many mothers who have never worked outside the home have done little to strengthen or bless the home. Gossiping, watching ungodly and immoral soap operas, and a host of other things can be as destructive as working away from home. But a woman's only opportunity to fulfill God's plan for her role as wife and mother is in the home.

Even widows or women whose husbands have left them are not expected to leave their domain and children to work outside the home. Paul declared, "If anyone does not provide for his own, and especially for those of his household, he has denied the faith, and is worse than an unbeliever" (1 Tim. 5:8). The reference is to the extended as well as the immediate family of a Christian man, and in the context pertains particularly to widows. If a woman has no husband and no financial resources of her own, her children or grandchildren are to take care of her (v. 4). If she has no children old enough to support her, the other men in her family have the obligation (v. 8). If she has no male relatives to support her, a female relative who has adequate resources is to care for her (v. 16a). If she has no such male or female relatives, or if they are unable or unwilling to support her, the church is obligated to care for her (v. 16b). The basic principle is that she should be cared for by other believers and not be forced to support herself by an outside work. As He was hanging on the cross, during the last moments of His life, Jesus took time in His agony to provide for His widowed mother by giving her into the care of John (John 19:26-27).

Widows who were over sixty years old, who had proven their faithfulness as wives and mothers, and who were known for their good works and their service to strangers and to fellow Christians, were put on the official widows' list (1 Tim. 5:9-10). We learn from extrabiblical sources that the widows on this list were fully supported by the local congregation and served the church in official ministries, as what might be called staff widows.

Younger widows, however, were not to be put on the list. They were likely to fall in love again and want to get married, forsaking their commitment to the ministry (vv. 11-12). They would also be more inclined to be lazy, and become "gossips and busybodies" (v. 13). Consequently, they were to be encouraged to "get married, bear children, keep house, and give the enemy no occasion for reproach," as some of them had already done in turning aside to follow Satan, perhaps in sexual sin or mixed marriage (vv. 14-15).

From the time of its inception, the early church recognized the high priority of its obligations to provide for widows. In order for them to be more carefully and fairly cared for, the apostles appointed the first deacons to be "in charge of this task" (Acts 6:3). Those chosen were among the most godly and capable men in the Jerusalem church and included Stephen and Philip.

If a woman still has children at home, her primary obligation is to them. If she has no children or they are grown, she has a responsibility to help teach the younger women and share the insights and wisdom she has gained from her own walk with the Lord. She should invest her time in teaching younger women much as she taught her own children. As a godly influence working in and out of her home, she bequeaths a spiritual legacy to succeeding generations even beyond the influence on her own family.

Some Christian women may have no choice but to work because they have no provider in their family and their church is unwilling to help them. But the great majority of women who work outside the home do so for the sake of some imagined need for personal fulfillment or extra income to increase their standard of living, rather than to provide for family necessities. Many young mothers leave their three- or four-month-old babies with baby-sitters in order to return to work so they can earn more money or sometimes just to get away from the responsibilities of the home. Some Christian churches, schools, and other institutions foster that practice by providing child care centers and nursery schools for mothers who work.

If the standard of living a family has cannot be maintained without the wife's working outside the home, that family should consider carefully whether their standard is God's will for them, and surely should not confuse the economic benefits of their presumption with blessing from God. Not only does the large number of working women damage the home but also the economy, by contributing to inflation and loss of jobs that men would otherwise fill.

Just as with the drinking of alcoholic beverages, the Bible does not specifically forbid a wife to work outside the home. But the biblical priorities are so clear that they can only be obeyed or rejected openly, and each woman must choose how she will honor those priorities.

When Samuel was still an infant, his father, Elkanah, wanted his mother to take the child and go up with the rest of the household to sacrifice in Jerusalem. But his mother, Hannah, replied, "I will not go up until the child is weaned; then I will bring him" (1 Sam. 1:21-22). Despite the importance of the yearly sacrifice, she knew that her primary responsibility at that time was to care for her baby. Realizing her priorities were right, Elkanah responded, "Do what seems best to you. Remain until you have weaned him; only may the Lord confirm His word" (v. 23).

The industrious and gifted woman who has time and energy remaining after taking care of her household responsibilities can channel them into many areas of service that do not take her out of the home on an all-day basis. The godly wife of Proverbs 31 took care of her husband and children, shopped carefully, supervised various business and financial dealings, helped the poor, gave encouraging and wise advice, was a kind teacher, and was highly respected by her husband, children, and the community (vv. 10-31). Yet she did all of that while operating primarily out of her home. With modern means of communication and transportation as well as countless other resources that the woman of Proverbs did not have, Christian women today have immeasurably more opportunities for productive, helpful, and rewarding service—without sacrificing the priority of their homes.

THE MANNER OF SUBMISSION

as to the Lord. (5:22b)

The manner or attitude of submission is to be **as to the Lord.** Everything we do in obedience to the Lord should also be done first of all for His glory and to please Him. Those to whom we submit, whether in mutual submission or in response to their functional authority, will often not inspire respect. Sometimes they will be thoughtless, inconsiderate, abusive, and ungrateful. But the Spirit-filled believer—in this instance, the wife—submits anyway, because that is the Lord's will and her submission is to Him. A wife who properly submits to her husband also submits **to the Lord.** And a wife who does not submit to her husband also does not submit to the Lord.

THE MOTIVE OF SUBMISSION

For the husband is the head of the wife, as Christ also is the head of the church, (5:23a)

The wife's supreme motive for submitting to her husband is the fact that he is her functional head in the family, just **as Christ also is the head of the church** (cf. 1 Cor. 11:3; Col. 1:18; and see Eph. 1:22-23). The head gives direction and the body responds. A physical body that does not respond to the direction of the head is crippled, paralyzed, or spastic. Likewise, a wife who does not properly respond to the direction of her husband manifests a serious spiritual dysfunction. On the other hand, a wife who willingly and lovingly responds to her husband's leadership as to the Lord is an honor to her Lord, her husband, her family, her church, and herself. She is also a beautiful testimony to the Lord before in view of the world around her.

THE MODEL OF SUBMISSION

He Himself being the Savior of the body. But as the church is subject to Christ, so also the wives ought to be to their husbands in everything. (5:23b-24)

The supreme and ultimate model of submission is Jesus Christ **Himself,** who performed the supreme act of submission by giving His own sinless life to save a sinful world. Christ is **the Savior of the body,** His church, for whom He died on the cross. He is the perfect Provider, Protector, and Head of His church, which is His **body.**

Jesus Christ is the divine role model for husbands, who should provide for, protect, preserve, love, and lead their wives and families as Christ cares for His church. Wives are no more to be co-providers, co-protectors, or co-leaders with their husbands than the church is have such joint roles with Jesus Christ. Just **as the church is subject to Christ, so also the wives ought to be to their husbands in everything.**

To follow God's plan for the family not only is pleasing to Him but is the only way to godlier, happier, and more secure homes. His plan is neither for the exaltation of man and suppression of woman nor the exaltation of woman and suppression of man, but for the perfection and fulfillment of both man and woman as He has ordained them to be. Such perfection and fulfilment is made possible by the filling of the Holy Spirit.

The Role and Priorities of the Husband

23

Husbands, love your wives, just as Christ also loved the church and gave Himself up for her; that He might sanctify her, having cleansed her by the washing of water with the word, that He might present to Himself the church in all her glory, having no spot or wrinkle or any such thing; but that she should be holy and blameless. So husbands ought also to love their own wives as their own bodies. He who loves his own wife loves himself; for no one ever hated his own flesh, but nourishes and cherishes it, just as Christ also does the church, because we are members of His body. For this cause a man shall leave his father and mother, and shall cleave to his wife; and the two shall become one flesh. This mystery is great; but I am speaking with reference to Christ and the church. Nevertheless let each individual among you also love his own wife even as himself; and let the wife see to it that she respect her husband. (5:25-33)

Life is made meaningful by relationships, the most meaningful of which is that between a man and woman in marriage. Peter called it "the grace of life" (1 Pet. 3:7). Yet the fulfillment of that relationship is elusive. A marriage that continually gets better, richer, and more satisfying is rare today.

From many voices today comes the claim that the very institution of marriage has failed to meet people's needs. But the fact is that it is not a matter of marriage having failed, since marriage has been increasingly avoided. Today, in place of exerting consistent effort and determination to fulfill the commitment it takes to make one's marriage work, the solution is to bail out.

In his book *Becoming Partners: Marriage and Its Alternatives,* Dr. Carl Rogers writes from the view of a humanistic unbeliever,

> To me it seems that we are living in an important and uncertain age, and the institution of marriage is most assuredly in an uncertain state. If 50-75 percent of Ford or General Motors cars completely fell apart within the early part of their lifetimes as automobiles, drastic steps would be taken. We have no such well organized way of dealing with our social institutions, so people are groping, more or less blindly, to find alternatives to marriage (which is certainly less than 50 percent successful). Living together without marriage, living in communes, extensive childcare centers, serial monogamy (with one divorce after another), the women's liberation movement to establish the woman as person in her own right, new divorce laws which do away with the concept of guilt—these are all gropings toward some new form of man-woman relationship for the future. It would take a bolder man than I to predict what will emerge. (New York: Dell, 1973, p. 11)

It does not take boldness to predict what will happen, but only a look at God's Word. "Realize this," Paul tells us; "in the last days difficult times will come. For men will be lovers of self, lovers of money, boastful, arrogant, revilers, disobedient to parents, ungrateful, unholy, unloving, irreconcilable, malicious gossips, without self-control, brutal, haters of good, treacherous, reckless, conceited, lovers of pleasure rather than lovers of God; holding to a form of godliness, although they have denied its power. . . . Evil men and impostors will proceed from bad to worse, deceiving and being deceived" (2 Tim. 3:1-5, 13).

In that awesome list of sins there are several—such as disobedience to parents, lack of love (the Greek term, *astorgos,* refers to lack of natural affection for one's family), and brutality—that are directly undermining the home today. But *every* sin that weakens the individual also weakens the home to some extent; *every* aspect of ungodliness weakens the relationships between husband and wife, parents and children, and brothers and sisters. The home has become fair game for every deceiver, every sexual pervert, every exploiter, as Satan mounts his great attack on that foundation stone of society.

Because of the curse on marriage at the Fall and the inclinations of man's fallen nature and of the world to oppose God's way, the family has always had difficulty. In the western culture of our day, however, it is under an onslaught seemingly unlike any other in this society's history. There is less chance than before of a family's living together in harmony, love, and mutual respect apart from God's provision in Christ. As every new corruption appears, a new philosophy arises to justify it. And those who persist in flouting God's way are destined, as Paul prophesied, to go from bad to worse. Marriage, along with every other institution and design of God, will be more and more debased, as men go deeper into sexual perversion and selfishness.

Before the Fall, Adam and Eve lived in the beautiful harmony and satisfaction of a perfect marriage. When Adam first saw Eve, he immediately recognized her as his perfect companion. "This is now bone of my bones, and flesh of my flesh," he said (Gen. 2:23). He saw no blemishes or shortcomings in her, because both her character and his attitude were pure. There was nothing to criticize in Eve and there was no critical spirit in Adam. Though they were both naked, they were not ashamed (v. 25), because there was no such thing as an evil, impure, or perverse thought.

Man was created first and was given headship over the woman and over creation. But their original relationship was so pure and perfect that his headship over her was a manifestation of his consuming love for her, and her submission to him was a manifestation of her consuming love for him. No selfishness or self-will marred their relationship. Each lived for the other in perfect fulfillment of their created purpose and under God's perfect provision and care.

The man and woman were so closely identified with each other that God's command was for "*them* [to] rule over the fish of the sea and over the birds of the sky and over the cattle and over all the earth. . . . God blessed *them;* and God said to *them,* 'Be fruitful and multiply, and fill the earth, and subdue it; and rule over the fish of the sea and over the birds of the sky, and over every living thing that moves on the earth'" (Gen. 1:26-28, emphasis added).

Marriage was instituted to procreate mankind, to raise up children to fill the earth (Gen. 1:28). It is also for the purpose of companionship, so that man would not be alone (2:18), and for the purpose of sexual fulfillment and pleasure (1 Cor. 7:4-5; cf. Heb. 13:4).

In the last chapter we discussed why the perfect marriage relationship of Adam and Eve was interrupted. The Fall itself involved a perversion of marital roles, and God's curse because of the Fall also affected marriage. Eve sinned not only in disobeying God's specific command but in acting independently of her husband and failing to consult Adam about the serpent's temptation. Adam sinned not only by disobeying God's command but by succumbing to Eve's leadership, thus failing to exercise his God-given authority. Because of her disobedience, God cursed the woman to pain in childbirth and to a perverted desire to rule over the man. The man was cursed to toil, to difficulty, to frustration in wresting sustenance from the land, and to conflict with his wife over her submission. Both were cursed with death as the penalty for their sin (Gen. 3:16-19; cf. Rom. 5:15-19).

Marriage was corrupted because both the man and the woman twisted God's plan for their relationship. They reversed their roles, and marriage has been a struggle ever since. Women's liberation reflects the woman's distorted desires, and male chauvinism the man's. The unredeemed nature of both men and women is to be self-preoccupied and self-serving—and those characteristics are no basis for harmonious relationships. God's way to successful marriage focuses on what husbands and wives put into it, not on what they can get out of it.

Throughout history the most dominant distortion of relationships has been on man's side. In most cultures of the ancient world, women were treated as little more than servants, and the practice is reflected in many parts of the world today. Marcius Cato, the famous Roman statesman of the second century B.C., wrote, "If you catch your wife in an act of infidelity, you can kill her without a trial. But if she were to catch you, she would not venture to touch you with her finger. She has no rights." That reflects the extreme of male chauvinism that comes out of the curse of the Fall and reflects the perversion of roles and responsibilities that God intends for husbands and wives.

Even in supposedly liberated societies, women are frequently looked on primarily as sex objects who exist for the sensual pleasures of men. Because modern man is inclined to view himself as merely a higher form of animal—with no divine origin, purpose, or accountability—he is even more disposed to see other people simply as things, to be used for his own pleasure and advantage.

As already pointed out, Satan's initial attack on God's supreme creation involved corruption of the family. Sin brought an alien, divisive influence into marriage and the family. The first murder was brother slaying brother (Gen. 4:8). A few generations later we see Lamech as a polygamist (Gen. 4:23), departing from God's design for one-man, one-woman marriage (2:24). We are not told exactly what happened when Ham saw his father, Noah, drunk and naked in his tent, but it apparently involved perverted sexual suggestions or attempts on Ham's part, because Noah cursed him for it (Gen. 9:25). When Sarah was not able to have children, she persuaded Abraham to have a child by Hagar, her maid, and thereby caused her husband to commit adultery (16:4). Because of their unbridled wickedness, especially in sexual perversions, God destroyed the cities of Sodom and Gomorrah (19:24-25). Since that day, Sodom has had the distinction of giving its name to a common term for homosexuality (sodomy). In Genesis 34 we read of Shechem's fornication with Dinah, one of Jacob's daughters (v. 3); and because the act was forceful, it was also rape. A few chapters later we read of another double sexual sin involving Judah and his daughter-in-law, Tamar, after she was widowed. Because she had no sons, she dressed up as a temple prostitute (which included wearing a veil) and enticed Judah as he passed down the road—who gave her the desired son, but at the cost of both prostitution and incest (38:13-18). In the next chapter we see the attempted seduction of Joseph by Potiphar's wife (39:7-12).

In this first book of the Bible we see the reversal of roles of husband and wife, fratricide, polygamy, perverted sexual suggestions, adultery, homosexuality, fornication, rape, prostitution, incest, and seduction—each of which directly attacks the sanctity and harmony of marriage and the family.

Yet in much of modern society those very sins are lauded. Young women who are virgins and husbands who are faithful to their wives are looked at askance and laughed at. Sexual purity and marital fidelity are standard fare for jesting in comedy and talk shows. It is difficult enough to make marriage work under the curse when most people recognize and seek to follow God's standards for morality and marriage. It is immeasurably more difficult when most people mock those standards. The only ones who can survive such a wicked and perverse generation are Christians who are filled with the Holy Spirit. Apart from His divine resources, a couple has no more chance of making their marriage what God intends it to be than Ponce de Leon did of finding the fountain of youth.

Satan knows by experience that when the home is weakened, all of society is weakened, because the heart of all human relationships is the family. The curse hits mankind at the base of its most needed human relationship, the need for men and women to have each other as helpers suitable for living productive, meaningful, and happy lives on earth. The world, inspired and led by Satan himself, tells us that meaning and happiness are found in serving and indulging self, in being free to express sexual desire however one wants—though promiscuity, unfaithfulness in marriage, partner swapping, homosexuality, bestiality, or any other way. And when men and women take that deceptive bait, they join Satan in undermining and destroying every meaningful and truly satisfying relationship in their lives—sexual as well as all others. And they bring on themselves the destruction and disease that God has ordained as the consequence of such sins.

Popular entertainment goes beyond reflecting the normal, realistic inner longings that every person has for relationships that are genuine and permanent. The fantasy of the perfect woman, the perfect man, the perfect romantic relationship become more and more elusive as the fantasy satisfactions of immorality are chosen over the real satisfactions that come only from God's standards of purity and unselfishness. The beautiful face, the athletic body, the winsome personality, and other such superficial attractions cannot hold two people together when their first priority in life is to serve and please themselves. The lie that no face is ever beautiful enough, no body ever sensual enough, no wardrobe ever glamorous enough, no physical pleasure ever fulfilling enough sends people on a path of self-destruction and emptiness.

Even when relationship after relationship proves disappointing, people continue to expect to find their fantasized satisfaction in the next person, the next experience, the next excitement. Because selfishness wants what it does not have, it therefore always wants more. Yet the more it possesses, the more it still wants and the less it is satisfied. As self is elevated above love, and immorality above purity, fantasy is inevitably elevated above reality—because reality becomes too disappointing to face. God destines the ungodly and immoral life to illusion and disappointment.

In Ephesians 5:25-33 Paul continues to describe the godly and moral life of the believer who is filled with the Holy Spirit and who is mutually submissive "in the fear of Christ" (v. 21). As he has already made clear (vv. 22-24), God has ordained the husband to be head over the wife. But the emphasis of the rest of the chapter in not on the husband's authority but on his duty to submit to his wife through his love for her. Verses 25-31 explain the manner of that love and verses 32-33 reveal its motive.

THE MANNER OF LOVE

Husbands, love your wives, just as Christ also loved the church and gave Himself up for her; that He might sanctify her, having cleansed her by the washing of water with the word, that He might present to Himself the church in all her glory, having no spot or wrinkle or any such thing; but that she should be holy and blameless. So husbands ought also to love their own wives as their own bodies. He who loves his own wife loves himself; for no one ever hated his own flesh, but nourishes and cherishes it, just as Christ also does the church, because we are members of His body. For this cause a man shall leave his father and mother, and shall cleave to his wife; and the two shall become one flesh. (5:25-31)

As just noted, the command, **husbands, love your wives,** continues Paul's explanation of the mutual submission mentioned in verse 21. The husband's primary submission to his wife is through his love for her, and the apostle makes clear that this is a boundless kind of love. Husbands are to love their wives **just as Christ also loved the church.** Jesus Christ loved the church before He brought the church into existence. He chose and loved His own even "before the foundation of the world" (1:4), because God's love is eternally present, having no past and no future.

Obviously no sinful human being has the capacity to love with the divine fullness and perfection with which **Christ . . . loved,** and will forever love, **the church.** However, because a Christian has Christ's own nature and Holy Spirit within him, God thereby provides for husbands to love their wives with a measure of Christ's own kind of love. The husband who submits to the Lord by being filled with His Spirit (v. 18) is able to love his wife with the same kind of love Jesus has for His own bride, the church. The Lord's pattern of love for His church is the husband's pattern of love for his wife.

In this passage Paul mentions four qualities of that divine love that husbands are to exemplify toward their wives. Like the Lord's, the husband's love is to be sacrificial, purifying, caring, and unbreakable.

SACRIFICIAL LOVE

and gave Himself up for her. (5:25b)

When Christ came to earth in human form, He knew that He came to be mocked, ridiculed, maligned, rejected, beaten, and crucified. He knew from eternity past what would be demanded of His eternal love if men were to be provided a way of salvation. He gave up His prerogatives as God's Son, not regarding "equality with God a thing to be grasped, but emptied Himself, taking the form of a bond-servant, . . . He humbled Himself by becoming obedient to the point of death, even death on a cross" (Phil. 2:6-8).

Because His sacrifice was determined in heaven before a single soul was created, and because every created soul became sinful in Adam's fall and only worthy of death (Rom. 1:32; 3:10-11, 23; 6:21), Jesus' sacrifice was purely of grace. Jesus loves and saves because it is His character to be gracious. "For one will hardly die for a righteous man; though perhaps for the good man someone would dare even to die. But God demonstrates His own love toward us, in that while we were yet sinners, Christ died for us" (5:7-8). Jesus' love for His church not only was sacrificial but *graciously* sacrificial. No person deserves to be saved, to be forgiven, cleansed, and placed within God's kingdom as His own child. He sacrificed not for the lovely or worthy but for the unlovely and unworthy.

The world's love is always object-oriented. A person is loved because of physical attractiveness, personality, wit, prestige, or some other such positive characteristic. In other words, the world loves those whom it deems worthy of love. Such love is necessarily fickle. As soon as a person loses a positive characteristic— or that characteristic is no longer appealing—the love based on the characteristic also disappears. It is because so many husbands and wives have only that kind of fickle love for each that their marriages fall apart. As soon as a partner loses his or her appeal, love is gone, because the basis for the love is gone.

God's love is not of that sort. He loves because it is His nature to love that which He has created and because the objects of His love *need* to be loved—not because they are attractive or deserve His love. If God loved as the world loves, He could not love a single human being. But in His marvelous graciousness, He loves because He cannot do otherwise.

God can command His own kind of love from those who belong to Him because He has given them the capacity to love as He loves (cf. Rom. 5:5; 1 Thess. 4:9) and because His commanded love must, therefore, be a matter of choice (cf. James 2:8; 1 John 3:7, 16-18, 23; 4:7, 11). It is an act of the will as well as of the heart. And it seems to be a principle that whatever we choose to love and practice loving soon becomes attractive to us. But a Christian's loving with Christ's kind of love is not based on the attractiveness of the one loved but on God's command to love. Loving as Christ loves does not depend in the least on what others are in themselves, but entirely on what we are in Christ.

A husband is not commanded to love his wife because of what she is or is not. He is commanded to love her because it is God's will for him to love her. It is certainly intended for a husband to admire and be attracted by his wife's beauty, winsomeness, kindness, gentleness, or any other positive quality or virtue. But though such things bring great blessing and enjoyment, they are not the bond of marriage. If every appealing characteristic and every virtue of his wife disappears, a husband is still under just as great an obligation to love her. If anything, he is under greater obligation, because her need for the healing and restorative power of his selfless love is greater. That is the kind of love Christ has for His church and is therefore the kind of love every Christian husband is to have for his wife.

The Good Samaritan's expression of love to the man who was beaten and robbed was based on his own generous character and on that man's severe need. Whether the man deserved his care did not enter into the picture. Jesus washed His disciples' feet because He loved them and sought to serve them, not because they deserved even that most menial of services. He loved them despite their selfishness, pride, ambition, self-indulgence, jealousy, and fickleness. No doubt He felt great sorrow and pain because of their continued selfishness after three years of being with Him in intimate fellowship. But He did not love and serve them on the basis of those feelings but on the basis of His own loving nature. He also washed their feet as an example of what every disciple of His is commanded to do. "If I then, the Lord and the Teacher, washed your feet, you also ought to wash one another's feet" (John 13:14). A short while later He said, "A new commandment I give to you, that you love one another, even as I have loved you, that you also love one another" (v. 34).

Where there is need, love acts, with no consideration of deserving or worth (cf. 1 John 3:16). God's love is its own justification; and when we love as He loves, our love is also its own justification, because it is like His love. God did not love the world and send His own Son to redeem it because it was worthy of that love. It was totally unworthy of His love; and when His love came in human flesh, the world despised it, rejected it, and threw it back in God's face. Yet Jesus Christ, as God's incarnate love, did not flinch or turn away or become resentful. He preached and taught and bled and died, because that is what divine love demanded.

Love does whatever needs to be done and does not count cost or merit. It reaches out and helps, leads, teaches, warns, or encourages. Whatever is needed it gives. Whether its help is received or rejected, appreciated or resented, love continues as long as the need continues.

Therefore the Christian who loves because of what other people may do for him or because they are attractive does not love as God loves. The husband who loves his wife only because of her physical attractiveness or pleasing temperament does not love her as **Christ . . . loved the church**. The husband who loves his wife for what she can give him loves as the world loves, not as Christ loves. The husband who loves his wife as Christ loves His church gives everything he has for his wife, including his life if necessary.

If a loving husband is willing to sacrifice his life for his wife, he is certainly willing to make lesser sacrifices for her. He puts his own likes, desires, opinions, preferences, and welfare aside if that is required to please her and meet her needs. He dies to self in order to live for his wife, because that is what Christ's kind of love demands. That is his submission.

The true spirituality of a church leader is not measured best by how well he leads a deacons' or elders' meeting, by the way he participates in Sunday school, or by the way he speaks from the pulpit—but by the way he treats his wife and children at home when no one else is around. Nowhere is our relationship to God better tested than in our relationship to our family. The man who plays the part of a spiritual shepherd in church but who lacks love and care in his home is guilty of spiritual fraud.

The world continually tells the man to be macho, to defend himself, assert himself, bring attention to himself, and live totally for himself. But God tells the

Christian man to give himself up for others, especially for his wife, just as Christ **gave Himself up for** the church.

To regularly remind myself of the essence of this self-sacrificing love, I have on my desk the following words from an unknown source:

> When you are forgotten or neglected or purposely set at naught, and you sting and hurt with the insult or the oversight, but your heart is happy, being counted worthy to suffer for Christ—that is dying to self. When your good is evil spoken of, when your wishes are crossed, your advice disregarded, your opinions ridiculed and you refuse to let anger rise in your heart, or even defend yourself, but take it all in patient loving silence—that is dying to self. When you lovingly and patiently bear any disorder, any irregularity, or any annoyance, when you can stand face to face with waste, folly, extravagance, spiritual insensibility, and endure it as Jesus endured it—that is dying to self. When you are content with any food, any offering, any raiment, any climate, any society, any attitude, any interruption by the will of God—that is dying to self. When you never care to refer to yourself in conversation, or to record your own good works, or itch after commendation, when you can truly love to be unknown—that is dying to self. When you see your brother prosper and have his needs met and can honestly rejoice with him in spirit and feel no envy nor question God, while your own needs are far greater and in desperate circumstances—that is dying to self. When you can receive correction and reproof from one of less stature than yourself, can humbly submit inwardly as well as outwardly, finding no rebellion or resentment rising up within your heart—that is dying to self.

PURIFYING LOVE

that He might sanctify her, having cleansed her by the washing of water with the word, that He might present to Himself the church in all her glory, having no spot or wrinkle or any such thing; but that she should be holy and blameless. (5:26-27)

For husbands to love their wives as Christ loves His church is to love them with a purifying love. Divine love does not simply condemn wrong in those loved but seeks to cleanse them from it. Christ's great love for His church does not allow Him to be content with any sin, any moral or spiritual impurity in it. God tells His people, "Though your sins are as scarlet, they will be as white as snow; though they are red like crimson, they will be like wool" (Isa. 1:18). He casts the sins of His forgiven children "into the depths of the sea" (Mic. 7:19), and He forgives their iniquity and remembers their sin no more (Jer. 31:34).

A believer is forgiven every sin the moment he trusts in Jesus Christ as Lord and Savior. After that initial and full purification from sin, as Jesus explained to Peter as he washed his feet, periodic cleansing is still necessary. "He who has bathed needs only to wash his feet, but is completely clean; and you are clean, but not all of you" (John 13:10). As we continue to confess our sins, Christ "is faithful and righteous to forgive us our sins and to cleanse us from all unrighteousness" (1 John 1:9). The **word** is the agent of this sanctification (cf. Titus 3:5), the objective of which is a blamelessness and holiness that makes us fit to be presented to Christ as His own beloved and eternal bride, to dwell in His glorious presence forever (cf. Rev. 21:1ff.).

Love wants only the best for the one it loves, and it cannot bear for a loved one to be corrupted or misled by anything evil or harmful. When a husband's love for his wife is like Christ's love for His church, he will continually seek to help purify her from any sort of defilement. He will seek to protect her from the world's contamination and protect her holiness, virtue, and purity in every way. He will never induce her to do that which is wrong or unwise or expose her to that which is less than good.

On a popular talk show some years ago the host interviewed two ministers. When asked what they thought of *Playboy* magazine, one of them replied, "I think it is despicable. I wouldn't read it or have it in my home. It dishonors God, it dishonors men and women, and it dishonors almost everything else that is good." The other minister said, "I am an evangelical Christian, and I want you to know that my wife and I both read *Playboy*. In fact she gave me a subscription to it. After 18 years of marriage we thought we needed a little something to stimulate our relationship." That man not only was defiling himself but encouraged his wife in the defilement. Whatever sensual desire motivated that couple to read such a magazine, it was not godly love for each other.

When a young man says he loves a young woman, but wants her to compromise her sexual purity before they are married, his love is the world's lust, not God's love; and it is selfish, not serving. That sort of love defiles rather than purifies. A husband who flirts with his secretary or a neighbor woman gives his wife cause to feel rejected and lonely—and perhaps to begin flirting herself. He not only jeopardizes his own moral purity, but his wife's as well, and shares responsibility for any indiscretion or immorality in which she might be tempted to become involved.

In ancient Greece, a bride-to-be would be taken down to a river to be bathed and ceremonially cleansed from every defilement of her past life. Whatever her life had been before, it was now symbolically purified and she would enter the marriage without any moral or social blemish—the past was washed away.

In an immeasurably greater way Christ gave Himself up for the church, **that He might sanctify her, having cleansed her by the washing of water with the word, that He might present to Himself the church in all her glory, having no spot or wrinkle or any such thing; but that she should be holy and blameless.** His cleansing of believers is not ceremonial and symbolic, but real and complete.

The soteriological truth in this analogy is that saving grace makes believers holy through the cleansing agency of the Word of God, so that they may be presented to Christ as His pure Bride, forever to dwell in His love. It is with that same purpose and in that same love that husbands are to cultivate the purity, righteousness, and sanctity of their wives.

CARING LOVE

So husbands ought also to love their own wives as their own bodies. He who loves his own wife loves himself; for no one ever hated his own flesh, but nourishes and cherishes it, just as Christ also does the church, because we are members of His body. (5:28-30)

For a husband's love for his wife to be like Christ's love for His Body, the church, it must also be affectionately caring—to the extent that he cares as much for her welfare as he does for the welfare of his own body.

Men and women have always been concerned about their bodies. But at no time in modern history have people more sinfully pampered, protected, nourished, and indulged the body as in our own day. The amount of money spent just to decorate, protect, enhance, comfort, and display the body is incalculable.

Because, as Christians, our bodies are temples of the Holy Spirit, we should be take proper care of them—giving them the right food, maintaining reasonable strength, getting enough rest, and so on. When our body is healthy we have a sense of well-being; and when a husband meets the needs of his wife—with the same care and concern with which he meets the needs of his own body—he will also have a sense of well-being and pleasure as a by-product of his love.

The husband who loves his wife as Christ loves the church will no more do anything to harm her than he would to harm **his own flesh**. His desire is to nourish and cherish her just as he **nourishes and cherishes** his own body—because that is how **Christ also does the church**.

When she needs strength, he gives her strength. When she needs encouragement, he gives her that. And so with every other thing she needs. Just as God supplies "all [our] needs according to His riches in glory in Christ Jesus" (Phil. 4:19), the loving husband seeks to supply all the needs of his wife. The blessed marriage is the marriage in which the husband loves his wife with unlimited caring. Something is basically wrong if she is looked at only as a cook, housekeeper, occasional companion, and sex partner. She is a God-given treasure to be loved, cared for, nourished, and cherished.

To nourish a wife is to provide for her needs, to give that which helps her grow and mature in favor with God and man. To cherish her is to use tender love and physical affection to give her warmth, comfort, protection, and security. Those responsibilities are primarily the husband's, not the wife's. As Christ provides for His church, so the husband provides for his wife and family.

Christ provides for us as His church **because we are members of His body**. Not to provide for His church would be not to provide for Himself. He shares common life with His church, and we are **members of His body**, His flesh and bones, His present incarnation on earth. Paul said, "The one who joins himself to the Lord is one spirit with Him" (1 Cor. 6:17), and again, "I have been crucified with Christ; and it is no longer I who live, but Christ lives in me; and the life which I now live in the flesh I live by faith in the Son of God, who loved me, and delivered Himself up for me" (Gal. 2:20).

UNBREAKABLE LOVE

For this cause a man shall leave his father and mother, and shall cleave to his wife; and the two shall become one flesh. (5:31)

For a husband to love his wife as Christ loves His church he must love her with an unbreakable love. In this direct quotation from Genesis 2:24 Paul emphasized the permanence as well as the unity of marriage. God's standard for marriage did not change from the time of Adam until the time of Paul, and it has not changed to this day.

One of the greatest barriers to successful marriage is the failure of one or both partners to **leave . . . father and mother.** In marriage, a new family is begun and the relationships of the former families are to be severed as far as authority and responsibilities are concerned. Parents are always to be loved and cared for, but they are no longer to control the lives of their children once they are married.

Proskollaō (**cleave**) literally means to be glued or cemented together. Husbands and wives are to **leave** their parents and to **cleave** to, be cemented to, each other. They break one set of ties as they establish the other, and the second is more binding and permanent than the first.

"'I hate divorce,' says the Lord, the God of Israel" (Mal. 2:16). God has always hated divorce and He will continue to hate it, because it destroys that which He has ordained to be unbreakable. He hates divorce on any terms and for any reason. He will tolerate it in certain instances, and will forgive it, as He will forgive any other sin; but He will never change His hatred for it, just as He will never change His hatred for any other sin.

Husbands and wives are not to be quick to divorce each other because of wrongs their spouses have done, not even for unfaithfulness. Just as Christ does not separate Himself from believers who sin against Him, husbands and wives are not to separate themselves from their partners who sin against them. As Christ is always forgiving of believers, husbands and wives should always be forgiving of each other.

Israel was repeatedly unfaithful to God, and that unfaithfulness is frequently referred to in the Old Testament as spiritual adultery. When God chose Israel to be His people, He determined to love them "with an everlasting love" (Jer. 31:3). It was only after unrelenting spiritual adultery and rejection of Him that God finally gave Israel a divorce (Jer. 3:8). But that was not to say He rejected the true believers within the nation, who were secure in His saving grace (see Mal. 3:16-18).

That is the sort of bond God ordained for marriage. It is not *ever*lasting as far as eternity is concerned, but it is lasting as far as the earthly lives of the husband and wife are concerned. Though He has made provision for divorce in the cases of unrepentant and continued adultery (Matt. 5:31-32; 19:4-10) and the departure of an unbelieving spouse (1 Cor. 7:15), death is God's only desired dissolution for marriage.

Just as the body of Christ is indivisible, God's ideal design for marriage is that it be indivisible. As Christ is one with His church, husbands are one with their wives. Therefore when a husband harms his wife he harms himself. A husband who violates his marriage violates himself. A husband who destroys his marriage destroys a part of himself.

When a man and woman are joined in marriage, Jesus said, "They are no longer two, but one flesh. What therefore God has joined together, let no man separate" (Matt. 19:6). When the Pharisees asked, "Why then did Moses command to give her a certificate and divorce her?" Jesus replied, "Because of your hardness of heart, Moses permitted you to divorce your wives; but from the beginning it has not been this way. And I say to you, whoever divorces his wife, except for immorality, and marries another woman commits adultery" (vv. 7-9).

Jesus made clear that God, through Moses, only "permitted" divorce; He never "commanded" it, as Jewish leaders had claimed for hundreds of years. The bill of divorcement was to protect the offended wife, who would then be allowed to marry again without becoming guilty of adultery. That is the only provision that either Moses or Jesus gives for divorce.

But it is not God's will that even adultery break the marriage relationship, and that is the message of the book of Hosea. Hosea's wife, Gomer, was unfaithful in the extreme, not only committing adultery but becoming a prostitute. Yet God's word to Hosea was to keep loving her and forgiving her. The more she sinned, the more he was to forgive—reflecting God's gracious forgiveness of His sinning people. Finally God restored the marriage of Hosea and Gomer, and He gave the promise to Israel, "I will heal their apostasy, I will love them freely, for My anger has turned away from them. I will be like the dew to Israel; he will blossom like the lily" (Hos. 14:4-5). That is the way God has always loved His people, the way Jesus Christ has always loved His church, and the way Christian husbands are always to love their wives. The Lord never puts us away. "If we confess our sins, He is faithful and righteous to forgive us our sins and to cleanse us from all unrighteousness" (1 John 1:9).

When a husband sees faults and failures in his wife—even if she is as unfaithful and wanton as Gomer—he should realize that she has not offended him to a fraction of the degree to which he has offended God. God has immeasurably more for which to forgive us than we could ever have for which to forgive others. (For a more detailed treatment of divorce, see the pertinent passages in the author's commentaries *Matthew 1-7* [Moody, 1985] and *First Corinthians* [Moody, 1984] as well as his book *The Family* [Moody, 1982].)

The early church Father John Chrysostom wrote,

Hast thou seen the measure of obedience? Here also is the measure of love. Wouldst thou that thy wife shouldst obey thee as the church doth love Christ? Then have care thyself for her as Christ does for the church, and if it be needful that thou shouldst give thy life for her, or be cut to pieces a thousand times, or endure anything whatsoever, refuse it not. Christ brought His church to His feet by His great love, not by threats or any such thing, and so do thou conduct thyself toward thy wife.

A man who was afraid that he loved his wife too much was asked if he loved her as much as Christ loved the church. When he answered no, he was told, "Then you must love her more."

Peter admonished, "You husbands likewise, live with your wives in an understanding way, as with a weaker vessel, since she is a woman; and grant her honor as a fellow heir of the grace of life, so that your prayers may not be hindered" (1 Pet. 3:7). Here we see at least three commands. First, a husband is to be considerate of his wife. To treat your wife in an understanding way is to treat her with sensitivity and consideration. Over and over we hear wives saying—usually with justification—that their husbands do not understand them, are not sensitive to their feelings and their needs, and do not communicate with them. The fact that a husband may have many pressures and worries of his own is no excuse for his being insensitive to his wife, whom God commands him to love and care for as Christ loves and cares for the church.

Second, Peter teaches that a husband is to be chivalrous to his wife as "a weaker vessel." True chivalry is not simply a formality of polite society; it reflects the attitude men should have toward all women, particularly their own wives. A husband's courtesy toward his wife not only pleases her but also God.

Third, Peter tells husbands to honor their wives "as a fellow heir of the grace of life." Husbands and wives should be the best of friends, not only in family matters and daily activities, but in spiritual things as well. A husband who is not considerate of his wife and who does not honor and respect her is defective in his spiritual life, and his prayers will "be hindered."

The husband who gives his wife consideration, courtesy, and honor contributes to the beauty and strength of his marriage and gives an invaluable example and legacy to his children.

The Motive for Loving Your Wife

This mystery is great; but I am speaking with reference to Christ and the church. Nevertheless let each individual among you also love his own wife even as himself; and let the wife see to it that she respect her husband. (5:32-33)

As Paul has pointed out in vv. 23-29, marriage is a picture of the church and its relationship to Christ. **This mystery**—this magnificent picture that men could never discover and that was unknown to the saints of the Old Covenant but is now revealed—**is great.** God's new people, **the church**, are brought into His kingdom and His family through faith in **Christ.** He is the Bridegroom and they are His bride (Rev. 21:9). A husband's greatest motive for loving, purifying, protecting, and caring for his wife is Christ's love, purifying, protecting, and caring for His own bride, the church. Christian marriage is to be loving, holy, pure, self-sacrificing, and mutually submissive because those virtues characterize the relationship of **Christ and the church**.

The sacred relationship between Christian husbands and wives is inextricably related to the sacred relationship between Christ and His church. Because of this great sacredness, Paul said, **Nevertheless let each individual among you also love his own wife even as himself; and let the wife see to it that she respect her husband**. The use of **nevertheless** (*plēn*) is intended to end the discussion and emphasize what in it is most essential to remember.

When Christian husbands and wives walk in the power of the Spirit, yield to His Word and His control, and are mutually submissive, they are brought much happiness, their children are brought much blessing, and God is brought much honor.

The Responsibilities of Children and Parents

24

Children, obey your parents in the Lord, for this is right. Honor your father and mother (which is the first commandment with a promise), that it may be well with you, and that you may live long on the earth. And, fathers, do not provoke your children to anger; but bring them up in the discipline and instruction of the Lord. (6:1-4)

The experiment is often recounted of placing a frog in a pan of cool water on a stove and of slowly increasing the heat. Because the rise in temperature is so gradual, it is imperceptible to the frog, and he remains in the pan even when the water begins to boil. He adjusts to the heat as it rises and eventually boils to death. That process illustrates what has happened to the American family, including many Christian families. The changed values in society have been so gradual that most people have hardly noticed them. Each small change in standards and values seems insignificant in itself. And because adjustments are gradually made to those lowered standards, the danger is not noticed even when the family and society start to disintegrate and crumble. Moral and spiritual standards have gradually eroded until countless families have been literally destroyed.

When the divorce rate among Christians is almost as high as that in the rest of society, it is clear that many believers should have jumped out of the pan long ago. It is high time we leave the evil system that is engulfing and destroying us and reestablish ourselves in God's revealed standards of fidelity and moral purity. We have long lost the luxury of living in a society that gives some nominal support to the church and to Christian values.

Christian seminars, books, and articles on marriage and the family continue to proliferate, and volumes of schemes and principles are proposed for strengthening them. Child psychology books are written almost ad infinitum. Yet God's Word gives the basis for right parent-child relationships in just four verses. When the other teachings of Scripture supportive of those verses are studied and applied, every parent and every child has all the foundational information necessary for godly and harmonious family living.

When God called the Hebrews to be His chosen people, He destined them to be the people through whom "all the families of the earth shall be blessed" (Gen. 12:3). At Sinai He commissioned them to be "a kingdom of priests and a holy nation" (Ex. 19:6). Israel was to be a witnessing nation, a witnessing people, for God. They were not called to be simply a repository of God's truth and blessing but to be a channel for His truth and blessing to be shared with the whole world.

The heart of God's truth is about God Himself. The central truth of Old Testament revelation is: "The Lord is our God, the Lord is one!" (Deut. 6:4). The corollary truth is about man's response to God: "And you shall love the Lord your God with all your heart and with all your soul and with all your might. And these words, which I am commanding you today, shall be on your heart" (vv. 5-6). That message Israel was to take for herself and then pass on to the world.

The first step in promulgating God's truth was to pass it on to their children. "And you shall teach them diligently to your sons and shall talk of them when you sit in your house and when you walk by the way and when you lie down and when you rise up" (v. 7). Parents were to continually speak about the things of God, so that knowledge and love of Him would become a matter of life and breath for the family. When the parents were not speaking the testimony would continue. "And you shall bind them as sign on your hand and they shall be as frontals on your forehead" (v. 8). Even when the parents were gone, the testimony remained, because it was to be written "on the doorposts of your house and on your gates" (v. 9). In other words, there was always to be both verbal and visible commitment to the Word of God in the home. It is God's plan for His Word to be passed on from one generation to the next. And His primary agent is the family.

But from the time of the Fall the family has been plagued with problems of every sort that weaken, undermine, and threaten to destroy it. The first cause of those problems—as of every human problem—is the sinful nature with which every person is born. The curse of the Fall is built into the family. It is the curse that causes men to be chauvinistic, women to usurp the place of men, children to be disobedient to their parents, and parents to be abusive to their children. Only where Christ is in control as Savior and Lord can a family live up to the standards and fulfill the ministry that God commands.

The Minnesota Crime Commission, demonstrating the truthfulness of the biblical view, issued a report which said, in part:

> Every baby starts life as a little savage. He is completely selfish and self-centered. He wants what he wants when he wants it: his bottle, his mother's attention, his playmate's toys, his uncle's watch, or whatever. Deny him these and he seethes with rage and aggressiveness which would be murderous were he not so helpless. He's dirty, he has no morals, no knowledge, no developed skills. This means that all children, not just certain children but all children, are born delinquent. If permitted to continue in their self-centered world of infancy, given free reign to their impulsive actions to satisfy each want, every child would grow up a criminal, a thief, a killer, a rapist.

The second cause of family problems is the satanic world system in which we live. Because God's plan is to build, strengthen, and protect the family, Satan's plan is to undermine, weaken, and destroy it. By every means possible he designs to push the family into the mold of his world system of values, so that it cannot function as God intends.

The world's mold should not be a perfect fit for the Christian. It should not fit at all. God commanded Moses to tell Israel, "You shall not do what is done in the land of Egypt where you lived, nor are you to do what is done is the land of Canaan where I am bringing you; you shall not walk in their statutes. You are to perform My judgments and keep My statutes, to live in accord with them; I am the Lord your God" (Lev. 18:3-4). "Do not defile yourselves by any of these things," he says later, referring specifically to various immoral sex practices. "For by all these the nations which I am casting out before you have become defiled" (v. 24). From the beginning it was God's intention for His people to be different and distinct, to be separated from the ways of the world.

A third major factor in the destruction of the home is the perverse influence of humanistic philosophy. At almost any secular college today one can hear so-called futuristic ideas being promoted by faculty members, visiting speakers, and campus organizations. One popular speaker says that he looks for a world where there will be no schools, no families, and no parent-child relationships. He says, "To free the child, we must do away with parenthood and marriage, we must settle for nothing less than the total elimination of the family."

At the first international seminar in preparation for the International Year of the Child (IYC) in 1977, the chairwoman of the Czechoslovak Women's Union said, "Long before the representatives of all the peoples of the world and the U. N. decided to adopt the declaration of the rights of the child and its ten principles, the socialist countries had gained vast experience in applying the ideas contained in the declaration in everyday life." One of the major goals of Marxist socialism is to liberate children from the home and make them wards of the state. A child out of the home will not be taught any moral, religious, social, patriotic, or political standards or attitudes that are contrary to what the state wants.

A letter I received from a man in my church who had emigrated with his family from Czechoslovakia includes these words:

> In Czechoslovakia the great majority of women work, and children are at kindergarten since several months of age. The impact on the family ties is horrible. My wife and I know it from our own experience. The godless doctrine pumped into little children's souls brought up the most cynical generation you can imagine. Most young people do not believe in anything, not even God. My wife recently visited our native country and returned with sadness in her heart. The godless system destroyed in great part the will of people, and produced an obeying array of cynical, indifferent, disposable robots. What scares me most is that the same process of liberation movement and jargon I heard twenty-five and thirty years ago is happening right now in this country, and we have to go through it a second time. We must tell you that this collapsing morality and growing indifference are some of the reasons we received Jesus Christ several months ago as our Savior, even though our background of dialectical materialism (that is another name for Communism) is enormous and unimaginable to the average American.

Among the things from which humanistic groups believe children must be liberated are: traditional morals and values, parental authority, physical punishment, religion, nationalism, patriotism, and capitalism. Among the things they believe children should be allowed to do and have are complete sexual freedom, including the right to homosexual "marriage," abortions, and free information and devices for contraception. Serious proposals have been made for children's rights to do such things as sue their parents for being forced to attend church, be paid minimum wage for doing household chores, and be allowed to choose their own family.

From the beginning of Scripture it is plain that children are a blessing from God. When Cain was born Eve exulted, "I have gotten a manchild with the help of the Lord" (Gen. 4:1), and when Seth was born she said, "God has appointed me another offspring in place of Abel" (v. 25). When God blessed Leah with sons because she was unloved by Jacob, she recognized His gracious hand in the births and said of Reuben, "Because the Lord has seen my affliction" and of Simeon, "Because the Lord has heard that I am unloved, He has therefore given me this son also" (Gen. 29:32-33). Throughout both Testaments children are shown to be the Lord's gifts—blessings to be cherished, loved, and cared for with gratitude and faithfulness. "Behold, children are a gift of the Lord; the fruit of the womb is a reward. Like arrows in the hand of a warrior, so are the children of one's youth. How blessed is the man whose quiver is full of them" (Ps. 127:3-5). The qualification for true blessing in parenthood is that of raising children to love the Lord and to follow His ways. It is the righteous, godly child who brings blessing and happiness to his parents. "The father of the righteous will greatly rejoice, and he who begets a wise son will be glad in him" (Prov. 23:24). Women make their most unique contribution to the church, as well as find their own highest fulfillment, in childrearing and in their involvement and activity in the home, which precludes their seeking the male role in the church (see 1 Tim. 2:15).

Parents who do not fully and tirelessly commit themselves to the godly teaching and training of their children are likely to wake up one day to find their sons and daughters inextricably enmeshed in the ungodly and immoral philosophies and practices of the world. Despite what the world may say, children are to obey and honor their parents. They are not to be liberated from their parents and enabled to choose whatever they want to do and the way they want to do it.

In God's Word, parents have every truth and every guideline necessary for raising their children in righteousness and godliness. And what a child needs to know about how he should relate and respond to his parents is there also. The Bible was completed two thousand years ago, but men have not changed since then and neither has God. What Scripture has to say is timeless and up-to-date. No human discovery, philosophy, or attitude is new or surprising to God or outside the scope and judgment of His revealed Word.

Ephesians 6:1-4 continues Paul's teaching on the mutual submission of believers (5:21) by moving to the family. Verses 1-3 focus on the submission of children and verse 4 focuses on the submission of parents.

THE SUBMISSION OF CHILDREN

Children, obey your parents in the Lord, for this is right. Honor your father and mother (which is the first commandment with a promise), that it may be well with you, and that you may live long on the earth. (6:1-3)

Tekna (**children**) does not refer particularly to young children but to all offspring. Sons and daughters still under their parents' roof are to **obey** and **honor** them. **Obey** has to do with action, and **honor** has to do with attitude. Although, as Paul has just mentioned, men and women are no longer under the authority of their parents once they themselves marry (5:31), special respect and concern for their parents should continue as long as they live. The child who is brought up to **obey** and **honor** his parents will always be sensitive to their wisdom, counsel, and welfare.

Hupakouō (**obey**) literally means "to hear under," that is, to listen with attentiveness and to respond positively to what is heard. **Children** are to put themselves under the words and authority of their **parents**.

In the Lord refers to the sphere of pleasing the Lord, to obeying **parents** for the Lord's sake. Children **obey** their parents as reflective of their obedience to the Lord. The context makes it clear that **in the Lord** applies to **honor** as well as to **obey**. **Parents** are to be obeyed and honored because to do so is to obey and honor **the Lord**.

Parents stand in the gap, so to speak, between children and God while the children are too young to have a full and mature relationship with Him themselves. Parents are God's stewards, His proxy authority, for their children, who are simply loaned to them in trust by their own heavenly Father. That is why children are commanded, "Be obedient to your parents in all things, for this is well-pleasing to the Lord" (Col. 3:20). The only exception to that obedience is in the matter of doing what is wrong. Every believer should refuse to do anything that is clearly against God's will as taught in Scripture. He should say with Peter and John, "Whether it is right in the sight of God to give heed to you rather than to God, you be the judge; for we cannot stop speaking what we have seen and heard" (Acts 4:19-20). Otherwise, however, a child is to obey his or her parents "in all things."

The basic reason for children to **obey** and **honor** their parents is simply that it **is right**. The rightness is not based on psychological case studies or other human evidence or theory, but on God's standard of right. God's declaration makes it **right**.

Dikaios (**right**) refers to that which is correct, just, righteous—to that which is exactly as it should be. For children to obey and honor their parents is *dikaios,* exactly as it should be, because everything God commands is *dikaios.* Ezra declared of God, "Then Thou didst come down on Mount Sinai, and didst speak with them from heaven; Thou didst give to them just [or right] ordinances and true laws, good statutes and commandments" (Neh. 9:13). "The precepts of the Lord are right, rejoicing the heart," David said; "the commandment of the Lord is pure, enlightening the eyes" (Ps. 19:8). Another psalmist wrote, "I know, O Lord, that Thy judgments are righteous," and "I esteem right all Thy precepts" (119:75, 128). Hosea closed his message with these beautiful words: "Whoever is wise, let him understand these things; whoever is discerning, let him know them. For the ways of the Lord are right, and the righteous will walk in them, but transgressors will stumble in them" (Hos. 14:9).

The **right** *attitude* behind the right *act* of obedience is **honor** (*timaō*), which means to value highly, to hold in the highest regard and respect. In both its verb and noun forms the word is often used as a term of reverence, preciousness, and honor regarding God the Father and Christ (1 Tim. 1:17; 1 Pet. 2:17; Rev. 4:9, 11; 5:12-13; etc.). It is also used by the Father in reference to the Son (Heb. 2:9; 2 Pet. 1:17).

Children are to **honor** both their **father and mother**, to hold them in the highest possible respect. When God first introduced His written law in the form of the Ten Commandments, the first law relating to human relationships was, "Honor your father and your mother, that your days may be prolonged in the land which the Lord your God gives you" (Ex. 20:12)—and that is the law Paul reiterates in this text. It is the only commandment of the ten that relates to the family, because that one principle alone, when obeyed, is enough to secure the right relationship of children to their parents. Not only that, but it is the key principle behind all right human relationships in society. A person who grows up with a sense of respect for and obedience to his parents will have the foundation for respecting the authority of other leaders and the rights of other people in general.

Respect for parents is of such grave importance to God that Moses commanded, "He who strikes his father or his mother shall surely be put to death," and "He who curses his father or his mother shall surely be put to death" (Ex. 21:15, 17; cf. Lev. 20:9). Either to physically or verbally abuse a parent was a capital offense in ancient Israel.

In the United States at least eight million serious assaults are made each year by children on their parents. In recent years, a number of children have been convicted of murdering or hiring the killing of their parents—usually for no greater reason than resentment of parental control or discipline. Children who are incessantly told they can do whatever they wish and can have their own way are children who will soon mock their parents, teachers, moral standards, the law, and society in general. All human relationships obviously grow out of those of children with parents. Children who respect and obey their parents will build a society that is ordered, harmonious, and productive. A generation of undisciplined, disobedient children will produce a society that is chaotic and destructive.

Honor of parents encompasses providing for them when they can no longer provide for themselves. Just as parents spend twenty or so years taking care of and providing for their children, their children are to spend whatever time and money is necessary to care and provide for their parents should the parents be no longer able to do so for themselves.

When some Pharisees and scribes reprimanded Jesus for allowing His disciples to eat without first ceremonially washing their hands, He countered: "And why do you yourselves transgress the commandment of God for the sake of your tradition? For God said, 'Honor your father and mother,' and 'He who speaks evil of father or mother, let him be put to death.' But you say, 'Whoever shall say to his father or mother, "Anything of mine you might have been helped by has been given to God," he is not to honor his father or his mother.' And thus you invalidated the word of God for the sake of your tradition" (Matt. 15:3-6). Jesus made it clear that honor of parents includes financial support of them when needed.

Obviously simply providing financial support for one's parents in their old age falls far short of honor if it is not done with loving personal involvement. Money can be an expression of love but never a substitute for love. A child can no more honor his parents by simply paying their bills than his parents could have responsibly raised him by only paying for his food, clothes, education, and other needs apart from loving care and personal involvement.

Children have to be trained to obey and honor their parents by their parents. The book of Proverbs is full of truths to guide parents in this training of their children and to guide children in obeying their parents. The proverbs are essentially a series of lessons for parents to teach their children, and its theme is: "Hear, my son, your father's instruction, and do not forsake your mother's teaching" (1:8). Parents are not infallible, but they are the child's primary God-given authority and source of training. "My son, do not forget my teaching, but let your heart keep my commandments" (3:1), the writer of Proverbs says. "Hear, O sons, the instruction of a father, and give attention that you may gain understanding, for I give you sound teaching; do not abandon my instruction. When I was a son to my father, tender and the only son in the sight of my mother, then he taught me and said to me, 'Let your heart hold fast my words; keep my commandments and live'" (4:1-4). The father taught his son what his father had taught him. God plans for believers to pass on His instruction from one generation to the next.

An old Chinese proverb says, "One generation plants the trees and the next gets the shade." The opportunities and freedoms we have to live and practice our faith were won by our forefathers centuries ago and passed on to us by those in between. Children raised in Christian families are blessed with the fruit from spiritual trees planted many years earlier by parents and grandparents. Conversely, it takes three or four generations to reverse the effects of one wicked group of fathers (cf. Ex. 20:5; 34:7; Num. 14:18; Deut. 5:9). The blessings we have from the preaching, teaching, and fellowship of our local church are fruit of the dedication and sacrifice of believers who have gone before us.

A child can have no greater inheritance than the godly teaching and example of his parents. "My son, keep my words, and treasure my commandments within you. Keep my commandments and live, and my teaching as the apple of your eye. Bind them on your fingers; write them on the tablet of your heart" (Prov. 7:1-3). The "apple of the eye" refers to the very front of the eye, the pupil. Because it is extremely sensitive, exposed to irritation, and is critical to vision, it is instinctively protected. An obedient child should cherish and protect the godly teaching of his parents more carefully than he protects his eyes.

Just as an obedient child brings happiness and tranquility to a family, a disobedient child brings the opposite. He brings "grief to his mother" (Prov. 10:1), unhappiness and destruction to his father (17:21; 19:13), and disgrace to them both (19:26). He uses them shamelessly to his own selfish ends (28:24).

The world today has much to say about children's so-called rights. But the emphasis should be on their responsibilities. Emphasis on rights—whether by children or adults—weakens and destroys relationships on every level. It is the sense of responsibility that builds right relationships as well as right character.

Although He was perfectly divine and free from sin, as a child even Jesus had to grow in the ways every child grows. Luke tells us that as a child Jesus was in perfect subjection to His parents. And as He grew to manhood, He "kept increasing in wisdom and stature, and in favor with God and men" (Luke 2:51-52). He grew intellectually, physically, spiritually, and socially.

Those are the ways in which every child must grow. He must grow intellectually. When a baby comes into the world, his mind is a blank. Childhood is a time of learning. Whatever children know they must be taught. They come into the world with no intellectual knowledge or judgment. The are inclined to choose junk food over what is nourishing, to play where it is dangerous rather than safe. They do not know the names of things or what they are used for. They do not know how to speak. Parents are therefore responsible for teaching their children what they need to know.

Every child must grow physically. When he is born he is extremely weak and physically undeveloped. He can do nothing for himself. He must be fed, changed, covered, protected from too much cold or heat, and so on. Gradually he is taught to do those things for himself, but in the meanwhile his parents must provide for him.

Like Jesus, every child must grow socially, in "favor with . . . men." A child's most dominant attitude is selfishness. His interests are totally self-centered. His own wants and needs are all he knows and all he cares about. That, of course, does not always remain a childhood trait. He must be *taught* to share, *taught* to be considerate of others, *taught* not to put his own interests above those of everyone else, and *taught* not to become disappointed or angry when he cannot have his own way.

And every child must grow spiritually, "in favor with God." Children do not know God naturally, much less love and obey Him naturally. A child must be taught about God, His nature, His care, His love, and His will. And when he is old enough, he must be taught His need to trust in Jesus Christ as His own Savior and Lord.

Paul said, "When I was a child, I used to speak as a child, think as a child, reason as a child" (1 Cor. 13:11). Children have deficiencies in every area of their lives, and it is the parents' responsibility to meet those needs for growth— including the need to develop in the truths of the Lord.

The command **honor your father and mother** is two-fold. **That it may be well with you** relates to the quality of life, and **that you may live long on the earth** relates to the quantity of life promised. The original promise was to Israel and involved many tangible, physical, earthly blessings. But Paul's reference to it here shows that it also extends to believers today. Though its blessings may not always be tangible, a family where children and parents live in mutual love and submission will have rich, God-given harmony and satisfaction that other families can never know. As for the promise of living **long on the earth**, the believer who honors his parents can know that his lifetime will be the full measure God intends, rather than cut short like those of Ananias and Sapphira (Acts 5:5-10) and certain members of the church at Corinth (1 Cor. 11:30).

If parents, who are much older and more experienced, cannot fulfill their responsibilities without being saved and being filled with the Holy Spirit, how much less can children be expected to fulfill their responsibilities without those spiritual requirements? The children Paul addresses in Ephesians 6:1 are just as much commanded to "be filled with the Spirit" (5:18) and to "be subject to one another in the fear of Christ" (5:21) as are the husbands and wives of 5:22-33 and the parents of 6:4.

Samuel's close relationship to the Lord started when he was very young, and King Josiah instigated spiritual revival in Judah when he was still a teenager. David was a boy when the Lord first started using him, and Queen Esther was a young woman when the Lord used her to save her people from annihilation. John the Baptist was filled with the Spirit from his mother's womb (Luke 1:15).

THE SUBMISSION OF PARENTS

And, fathers, do not provoke your children to anger; but bring them up in the discipline and instruction of the Lord. (6:4)

THE NEGATIVE COMMAND

Paul's first command to parents is negative: **fathers, do not provoke your children to anger.** That was a totally new concept for Paul's day, especially in such pagan strongholds as Ephesus. Most families were in shambles, and mutual love among family members was almost unheard of. A father's love for his children would have been hard even to imagine. By the Roman law of *patria potestas* a father had virtual life and death power not only over his slaves but over his entire household. He could cast any of them out of the house, sell them as slaves, or even kill them—and be accountable to no one. A newborn child was placed at its father's feet to determine its fate. If the father picked it up, the child was allowed to stay in the home; if the father walked away, it was simply disposed of—much as aborted babies are in our own day. Discarded infants who were healthy and vigorous were collected and taken each night to the town forum, where they would be picked up and raised to be slaves or prostitutes.

A letter written in 1 B.C. by a man named Hilarion to his wife, Alis, reads, "Heartiest greetings. Note that we are still even now in Alexandria. Do not worry if when all others return I remain in Alexandria. I beg and beseech you to take care of the little child, and as soon as we receive wages I will send them to you. If—good luck to you—you have another child, if it is a boy, let it live; if it is a girl, expose it" (Papyri Oxyrhynchus 4.744). Seneca, a renowned statesman in Rome at the time Paul wrote the Ephesian letter, said, "We slaughter a fierce ox; we strangle a mad dog; we plunge a knife into a sick cow. Children born weak or deformed we drown."

Such callousness is chilling. Yet, according to a recent report, the primary cause for children being in foster homes today is not the divorce, financial destitution, or death of their parents, but simply the disinterest of their parents. And perhaps the most devastating abuse a child can experience is that of being neglected, treated almost as if he did not exist.

Though *patēres* (**fathers**) usually referred to male parents, it was sometimes used of parents in general. Paul has been speaking about both parents in the preceding three verses, and it seems likely that he still has both in mind in this term in verse 4. The same word is used in Hebrews 11:23 to refer to Moses' parents.

Because a father was by far the dominant figure in the households of that day, he was the parent who would most often **provoke** his **children to anger**. But a mother is obviously capable of doing the same thing, and she is no more justified in doing it than is a father.

Harvard University sociologists Sheldon and Eleanor Glueck developed a test (that proved to be 90 percent accurate) to determine whether or not five- and six-year-olds would become delinquent. They discovered that the four primary factors necessary to prevent delinquency are: the father's firm, fair, and consistent discipline; the mother's supervision and companionship during the day; the parent's demonstrated affection for each other and for the children; and the family's spending time together in activities where all participated (*Unraveling Juvenile Delinquency* [Cambridge, Mass.: Harvard Univ. Press, 1950], pp. 257-71).

The Christian psychiatrist Dr. Paul Meier gives a similar list of factors that produce right parent-child relations: genuine love of the parents for each other and for the children; firm, consistent discipline; consistency of standards for parents and children; the right example by parents; and the father as true head of the home.

He also comments that the vast majority of neurotics have grown up in homes where there was no father or where he was dominated by the mother (*Christian Child-Rearing and Personality Development* [Grand Rapids: Baker, 1980], pp. 81-82).

To provoke . . . to anger suggests a repeated, ongoing pattern of treatment that gradually builds up a deep-seated anger and resentment that boils over in outward hostility.

Such treatment is usually not *intended* to provoke . . . anger. Often it is thought to be for the child's good. Well-meaning overprotection is a common cause of resentment in children. Parents who smother their children, overly restrict where they can go and what they can do, never trust them to do things on their own, and continually question their judgment build a barrier between themselves and their children—usually under the delusion that they are building a closer relationship. Children need careful guidance and certain restrictions, but they are individual human beings in their own right and must learn to make decisions on their own, commensurate with their age and maturity. Their wills can be guided but they cannot be controlled.

Another common cause of provoking children to anger is favoritism. Isaac favored Esau over Jacob and Rebekah preferred Jacob over Esau. That dual and conflicting favoritism not only caused great trouble for the immediate family but has continued to have repercussions in the conflicts between the descendants of Jacob and Esau until our present day!

For parents to compare their children with each other, especially in the children's presence, can be devastating to the child who is less talented or favored. He will tend to become discouraged, resentful, withdrawn, and bitter. Favoritism by parents generally leads to favoritism among the children themselves, who pick up the practice from their parents. They will favor one brother or sister over the others and will often favor one parent over the other.

A third way parents provoke their children is by pushing achievement beyond reasonable bounds. A child can be so pressured to achieve that he is virtually destroyed. He quickly learns that nothing he does is sufficient to please his parents. No sooner does he accomplish one goal than he is challenged to accomplish something better. Fathers who fantasize their own achievements through the athletic skills of their sons, or mothers who fantasize a glamorous career through the lives of their daughters prostitute their responsibility as parents.

I once visited a young woman who was confined to a padded cell and was in a state of catatonic shock. She was a Christian and had been raised in a Christian family, but her mother had ceaselessly pushed her to be the most popular, beautiful, and successful girl in school. She became head cheerleader, homecoming queen, and later a model. But the pressure to excel became too great and she had a complete mental collapse. After she was eventually released from the hospital, she went back into the same artificial and demanding environment. When again she found she could not cope, she committed suicide. She had summed up her frustration when she told me one day, "I don't care what it is I do, it never satisfies my mother."

A fourth way children are provoked is by discouragement. A child who is never complimented or encouraged by his parents is destined for trouble. If he is always told what is wrong with him and never what is right, he will soon lose hope and become convinced that he is incapable of doing anything right. At that point he has no reason even to try. Parents can always find something that a child genuinely does well, and they should show appreciation for it. A child needs approval and encouragement in things that are good every bit as much as he needs correction in things that are not.

A fifth way provocation occurs is by parents' failing to sacrifice for their children and making them feel unwanted. Children who are made to feel that they are an intrusion, that they are always in the way and interfere with the plans and happiness of the parents, cannot help becoming resentful. To such children the parents themselves will eventually become unwanted and an intrusion on the children's plans and happiness.

A sixth form of provocation comes from failing to let children grow up at a normal pace. Chiding them for always acting childish, even when what they do is perfectly normal and harmless, does not contribute to their maturity but rather helps confirm them in their childishness.

A seventh way of angering children is that of using love as a tool of reward or punishment—granting it when a child is good and withdrawing it when he is bad. Often the practice is unconscious, but a child can sense if a parent cares for him less when is he disobedient than when he behaves. That is not how God loves and is not the way he intends human parents to love. God disciplines His children just as much out of love as He blesses them. "Those whom the Lord loves He disciplines" (Heb. 12:6). Because it is so easy to punish out of anger and resentment, parents should take special care to let their children know they love them when discipline is given.

An eighth way to provoke children is by physical and verbal abuse. Battered children are a growing tragedy today. Even Christian parents—fathers especially—sometimes overreact and spank their children much harder than necessary. Proper physical discipline is not a matter of exerting superior authority and strength, but of correcting in love and reasonableness. Children are also abused verbally. A parent can as easily overpower a child with words as with physical force. Putting him down with superior arguments or sarcasm can inflict serious harm, and provokes him to anger and resentment. It is amazing that we sometimes say things to our children that we would not think of saying to anyone else—for fear of ruining our reputation!

One Christian father confesses,

> My family's all grown and the kids are all gone. But if I had to do it all over again, this is what I would do. I would love my wife more in front of my children. I would laugh with my children more—at our mistakes and our joys. I would listen more, even to the littlest child. I would be more honest about my own weaknesses, never

pretending perfection. I would pray differently for my family; instead of focusing on them, I'd focus on me. I would do more things together with my children. I would encourage them more and bestow more praise. I would pay more attention to little things, like deeds and words of thoughtfulness. And then, finally, if I had to do it all over again, I would share God more intimately with my family; every ordinary thing that happened in every ordinary day I would use to direct them to God.

THE POSITIVE COMMAND

The positive command to parents is for them to **bring up** [their children] **in the discipline and instruction of the Lord**. *Paideia* (**discipline**) comes from the word *pais* (child) and refers to the systematic training of children. It includes the idea of correction for wrongdoing, as seen in the well-known proverb, "He who spares his rod hates his son, but he who loves him disciplines him diligently" (Prov. 13:24). In the several uses of the term in Hebrews 12:5-11, the translators of the Authorized Version rendered it "chastening," which is clearly the emphasis of that context. Paul's meaning here is expressed even more fully, however, in the proverb "Train up a child in the way he should go, even when he is old he will not depart from it" (22:6). **Discipline** has to do with the overall training of children, including punishment.

Susannah Wesley, the mother of John and Charles Wesley, raised seventeen children and had these words to say about raising children: "The parent who studies to subdue [self-will] in his child works together with God in the renewing and saving a soul. The parent who indulges it does the devil's work, makes religion impracticable, salvation unattainable, and does all that in him lies to damn his child, soul and body forever" (cited in *The Journal of John Wesley* [Chicago: Moody, n. d.], p. 106).

Nouthesia (**instruction**) is literally a "putting in mind" and also includes the connotation of correction. It refers to the type of instruction found in the book of Proverbs, where the primary focus is on the training and teaching of children. It does not have as much to do with factual information as with right attitudes and principles of behavior.

The key to right **discipline** and **instruction** of children is its being **of the Lord**. Everything parents do for their children is to be of Him—according to the teaching of His Word, by the guidance and power of His Holy Spirit, in the name of His Son, Jesus Christ, and to His own glory and honor.

Spirit-Filled Labor Relations

25

Slaves, be obedient to those who are your masters according to the flesh, with fear and trembling, in the sincerity of your heart, as to Christ; not by way of eyeservice, as men-pleasers, but as slaves of Christ, doing the will of God from the heart. With good will render service, as to the Lord, and not to men, knowing that whatever good thing each one does, this he will receive back from the Lord, whether slave or free. And, masters, do the same things to them, and give up threatening, knowing that both their Master and yours is in heaven, and there is no partiality with Him. (6:5-9)

In this passage Paul gives his final illustration of the principle of Spirit-produced mutual submission, "and be subject to one another in the fear of Christ" (5:21), applying it to relations between slaves and masters—and, by extension, to all employer-employee relationships.

In our day the struggle between employers and employees has reached monumental levels. Conflicts rage constantly between workers and management, with each side accusing the other of selfishness and unreasonableness. Employees want smaller work loads, fewer hours, more vacation, and more pay and benefits. Employers want more productivity, more profits, and greater control of management policies and practices. Both sides want lower taxes for themselves while

321

expecting greater government protection and sometimes even subsidy.

It is not hard to see that the heart of the problem on both sides is greed. The sin of greed is the primary fuel that feeds the inflationary spiral that has become a common part of modern life in most parts of the world. When everyone wants more, prices must rise to pay for higher wages and profits. And as prices rise and money therefore buys less, people want still higher pay or profits to make up the difference. When the government becomes heavily involved in various subsidies and supports, then taxes, the national debt, or both must be raised. If the government prints more money without backing, the value of all its money is decreased, and again people want more income to make up the difference.

Added to all of that is the principle that, as possessions increase so does greed, because greed is by nature insatiable. It is likely that modern Western society is the greediest in history. Everyone wants more for less, and the ascending spirals of inflation, debt, and taxation are unabated.

How are such seemingly irreconcilable problems to be resolved? Many people advocate some form of socialism, in which the government has total control of the economy. As greed increases and self-interest becomes more hardened, more government control may be required to prevent anarchy. Revelation 18 suggests that the final Antichrist will come into power through a great worldwide economic system in which virtually all power is centered in the hands of a few elite leaders.

But God did not design man's freedom to work against man. He designed it to allow us to earn a living, provide for our families, and be of service to others. Yet, as in every other area of life, man's depraved nature turns God's provisions to selfish ends. As with problems in relations between husbands and wives and parents and children (Eph. 5:22—6:4), the solution to labor relations problems must begin with God's solution—salvation through Jesus Christ and the empowerment of His Holy Spirit.

In every aspect of human life God's plan is one of authority and submission, and those two pillars are the bedrock of biblical labor relations. To avoid chaos and anarchy, someone must lead, and others must follow. The mutual submission Paul teaches in relation to masters and servants, just as that between husbands and wives and parents and children, is in the context of the God-designated roles of authority—of husbands over wives, parents over children, and masters over servants. But that authority is not based on any inherent superiority of husbands, parents, or masters. They possess their authority as a stewardship from God, to be used for His purposes and according to His principles. Their authority is not total or unrestricted and is to be used only to serve God and to serve those over whom they have been given the authority. Submission, therefore, is not one-way but mutual.

Paul's instructions to masters and slaves continues in the setting of the household. The vast majority of businesses in New Testament times were family operated, and therefore most servants were part of an extended household. In agrarian situations the servants, or slaves, worked in the fields or tended the flocks. If the master had a shop the servants worked as craftsmen or helpers. If he was a merchant they would do whatever chores were required to help in the business. In any case, the head of the household was also head of the business. He was usually the employer and the servants were his employees.

In this passage Paul continues to deal with the practical effects of the Spirit-filled life (5:18), without which none of God's righteous standards can be met, including those which regulate working relationships. Verses 5-8 teach about the submission of slaves, or workers, and verse 9 teaches about the submission of masters, or employers.

THE SUBMISSION OF EMPLOYEES

Slaves, be obedient to those who are your masters according to the flesh, with fear and trembling, in the sincerity of your heart, as to Christ; not by way of eyeservice, as men-pleasers, but as slaves of Christ, doing the will of God from the heart. With good will render service, as to the Lord, and not to men, knowing that whatever good thing each one does, this he will receive back from the Lord, whether slave or free. (6:5-8)

Slaves translates the Greek *douloi,* and indicates subjection and usually bondage. In biblical times slavery was common and much abused. In both Greek and Roman cultures, most slaves had no legal rights and were treated as commercial commodities. Roman citizens came to look on work as beneath their dignity, and the entire empire gradually came to function largely by slave power. Slaves were bought, sold, traded, used, and discarded as heartlessly as if they were animals or tools. Considerate masters such as Pliny the Elder, who was deeply grieved over the death of some of his slaves, were exceptional.

One Roman writer divided agricultural instruments into three classes—the articulate, who were slaves; the inarticulate, which were animals; and the mute, which were tools and vehicles. A slave's only distinction above animals or tools was that he could speak! The Roman statesman Cato said, "Old slaves should be thrown on a dump, and when a slave is ill do not feed him anything. It is not worth your money. Take sick slaves and throw them away because they are nothing but inefficient tools." Augustus crucified a slave who accidentally killed his pet quail, and a man named Pollio threw a slave into a pond of deadly lamprey eels for breaking a crystal goblet. Juvenal wrote of a slave owner whose greatest pleasure was "listening to the sweet song of his slaves being flogged." (The previous material is cited in William Barclay, *The Daily Bible Study Series: The Letters to the Galatians and Ephesians* [Philadelphia: Westminster, 1958], pp. 212-14.)

Although Scripture does not speak against slavery as such, it clearly speaks against the kidnapping of anyone for the purpose of making him or her a slave (Ex. 21:16). The European and American slave trade that lasted past the middle of the nineteenth century was therefore in clear violation of Scripture, despite the rationalizations of many Christians who were involved in it.

Certain types of nonabusive and beneficial slavery were permitted, or even advocated, in the Old Testament. For example, a thief who could not make restitution could be indentured until repayment was worked out—a plan far superior to the modern prison sentence which provides for no restitution of property or money to the victim or restoration of dignity for the thief. Israelites were allowed to buy slaves from the pagan nations around them (Lev. 25:44), but fellow Israelites could not be bought or sold, although they could voluntarily indenture themselves until the year of jubilee (vv. 39-40). During their time of service they were to be treated as hired workers, not as slaves (v. 40-41, 46). Even pagan slaves were not to be abused and were given their freedom if seriously injured by their master (Ex. 21:26-27). A slave who fled from an oppressive master was to be given asylum and protection (Deut. 23:15-16). A fellow Israelite could not be used as a slave for more than six years, at the end of which he was to be given liberal provisions as a form of severance pay (Ex. 21:2; Deut. 15:13-14). Every fiftieth year, the year of jubilee, all slaves were to be freed and returned to their families (Lev. 25:10). A slave who loved his master and preferred to remain with him could voluntarily indenture himself for life by having his ear pierced by his master (Ex. 21:5-6). The kind of slavery controlled by scriptural teaching was a blessing to both employer and employee and was a rewarding and fulfilling relation between them.

Although slavery is not uniformly condemned in either the Old or New Testaments, the sincere application of New Testament truths has repeatedly led to the elimination of its abusive tendencies. Where Christ's love is lived in the power of His Spirit, unjust barriers and relationships are inevitably broken down. As the Roman empire disintegrated and eventually collapsed, the brutal, abused system of slavery collapsed with it—due in great measure to the influence of Christianity. In more recent times the back of the black slave trade was broken in Europe and America due largely to the powerful, Spirit-led preaching of such men as John Wesley and George Whitefield and the godly statesmanship of such men as William Wilberforce and William Pitt.

New Testament teaching does not focus on reforming and restructuring human systems, which are never the root cause of human problems. The issue is always the heart of man—which when wicked will corrupt the best of systems and when righteous will improve the worst. If men's sinful hearts are not changed, they will find ways to oppress others regardless of whether or not there is actual slavery. On the other hand, Spirit-filled believers will have just and harmonious relationships with each other, no matter what system they live under. Man's basic problems and needs are not political, social, or economic but spiritual, and that is the area on which Paul here concentrates.

Throughout history, including in our own day, working people have been oppressed and abused by economic intimidation that amounts to virtual slavery—regardless of the particular economic, social, or political system. Paul's teaching therefore applies to every business owner and every worker.

Because the command of mutual submission is possible only to the Spirit-filled believer, Paul is addressing Christian **slaves**, just as he later addresses

Christian masters (v. 9). He calls them to have the right behavior, the right perspective, the right attitude, and the right commitment that reflect their right relationship to God through Jesus Christ.

THE RIGHT BEHAVIOR

Slaves are commanded to **be obedient to those who are** [their] **masters. Be obedient** is in the present tense in the Greek, indicating uninterrupted obedience. Believers are not to obey simply when they desire to or when their employers are fair and reasonable. They are to obey in everything and at all times, the only exception being when they are instructed to do something immoral, idolatrous, blasphemous, or the like. Speaking of household workers, Peter said, "Servants, be submissive to your masters with all respect, not only to those who are good and gentle, but also to those who are unreasonable. For this finds favor, if for the sake of conscience toward God a man bears up under sorrows when suffering unjustly. For what credit is there if, when you sin and are harshly treated, you endure it with patience? But if when you do what is right and suffer for it you patiently endure it, this finds favor with God" (1 Pet. 2:18-20).

In New Testament times many slaves became Christians and thereby became children of God and joint heirs with Jesus Christ, as Paul has already reminded his readers (1:5-14). Therefore the natural response of many Christian slaves was to look upon their bondage as completely incongruous with their new standing before God. They reasoned that God's own children, who will reign with Him forever, should not be subservient to any human being, certainly not to a ruthless pagan. As spiritual nobility, they deserved more than common slavery.

Yet Paul tells them plainly and simply to **be obedient.** The first obligation of a Christian is to please his Lord and to be a faithful testimony to Him. One way to do this, the apostle says, is to give willing obedience to those under whom you work, regardless of who they are or what their character is like. Being a Christian should always make a person a better, more productive, and more agreeable worker. People will not be inclined to listen to the testimony of a Christian who does shoddy, careless work or who is constantly complaining. If a Christian finds an employment situation to be intolerable, he should quit and look for something else. But as long as he is employed he should do the work to the best of his ability.

Some Christians might reason that, if they work for a fellow believer, they need not be cautious and responsible in the manner of their spiritual life because their testimony before him does not matter since he already believes. Others might feel that their employers are obligated to give them preferential treatment since they are fellow Christians. But that sort of thinking is presumptuous, carnal, and unscriptural. Paul wrote, "Let those who have believers as their masters not be disrespectful to them because they are brethren, but let them serve them all the more, because those who partake of the benefit are believers and beloved" (1 Tim. 6:1-2). If we are to be respectful and obedient to unbelieving masters, how much more so should we be to our brothers in Christ?

An employer is an employer, no matter who he is, and he deserves the best effort in whatever work one does for him. Saints are to submit to the authority of anyone to whom they report. Pastors and other Christian workers are not exempt from that principle. They are responsible to submit to a church, a board, another staff member, or to whomever else has supervision over them.

When a believer sits beside his boss in a worship service or works beside him in Christian service, he does so as a completely equal brother in Christ. But on the job he is to submit to the authority of his boss, because that witnesses his submission to the higher authority of God's Word.

So whether his boss is kind or cruel, believing or pagan, a Christian is **obedient** to him because that is God's will. "Bondslaves," Paul said to Titus, are "to be subject to their own masters in everything, to be well-pleasing, not argumentative, not pilfering, but showing all good faith that they may adorn the doctrine of God our Savior in every respect" (Titus 2:9-10). How a believer works in his job reflects on His Lord, regardless of who his human master or employer may be.

THE RIGHT PERSPECTIVE

A Christian worker's submission to his employer is done under the employer's authority **according to the flesh.** The intent of that prepositional phrase is to emphasize that, while the authority-submission relationship is important and is to be respected, it is only temporal. It lasts only in this life and does not apply to moral and spiritual concerns at any time or under any circumstances.

THE RIGHT ATTITUDE

The believer's attitude in obeying his employer is to be one of **fear and trembling.** The idea is not that of cowering fright but of the honor and respect that make a person anxious to please. If he cannot honor and respect his employer for the employer's own sake, he respects him for the Lord's sake as one under whom he is to submit. Although men terribly abuse it, the principle of authority and submission is God-given and is always to be honored. God has allowed bosses to be where they are and subordinates to be where they are, and the faithful believer willingly and graciously submits to those under whose authority God has placed him.

The place where a believer works is part of his field of service for the Lord, and it is often a mission field. When he does his work carefully and respectfully it is a testimony to unbelievers, an encouragement to believers, and an act of service to God.

THE RIGHT COMMITMENT

The fourth qualification for proper submission to masters, or employers, is that of **sincerity of heart.** It is not hypocritical and superficial but genuine and thorough.

Paul told the Thessalonian believers to "excel still more, and to make it your ambition to lead a quiet life and attend to your own business and work with your hands, just as we commanded you; so that you may behave properly toward outsiders and not be in any need" (1 Thess. 4:10-12). The idea is to do well the work we are assigned to do, without complaining, bragging, criticizing the work of others, or in any other way being disruptive.

THE RIGHT MOTIVE

A Christian's primary concern about his job should be simply to do it well to the glory of God, **as to Christ**. Being filled with the Spirit brings practical results, including those of being a reliable, productive, and cooperative worker. And whenever a Christian is submissive to the Holy Spirit his accomplishments are **as to Christ**, because Christ is both the origin and the goal of his obedience. He does everything out of love for Christ, by the power of Christ, and to the glory of Christ. "Whether, then, you eat or drink or whatever you do," Paul says, "do all to the glory of God" (1 Cor. 10:31).

It is not God's plan to call every believer into preaching, Christian education, missionary service, or other such church-related ministries. Those ministries are no more spiritual than any other into which God may call a believer. But because those ministries more directly and obviously represent the Lord's work, He will not call a person into them who has not been faithful in whatever other work he has been doing. A person who has not been faithful to the Lord as a salesman, secretary, clerk, or carpenter cannot expect God to give a call to a more influential ministry. The Lord only appoints those over much who have been faithful over little (Matt. 25:21).

THE RIGHT DILIGENCE

When Spirit-filled Christians are sincerely obedient to their employers as to Christ, they will not work **by way of eyeservice, as men-pleasers, but as slaves of Christ, doing the will of God from the heart**.

The faithful believer does not simply do the minimum his job requires, much less work only when his supervisor or other workers are watching, that is, **by way of eyeservice**. He does not need to be checked up on, because he always does his work to the best of his ability, whether or not anyone else is around. And he works just as hard when he is passed over for a raise or promotion as when he is being considered for them. He does not do a good job to make a good impression on other people (as do **men-pleasers**) or to promote his own welfare. If he gains those things, they are incidental to his primary motive and intention. He works diligently because to do so is **the will of God** and is the sincere desire of his own **heart**.

With good will render service, as to the Lord, and not to men repeats and reinforces what Paul has just said. **With good will** expresses the attitude of the worker who does not need prompting or compelling. When a Christian is where God wants him to be and is obedient to **render service, as to the Lord,** that is the most challenging, productive, and rewarding place to be.

With good will render service, as to the Lord, and not to men repeats and reinforces what Paul has just said. **With good will** expresses the attitude of the worker who does not need prompting or compelling. When a Christian is where God wants him to be and is obedient to **render service, as to the Lord,** that is the most challenging, productive, and rewarding place to be.

Every day should be a day of service to the Lord. "Whatever your hand finds to do," Solomon tells us, "do it with all your might" (Eccles. 9:10). In his letter to Rome, Paul tells us not to lag behind in diligence but to be "fervent in spirit, serving the Lord" (12:11), and in Colossians, "Whatever you do, do your work heartily, as for the Lord rather than for men" (3:23). That is the work attitude of the Spirit-filled Christian.

A believer does his work diligently for the Lord's sake in the assurance **that whatever good thing each one does, this he will receive back from the Lord, whether slave or free.** God's credits and rewards are always dependable and always appropriate. An employer may not appreciate or even be aware of the good work done, perhaps because he is indifferent or because someone else takes credit for what is done. But God knows and God rewards. No good thing done in His name and for His glory can pass His notice or fail to receive His blessing.

The story is told of an elderly missionary couple who were returning home on a ship after many years of sacrificial service in Africa. On the same ship was Theodore Roosevelt, who had just completed a highly successful big game hunt. As the ship docked in New York harbor, thousands of well-wishers and dozens of reporters lined the pier to welcome Roosevelt home. But not a single person was there to welcome the missionaries. As the couple rode to a hotel in a taxi, the man complained to his wife, "It just doesn't seem right. We give forty years of our lives to Jesus Christ to win souls in Africa, and nobody knows or cares when we return. Yet the president goes over there for a few weeks to kill some animals and the whole world takes notice." But as they prayed together that night before retiring, the Lord seemed to say to them, "Do you know why you haven't received your reward yet, My children? It is because you are not home yet."

THE SUBMISSION OF EMPLOYERS

And, masters, do the same things to them, and give up threatening, knowing that both their Master and yours is in heaven, and there is no partiality with Him. (6:9)

Paul's closing remarks about the mutual submission of Spirit-filled believers are addressed to **masters,** and, by extension, to Christian employers of every sort. Their attitude toward their workers is to be basically the same as that which the workers should have for them: **do the same things to them.**

The antecedent of **the same things** most likely is the command at the end of verse 6, "doing the will of God from the heart," on which verses 7-8 are a commentary. A Christian employer's relationship to his employees should have the same motivation and goal as a Christian worker's relationship to his employer: the desire to obey and please the Lord. An employer is to use his authority "as to the Lord," just as workers are to submit to authority "as to the Lord." That is an expression of their mutual submission in being "subject to one another in the fear of Christ" (5:21).

A Christian employer's first work, just as a Christian employee's first work, is to do God's will and to manifest Christlikeness in all that he does. He makes business decisions first of all on the basis of God's standards of righteousness, truth, and honesty—seeking to manifest the nature and will of his heavenly Father in everything he does. He deals with his employees on the basis of their own welfare and best interests as well as of those of business. He deals with them fairly because that is His Lord's will. He treats them with respect because to do so is to respect and honor the Lord.

The Spirit-filled employer is careful to **give up threatening.** The term used suggests the idea of loosening up, or releasing. He uses his authority and power as little as possible and does not throw his weight around or lord it over those under him. He is never abusive or inconsiderate. He realizes that his own authority, though God-given, is strictly functional and temporary. He knows that he and his workers alike are under the supreme authority of God, **that their Master** and his is not on earth but **in heaven.** The faithful Christian employer knows that he is a fellow servant of Jesus Christ with his employees, and is accountable to the same **Master.**

He also knows that before God he is no more important or worthy in himself than the least of his employees, because **there is no partiality with Him** (cf. Acts 10:34; Rom. 2:11; James 2:9). And he plays no favorites because God plays no favorites.

God's impartiality is the closing truth in Paul's discourse on being "subject to one another in the fear of Christ" (5:21). Spirit-filled believers—whether husbands or wives, parents or children, employers or employees—are to be mutually submissive because they are equally loved, equally cared for, and equally subservient to a common **Master,** their Savior and Lord, Jesus Christ.

The Believer's
Warfare

26

Finally, be strong in the Lord, and in the strength of His might. Put on the full armor of God, that you may be able to stand firm against the schemes of the devil. For our struggle is not against flesh and blood, but against the rulers, against the powers, against the world forces of this darkness, against the spiritual forces of wickedness in the heavenly places. Therefore, take up the full armor of God, that you may be able to resist in the evil day, and having done everything, to stand firm. (6:10-13)

The true Christian described in Ephesians 1-3 who lives the faithful life described in 4:1—6:9 can be sure that he will be involved in the spiritual warfare described in 6:10-20. The faithful Christian life is a battle; it is warfare on a grand scale—because when God begins to bless, Satan begins to attack.

If we are walking worthy of our calling, in humility rather than pride, in unity rather than divisiveness, in the new self rather than the old, in love rather than lust, in light rather than darkness, in wisdom rather than foolishness, in the fullness of the Spirit rather than the drunkenness of wine, and in mutual submission rather than self-serving independence, then we can be absolutely certain we will have opposition and conflict.

Jesus' ministry began in a great battle with Satan that lasted forty days

(Luke 4:2). As Jesus' ministry ended, Satan besieged Him again in the Garden of Gethsemane with such force that He sweat great drops of blood (22:44). Among many other instructive truths, those two accounts teach us that the battle may not become easier as we grow in obedience to God. If anything, Satan will intensify his efforts against those who continue to effectively serve the Lord. As believers grow stronger, so will Satan's attacks.

The Christian who continually seeks to grow in his knowledge of and obedience to the Word and to serve the Lord more faithfully will not find ministry becoming easier. As the Lord gives mastery over certain temptations and weaknesses, Satan will attack elsewhere. Faithful witnessing, preaching, teaching, visiting, and every other service for the Lord not only will bring victories but will also bring their own special difficulties and opposition. A Christian who no longer has to struggle against the world, the flesh, and the devil is a Christian who has fallen either into sin or into complacency. A Christian who has no conflict is a Christian who has retreated from the front lines of service.

When Paul first went to Ephesus he immediately began to preach the gospel. He led some disciples of John the Baptist to saving faith in Jesus Christ and spoke three months in the local synagogue and then in the school of Tyrannus. "And this took place for two years, so that all who lived in Asia heard the word of the Lord, both Jews and Greeks. And God was performing extraordinary miracles by the hand of Paul" (Acts 19:10-11). He led many Jews and Gentiles to the knowledge of Christ. Those who had practiced magic burned their books, and "the word of the Lord was growing mightily and prevailing" (vv. 17-20). But from the beginning he faced opposition. He was run out of the synagogue by unbelieving Jewish leaders (vv. 8-9), mimicked by apostate Jewish exorcists (vv. 13-16), and threatened by Demetrius and his fellow silversmiths, whose idol-making business was suffering because of Paul's ministry (vv. 23-40).

Paul knew that where there was the greatest spiritual challenge there was also likely to be the greatest danger and opposition. As he explained to the believers at Corinth, he was determined to stay a while longer in Ephesus because "a wide door for effective service has opened to me, and there are many adversaries" (1 Cor. 16:8-9). Many pastors are tempted to leave a church or other field of service when things begin to get difficult. But an easy ministry may be a weak ministry, because where the Lord's work is genuinely being done Satan will not fail to oppose it. As believers in Jesus Christ, we are not only God's sons and servants but also His soldiers—and a soldier's job is to fight the enemy.

Even God's holy angels face opposition when they minister for Him. The angel sent to Daniel was opposed by a demon for twenty-one days and had to be assisted by the archangel Michael (Dan. 10:13), and Michael even had a battle with Satan himself over the body of Moses (Jude 9).

To the Thessalonian church Paul reflected on his battle when he said, "For we wanted to come to you—I, Paul, more than once—and yet Satan thwarted us" (1 Thess. 2:18). Believers are attacked personally and corporately.

Paul warned the elders from Ephesus, "I know that after my departure savage wolves will come in among you, not sparing the flock; and from among your own selves men will arise, speaking perverse things, to draw away the disciples after them" (Acts 20:29-30). They would be attacked both from the outside and the inside. Satan is always on the prowl, and the biblically-taught Christian is "not ignorant of his schemes" (2 Cor. 2:11).

Although it is a digression from the present passage, a look at the letters of the Lord to the seven churches of Asia Minor, the first of which was to the church at Ephesus, will assist us in understanding how Satan attacks the church. Those seven historical churches were prototypes of churches that have existed through the centuries since that time. In his vision on Patmos, John saw Jesus Christ in His kingly, priestly, and prophetic robe evaluating the churches and commanding letters to be sent to each one. Only two of the letters—those to Smyrna and Philadelphia—do not contain some form of warning and condemnation. The church at Smyrna suffered great persecution as it held forth the gospel, and it could well have been persecution that kept it strong in the faith. The church at Philadelphia also knew satanic attack, yet was an aggressive, evangelistic church. Both churches knew the attacks of what our Lord calls "the synagogue of Satan" (Rev. 2:9; 3:9), a group of blaspheming Jewish persecutors of the church. Persecution and evangelism were purifying, because they kept believers' attention off themselves and on God's will and power.

In the letters to the other five churches there is a progression in the seriousness of the warnings. The Christians at Ephesus were active in good works, persevering, intolerant of sin, opposed false teaching, and patiently endured hardship for Christ's sake. They had nevertheless left their first love—their original, single-minded, and devoted love for the Lord Himself (Rev. 2:2-4). Although they lived in the midst of one of the most corrupt cities of the Roman world, a center of pagan idolatry and of gross immorality, they faithfully maintained right doctrine and pure moral standards. But their fatal flaw—one that seems small compared to their areas of great faithfulness—was loss of love. The thrill was gone, enthusiasm was low, and zeal had flattened out into orthodox habit and tradition.

Orthodox, fundamental believers are inclined to believe that they love God because they have such high regard for and obedience to His Word. Peter was shocked and offended when Jesus three times questioned whether he really loved Him (John 21:15-17). Peter's theology and morality were sound, but his heart was not yet fully devoted to Christ. As important as right doctrine and right living are, they are no substitute for love and, in fact, become cold and sterile apart from love. Lovelessness not only grieves the Lord but gives Satan a foothold in a believer's life. When a believer, or a body of believers, loses its deep sense of love for the Lord, that believer or that church is on the brink of spiritual disaster.

Spiritual defection usually begins simply with forgetting the joy of those first experiences after salvation, including the thrill of Bible study, prayer, worship, and the sense of belonging to the Lord Jesus. Therefore Christ said to the church at Ephesus, "Remember therefore from where you have fallen" (Rev. 2:5*a*). "Remember how you were before your love became cold," He was saying. Second, spiritual defection always involves sin, and the Lord next told them to repent (v. 5b). Sinning believers—which includes the loveless—must be cleansed by the Lord before they are useful to Him again. Third, spiritual defection always involves a decrease in the quality, if not the quantity, of Christian service, and the Lord therefore told the Ephesians, "do the deeds you did at first" (v. 5c).

Orthodox but loveless activities are done in the flesh, and though they appear to be godly they are not. The only true spiritual service is loving service. The Lord was saying, in effect, "Get back to the fire, to the source of your power and help. Get back to the Word and to prayer and close Christian fellowship. Get back to praising the Lord." But the church at Ephesus did not do that, and, as He had warned (v. 5d), the Lord removed her lampstand. That church—though orthodox, evangelical, and active in good works—soon went out of existence.

The church at Pergamum (or Pergamos) also had many good things for which the Lord commended it. Despite living in a fiercely pagan city and having endured persecution and the martyrdom of one of its leading members, the church did not deny the faith (Rev. 2:13). Pergamum was a center of emperor worship and of the worship of Zeus, chief of the Roman mythological deities. It is probably to his altar that "Satan's throne" refers. The city was also closely associated with Aesculapius, the god of healing, whose snake symbol is still seen today on medical insignias. The floor of his temple was covered with nonpoisonous snakes that crawled over the bodies of the sick and crippled for the purpose of bringing healing. Satan no doubt did enough supernatural healings to keep the people in this lying religion.

Being a Christian in Pergamum was difficult, and the Lord's people there were basically faithful. But they had compromised in some important areas. The "teaching of Balaam," which some of them held, was probably the practice of intermarriage with unbelievers, the sin by which Balak and Balaam managed to lead the Israelites astray (Rev. 2:14; cf. Num. 24:10—25:3). They also were eating things sacrificed to idols and committing acts of immorality by engaging in the orgiastic idolatry of the unregenerate pagans (Rev. 2:14). In short, they were aping the world, falling into sinful habits and practices contrary to God's standards while attempting to maintain the church (cf. 1 Cor. 10:20-22).

That is one of the greatest dangers in the church today. Many believers are inclined to accommodate to nearly every worldly practice. Under the pretense of relevance, they copy the world's materialistic and immoral ways. When the world becomes preoccupied with material things, so has the church. When the world lowers its sexual standards, so has the church. When the world becomes entertainment crazed, so has the church. When the world glorifies self-worth and self-fulfillment, so has the church.

The third church to whom the Lord sent a letter of warning was at Thyatira, and her problem was toleration of sin. The Lord said to her, "I know your deeds, and your love and faith and service and perseverance, and that your deeds of late are greater than at first. But I have this against you, that you tolerate the woman

Jezebel, who calls herself a prophetess, and she teaches and leads My bond-servants astray, so that they commit acts of immorality and eat things sacrificed to idols" (Rev. 2:19-20). The church had many good things to commend it, but it became the victim of a false teacher who masqueraded as a teacher of God. She led many of the believers into idol worship and the sexual immorality associated with it, and the church and its leaders tolerated her and her doctrine.

Christians still succumb in similar ways. When the things of the world are idolized, as they frequently are even by believers, it is impossible not to be drawn into the moral and spiritual compromises that such idolatry demands. When a person longs to be like the world and insists on aping, he soon will be thinking and acting like it.

The Lord does not tolerate sin in His church, and righteousness is not a matter of balancing good things with bad. Thyatira's good list was longer than her bad, but that did not protect her from judgment. The Lord had given her ample time to repent, and when she refused, He said, "Behold, I will cast her upon a bed of sickness, and those who commit adultery with her into great tribulation, unless they repent of her deeds. And I will kill her children with pestilence; and all the churches will know that I am He who searches the minds and hearts; and I will give to each one of you according to your deeds" (Rev. 2:22-23). The bed of vice would be turned into a bed of death for all who remained in the sin, and other churches would be warned by the judgment on those believers.

Many churches are afraid to deal with known sin in their midst. They do not want to confront members with their immorality or unbiblical ideas, for fear of losing those members or of being called prudish, old fashioned, or unloving. But love does not wink at sin and never condones wickedness and unrighteousness (1 Cor. 13:6).

The Lord's judgment was only on those church members involved in the idolatry and immorality. To the faithful ones Jesus said, "I place no other burden on you. Nevertheless what you have, hold fast until I come" (Rev. 2:24-25). In other words, Jesus warned, even the most faithful believers are never beyond danger until they are one day with the Lord. Until that day—whether it comes by death or the Lord's return—the exhortation is to "hold fast" to Christ and the standards of His Word.

The church at Sardis was worse still. Because it had a large congregation and many activities, it had a reputation for being alive, but the Lord declared it to be dead (Rev. 3:1). Like the ship in Coleridge's "Rhyme of the Ancient Mariner," which had corpses to row and steer it, the church at Sardis was being operated by members who were spiritually dead. The city of Sardis was synonymous with wealth. The expression "rich as Croesus" comes from the extreme wealth of King Croesus, who ruled over the ancient kingdom of Lydia, of which Sardis was the capital. But the superficial activities of the church there could no more keep it spiritually alive than the great wealth and reputation of the city could keep it politically alive. Both city and church went out of existence shortly after New Testament times.

When a church substitutes programs, activities, ceremonies, and human issues for the Lord and His work, it becomes a spiritual corpse, despite its appearance of vitality. It has no spiritual life because God is not there. It becomes an Ichabod, because the glory of the Lord departs from it (see 1 Sam. 4:21). When lovelessness, immorality, empty ritual, and self-satisfaction overcome a church, the result is spiritual lifelessness. The few believers in Sardis who had "not soiled their garments" were encouraged by the Lord with the promise of one day walking with Him in white in His glorious heavenly kingdom (Rev. 3:4-5). That faithful remnant prevented the church as a whole from losing its lampstand and falling into oblivion.

The fifth church warned by the Lord was at Laodicea. This church had absolutely nothing to commend it, not even a superficial semblance of life. Its members were totally indifferent to the things of the Lord (Rev. 3:15-16). Indifference is a seemingly harmless spiritual disease that has probably killed the effectiveness of more believers and churches than any other. The Laodicean Christians identified themselves as a church, but they had no part in the things of the Lord. They said, "I am rich, and have become wealthy, and have need of nothing." But the Lord said, "You do not know that you are wretched and miserable and poor and blind and naked" (Rev. 3:17). Indifferent, hypocritical, religious self-satisfaction is even more nauseating to God than outright immorality. The cold heart God seeks to woo with His love and grace, and the warm heart He embraces to His bosom. But the lukewarm heart He spits out of His mouth in disgust (v. 16).

The church at Laodicea was totally hypocritical, the phony church that is no church. It is the liberal church of today that calls itself Christian, yet denies Christ's deity and atoning sacrifice, rejects His Word, and disregards His standards. It is humanistic—man-centered and man-worshiping. It may have an ecclesiastical shell, great wealth, and worldwide influence. But it has no love for the things of the Lord and no sense of need for the Lord, having everything it wants in itself. It members are apostate, and because they reject the Lord, He will reject them by spitting them out of His mouth.

The pattern of regression in the five churches is clear: from loss of first love for Christ, to compromise with the world, to tolerance of sin, to contentment with programs and activities, to satisfaction with possessions and self. The adversary attacks the whole church in this fashion by tempting individuals in the church to fall into such sins. There is no attack on the purity and holiness of the church that is not a personal attack on the people within that congregation. This attack can be seen in the experience of Peter (Luke 22:31-32; 1 Pet. 5:8) and of Paul (2 Cor. 12:7; 1 Thess. 2:18). No believer is exempt.

Recognizing Satan's schemes, Paul closes his letter to Ephesus by giving his brothers and sisters there both encouragement and warning, much as Jesus did in His letters to the seven churches of Asia Minor over 30 years later. In 6:10-13 the apostle outlines the necessary information in regard to the preparation, the armor, the enemy, the battle, and the victory of the believer's warfare.

THE PREPARATION: STRENGTH IN THE LORD

Finally, be strong in the Lord, and in the strength of His might. (6:10)

Basic to the effective Christian life is preparation. The unprepared believer becomes the defeated believer who seeks to serve the Lord in his own wisdom and power. The strength of the Christian life is dependence on God, being **strong in the Lord, and in the strength of His might.** Any other strength proves to be impotent.

The cardinal reality presented in the book of Ephesians is that, as believers, we are in Christ and are one with Him. His life is our life, His power our power, His truth our truth, His way our way, and, as Paul goes on to say here, His **strength** is our strength.

The Lord's **strength** is always more than sufficient for the battle. When Jesus told the church at Philadelphia, "I have put before you an open door which no one can shut, because you have a little power, and have kept My word, and have not denied My name" (Rev. 3:8), He was affirming that even a little power was enough to preserve them, because it was the Lord's supernatural power. Our own strength is never strong enough to oppose Satan, but when we are **strong in the Lord,** even a little of His strength is sufficient to win any battle. "I can do all things through Him who strengthens me," Paul said (Phil. 4:13). It is not the amount of the strength we have that is important—only its source.

In the ultimate sense, the church's battles with Satan are already won. In his crucifixion and resurrection Jesus destroyed Satan and his power of sin and death (Rom. 5:18-21; 1 Cor. 15:56-57; Heb. 2:14). Trust in Jesus Christ initiates a person into that victory. To the extent that a Christian is **strong in the Lord,** his victory over the worst that Satan has to offer is guaranteed. We are in a war—a fierce and terrible war—but we have no reason to be afraid if we are on the Lord's side. Appropriation of that **strength** comes through the means of grace—prayer, knowledge of and obedience to the Word, and faith in the promises of God.

After several years of ministry, Timothy became fearful and timid. He faced stronger temptations than he had expected and considerably more opposition. Paul wrote to him, "I remind you to kindle afresh the gift of God which is in you through the laying on of my hands. For God has not given us a spirit of timidity, but of power and love and discipline. Therefore do not be ashamed of the testimony of our Lord. . . . You therefore, my son, be strong in the grace that is in Christ Jesus" (2 Tim. 1:6-8; 2:1).

THE PROVISION: THE ARMOR OF GOD

Put on the full armor of God, that you may be able to stand firm (6:11a)

In order to take advantage of the strength of God's might, a believer must also **put on the full** spiritual **armor** that He supplies (cf. 2 Cor. 10:3-5). *Enduō* (**put** on) carries the idea of once and for all, of permanence. **The full armor of God** is not something to be put on and taken off occasionally but is something to be **put on** permanently. It is not a uniform to wear only while playing a game and then to remove when the game is over. **The armor of God** is to be the Christian's lifelong companion. It provides believers with divine power from "Him who is able to keep you from stumbling, and to make you stand in the presence of His glory blameless with great joy" (Jude 24).

Paul was probably chained to a Roman soldier when he penned the words of Ephesians, and looking at the soldier's armor, he was inspired by the Holy Spirit to see in it the analogy of God's spiritual provision for our battle with Satan and his angels (vv. 14-17). As the apostle explains in those verses, the believer's **armor** equips him beyond the initial facts of the gospel. It is *living* the obedient, Scripture-dominated, Spirit-empowered life that enables us to **stand firm.**

To stand firm (from *histēmi*), when used in a military sense, had the idea of holding a critical position while under attack. The intent of the exhortation here is not unlike that of our Lord to the embattled church at Thyatira, whom He commanded, "hold fast until I come" (Rev. 2:25).

THE ENEMY: SATAN

against the schemes of the devil. (6:11b)

The enemy against which we need God's strength and armor is Satan, **the devil.** Because he is God's enemy, he is our enemy, and the only way he can attack God is through us. We can therefore be sure that he will seek us out and attack us with his **schemes.**

Methodia (**schemes**), from which comes the English *method,* carries the idea of craftiness, cunning, and deception (see also 4:14). The term was often used of a wild animal who cunningly stalked and then unexpectedly pounced on its prey. Satan's evil **schemes** are built around stealth and deception.

In modern times a strange phenomenon exists. Along with increased disbelief even in the existence of **the devil** there is also increased demonic/occultic involvement—both of which play into Satan's hands.

Scripture is clear about Satan's very real and personal existence. He was once the chief angel, the anointed cherub, the star of the morning, who sparkled with all the jewels of created beauty—until he rebelled against his Creator and tried to usurp His power and glory (see Isa. 14:12-17; Ezek. 28:1-10; Rev. 12:7-9). He first appears in Scripture in the form of a serpent, as he tempted Adam and Eve (Gen. 3:1). Jesus not only spoke about Satan (Luke 10:18; John 8:44; 12:31) but spoke with him (Matt. 4:3-10). Paul, Peter, James, John, and the writer of Hebrews all speak of him as a personal being (Rom. 16:20; 2 Cor. 2:11; 1 Thess. 2:18; Heb. 2:14; James 4:7; 1 Pet. 5:8; Rev. 12:9). We see him opposing God's work (Zech. 3:1), perverting God's Word (Matt. 4:6), hindering God's servant (1 Thess. 2:18), hindering the gospel (2 Cor. 4:4), snaring the wicked (1 Tim. 3:7), appearing as an angel of light (2 Cor. 11:14), and fighting with the archangel Michael (Jude 9). He brought sin into the world and the whole world now lies in his power (1 John 5:19).

The Bible refers to **the devil** by such personal names and descriptions as "the anointed cherub" (Ezek. 28:14), "the ruler of demons" (Luke 11:15), "the ruler of this world" (John 16:11), "the god of this world" (2 Cor. 4:4), "the prince of the power of the air" (Eph. 2:2), and numerous others. He is identified as the great dragon, a roaring lion, the vile one, the tempter, the accuser, and the spirit working in the sons of disobedience. Fifty-two times he is called Satan, which means "adversary," and thirty-five times the devil, which means "slanderer." This fallen archangel and his fallen angels who became demons have been tempting and corrupting mankind since the Fall. They are an evil, formidable, cunning, powerful, and invisible foe against whom no human being in his own power and resources is a match.

Evidence of Satan's great power and deception can be seen in the fact that, despite God's miraculous deliverance of Israel from Egypt, His immeasurable blessings, protection, and provisions in the wilderness and in Canaan, His chosen people repeatedly fell for Satan's seductions, worshiping the hideous and demonic idols of paganism. After all of the predictions of the Messiah given in the Old Testament and after Jesus' preaching, teaching, and miraculous healings, Satan managed to induce Israel to reject and crucify her own Messiah! In the last days his final deception of Israel will be to persuade her that the antichrist is instead the Christ (see Dan. 9:26-27).

In our own day the world is rushing to accept such demonic deceptions as the woman's liberation movement, which denies God's order for the family; the new morality, which is no morality; and homosexuality, which is total perversion of sexuality. The proliferation of pagan and apostate Christian cults and religious/philosophical isms experienced by no other age in history reflects the work of "seducing spirits" and "the doctrines of demons" (1 Tim. 4:1). Even in the name of Christianity, Jesus' deity, miracles, resurrection, atoning sacrifice, second coming, and judgment are denied. The church is being seduced away from Scripture by liberal theology, psychology, mysticism, and even the occult.

All of these things are but manifestations of **the schemes of the devil** against mankind. In every confusing and deceptive way he can devise "the devil comes and takes away the word from their heart, so that they may not believe and be saved" (Luke 8:12). On another occasion the Lord warned that "false Christs and false prophets will arise and will show great signs and wonders, so as to mislead, if possible, even the elect" (Matt. 24:24).

The schemes of the devil include the propagation of individual beliefs and life-styles that corrupt and damn. They include evil national and international policies and practices that deceive and destroy. They include the doubts placed in believers' minds to lead them away from trust in their holy and loving Father. They include temptations of God's children to immorality, worldliness, pride, self-reliance, and self-satisfaction. They include slander, ridicule, and persecution of

His saints. The apostle John summarizes the attack points of the devil with the exhortation in his first epistle: "Do not love the world, nor the things in the world. If anyone loves the world, the love of the Father is not in him. For all that is in the world [Satan's present domain], the lust of the flesh and the lust of the eyes and the boastful pride of life, is not from the Father" (1 John 2:15-16).

The Battle: Against Demons

For our struggle is not against flesh and blood, but against the rulers, against the powers, against the world forces of this darkness, against the spiritual forces of wickedness in the heavenly places. (6:12)

One of Satan's most effective strategies, and therefore one of a believer's greatest dangers, is the delusion that no seriously threatening conflict between good and evil is really raging in the invisible and supernatural realm. After all, it is argued, there appear to be many good things in the world today. Numerous ancient evils, such as slavery and race hatred, have disappeared or improved dramatically. People have never been so concerned about getting along together, understanding one another, and working with one another to improve individual lives and society as a whole. Not only that, but evangelicalism is riding a crest of popularity, growth, and influence unknown for over a century.

But that sort of thinking not only is naive but inevitably leads to lethargy, indifference, indolence, and spiritual stagnation. A biblical perspective on the situation and a clear perception of the direction things are really moving—especially in light of Scripture's teaching about the end times—does not leave room for such delusion in the mind of any believer. The war between God and Satan has not diminished but intensified, and so has its front on this earth.

Palē (**struggle**) was used of hand-to-hand combat and especially of wrestling. As in our own day, wrestling was characterized by trickery and deception—with the difference that in fights in ancient Rome the conflict was real and often a matter of life for the winner and death for the loser. Though Satan and his minions know they are sentenced eternally to the bottomless pit prepared in hell for them, they seek desperately to change that fate if they can—warring ceaselessly to break the power of God and destroy the things of God, especially the church.

Paul here reminds his readers that the Christian's **struggle** is not only against Satan himself but also against a host of his demon subordinates, a vast array of adversaries who, like the devil, are not **flesh and blood.** Our greatest enemy is not the world we see, corrupt and wicked as it is, but the world we cannot see.

Rulers, . . . powers, . . . world forces of this darkness, . . . and **spiritual forces of wickedness** describe the different strata and rankings of those demons and the evil, supernatural empire in which they operate. Human beings who promote paganism, the occult, and various other ungodly and immoral movements and programs are but dupes of Satan and his demons—trapped by sin into unwittingly helping to fulfill his schemes.

The mention of each of these supernatural powers is preceded by **against**, and each seems to represent a particular category of demon activity and level of authority. Satan's forces of darkness are highly organized and structured for the most destructive warfare possible. Like the unfallen holy angels, demons do not procreate and their number is fixed. But they are a great and ancient multitude and constitute a formidable and highly experienced supernatural enemy.

The demonic categories are not explained, but **rulers** no doubt reflects a high order of demons (linked with "authorities" in Col. 2:15), **powers** are another rank (mentioned in 1 Pet. 3:22), and **world forces of this darkness** perhaps refers to demons who have infiltrated various political systems of the world, attempting to pattern them after Satan's realm of darkness (see Dan. 10:13; Col. 1:13). Many stories are told of world-wide conspiracies, ranging from those mentioned in ancient Egyptian writings to supposed modern cabals. We have no way of absolutely identifying the networking of the various **schemes** of Satan and should be wary of those who claim to do so. But we can be certain that he is active behind the scenes of Christless human endeavors—both in the overt, obviously evil works of men as well as in the many covert and seemingly innocent and good works of humanistic endeavors.

The **spiritual forces of wickedness** are possibly those demons who are involved in the most wretched and vile immoralities—such as extremely perverse sexual practices, the occult, Satan worship, and the like.

Paul's purpose, however, is not to explain the details of the demonic hierarchy but to give us some idea of its sophistication and power. We are pitted against an incredibly evil and potent enemy. But our need is not to specifically recognize every feature of our adversary but to turn to God, who is our powerful and trustworthy source of protection and victory.

Much today is being said about Christian exorcism of demons, although Scripture teaches no such practice. Rituals of exorcism are foreign to the Bible, which does not record a single instance of a demon being cast out of a believer, at any time or place by anyone. Nor does Scripture give any formula or method for such exorcism. Whenever Satan is confronted by Christians, the means of opposition is the strength of the Lord and the provision He has already made for all believers. Every believer has already experienced "the surpassing greatness of [God's] power toward us who believe. These are in accordance with the working of the strength of His might which He brought about in Christ, when He raised Him from the dead, and seated Him at His right hand in the heavenly places" (Eph. 1:19-20). The power that raised Jesus from the dead and exalted Him in heaven is *our* power, bequeathed to us as joint heirs with Him.

Dealing with demons in one's Christian life is not a matter of finding the technique to send them away, but of being committed to the spiritual means of grace that purifies the soul, so that there is no unclean place that demons could occupy or by which they might gain advantage. James gives the only formula for deliverance from the demons or the devil himself: "Resist the devil and he will flee from you" (James 4:7).

There is no believer who cannot deal with Satan on the terms of the resurrection power of Jesus Christ in which he participates as a Christian. Paul prayed for the Colossians that they would be "strengthened with all power, according to His glorious might, for the attaining of all steadfastness and patience; joyously giving thanks to the Father, who has qualified us to share in the inheritance of the saints in light. For He delivered us from the domain of darkness, and transferred us to the kingdom of His beloved Son" (Col. 1:11-13). No Christian is any longer in Satan's domain, and every Christian has the resources of God's own Holy Spirit within him to free himself from any demonic entanglement, no matter how severe. Where sin is confessed and put away, Satan and his demons are expelled.

On the other hand, it is dangerous to become presumptuous, thinking that we are free from any danger. "Therefore let him who thinks he stands take heed lest he fall," Paul warned (1 Cor. 10:12). Imagining that one has mastered Scripture, or any part of it, or has become strong enough to live in personal power, renders such a person the weakest and most vulnerable. Only where trust is completely in the Lord's power is there safety. As the apostle went on to say, "God is faithful, who will not allow you to be tempted beyond what you are able, but with the temptation will provide the way of escape also, that you may be able to endure it" (v. 13).

It is recognition of our weakness that makes us the strongest. "Most gladly, therefore, I will rather boast about my weaknesses," Paul declared, "that the power of Christ may dwell in me. . . . For when I am weak, then I am strong" (2 Cor. 12:9-10).

A guard who sees the enemy approaching does not run out and start fighting. He reports the attack to his commanding officer, who then organizes the defense. When Satan attacks, it is foolish to try to do battle with him alone. Like the soldier on guard duty, we should simply report to the Commander and leave the defense in His hands. As the Lord assured King Jehoshaphat as his army faced the greatly superior forces of Moab and Ammon, "Do not fear or be dismayed because of this great multitude, for the battle is not yours but God's" (2 Chron. 20:15).

My friend John Weldon, who has devoted many years of his life to the study of cults and false religions, warns believers:

> God did not make us in such a way that we can function either safely or effectively in a demon environment. Even if it is neutral, which it clearly is not, who knows what demons can do in their own environment and what interrelationships exist or can be manufactured between their world and ours? We were not made to fly around in astral realms. Granted the existence of the demonic, one is playing in an astral pigpen filled with evil and hostility. We were not made with the intellectual capacities to separate the good from the evil, the true from the false, in the occult realm. For example, the prophet Daniel was a brilliant and godly young man;

however, even he had to be given additional wisdom from God in a special way to be able to have discernment in occult matters. Thus involvement in such things will always produce faulty conclusions, because man as a fallen creature does not have the necessary equipment or ability to sort out demonic matters.

We know from God's Word that Satan and his invisible demons are continually at work in the world and all around us. But we do not have the wisdom to discern exactly when they are present, how many there are, what kind they are, or what they are doing. Saints tread on dangerous ground when they try to deal with things for which Scripture gives no instruction or guidance. We are to put on God's armor and report to Him, perfectly confident in the knowledge that "greater is He who is in [us] than he who is in the world" (1 John 4:4). The very "gates of Hades shall not overpower" Christ's church (Matt. 16:18).

THE VICTORY: IN STANDING FIRM

Therefore, take up the full armor of God, that you may be able to resist in the evil day, and having done everything, to stand firm. (6:13)

It is easy for believers—especially in the Western world, where the church is generally prosperous and respected—to be complacent and become oblivious to the seriousness of the battle around them. They rejoice in "victories" that involve no battles and in a kind of peace that is merely the absence of conflict. Theirs is the victory and peace of the draft dodger or defector who refuses to fight. They are not interested in **armor** because they are not engaged in the war.

It is possible to live the Christian life in lethargy, indifference, and in perfect satisfaction with the way things are—and still spend eternity with the Lord, because He has eternally secured the salvation of every believer (John 10:28-29). We cannot lose the ultimate war, because we belong to the Lord and the battle is His. But we disregard obedience to Him at great cost. We bring our heavenly Father and ourselves grief instead of joy; we leave lost souls in darkness and damnation instead of bringing them to the light of salvation; and we see our work burned up with fire like so much hay, as we forfeit the reward that faithful service would bring.

God gives no deferments or exemptions. His people are at war and will continue to be at war until He returns and takes charge of earth. But even the most willing and eager soldier of Christ is helpless without God's provision. That is Paul's point here: **take up the full armor of God.** We have His provision in being His children, in having His Word, in possessing His indwelling Holy Spirit, of having every resource of our heavenly Father. God is our strength, but His strength is appropriated only through obedience; His mighty **armor** must be put on (v. 11) and taken up (v. 13).

Every day since the Fall has been an **evil day** for mankind, and every day will continue to be evil until the usurper and his forces are thrown forever into the bottomless pit. In the meanwhile the Lord makes us **able to resist in the evil day** as we take advantage of the **armor** He supplies.

Our responsibility is to **resist** and **stand firm**. When Martin Luther stood before the Diet of Worms he was accused of heresy. After being condemned for declaring that men are saved by faith alone in Christ alone, he declared, "My conscience is captive to the Word of God. . . . Here I stand, I cannot do otherwise." Every believer who is faithful to God's Word cannot do otherwise than **stand firm**.

Some forty years ago three men conducted evangelistic campaigns together in Ireland and saw much fruit from their labors there. Years later an Irish pastor who was converted in those meetings asked about the three men. He was told that only one was still faithful to the Lord. Of the other two, one had become apostate and the other had died an alcoholic. Some believers **have done everything** well in the Lord's work, but they do not continue to **stand firm**. The issue is not in what a believer has done, but, when the battle is over and the smoke clears, whether he is found standing true to the Savior.

John warned, "Watch yourselves, that you might not lose what we have accomplished, but that you may receive a full reward" (2 John 8). Paul's one great fear was that, "possibly, after I have preached to others, I myself should be disqualified" (1 Cor. 9:27). He was not afraid of losing his salvation but his reward and, even more importantly, his usefulness to the Lord. Countless men and women have faithfully taught Sunday school for years, led many people to Jesus Christ, pastored a church, led Bible studies, ministered to the sick, and done every sort of service in the Lord's name—only to one day give up, turn their backs on His work, and disappear into the world. The circumstances differ, but the underlying reason is always the same: they took God's **armor** off and thereby lost the courage, the power, and the desire to **stand firm**.

In the great spiritual warfare in which we do battle, we are only called to **resist** and to **stand firm**. As noted earlier, James says, "Resist the devil and he will flee from you" (James 4:7). Peter counsels us to "be of sober spirit, be on the alert. Your adversary, the devil, prowls about like a roaring lion, seeking someone to devour. But resist him, firm in your faith" (1 Pet. 5:8-9).

The greatest joys come in the greatest victories, and the greatest victories come from the greatest battles—when they are fought in the power and with the armor of the Lord.

The Believer's Armor—part 1

27

Stand firm therefore, having girded your loins with truth, and having put on the breastplate of righteousness, and having shod your feet with the preparation of the gospel of peace; (6:14-15)

The great supernatural warfare raging throughout the universe that Paul describes in 6:11-12 is between God and His angels and the forces of Satan. Because Christians belong to God they are drawn into this spiritual conflict as they are attacked by the various "schemes of the devil." God's enemy becomes their enemy.

This is the supernatural enemy who rebelled against God in His own heavens, who succeeded in luring man from innocence to sin in the Garden of Eden, who repeatedly tried to destroy God's chosen people, Israel. This is the enemy who tried to stop the birth, ministry, and resurrection of God's own Son, Jesus Christ. This is the enemy of unequalled wickedness who seeks to thwart Christ's coming again and who will oppose Him with desperate and unprecedented fierceness when He does return.

Because the "struggle is not against flesh and blood" (v. 12), the Christian cannot fight it in the power of his own flesh and blood (2 Cor. 10:3-5). It is first of all God's battle and it can be fought only in God's power and in God's armor.

Satan opposes the believer in many ways, some of them direct and obvious and others of them indirect and subtle. First of all, he attempts to impugn God's character and credibility, just as he did with Adam and Eve. Because man's greatest strength is to trust God, Satan's objective is to make him distrust God. In countless variations Satan continues to tempt men to doubt God's will ("Indeed, has God said?") and to doubt His motives ("For God knows that in the day you eat from it your eyes will be opened, and you will be like God," Gen. 3:1, 5). The devil's supreme desire is to convince men that God is untrustworthy, to cause them to deny God's Word and to make Him a liar (see 1 John 5:10). Satan paints the Father of truth in his own perverse image as "the father of lies" (John 8:44).

When a believer doubts God's goodness, love, power, grace, mercy, or sufficiency, he joins Satan in impugning God's truthfulness. When a believer becomes anxious, despondent, depressed, and hopeless, he joins Satan in impugning God's trustworthiness. He entices some believers even to commit murder against themselves through suicide, because they will not recognize or accept the forgiveness their heavenly Father continually and freely offers (1 John 1:9). When a young child dies or is permanently crippled, a husband or wife is taken away, a child turns away from the Lord, or we lose our business or our health, Satan or his demons may attempt to generate thoughts in the mind that place the blame on God. This arena of conflict also involves attacking the truthfulness and sufficiency of Scripture.

Second, Satan tries to undermine present victory by generating trouble that makes life difficult, thereby tempting us to forsake obedience to God's standards and calling. His most extreme tactic is persecution. Throughout the history of the church, believers have had to pay for their faith with their reputation, their freedom, their jobs, their families, and even their lives. Perhaps the devil's most common and effective persecution of Christians comes in the form of peer pressure. Fear of criticism and the desire to be accepted by friends leads believers to compromise God's Word. Satan may even reverse his approach and undercut faithful Christian living by making it easy. Without hardships there is the inclination to lose the sense of dependence on the Lord. The easiest circumstances are often the hardest ones in which to be faithful. Many believers whose faith is strengthened by hard times find it is weakened when the battlefield is quiet. Christianity is often impotent when it is acceptable.

Third, Satan attacks believers through doctrinal confusion and falsehood. Christians who are untaught in God's Word fall easy prey to wrong ideas about the things of God—about salvation, sanctification, morality, heaven and hell, the second coming, and every other biblical truth. The believer who is confused about God's Word cannot be effective in God's work. He is "tossed here and there by waves, and carried about by every wind of doctrine" (Eph. 4:14). The enemy continually tries to convince Christians that Scripture is difficult to understand and insufficient to deal with complex issues, so that the average person cannot possibly expect to make sense or application of it and might as well give up trying. When believers hear preachers and teachers giving conflicting and even contradictory interpretations of doctrine, their fears about Scripture being difficult to understand are reinforced. And instead of studying God's Word for themselves, many become willing sheep for false shepherds to lead astray. In the process they send millions of dollars of the Lord's money to support unworthy causes.

Fourth, Satan attacks God's people by hindering their service to Him. He opposes every faithful life and every effective ministry. He opposed Paul's work in Ephesus through "many adversaries" (1 Cor. 16:9) and even gave the apostle "a thorn in the flesh, a messenger of Satan to buffet [him]" (2 Cor. 12:7), and hindered his plans for Thessalonica (1 Thess. 2:18). The Lord used that thorn to strengthen Paul's ministry by keeping him dependent and humble and He used that hindrance to accomplish His priority work elsewhere, but Satan's purpose was to undermine and weaken the work.

Fifth, Satan attacks believers by causing divisions. That is why Jesus prayed so earnestly and repeatedly for the unity of His followers (John 17:11, 21-23) and commands them to be quickly and willingly reconciled to each other (Matt. 5:24). Nothing more clearly evidenced the carnality of the Corinthian church than its divisiveness (see 1 Cor. 1-3), and one of Paul's great concerns for the Ephesian believers was that they be "diligent to preserve the unity of the Spirit in the bond of peace" (Eph. 4:3). The enemy knows God cannot work effectively in or through a body of believers who will not work lovingly with each other.

Sixth, Satan attacks believers by persuading them to trust their own resources. To attempt to do the Lord's work in our own power is not to do His work at all. After David had experienced many years of successful rule over Israel and of defeating her enemies, "Satan stood up against Israel and moved David to number Israel." Instead of relying on the Lord as he had in the past, David decided to count his own resources in terms of soldiers. "God was displeased with this thing, so He struck Israel" with judgment. "And David said to God, 'I have sinned greatly, in that I have done this thing. But now, please take away the iniquity of Thy servant, for I have done very foolishly'" (1 Chron. 21:1-8).

It is easy for believers to rely on their knowledge of God's Word instead of on the One who gives the Word and makes it effective. No matter how orthodox and comprehensive our theology and no matter how solid the scriptural foundation of our understanding, if we do not rely day by day on God's leading and provision, living in constant faith and dependent prayer, we are unprepared soldiers of Christ and are vulnerable to our spiritual adversaries. Being filled with God's Word but not obedient to His Spirit has caused the downfall of many believers. Right doctrine without right devotion is a serious pitfall for many Christians. The person who trusts in his own understanding instead of the Lord Himself (Prov. 3:5) plays into Satan's hands. As we noted with this very church at Ephesus, within a few years it became cold and mechanical in the expression of its orthodoxy. Right theology without deep devotion to Christ cannot prevent the death of a church.

Seventh, Satan attacks believers by leading them into hypocrisy. One of his greatest successes throughout the history of the church is that of populating the church with religious unbelievers and with real believers who live disobedient lives. The believer who is more concerned about his outward reputation than his inner spirituality does the devil's work, not the Lord's. To be satisfied with covering our sins and spiritual weaknesses with a mask of piety, rather than bringing them to the Lord for cleansing and strengthening, is to play Satan's game.

Eighth, Satan attacks believers by leading them into worldliness, by enticing them to let the world squeeze them "into its own mold" (see Rom. 12:2, Phillips). In times of prosperity he finds it particularly easy to lead God's people into materialism, self-satisfaction, self-indulgence, hedonism, and contentedness with the things of this world. Again reflecting on the warning of John, we are reminded, "Do not love the world, nor the things in the world. If anyone loves the world, the love of the Father is not in him. For all that is in the world, the lust of the flesh and the lust of the eyes and the boastful pride of life, is not from the Father, but is from the world" (1 John 2:15-16).

Ninth, in a way that encompasses all the others, Satan attacks believers by leading them to disobey God's Word. Because God wants us to act faithfully, the enemy encourages us to act unfaithfully. Because God wants us to live morally, the enemy solicits us to live immorally. Because God wants us to speak the truth, the enemy tempts us to lie. Because God wants us to love, the enemy tempts us to hate. Because God wants us to be content with what we have, the enemy tempts us to covet. Because God wants us to live by faith, the enemy tempts us to live by sight. And so with every command and standard of Scripture.

Yet, although we should be aware of these devices of Satan, our defense against them is not simply our knowledge of them but rather God's provision to meet them. "Therefore, take up the full armor of God," Paul says, "that you may be able to resist in the evil day, and having done everything, to stand firm" (Eph. 6:13). Partial armor is not enough. Jesus asked, "What king, when he sets out to meet another king in battle, will not first sit down and take counsel whether he is strong enough with ten thousand men to encounter the one coming against him with twenty thousand?" (Luke 14:31). We cannot know exactly when, where, or how the enemy will attack. We therefore need to have on *all* of God's armor all the time. When the believer has on God's full armor, it is not necessary to fully know or specifically understand the devil's schemes. In fact, many times the Christian soldier will not even be aware of a danger from which God's armor is at that moment protecting him.

In Ephesians 6:14-17 Paul tells us of the seven pieces of armor with which God supplies His children to withstand the onslaughts of Satan and his hosts.

As indicated by **having** . . . (representing the Greek aorist tense), the first three pieces of armor are permanent, and the believer is never to be without them.

THE GIRDLE OF TRUTH

Stand firm therefore, having girded your loins with truth, (6:14a)

The Roman soldier always wore a tunic, an outer garment that served as his primary clothing. It was usually made of a large, square piece of material with holes cut out for the head and arms. Ordinarily it draped loosely over most of the soldier's body. Since the greatest part of ancient combat was hand-to-hand, a loose tunic was a potential hindrance and even a danger. Before a battle it was therefore carefully cinched up and tucked into the heavy leather belt that **girded** the soldier's **loins**.

The ordinary citizen of the Near East had a similar problem with his robe. When he was in a hurry or had heavy work to do, he either took the robe off or tucked it around his waist. As God prepared the children of Israel to eat the Passover meal before they left Egypt, He instructed Moses to tell them, "Now you shall eat it in this manner: with your loins girded, your sandals on your feet, and your staff in your hand; and you shall eat it in haste" (Ex. 12:11). Concerning His second coming, Jesus tells us to "be dressed in readiness" (Luke 12:35), which is literally, "have your loins girded." Peter used the same expression when he said, "Therefore, gird your minds [lit., "gird up the loins of your minds"] for action, keep sober in spirit, fix your hope completely on the grace to be brought to you at the revelation of Jesus Christ" (1 Pet. 1:13). Girding the loins was a mark of preparedness, and the soldier who was serious about fighting was sure to secure his tunic with his belt.

The belt that **girded** it all securely together and demonstrates the believer's readiness for war is **truth**. *Alētheia* (**truth**) basically refers to the content of that which is true. The content of God's **truth** is absolutely essential for the believer in his battle against the schemes of Satan. Without knowledge of biblical teaching, he is, as the apostle has already pointed out, subject to being "carried about by every wind of doctrine, by the trickery of men, by craftiness in deceitful scheming" (4:14). In his first letter to Timothy, Paul warns that "the Spirit explicitly says that in later times some will fall away from the faith, paying attention to deceitful spirits and doctrines of demons" (1 Tim. 4:1). The "doctrines of demons" taught by cults and false religions have their origin in the "deceitful spirits" that in Ephesians Paul calls "rulers, . . . powers, . . . world forces of this darkness, . . . [and] spiritual forces of wickedness in the heavenly places" (6:12). These false schemes of Satan can be successfully encountered only with the **truth** of the Word of God.

But *alētheia* (**truth**) can also refer to the attitude of truthfulness. It represents not only the accuracy of specific truths but the quality of truthfulness. That seems to be the primary meaning Paul has in mind here. The Christian is to gird himself in an attitude of total truthfulness. To be **girded . . . with truth** therefore shows an attitude of readiness and of genuine commitment. It is the mark of the sincere believer who forsakes hypocrisy and sham. Every encumbrance that might hinder his work for the Lord is gathered and tucked into his belt of truthfulness so that it will be out the way. Just as the serious runner takes off every unnecessary piece of clothing before the race (Heb. 12:1), the serious soldier tucks in every loose piece of clothing before the battle.

How much more important is the Christian's preparedness as he faces the forces of Satan. "No soldier in active service," Paul says, "entangles himself in the affairs of everyday life, so that he may please the one who enlisted him as a soldier" (2 Tim. 2:4). It is sad that so many Christians are content to let the "tunics" of their daily cares and concerns flap in the breeze around them—continually interfering with their faithfulness to the Lord and giving the devil every opportunity to entangle and defeat them with their own immature habits and interests.

I believe that being **girded . . . with truth** primarily has to do with the self-discipline of total commitment. It is the committed Christian, just as it is the committed soldier and the committed athlete, who is prepared. Winning in war and in sports is often said to be the direct result of desire that leads to careful preparation and maximum effort. It is the army or the team who wants most to win who is most likely to do so—even against great odds.

Some years ago I was told of a young Jewish man from the United States who decided to go to Israel and live. After working there for two years he was required either to serve in the army for a given period of time or to return home. He decided to join the army. His father was a good friend of an Israeli general, who at first was afraid the young man would use that friendship to secure an easy, safe assignment. Instead, he went to the general and said, "My present duty is too easy. I want to be in the finest, most strategic, diligent, and difficult regiment in the Israeli army." Commenting on that spirit of dedication, the general said, "People think Israelis are so successful at war because we are a super people or that we have super intellect or super strength. But our success is not built on any of those things; it is built on commitment, unreserved and sacrificial commitment."

If athletes so dedicate and discipline themselves in order to *possibly* win a race and receive "a perishable wreath" from the world, how much more should believers in Jesus Christ dedicate and discipline themselves to *absolutely* win in their struggle against Satan and receive an "imperishable" wreath from God (1 Cor. 9:25)?

Being **girded . . . with truth** is being renewed in the mind, in order to "prove what the will of God is, that which is good and acceptable and perfect" (Rom. 12:2). When the mind is renewed in commitment to God's **truth**, there is empowerment for the Christian soldier to become "a living and holy sacrifice" that please God and is that believer's "spiritual service of worship" (v. 1). In many ways it is more difficult and more demanding to be a living sacrifice than a dying one. To be burned at the stake for one's faith would be painful, but it would soon be over. To live a lifetime of faithful obedience can also be painful at times, and its demands go on and on. It requires staying power that only continual and total commitment to the Lord can provide. It demands that love "abound still more and more in real knowledge and all discernment, so that [we] may approve the things that are excellent, in order to be sincere and blameless until the day of Christ; having been filled with the fruit of righteousness which comes through Jesus Christ, to the glory and praise of God" (Phil. 1:9-11). Love, knowledge, and understanding of God all need to grow in us. And when those grow, so does our commitment to the Lord for excellence in all things—the ultimate goal of which is "the glory and praise of God."

To be content with mediocrity, lethargy, indifference, and half-heartedness is to fail to be armored with the belt of God's **truth** and to leave oneself exposed to Satan's schemes.

John Monsell's hymn focuses on the virtue of true commitment:

> Fight the good fight with all thy might;
> Christ is thy strength, and Christ thy right.
> Lay hold on life, and it shall be
> Thy joy and crown eternally.
>
> Run the straight race through God's good grace,
> Lift up thine eyes, and seek His face;
> Life with its way before thee lies,
> Christ is the path, and Christ the prize.
>
> Cast care aside, lean on thy Guide;
> His boundless mercy will provide;
> Trust, and thy trusting soul shall prove
> Christ is its life, and Christ its love.

THE BREASTPLATE OF RIGHTEOUSNESS

and having put on the breastplate of righteousness, (6:14b)

No Roman soldier would go into battle without his **breastplate**, a tough, sleeveless piece of armor that covered his full torso. It was often made of leather or heavy linen, onto which were sewn overlapping slices of animal hooves or horns or pieces of metal. Some were made of large pieces of metal molded or hammered to conform to the body. The purpose of that piece of armor is obvious—to protect the heart, lungs, intestines, and other vital organs.

In ancient Jewish thinking, the heart represented the mind and the will and the bowels were considered the seat of emotions and feelings. The mind and the emotions are the two areas where Satan most fiercely attacks believers. He creates a world system, a sinful environment by which he tempts us to think wrong thoughts and to feel wrong emotions. He wants to cloud our minds with false doctrine, false principles, and false information in order to mislead and confuse us. He also wants to confuse our emotions and thereby pervert our affections, morals, loyalties, goals, and commitments. He desires to snatch the Word of God from our minds and replace it with his own perverse ideas. He seeks to undermine pure living and replace it with immorality, greed, envy, hate, and every other vice. He wants us to laugh at sin rather than mourn over it, and to rationalize it rather than confess it and bring it to the Lord for forgiveness. He seduces us to become so used to sin in us and around us that it no longer bothers our conscience.

The protection against those attacks of Satan is **the breastplate of**

righteousness. Righteousness is to be taken and wrapped around our whole being, as it were, just as ancient soldiers covered themselves with breastplates of armor.

Paul is obviously not speaking here of self-righteousness, which is not righteousness at all but the worst form of sin. It is, however, with this sort of righteousness that many Christians clothe themselves, thinking that their own character and legalistic behavior and accomplishments please God and will bring His reward. But far from protecting a believer, a cloak of self-righteousness gives Satan a ready-made weapon to stifle and smother our spiritual life and service. Self-righteousness will as surely keep a believer out of the power of fellowship with God as it will keep an unbeliever out of His kingdom (Matt. 5:20). Our own righteousness, even as believers, is nothing more than filthy garments (Isa. 64:6). It brings us no favor with God and no protection from Satan.

Nor is Paul speaking here of imputed righteousness, the perfect righteousness God applies to the account of every Christian the moment he believes in Christ (Rom. 4:6, 11, 22-24). God made Christ, "who knew no sin to be sin on our behalf, that we might become the righteousness of God in Him" (2 Cor. 5:21). We cannot **put on** what God has already clothed us with. We are permanently dressed in that righteousness, throughout our lives on earth and throughout all eternity.

God's imputed righteousness is the basis of our Christian life and of our Christian living. It protects us from hell, but it does not, in itself, protect us from Satan in this present life. The **breastplate of righteousness** that we **put on** as spiritual armor against our adversary is the *practical* righteousness of a life lived in obedience to God's Word. (Cf. the putting on of righteous behavior in line with the "new self" in 4:24-27, which having been done, will "not give the devil an opportunity." See also the putting on of righteous deeds in Col. 3:9-14.)

Paul shows the relationship between these two forms of true righteousness in Philippians 3. His salvation, he tells us, was based solely on God's imputed righteousness, "not having a righteousness of [his] own derived from the Law, but that which is through faith in Christ, the righteousness which comes from God on the basis of faith" (v. 9). But his Christian living involved another kind of righteousness, the practical working out of his imputed righteousness: "Not that I have already obtained it, or have already become perfect, but I press on in order that I may lay hold of that for which also I was laid hold of by Christ Jesus. Brethren, I do not regard myself as having laid hold of it yet; but one thing I do: forgetting what lies behind and reaching forward to what lies ahead, I press on toward the goal for the prize of the upward call of God in Christ Jesus" (vv. 12-14). Imputed righteousness makes practical righteousness possible, but only obedience to the Lord makes practical righteousness a reality.

Paul gloried in his imputed righteousness, which only God's saving grace can bestow. But he did not presume on it as many believers throughout the history of the church have done. Christians who say that it doesn't really matter how they think or talk or act, because all sins—past, present, and future—are covered by Christ's blood, reflect this presumption and vulnerability to the enemy. It is this irrational and unscriptural argument that Paul counters in Romans 6. "Are we to continue in sin that grace might increase? May it never be! How shall we who died to sin still live in it? . . . Even so consider yourselves to be dead to sin, but alive to God in Christ Jesus. Therefore do not let sin reign in your mortal body that you should obey its lusts, and do not go on presenting the members of your body to sin as instruments of unrighteousness; but present yourselves to God as those alive from the dead, and your members as instruments of righteousness to God" (vv. 1-2, 11-13). Jesus died to save us from every aspect of sin, its presence as well as its power and penalty.

To **put on the breastplate of righteousness** is to live in daily, moment-by-moment obedience to our heavenly Father. This part of God's armor is holy living, for which God supplies the standard and the power but for which we must supply the willingness. God Himself puts on our imputed righteousness, but we must put on our practical righteousness.

Not to be armored with the **breastplate of righteousness** will first of all cost the Christian his joy. John's first epistle contains many warnings and commands to believers, and these are given—along with the other truths of the letter—"so that our joy may be made complete" (1 John 1:4). In other words, lack of obedience brings lack of joy. The only joyful Christian is the obedient Christian.

Many, if not most, of the emotional and relational problems Christians experience are caused by lack of personal holiness. Many of our disappointments and discouragements do not come from circumstances or from other people but from our own unconfessed and uncleansed sin. And when circumstances and other people do manage to rob us of happiness, it is because we are unprotected by the armor of a holy life. In either case the cause of unhappiness is our own sin. After David committed adultery with Bathsheba and ordered the death of her husband, Uriah, he had no peace. That is why his great psalm of penitence for those sins includes the plea, "Restore to me the joy of Thy salvation" (Ps. 51:12). Unholy living does not rob us of salvation, but it robs us of salvation's joy.

The church today is often guilty of supplying believers with the paper armor of good advice, programs, activities, techniques, and methods—when what they need is godly armor of holy living. No program, method, or technique can bring wholeness and happiness to the believer who is unwilling to confront and forsake his sin.

Second, failure to be armed with practical righteousness will cause fruitlessness. The disobedient Christian is unproductive in the things of the Lord. Whatever accomplishments he may seem to achieve will be sham, hollow hulls that have no spiritual fruit inside.

Third, unholy living brings loss of reward. Whatever the worldly, fleshly believer does will never amount to anything worthy of heavenly praise. It is no more than wood, hay, or straw in God's sight, and when he faces the Lord his worthless work will be burned up and his reward forfeited (1 Cor. 3:12-15).

Fourth, unholy living brings reproach on God's glory. The greatest evil of a Christian's sin is its reflection on his heavenly Father. Unholiness fails to "adorn the doctrine of God our Savior in every respect" (Titus 2:10).

"Beloved," Peter implores, "I urge you as aliens and strangers to abstain from fleshly lusts, which wage war against the soul" (1 Pet. 2:11). Fleshly lusts and every other form of sin are part of Satan's arsenal with which he wages war against our very souls. Our armor must therefore include the **breastplate of righteousness**, the genuine holiness of the genuine Christian whose "every thought [is] captive to the obedience of Christ" (2 Cor. 10:5) and whose mind is set "on the things above, not on the things that are on earth" (Col. 3:2). "The night is almost gone," Paul says, "and the day is at hand. Let us therefore lay aside the deeds of darkness and put on the armor of light. . . . Put on the Lord Jesus Christ, and make no provision for the flesh in regard to its lusts" (Rom. 13:12, 14).

FEET SHOD WITH THE GOSPEL

and having shod your feet with the preparation of the gospel of peace; (6:15)

Today we have shoes for every conceivable type of activity. We have dress shoes, work shoes, leisure shoes. In athletics there are special shoes for every sport, sometimes several types for a given sport. A tennis player might wear one type of shoe on a concrete court, another kind on clay, and still another on grass. Likewise, football and baseball players wear different shoes to play on different surfaces.

A soldier's shoes are more important even than an athlete's, because his very life could depend on them. As he marches on rough, hot roads, climbs over jagged rocks, tramples over thorns, and wades through streambeds of jagged stones, his feet need much protection. A soldier whose feet are blistered, cut, or swollen cannot fight well and often is not even be able to stand up—a perilous situation in battle. He cannot very well handle his sword or shield and cannot advance rapidly or even retreat.

In addition to being made tough and durable to protect his feet, the Roman soldier's shoes, or boots, were usually impregnated with bits of metal or nails to give him greater traction as he climbed a slippery cliff and greater stability as he fought.

A Christian's spiritual footwear is equally important in his warfare against the schemes of the devil. If he has carefully girded his loins with truth and put on the breastplate of righteousness, but does not properly **shod** his **feet with the preparation of the gospel of peace**, he is destined to stumble, fall, and suffer many defeats.

Hetoimasia (**preparation**) has the general meaning of readiness. In Titus 3:1 Paul uses the term to exhort believers "to *be ready* for every good deed" (emphasis added). A good pair of boots allows the soldier to be ready to march, climb, fight, or do whatever else is necessary. Christ demands the same readiness of His people.

Because Paul quoted Isaiah 52:7 in the context of preaching the gospel ("How beautiful are the feet of those who bring glad tidings of good things!" Rom.

10:15), many commentators also interpret Ephesians 6:15 as a reference to preaching. But in the Ephesians text Paul is not talking about preaching or teaching but about fighting spiritual battles. And he is not talking about traveling about but standing firm (vv. 11, 13, 14). His subject is not evangelizing the lost but fighting the devil.

In this passage **the gospel of peace** refers to the good news that believers are at peace with God. The unsaved person is helpless, ungodly, sinful, and an enemy of God (Rom. 5:6-10). The saved person, on the other hand, is reconciled to God through faith in His Son (vv. 10-11). As Paul had proclaimed a few verses earlier, "We have peace with God through our Lord Jesus Christ" (5:1). "And although you were formerly alienated and hostile in mind, engaged in evil deeds," Paul explained to the Colossians, "yet He has now reconciled you in His fleshly body through death, in order to present you before Him holy and blameless and beyond reproach" (1:21-22).

The gospel of peace is the marvelous truth that in Christ we are now at peace with God and are one with Him. Therefore, when our **feet** are **shod** with **the preparation of the gospel of peace**, we stand in the confidence of God's love for us, His union with us, and His commitment to fight for us.

When Peter took out his sword as the soldiers came to arrest Jesus in the Garden of Gethsemane, he considered himself invincible, because he had just seen all the soldiers fall to the ground simply at Jesus' words, "I am He" (John 18:6). As the children of Israel faced the great Midianite army that numbered some thirty-two thousand men, the Lord told Gideon, "The people who are with you are too many for Me to give Midian into their hands, lest Israel become boastful, saying 'My own power has delivered me'" (Judg. 7:2). After Gideon had trimmed his own force down to but three hundred men, the Lord gave Israel an astounding victory without their using a single weapon (v. 22). As Judah was about to be invaded by the powerful armies of Ammon and Moab, the Lord promised King Jehoshaphat, "Do not fear or be dismayed because of this great multitude, for the battle is not yours but God's" (2 Chron. 20:15). As His people "began singing and praising, the Lord set ambushes against the sons of Ammon, Moab, and Mount Seir, who had come against Judah; so they were routed. For the sons of Ammon and Moab rose up against the inhabitants of Mount Seir destroying them completely, and when they had finished with the inhabitants of Seir, they helped to destroy one another. When Judah came to the lookout of the wilderness, they looked toward the multitude; and behold, they were corpses lying on the ground, and no one had escaped" (vv. 22-24). As with Gideon's band against Midian, the Lord won the victory without His people raising a weapon.

The believer who stands in the Lord's power need not fear any enemy, even Satan himself. When he comes to attack us, our feet are rooted firmly on the solid ground of **the gospel of peace**, through which God changed from our enemy to our defender. We who were once His enemies are now His children, and our heavenly Father offers us His full resources to "be strong in the Lord, and in the strength of His might" (Eph. 6:10). "If God is for us, who is against us?" Paul asks. "But in all these things we overwhelmingly conquer through Him who loved us. For I am convinced that neither death, nor life, nor angels, nor principalities, nor things present, nor things to come, nor powers, nor height, nor depth, nor any other created thing, shall be able to separate us from the love of God, which is in Christ Jesus our Lord" (Rom. 8:31, 37-39).

The Spirit-filled believer who is fully clad in God's armor can sing confidently with John Newton,

> Though many foes beset you round,
> And feeble is your arm,
> Your life is hid with Christ in God
> Beyond the realm of harm.
>
> Weak as you are you shall not fade,
> Or fainting shall not die;
> Jesus the strength of every saint
> Will aid you from on high.
>
> Though unperceived by mortal sense,
> Faith sees Him always near,
> A guide, a glory, a defense,
> What have you to fear?
>
> As surely as He overcame,
> And triumphed once for you,
> So surely you that love His name
> Shall in Him triumph too.

The Believer's Armor—part 2

28

In addition to all, taking up the shield of faith with which you will be able to extinguish all the flaming missiles of the evil one. And take the helmet of salvation, and the sword of the Spirit, which is the word of God. (6:16-17)

In addition to all introduces the last three pieces of armor. The first three—girdle, breastplate, and shoes (vv. 14-15)—were for long-range preparation and protection and were never taken off on the battlefield. The **shield, helmet,** and **sword,** on the other hand, were kept in readiness for use when actual fighting began, hence the verbs **taking up** and **take.**

THE SHIELD OF FAITH

the shield of faith with which you will be able to extinguish all the flaming missiles of the evil one. (6:16)

Roman soldiers used several kinds of shields, but two were the most common. The first was a rather small round shield, perhaps two feet in diameter, that was secured to the arm by two leather straps. It was relatively lightweight and was used to parry the sword blows of one's opponent in hand-to-hand fighting.

The second kind was the *thureos,* to which Paul refers here. This **shield** was about two and half feet wide and four and a half feet high, designed to protect the entire body of the soldier—who was considerably smaller than the average man today. The **shield** was made of a solid piece of wood and was covered with metal or heavy oiled leather.

The soldiers who carried these shields were in the front lines of battle, and normally stood side by side with their shields together, forming a huge phalanx extending as long as a mile or more. The archers stood behind this protective wall of shields and shot their arrows as they advanced against the enemy. Anyone who stood or crouched behind such shields was protected from the barrage of enemy arrows and spears.

The **faith** to which Paul refers here is not the body of Christian beliefs (for which the term is used in 4:13), but basic trust in God—the faith in Christ that appropriates salvation and continues to bring blessing and strength as it trusts Him for daily provision and help. The substance of Christianity is believing that God exists and that He rewards those who seek Him (Heb. 11:6); putting total trust in His Son as the crucified, buried, risen, and ascended Savior; obeying Scripture as His infallible and authoritative Word; and looking forward to the Lord's coming again. Habakkuk's great declaration that "the righteous will live by his faith" (Hab. 2:4) is quoted and reaffirmed twice by Paul (Rom. 1:17; Gal. 3:11) and once by the writer of Hebrews (10:38).

Every person lives by some form of faith. We cross a bridge with the faith that it will support us. We eat food trusting that it is not poisoned. We put our lives in the security of airplanes, trains, ships, buses, and automobiles, confident that they are safe. The fact that faith in such things is usually well founded makes life and society as we know it possible. Reflecting on this fact in a more philosophical manner, Oliver Wendell Holmes said, "It is faith in something that makes life worth living."

But **faith** in God is immeasurably more reliable and more important than the practical, everyday faith by which we live. And it is far from being simply "faith in something." Faith is only as reliable and helpful as the trustworthiness of its object; and Christian **faith** is powerful and effective because the object of faith, Jesus Christ, is infinitely powerful and absolutely dependable. Christian faith never fails, because the One in whom that faith is placed never fails.

When John Paton was translating the Bible for a South Seas island tribe, he discovered that they had no word for trust or faith. One day a native who had been running hard came into the missionary's house, flopped himself in a large chair and said, "It's good to rest my whole weight on this chair." "That's it," said Paton. "I'll translate faith as 'resting one's whole weight on God.'"

In New Testament times the tips of arrows would often be wrapped in pieces of cloth that had been soaked in pitch. Just before the arrow was shot, the tip would be lighted and the **flaming missile** would be shot at the enemy troops. The pitch burned fiercely, and on impact it would spatter burning bits for several feet, igniting anything flammable it touched. In addition to piercing their bodies, it could inflict serious burns on enemy soldiers and destroy their clothing and gear. The most reliable protection against such **flaming missiles** was the *thureos* **shield**, whose covering of metal or leather soaked in water would either deflect or **extinguish** them.

The spiritual **flaming missiles** against which believers need protection would seem primarily to be temptations. Satan continually bombards God's children with temptations to immorality, hatred, envy, anger, covetousness, pride, doubt, fear, despair, distrust, and every other sin.

Satan's initial temptation to Adam and Eve was to entice them to doubt God and instead to put their trust in his lies. That was the first of his **flaming missiles**, from which all the others have lighted their flames. Every temptation, directly or indirectly, is the temptation to doubt and distrust God. The purpose of all of Satan's **missiles**, therefore, is to cause believers to forsake their trust in God, to drive a wedge between the Savior and the saved. He even tempted God's own Son to distrust Him in the wilderness—first to distrust His Father's provision, then to distrust His protection and His plan (Matt. 4:3-9).

Efforts to justify fornication or adultery in the name of God's grace—arguing, as some do, that sex was created by God and that everything He created is good—pervert logic, contradict God's Word, and impugn His integrity. Trying to justify marriage to an unbeliever—arguing that the relationship is so beautiful that it must be of God—follows Satan's will instead of God's. Doubting God is to disbelieve God, which, as the apostle John tells us, makes a liar of Him who cannot lie (1 John 5:10; cf. Titus 1:2). Whenever and however we try to justify any sin, we degrade God's character and elevate Satan's. To sin is to believe Satan, and to follow righteousness is to believe God. Therefore, all sin results from failure to act in faith in who God is and in what He is. **Faith**, then, is the **shield**.

Sin forsakes and contradicts God's promises that the person who listens to Him is blessed (Prov. 8:34), that He will never give His children a stone when they ask for a fish (Matt. 7:9), that He will open the windows of heaven and pour out immeasurable blessings on His faithful children (Mal. 3:10), that He has given "every good thing bestowed and every perfect gift" (James 1:17), that He will "supply all [our] needs according to His riches in glory" (Phil. 4:19), that He has already "blessed us with every spiritual blessing in the heavenly places in Christ" (Eph. 1:3), and a hundred other such promises.

The only way to **extinguish** Satan's **flaming missiles** of temptation to doubt God is to *believe* God, **taking up the shield of faith.** "Every word of God is tested," the writer of Proverbs tells us. "He is a shield to those who take refuge in Him. Do not add to His words lest He reprove you, and you be proved a liar" (Prov. 30:5-6). David reminds us that "the word of the Lord is tried; He is a shield to all who take refuge in Him" (Ps. 18:30). "This is the victory that has overcome the world—our faith" (1 John 5:4).

The evil one (or "vile, wretched one," *ponēros*) refers to the devil, whose supernaturally evil schemes we are to stand firm against and "to resist in the evil day" with the armor God supplies (vv. 11-13). Paul here again emphasizes that our struggle is against *personal* forces of evil—not simply against bad philosophies or wrong ideas, as liberal theologians and preachers have long maintained. Our battle is not against abstract evil influences but the personal **evil one** and his hordes of personal demons.

THE HELMET OF SALVATION

And take the helmet of salvation, (6:17a)

The fifth piece of God's armor is represented by the Roman soldier's **helmet**, without which he would never enter battle. Some of the helmets were made of thick leather covered with metal plates, and others were of heavy molded or beaten metal. They usually had cheek pieces to protect the face.

The purpose of the **helmet**, of course, was to protect the head from injury, particularly from the dangerous broadsword commonly used in the warfare of that day. That was not the much smaller sword mentioned later in this verse, but was a large two-handed, double-edged sword (*rhomphaia,* see Rev. 1:16; 2:12; 6:8) that measured three to four feet in length. It was often carried by cavalrymen, who would swing at the heads of enemy soldiers to split their skulls or decapitate them.

The fact that the **helmet** is related to **salvation** indicates that Satan's blows are directed at the believer's security and assurance in Christ. The two dangerous edges of Satan's spiritual broadsword are discouragement and doubt. To discourage us he points to our failures, our sins, our unresolved problems, our poor health, or to whatever else seems negative in our lives in order to make us lose confidence in the love and care of our heavenly Father.

As Elijah discovered, we are sometimes most vulnerable to discouragement just after we have experienced success. By calling down fire to consume the sacrifices on a Mount Carmel altar drenched with water, the prophet had demonstrated that the Lord of Israel was the true God. He then killed the 450 false prophets of Baal and reported to King Ahab that rain would at last return to Israel. But when Queen Jezebel, who had brought the false prophets to Israel, heard of their slaughter, she sent word to Elijah, saying, "So may the gods do to me and even more, if I do not make your life as the life of one of them by tomorrow about this time." Then the prophet who had stood fearlessly before the hundreds of false prophets became frightened for his life at the threat of this one woman. Although he was perhaps eighty years old at that time, Elijah "was afraid and arose and ran for his life" down to Beersheba and on into the wilderness. There he "sat down under a juniper tree; and he requested for himself that he might die, and said, 'It is enough; now, O Lord, take my life, for I am not better than my fathers.'" But instead of letting his prophet die, the Lord twice sent an angel to him with food and water, and in the strength of that food Elijah travelled forty days and nights farther to Mount Horeb, where the Lord twice asked him, "What are you doing here, Elijah?" After Elijah twice replied, in effect, that everything was hopeless and that he was the only faithful Israelite left alive, the Lord assured him in a gentle voice that He was still in control. He then gave His prophet his next assignment and assured him that 7,000 of his fellow countrymen had not bowed to Baal (1 Kings 18:27—19:18).

We learn from Elijah's experience that we need the Lord's strength and provision after a victory as well as during the battle. For Satan, the battle is never over, and he loves to attack us with discouragement the moment we think we are safe. The Lord told the disciples the parable of the importunate widow "to show that at all times they ought to pray and not to lose heart" (Luke 18:1).

When the coal truck delivered a ton of coal on the sidewalk in front of her house, a little London girl took her small shovel and began carrying the coal into the basement. When a neighbor man who was watching told her, "You'll never be able to get it all in," she replied, "Oh, I will sir, if I work long enough."

The test of a person's character is what it takes to stop him. Some people retreat as soon as the first shot is fired, while others fight through battle after battle with no thought of giving up. Satan will try every means to discourage and deter us, reminding us of defeats and dangers and setting every possible object in our way to destroy our assurance in Christ. The Lord allowed Satan to strip Job of every good thing he possessed except his life, yet that man of God declared, "Though He slay me, I will hope in Him" (Job 13:15). The book of Job demonstrates the character of true saving faith in revealing that it is not connected to what benefits and blessings a person has or loses. Job's helmet deflected every blow against him, and he maintained his faith in God's love and care. When God first called Jeremiah, He told the prophet that no one would listen to him and that he would be rejected and afflicted; yet he testified, "Thy words were found and I ate them, and Thy words became for me a joy and the delight of my heart; for I have been called by Thy name, O Lord God of hosts" (Jer. 15:16).

Satan also tempts us to become discouraged when we see other believers going through times of trial. Realizing the Ephesians' deep concern about his imprisonment, Paul told them, "I ask you not to lose heart at my tribulations on your behalf, for they are your glory" (Eph. 3:13). He tempts us to give up when we cannot see results from our service to the Lord. When the Galatian believers faced that problem, Paul told them, "Let us not lose heart in doing good, for in due time we shall reap if we do not grow weary" (Gal. 6:9).

Because the adversary will never lay down his sword against us as long as we are on earth, God's armor is a constant necessity until we leave this earth forever. Only when our work on earth is finished can we say with Paul, "I have fought the good fight, I have finished the course, I have kept the faith" (2 Tim. 4:7). In His brief letter to the Ephesian church recorded in the book of Revelation, the Lord wrote these words of encouragement: "You have perseverance and have endured for My name's sake, and have not grown weary" (Rev. 2:3).

Discouragement in praying for an unsaved husband who continues to reject the gospel or a child who refuses to follow the ways of the Lord he has been taught is common. The temptation is to lose heart when, like Paul, we repeatedly pray for a physical healing that does not come. God answered the apostle's prayer in words that apply to every believer in every circumstance: "My grace is sufficient for you, for power is perfected in weakness." We need to respond as Paul did: "Most gladly, therefore, I will rather boast about my weaknesses, that the power of Christ may dwell in me" (2 Cor. 12:9). It is also helpful to remember with him that "now salvation is nearer to us than when we believed" (Rom. 13:11).

As my dedicated grandfather, who had preached the gospel faithfully all through his ministry, lay dying of cancer, he told my father, "I wish I could just preach this one last sermon I've prepared." He was never personally able to preach that sermon from a pulpit, but my father had it printed and distributed to the congregation at the funeral. Even from his deathbed he longed to serve, never losing heart or giving up. As Isaiah tells us, the Lord "gives strength to the weary, and to him who lacks might He increases power. Though youths grow weary and tired, and vigorous young men stumble badly, yet those who wait for the Lord will gain new strength; they will mount up with wings like eagles, they will run and not get tired, they will walk and not become weary" (Isa. 40:29-31).

In the name of grace, some Christians insist that a believer's only responsibility is to "let go and let God." The statement made to King Jehoshaphat, "The battle is not yours but God's," has been taken to mean that believers have only to sit back and watch God work. That ever-present philosophy was held by the Quakers and Quietists of past centuries, who emphasized surrender and passivity above commitment and self-discipline. Abiding in Jesus does not mean we are to do nothing ourselves. In the same passage in which He tells us to abide in Him, He explains that this abiding involves keeping His commandments (John 15:4-10; cf. 1 John 3:24). The truly surrendered life is the life committed to aggressive, confrontive, and unreserved obedience to all of God's commands.

Some advocates of that truncated view of the surrendered life have taught that the person who is fully surrendered will never experience temptation, because Christ intercepts every effort of Satan to tempt us. This philosophy is perhaps most clearly and popularly presented in Hannah Whithall Smith's *The Christian's Secret of a Happy Life*. In that book she says,

> What *can* be said about man's part in this great work but that he must continually surrender himself and continually trust? But when we come to God's side of the question, what is there that may not be said as to the manifold and wonderful ways in which He accomplishes the work entrusted to Him? It is here that the growing comes in. The lump of clay could never grow to a beautiful vessel if it stayed in the clay pit for thousands of years; but when it is put into the hands of a skillful potter it grows rapidly, under his fashioning, into the vessel he intends it to be. And in the same way the soul, abandoned to the working the Heavenly Potter, is made into a vessel unto honor, sanctified, and meet for the Master's use. ([Westwood, N.J.: Revell, 1952], p. 32)

One of the problems with that view is that it makes no allowance for sin. John says unequivocally that "if we say that we have no sin, we are deceiving ourselves, and the truth is not in us" (1 John 1:8). Does such a surrendered believer occasionally jump out of the divine Potter's hand into sin? If so, what does that say about the Potter, who, according to this view, has complete control over the clay?

Even more importantly, that view is not supported by Scripture. Surrender and submission to the Lord are cardinal and oft-repeated New Testament truths, but they do not stand apart from—much less opposed to—the many other New Testament commands for Christians to be actively involved in the Lord's work. To "depend on God for everything" and then not use His provision to do the other things He commands is not dependence but presumption.

Paul's letter to the Ephesians is replete with commands for Christians to do things other than simply submit to God. As soon as he has finished saying, "For by grace you have been saved through faith; and that not of yourselves, it is the gift of God; not as a result of works, that no one should boast," the apostle goes on to say, "For we are His workmanship, created in Christ Jesus for good works, which God prepared beforehand, that we should walk in them" (2:8-10). Later he entreats us "to walk in a manner worthy of the calling with which [we] have been called" (4:1); to "walk no longer just as the Gentiles also walk" (4:17); to "be imitators of God, as beloved children; and walk in love, just as Christ also loved you" (5:1-2); and to "be filled with the Spirit" and "be subject to one another" (5:18, 21). He commands wives to be subject to their husbands, husbands to love their wives, children to obey their parents, and slaves to be obedient to their masters (5:22, 25; 6:1, 5). In the passage about the Christian's armor (6:10-17) he commands believers to "be strong," to "put on the full armor of God," "to stand firm" (three times), and, as they struggle against the devil and his forces, to "take up the full armor of God," to "resist in the evil day," to gird their loins, "put on the breastplate of righteousness," take up "the shield of faith," and "take the helmet of salvation, and the sword of the Spirit." Paul says nothing here about surrender, but a great deal about fighting, commitment, and disciplined living. The faithful believer must always be submissive to the Lord, but submission to Him is the furthest thing from passivity.

Christians are not onlookers to God's work. They are called runners (1 Cor. 9:24; Heb. 12:1), fighters (1 Cor. 9:26), soldiers (2 Tim. 2:3), doers of good deeds (Titus 3:8), opponents of Satan (1 Pet. 5:8-9), seekers after holiness (2 Cor. 7:1), and countless other names that denote active obedience.

Spiritual resources given by God are for His children to use, not simply to keep. Peter declared, "His divine power has granted to us everything pertaining to life and godliness, through the true knowledge of Him who called us by His own glory and excellence." But then he admonished, "Now for this very reason also, applying all diligence, in your faith supply moral excellence, and in your moral excellence, knowledge; and in your knowledge, self-control, and in your self-control, perseverance, and in your perseverance, godliness; and in your godliness, brotherly kindness, and in your brotherly kindness, love. For if these qualities are yours and are increasing, they render you neither useless nor unfruitful in the true knowledge of our Lord Jesus Christ. . . . For as long as you practice these things, you will never stumble" (2 Pet. 1:3, 5-8, 10). The Lord gives us commands to *obey* and equipment to *use*.

In Philippians 2 Paul presents the two sides of God's provision and man's obedience. "So then, my beloved, just as you have always obeyed, not as in my presence only, but now much more in my absence, work out your salvation with fear and trembling; for it is God who is at work in you, both to will and to work for His good pleasure" (vv. 12-13). Again, in Colossians he gives the balance: "For this purpose also I labor, striving according to His power, which mightily works within me" (1:29).

The faithful servant of Jesus Christ does not simply look on as His Master works, but continually toils in the Master's work in the Master's power. When he does that, he not only receives God's strength and blessings but also, like Paul, finds himself involved in such things as afflictions, hardships, distresses, beatings, imprisonments, labors, sleeplessness, hunger, glory and dishonor, evil report and good report, punishment, sorrow, and poverty (2 Cor. 6:4-10; cf. 4:8-18; 11:23-28). Those things came as a direct result of Paul's diligent ministry for the Lord, and he wore them gladly as badges of faithfulness. Christians do not grow and earn reward by minimum effort, much less by no effort, but by maximum effort. And it is the active, working, striving believer who is most tempted by Satan's sword of discouragement. The person who never attempts anything has little to be discouraged about.

The other, and closely related, edge of Satan's two-edged sword is the doubt that often brings discouragement. Doubts about the truths of God, including doubt about one's salvation, are the worst discouragements for a believer. If a believer doubts God's goodness or dependability, or if his relation to God seems uncertain, he has no ground for hope and therefore no protection from discouragement. The person who thinks he has nothing worthwhile to look forward to has no reason to fight, work, or live responsibly. If our often unpleasant and disappointing earthly life is all we can be certain of, then Christians are indeed "of all men most to be pitied" (1 Cor. 15:19).

Satan's most disturbing attack against believers is in tempting them to believe they have lost, or could lose, their salvation. Few things are more paralyzing, unproductive, or miserable than insecurity. Jesus said, "Peace I leave with you; My peace I give to you; not as the world gives, do I give to you. Let not your heart be troubled, nor let it be fearful" (John 14:27). He said, "These things I have spoken to you, that in Me you may have peace" (16:33). But how can a doubting heart have peace? How can a person who lives in continual uncertainty about his salvation be comforted by such promises—when he is not sure that they apply to him or that they will always apply to him? If he loses his salvation, he obviously loses those promises as well. How could such a person not have a troubled and fearful heart? Those promises would be a mockery to him.

One of the central truths of John's first epistle is that of the certainty of the believer's spiritual knowledge—"By this we know that we have come to know Him" (2:3); "I am writing to you, fathers, because you know Him . . . to you, young men, because you have overcome the evil one . . . to you, children, because you know the Father" (2:13); "We know that, when He appears, we shall be like Him, because we shall see Him just as He is" (3:2); "We shall know by this that we are of the truth, and shall assure our heart before Him" (3:19); and so on. John's specific purposes in writing the letter were "that our joy may be made complete" (1:4) and "that you may know that you have eternal life" (5:13).

Satan's purposes for believers are the opposite. His plan is to cause them to doubt God's promises, His power, His goodness, His truth, and, above all, His willingness or ability to keep them saved. If he succeeds in those he also succeeds in robbing believers of joy. Knowing Satan's strategy, Jesus assures us that "all that the Father gives Me shall come to Me, and the one who comes to Me I will certainly not cast out. . . . And this is the will of Him who sent Me, that of all that He has given Me I lose nothing, but raise it up on the last day" (John 6:37, 39). Absolutely no circumstance—no failure, shortcoming, or sin, no matter how serious—can cause either Jesus or His Father to disown a person who is saved. Nor can any other person or thing ever snatch them out of the hand of the Son or the hand of the Father (John 10:28-29). That is why Paul could declare with such confidence that "neither death, nor life, nor angels, nor principalities, nor things present, nor things to come, nor powers, nor height, nor depth, nor any other created thing, shall be able to separate us from the love of God, which is in Christ Jesus our Lord" (Rom. 8:38-39) and that "He who began a good work in you will perfect it until the day of Christ Jesus" (Phil. 1:6).

Since Paul is addressing believers, putting on the **helmet of salvation** cannot refer to receiving Christ as Savior. The only ones who can take up any piece of God's armor, and the only ones who are involved in this supernatural struggle against Satan and his demon forces, are those who are already saved.

Trusting in Jesus Christ, immediately saves from the penalty of sin. For believers, this first aspect of salvation, which is justification, is past. It was accomplished the moment we trusted in Christ, and that particular act of faith need never be repeated, because we are secure in our Father's hands—from whom, as we have just seen, we can never be snatched (John 10:28-29). We are forever saved from condemnation (Rom. 8:1).

The second aspect of salvation, which is sanctification, involves our life on earth, during which time we experience a measure of freedom from the dominating power of sin. Being now under God's grace, sin no longer has mastery or dominion over us; we are no longer sin's slave but God's (Rom. 6:14, 18-22). Paul shows these first two aspects of salvation side by side in the previous chapter of Romans: "For if while we were enemies, we were reconciled to God through the death of His Son, much more, having been reconciled, we shall be saved by His life" (5:10). Christ's death saved us once and for all from sin's penalty, and His life within us now is saving us day to day from sin's power and mastery.

The third aspect of salvation is future, the aspect of glorification, when we shall one day be saved altogether and forever from sin's presence. Looking forward to that glorious time, John says, "Beloved, now we are children of God, and it has not appeared as yet what we shall be. We know that, when He appears, we shall be like Him, because we shall see Him just as He is" (1 John 3:2). To be like God is to be without sin. We rejoice that this aspect of our salvation "is nearer than when we believed" (Rom. 13:11).

It is this final aspect of **salvation** that is the real strength of the believer's **helmet.** If we lose hope in the future promise of salvation, there can be no security in the present. This, no doubt, is why Paul calls this same piece of armor "the helmet" which is "the hope of salvation" (1 Thess. 5:8). "Having the first fruits of the Spirit," Paul explains in Romans, "even we ourselves groan within ourselves, waiting eagerly for our adoption as sons, the redemption of our body. For in hope we have been saved" (8:23-24). **The helmet of salvation** is that great hope of final salvation that gives us confidence and assurance that our present struggle with Satan will not last forever and we will be victorious in the end. We know the battle is only for this life, and even a long earthly life is no more than a split second compared to eternity with our Lord in heaven. We are not in a race we can lose. We have no purgatory to face, no uncertain hope that our own continued efforts or those of our loved ones and friends will perhaps some day finally make us acceptable to God. We know that whom God "predestined, these He also called; and whom He called, these He also justified; and whom He justified, these He also glorified" (Rom. 8:30). There is not the loss of a single soul from predestination to justification to sanctification to glorification. That is God's unbroken and unbreakable chain of salvation (cf. John 6:39-40; 10:27-30).

We have a certain hope, "a living hope," as Peter calls it. "Blessed be the God and Father of our Lord Jesus Christ," he exults in his first epistle, "who according to His great mercy has caused us to be born again to a living hope through the resurrection of Jesus Christ from the dead, to obtain an inheritance which is imperishable and undefiled and will not fade away, reserved in heaven for you, who are protected by the power of God through faith for a salvation ready to be revealed in the last time" (1 Pet. 1:3-5). When the **helmet** of that hope is in place, we can "greatly rejoice, even though now for a little while, if necessary, [we] have been distressed by various trials, that the proof of [our] faith, being more precious than gold which is perishable, even though tested by fire, may be found to result in praise and glory and honor at the revelation of Jesus Christ; and though [we] have not seen Him, [we] love Him, and though [we] do not see Him now, but believe in Him, [we] greatly rejoice with joy inexpressible and full of glory, obtaining as the outcome of [our] faith the salvation of [our] souls" (vv. 6-9). That is the **salvation** which is our **helmet.** Our **helmet** is the certain prospect of heaven, our ultimate **salvation,** which "we have as an anchor of the soul" (Heb. 6:19).

Often when a runner is on the home stretch of a race he suddenly "hits the wall," as the expression goes. His legs wobble and refuse to go any farther. The only hope for the runner is to keep his mind on the goal, on the victory to be won for himself and his team. It is that hope that keeps him going when every other part of his being wants to give up.

To the persecuted and discouraged believers at Thessalonica, Paul wrote words parallel to the thought here in Ephesians: "Since we are of the day, let us be sober, having put on the breastplate of faith and love, and as a helmet, the hope of salvation. For God has not destined us for wrath, but for obtaining salvation through our Lord Jesus Christ, who died for us, that whether we are awake or asleep, we may live together with Him. Therefore encourage one another, and build up one another, just as you also are doing" (1 Thess. 5:8-11).

To the worldly, fleshly Corinthians who were self-centered, divisive, and confused about the resurrection, Paul said, "If from human motives I fought with wild beasts at Ephesus, what does it profit Me? If the dead are not raised, let us eat and drink, for tomorrow we die" (1 Cor. 15:32). If the Christian has no future element of salvation to look forward to, if, as the apostle had said a few verses earlier, "we have hoped in Christ in this life only," then "we are of all men most to be pitied" (v. 19). Paul's own spiritual **helmet** was his firm hope in the completion of his **salvation.** "Momentary, light affliction is producing for us an eternal weight of glory far beyond all comparison, while we look not at the things which are seen, but at the things which are not seen; for the things which are seen are temporal, but the things which are not seen are eternal" (2 Cor. 4:17-18). The faithful believer does not "lose heart in doing good," because he knows that "in due time we shall reap if we do not grow weary" (Gal. 6:9).

To the persecuted and beleaguered Christians to whom he wrote, Jude gave sobering warnings about false teachers, "ungodly persons who turn the grace of our God into licentiousness and deny our only Master and Lord, Jesus Christ" (v. 4). But he began the letter by addressing believers as "those who are the called, beloved in God the Father, and kept for Jesus Christ" (v. 1). *Tēreō* (the verb behind "kept") means to guard, keep watch over, and protect. God Himself guards, watches over, and protects every person who belongs to Him. Jude ended the letter by assuring believers that He "is able to keep you from stumbling, and to make you stand in the presence of His glory blameless with great joy" (v. 24; cf. 1 Thess. 5:23). The word behind "keep" in this verse is not *tēreō,* as in verse 1, but *phulassō,* which has the basic idea of securing in the midst of an attack. No matter what our spiritual enemies may throw against us, we are secured by God's own power.

We sing of this assurance in Samuel Stone's beloved hymn "The Church's One Foundation":

> 'Mid toil and tribulation, and tumult of her war,
> She waits the consummation of peace for evermore;
> Till, with the vision glorious, her longing eyes are blest,
> And the great church victorious shall be the church at rest.

THE SWORD OF THE SPIRIT

and the sword of the Spirit, which is the word of God. (6:17b)

The **sword** to which Paul refers here is the *machaira,* which varied in length from six to eighteen inches. It was the common sword carried by Roman foot soldiers and was the principal weapon in hand-to-hand combat. Carried in a sheath or scabbard attached to their belts, it was always at hand and ready for use. It was the sword carried by the soldiers who came to arrest Jesus in the Garden (Matt. 26:47), wielded by Peter when he cut off the ear of the high priest's slave (v. 51), and used by Herod's executioners to put James to death (Acts 12:2).

Of the Spirit can also be translated "by the Spirit" or as "spiritual," referring to the nature of the sword rather than its source. From the context we know that it is a spiritual weapon, to be used in our struggle against spiritual enemies. The same Greek phrase (*tou pneumatos*) is translated "spiritual" in Ephesians 1:3 and 5:19. Although this meaning is perfectly consistent with the context of 6:10-17, the preferred rendering is as a genitive of origin, **of the Spirit**, indicating the Holy Spirit as the origin of **the sword**. As the Spirit of truth (John 14:17), the Holy Spirit is the believer's resident truth Teacher, who teaches us all things and brings God's Word to our remembrance (v. 26).

The emphasis of the present passage is on how believers are to use **the sword of the Spirit**. It is not a physical weapon designed by human minds or forged by human hands (as noted in 2 Cor. 10:3-5) but the perfect spiritual weapon of divine origin and power. Like the shield of faith and the helmet of salvation, it is always to be at hand, ready to be taken up (vv. 16a and 17a) and used when a battle begins.

Paul explicitly states that **the sword of the Spirit** is Scripture, **the word of God**. The Scottish pastor and writer Thomas Guthrie said, "The Bible is an armory of heavenly weapons, a laboratory of infallible medicines, a mine of exhaustless wealth. It is a guidebook for every road, a chart for every sea, a medicine for every malady, and a balm for every wound. Rob us of our Bible and our sky has lost its sun."

From an unknown source comes this tribute to Scripture:

> There are words written by kings, by emperors, by princes, by poets, by sages, by philosophers, by fishermen, by statesmen, by men learned in the wisdom of Egypt, educated in the schools of Babylon, and trained at the feet of rabbis in Jerusalem. It was written by men in exile, in the desert, in shepherd's tents, in green pastures, and beside still waters. Among its authors we find a tax-gatherer, a herdsman, a gatherer of sycamore fruit. We find poor men, rich men, statesmen, preachers, captains, legislators, judges, and exiles. The Bible is a library full of history, genealogy, ethnology, law, ethics, prophecy, poetry, eloquence, medicine, sanitary science, political economy, and the perfect rules for personal and social life. And behind every word is the divine author, God Himself.

Of the divine authorship of Scripture John Wesley said, "The Bible must have been written by God or good men or bad men or good angels or bad angels. But bad men and bad angels would not write it because it condemns bad men and bad angels. And good men and good angels would not deceive by lying about its authority and claiming that God wrote it. And so the Bible must have been written as it claims to have been written—by God who by His Holy Spirit inspired men to record His words using the human instrument to communicate His truth."

Scripture teaches many truths about itself. First, and most importantly, it claims God as its author. "All Scripture is inspired by God," Paul declared (2 Tim. 3:16). "Know this first of all," Peter said, "that no prophecy of Scripture is a matter of one's own interpretation, for no prophecy was ever made by an act of human will, but men moved by the Holy Spirit spoke from God" (2 Pet. 1:20-21).

The Bible also claims that it is inerrant and infallible, containing no errors or mistakes. It is flawless, faultless, and without blemish. As God's own Word it could not be otherwise. David tells us that "the law of the Lord is perfect, . . . the testimony of the Lord is sure, . . . the precepts of the Lord are right, . . . the commandment of the Lord is pure" (Ps. 19:7-8). The proverb writer tells us, "Every word of God is tested; . . . Do not add to His words lest He reprove you, and you be proved a liar" (Prov. 30:5-6).

The Bible claims that it is complete. Echoing the words of Proverbs just quoted, as well as those of Deuteronomy 4:2 and 12:32, John said at the close of the last book of the Bible, "I testify to everyone who hears the words of the prophecy of this book: if anyone adds to them, God shall add to him the plagues which are written in this book; and if anyone takes away from the words of the book of this prophecy, God shall take away his part from the tree of life and from the holy city, which are written in this book" (Rev. 22:18-19).

The Bible claims to be authoritative. Isaiah declared, "Listen, O heavens, and hear, O earth; for the Lord speaks" (Isa. 1:2). It claims to be sufficient for our needs. "All Scripture is inspired by God and profitable for teaching, for reproof, for correction, for training in righteousness; that the man of God may be adequate, equipped for every good work" (2 Tim. 3:16-17).

The Bible claims to be effective. When its truths are proclaimed and applied, things happen. "So shall My word be which goes forth from My mouth; it shall not return to Me empty, without accomplishing what I desire, and without succeeding in the matter for which I sent it" (Isa. 55:11).

The Bible also claims to be determinative. What a person does with God's Word evidences his relationship to God Himself. "He who is of God," Jesus said, "hears the words of God" (John 8:47). Those who listen to God's Word and heed it give evidence that they belong to God, and those who deny and contradict His Word give evidence that they do not belong to Him.

As **the sword of the Spirit**, the Bible offers limitless resources and blessings to the believer. First of all, it is the source of truth. "Thy Word is truth," Jesus said to His Father (John 17:17). People today look everywhere for answers to life, to try to find out what is worth believing and what is not. The source of all truth about God and man, life and death, time and eternity, men and women, right and wrong, heaven and hell, damnation and salvation, is God's own **word**.

The Bible is also a source of happiness. Speaking of God's wisdom, the writer of Proverbs said, "Blessed [or happy] is the man who listens to me" (Prov. 8:34). Jesus said, "Blessed are those who hear the word of God, and observe it"

(Luke 11:28). No person can be happier than when he discovers, accepts, and obeys God's Word.

The Bible is the source of spiritual growth. "Like newborn babes," Peter admonished, "long for the pure milk of the word, that by it you may grow in respect to salvation" (1 Pet. 2:2).

It is the source of power, "living and active and sharper than any two-edged sword, and piercing as far as the division of soul and spirit" (Heb. 4:12); the source of guidance, "a lamp to [our] feet, and a light to [our] path" (Ps. 119:105); the source of comfort (Rom. 15:4); the source of perfection (2 Tim. 3:16). And **the word of God** is the source of victory over our great spiritual enemy, our most powerful weapon against Satan.

The sword of the Spirit is first of all a defensive weapon, capable of deflecting the blows of an opponent. It is the believer's supreme weapon of defense against the onslaughts of Satan. Unlike the shield, however, which gives broad and general protection, the sword can deflect an attack only if it is handled precisely and skillfully. It must parry the enemy weapon exactly where the thrust is made. When Jesus was tempted by Satan in the wilderness, His defense for each temptation was a passage of Scripture that precisely contradicted the devil's word (Matt. 4:4, 7, 10). The Christian who does not know God's Word well cannot use it well. Satan will invariably find out where we are ignorant or confused and attack us there. Scripture is not a broadsword (*rhomphaia*) to be waved indiscriminately, but a dagger to be used with great precision.

Christians who rely simply on their experience of salvation and their feelings to get them through are vulnerable to every sort of spiritual danger. They get into countless compromising situations and fall prey to innumerable false ideas and practices, simply because they are ignorant of the specific teachings of Scripture.

The term Paul uses here for **word** is not *logos,* which refers to general statements or messages, but is *rhēma,* which refers to individual words or particular statements. The apostle is therefore not talking here about general knowledge of Scripture, but is emphasizing again the precision that comes by knowledge and understanding of specific truths. Like Jesus did in the wilderness, we need to use specific scriptural truths to counter specific satanic falsehoods. That is why Paul counseled Timothy, "Be diligent to present yourself approved to God as a workman who does not need to be ashamed, handling accurately the word of truth" (2 Tim. 2:15). The faithful believers of Revelation 12 "overcame him [the accuser] because of the blood of the Lamb and because of the word of their testimony" (v. 11).

The sword of the Spirit is also an offensive weapon, capable of inflicting blows as well as deflecting those of the enemy. Scripture is "living and active and sharper than any two-edged sword, and piercing as far as the division of soul and spirit, of both joints and marrow, and able to judge the thoughts and intentions of the heart. And there is no creature hidden from His sight, but all things are open and laid bare to the eyes of Him with whom we have to do" (Heb. 4:12-13). When **the word of God** is preached, it brings God's judgment to bear on lives as it infallibly sifts the evidence of sin and guilt.

The word of God is so powerful it transforms men from the realm of falsehood to that of truth, from the realm of darkness to that of light, and from the realm of sin and death to that of righteousness and life. It changes sadness into joy, despair into hope, stagnation into growth, childishness into maturity, and failure into success.

Every time God's Word is used to lead a person to salvation it gives witness to its power to cut a swath through Satan's dominion of darkness and bring the light of life to a lost soul.

Testifying to His Word in our family, among our friends, at work, at school, in the classroom or pulpit, or as we travel, uses the most powerful spiritual weapon in the universe, which no power of Satan can withstand.

For the very reason that God's Word is so powerful and effective, that is where Satan's greatest offensives are mounted. He will do anything and everything to undermine God's Word and those who preach and teach it. As Jesus makes clear in the parable of the sower, Satan is quick to snatch God's Word from a hearer's heart before it has a chance to take root (Matt. 13:19). Many people gladly listen to the gospel, but before their decision is made, some intrusion distracts them and the effectiveness of the witness is lost, along with the soul of that hearer. In another person's heart the word is accepted at first with joy, but when Satan sends "affliction or persecution . . . because of the word, immediately he falls away" (vv. 20-21). Many people seem to be genuine and faithful believers—until hardship, criticism, or persecution come. When the price for faithfulness becomes too high, they reveal that they never had true faith in the first place. Still another hearer also accepts the word in a superficial and temporary way, but as he trusts in his wealth the word is choked and "it becomes unfruitful" (v. 22). Because he wants the world, he forsakes the word.

But when the seed of God's Word is "sown on the good soil," the hearer understands it and "indeed bears fruit, and brings forth, some a hundredfold, some sixty, and some thirty" (v. 23). It is here that the great offensive power of **the sword of the Spirit** is seen as it converts a soul from sin to salvation.

Offensively, as well as defensively, the use of God's Word needs to be specific in order to be effective. Romans 10:17 is more accurately and clearly translated "faith comes from hearing, and hearing comes by *a word* [*rhēma*, a particular word] of God" (emphasis added). It is not from just any part of Scripture that men come to faith, but from those parts that declare the gospel. Saving faith does not come from believing just any truth of Scripture, but from believing that Jesus Christ died for the sins of the world and trusting in His death to cleanse our own sins.

The Christian who misquotes and is confused about scriptural truths will not be a successful witness. The effective teacher, preacher, and witness must "be ready in season and out of season" (2 Tim. 4:2). The more we know and understand Scripture, the more we will be able to march through Satan's strongholds and lead people from his kingdom to God's.

No believer has excuse for not knowing and understanding God's Word. Every believer has God's own Holy Spirit within Him as his own divine teacher of God's divine Word. Our only task is to submit to His instruction by studying the Word with sincerity and commitment. We cannot plead ignorance or inability, only disinterest and neglect.

H. P. Barker gives a graphic illustration that points up the need for both knowing and applying the Bible's truths.

> As I looked out into the garden one day, I saw three things. First, I saw a butterfly. The butterfly was beautiful, and it would alight on a flower and then it would flutter to another flower and then to another, and only for a second or two it would sit and it would move on. It would touch as many lovely blossoms as it could, but derived absolutely no benefit from it. Then I watched a little longer out my window and there came a botanist. And the botanist had a big notebook under his arm and a great big magnifying glass. The botanist would lean over a certain flower and he would look for a long time and then he would write notes in his notebook. He was there for hours writing notes, closed them, stuck them under his arm, tucked his magnifying glass in his pocket and walked away. The third thing I noticed was a bee, just a little bee. But the bee would light on a flower and it would sink down deep into the flower and it would extract all the nectar and pollen that it could carry. It went in empty every time and came out full. (A. Naismith, *1200 Notes, Quotes and Anecdotes* [Chicago: Moody, 1962], p. 15.)

Some Christians, like that butterfly, flit from Bible study to Bible study, from sermon to sermon, and from commentary to commentary, while gaining little more than a nice feeling and some good ideas. Others, like the botanist, study Scripture carefully and take copious notes. They gain much information but little truth. Others, like the bee, go to the Bible to be taught by God and to grow in knowledge of Him. Also like the bee, they never go away empty.

D. Martyn Lloyd-Jones wrote of Martin Luther:

> Luther was held in darkness by the devil, though he was a monk. He was trying to save himself by works. He was fasting, sweating, and praying; and yet he was miserable and unhappy, and in bondage. Superstitious Roman Catholic teaching held him captive. But he was delivered by the word of Scripture—"the just shall live by faith." From that moment he began to understand this Word as he had never understood it before, and the better he understood it the more he saw the errors taught by Rome. He saw the error of her practice, and so became more intent on the reformation of the church. He proceeded to do all in terms of exposition of the Scriptures. The great doctors in the Roman church stood against him. He sometimes had to stand alone and meet them in close combat, and invariably he

took his stand upon the Scripture. He maintained that the church is not above the Scriptures. The standard by which you judge even the church, he said, is the Scripture. And though he was one man, at first standing alone, he was able to fight the papal system and twelve centuries of tradition. He did so by taking up "the sword of the Spirit, which is the word of God." (*The Christian Soldier* [Grand Rapids: Baker, 1977], p. 331.)

It was William Tyndale's vow that every English plowman and every boy that pulled a plow would one day be able to read and understand the Scriptures, and to that end he devoted his life to translating it into the English language. It is essential for the Word of God to be known, and loved, and practiced if we are to win the battle against Satan.

Praying at All Times

With all prayer and petition pray at all times in the Spirit, and with this in view, be on the alert with all perseverance and petition for all the saints, and pray on my behalf, that utterance may be given to me in the opening of my mouth, to make known with boldness the mystery of the gospel, for which I am an ambassador in chains; that in proclaiming it I may speak boldly, as I ought to speak.

But that you also may know about my circumstances, how I am doing, Tychicus, the beloved brother and faithful minister in the Lord, will make everything known to you. And I have sent him to you for this very purpose, so that you may know about us, and that he may comfort your hearts.

Peace be to the brethren, and love with faith, from God the Father and the Lord Jesus Christ. Grace be with all those who love our Lord Jesus Christ with a love incorruptible. (6:18-24)

In the seventeenth century a man named Johann Burchard Freystein wrote the following hymn:

> Rise my soul to watch and pray,
> From thy sleep awaken,

> Be not by the evil day
> Unawares or taken.
> For the foe well we know.
> Oft his harvest reapeth
> While the Christian sleepeth.
> Watch against the devil's snares
> Lest asleep he find thee,
> For indeed no pains he spares
> To deceive and blind thee.
> Satan's prey oft are they
> Who secure are sleeping
> And no watch are keeping.
> But while watching also
> Pray to the Lord unceasing.
> O Lord, bless in distress
> And let nothing swerve me
> From the will to serve Thee.

Over a hundred years ago Charlotte Elliot wrote the words for another hymn:

> Christian, seek not yet repose,
> Cast thy dreams of ease away;
> Thou art in the midst of foes;
> Watch and pray.
>
> Principalities and power,
> Mustering their unseen array,
> Wait for thy unguarded hours;
> Watch and pray.
>
> Watch as if on that alone
> Hung the issue of the day,
> Pray that help may be sent down;
> Watch and pray.

Both of those hymns point up the reality that victory over Satan and his hosts in the great spiritual warfare in which we are engaged demands unceasing and diligent commitment to prayer. That is exactly what the apostle Paul says as he closes his appeal for Christians to put on the full armor of God. Is it perhaps this passage that inspired still another hymnist to write, "Put on the gospel armor, each piece put on with prayer."

In his *Pilgrim's Progress* John Bunyan tells of Christian's weapon called prayer, which, when everything else failed, would enable him to defeat the fiends in the valley of the shadow. Prayer is the closing theme of Ephesians, and though closely related to God's armor, it is not mentioned as part of it, because it is much more than that. Prayer is not merely another godly weapon, as important as those weapons are. All the while that we are fighting in the girdle of truth, the breastplate of righteousness, the shoes of the gospel of peace, the shield of faith, the helmet or salvation, and the sword of the Spirit, we are to be in prayer. Prayer is the very spiritual air that the soldier of Christ breathes. It is the all-pervasive strategy in which warfare is fought.

Jesus urged His disciples to pray always and not to lose heart (Luke 18:1). He knows that when the battle gets hard soldiers easily become tired, weak, and discouraged. In the struggle with Satan, it is either pray or faint. Paul's closing admonition for believers to "pray at all times" is not accidental. Not only does it give final instruction about the believer's warfare but it is the climactic truth of the entire epistle, because prayer fills all of Christian life. Prayer is the crescendo at the end of Paul's anthem of Ephesians.

No New Testament book so fully delineates the resources and blessings of the believer as does Ephesians. Throughout the book Paul magnifies and expands the truth that he briefly mentioned in Colossians, "in Him you have been made complete" (2:10) and that Peter touched on in his second epistle, "His divine power has granted to us everything pertaining to life and godliness" (1:3). Here is a monumental catalog of all that is ours in Jesus Christ.

Paul begins Ephesians with the comprehensive declaration that "the God and Father of our Lord Jesus Christ . . . has blessed us with every spiritual blessing in the heavenly places in Christ" (1:3). He then proceeds to tell us that we are chosen, predestined, and adopted as God's children (1:4-5); lavished with His grace (1:6, 8; 2:7); redeemed and forgiven (1:7; 4:32); given the mystery of His will (1:9; 3:4-6); receivers of an inheritance (1:11); have been sealed with the Holy Spirit (1:13-14; 4:30); greatly loved by God (2:4; 5:25); made alive with new life (2:5-6); the workmanship of Christ, created by Him for doing good works (2:10); given God's own peace (2:14); made one with Christ and with every other believer as His own Body (2:13-19; 3:4-6); made citizens of God's kingdom and members of His family (2:19); built into God's own temple and the dwelling place of His Spirit (2:20-22); given boldness and confident access to God (3:12); made powerful beyond our imagination (3:20); given the unity of the Spirit in the bond of peace (4:3); individually and uniquely gifted by Christ (4:7); blessed with specially gifted leaders to equip us in the work of ministry (4:11-12); taught by Jesus Christ Himself (4:20-21); given a new self in God's holy likeness (4:24); made light (5:8); offered the fullness of the Holy Spirit (5:18); given the instructions and resources to make all relationships with others what God intends them to be (5:21—6:9); and given God's full armor to make us invincible against Satan and his demonic forces (6:10-17).

After a believer contemplates that breathtaking list of blessings he possesses as an exalted child of God, Paul realizes the great danger that is likely to follow: temptation to self-satisfaction and spiritual arrogance. The student of Ephesians does well to take to heart Paul's warning to the Corinthians: "Let him who thinks he stands take heed lest he fall" (1 Cor. 10:12). The magnificent and boundless blessings described in Ephesians are so enriching that Satan will try to use them to turn our thoughts to ourselves as the blessed ones rather than to the

One who gives us the blessings. In light of our immeasurable and wondrous privileges, we can easily begin to think we are adequate in ourselves and thereby lose the essential sense of dependence on God.

Each time his team loses a game, a well-known professional football coach tells the players in the locker room afterward: "Gentlemen, I told you how to win. You didn't do what I told you, and you lost." Just like an athlete, a Christian can have great skills, the best training, the best equipment, and a good understanding of what he is supposed to do—and yet fail because he does not follow instructions. If a football player does poorly when he fails to follow his coach, how much worse does a Christian fare when he fails to follow his Lord?

It is especially easy for Christians who live in a free and prosperous society to feel secure just as they are, presuming on instead of depending on God's grace. It is easy to become so satisfied with physical blessings that we have little desire for spiritual blessings, and to become so dependent on our physical resources that we feel little need for spiritual resources. When programs, methods, and money produce such obvious and impressive results, there is a proneness to confuse human success with divine blessing. A happy marriage, where children are well behaved and all are enjoying a church that is growing, tends to make people smug and self-satisfied. They can even become practical humanists, living as if God were not necessary. When that happens, passionate longing for God and yearning for His help will be missing—along with God's empowerment. It is because of this great and common danger that Paul closes this epistle with an urgent call to prayer.

Ephesians begins by lifting us up to the heavenlies, and ends by pulling us down to our knees. "Don't think," Paul concludes, in effect, "that because you have all these blessings and resources that you can now live the Christian life without further help from God." God's armor is neither mechanical nor magical. We cannot simply take hold of it on our own and expect it automatically to produce supernatural feats. If James Russell Lowell's eloquent saying, "The gift without the giver is bare," is true in human relationships, it is immeasurably truer in our relationship to God. Our divine gifts—marvelous as they are—are bare without the divine Giver.

In the closing verses of this letter Paul first gives believers some general instruction about prayer, then a specific illustration of prayer, and finally a benediction.

THE GENERAL INSTRUCTION

With all prayer and petition pray at all times in the Spirit, and with this in view, be on the alert with all perseverance and petition for all the saints. (6:18)

The four **alls** introduce the five emphases Paul makes regarding the general character of the believer's prayer life: the variety, the frequency, the power, the manner, and the objects of prayer.

THE VARIETY OF PRAYER

Proseuchē (**prayer**) refers to general requests, while *deēsis* (**petition**) refers to those that are specific. The use of both words points to the idea that we are to be involved in **all** kinds of prayer, every form of prayer that is appropriate. Scriptural precept and allowance suggest we may pray publicly or privately; in loud cries, in soft whispers, or silently; deliberately and planned or spontaneously; while sitting, standing, kneeling, or even lying down; at home or in church; while working or while traveling; with hands folded or raised; with eyes open or closed; with head bowed or erect. The New Testament, like the Old, mentions many forms, circumstances, and postures for prayer but prescribes none. Jesus prayed while standing, while sitting, while kneeling, and quite probably in other positions as well. We can pray wherever we are and in whatever situation we are in. "Therefore I want the men in every place to pray" (1 Tim. 2:8), Paul said. For the faithful, Spirit-filled Christian, every place becomes a place of prayer.

THE FREQUENCY OF PRAYER

The Jewish people of Paul's day had several prescribed times for daily prayer, but the coming of the New Covenant and the birth of the church brought a new dimension to prayer as it did to everything else. Jesus said, "Keep on the alert at all times, praying in order that you may have strength to escape all these things that are about to take place" (Luke 21:36). Among other things, the earliest Christians in Jerusalem "were continually devoting themselves . . . to prayer" (Acts 2:42). The God-fearing Cornelius, to whom the Lord sent Peter with the message of salvation, "prayed to God continually" (Acts 10:2). In many of his letters Paul urged his readers to regularly devote themselves to prayer (Rom. 12:12; Phil. 4:6; Col. 4:2; 1 Thess. 5:17). The apostle assured Timothy, his beloved son in the Lord, that he prayed for him "night and day" (2 Tim. 1:3). The early church knew the importance of prayer, and God honored their prayers, even when faith was sometimes weak— as in the case of those who were praying for Peter's release from prison but did not believe Rhoda when she reported that he was knocking at the door (Acts 12:12-15).

David said, "Evening and morning and at noon, I will complain and murmur, and He will hear my voice, . . . God will hear and answer" (Ps. 55:17, 19). There is no time when we do not need to pray and no time when God will not hear our prayers. In many ways prayer is even more important than knowledge about God. In fact, only through a regular and sincere prayer life can God's Holy Spirit add spiritual wisdom to our knowledge. D. Martyn Lloyd-Jones wrote, "our ultimate position as Christians is tested by the character of our prayer life." A person may be a Bible school or seminary graduate, a pastor or a missionary, but his deep knowledge of and relationship to God are measured by his prayer life. If knowledge about God and the things of God do not drive us to know Him more personally, we can be sure that our true motivation and commitment are centered in ourselves rather than Him. Jesus' deepest prayer for His disciples was not that they simply know the truth about God but that "they may know Thee, the only true God, and Jesus Christ whom Thou hast sent" (John 17:3). Studying and learning God's Word in the right spirit will always drive the believer to know Him more intimately and to commune with Him more faithfully in prayer.

To **pray at all times** obviously does not mean we are to pray in formal or noticeable ways every waking moment of our lives. Jesus did not do that, nor did the apostles. And it certainly does not mean we are to devote ourselves to ritualistic patterns and forms of prayer that are recited mechanically from a prayer book or while counting beads. That amounts to no more than the "meaningless repetition" that characterizes pagan worship (Matt. 6:7).

To **pray at all times** is to live in continual God consciousness, where everything we see and experience becomes a kind of prayer, lived in deep awareness of and surrender to our heavenly Father. To obey this exhortation means that, when we are tempted, we hold the temptation before God and ask for His help. When we experience something good and beautiful, we immediately thank the Lord for it. When we see evil around us, we pray that God will make it right and be willing to be used of Him to that end. When we meet someone who does not know Christ, we pray for God to draw that person to Himself and to use us to be a faithful witness. When we encounter trouble, we turn to God as our Deliverer. In other words, our life becomes a continually ascending prayer, a perpetual communing with our heavenly Father. To **pray at all times** is to constantly set our minds "on the things above, not on the things that are on earth" (Col. 3:2).

The ultimate purpose of our salvation is to glorify God and to bring us into intimate, rich fellowship with Him; and to fail to come to God in prayer is to the deny that purpose. "What we have seen and heard we proclaim to you also," John said, "that you also may have fellowship with us; and indeed our fellowship is with the Father, and with His Son Jesus Christ" (1 John 1:3). Our fellowship with God is not meant to wait until we are in heaven. God's greatest desire, and our greatest need, is to be in constant fellowship with Him *now*, and there is no greater expression or experience of fellowship than prayer.

THE POWER OF PRAYER

The most important and pervasive thought Paul gives about prayer is that it should be **in the Spirit**. This supreme qualification for prayer has nothing to do with speaking in tongues or in some other ecstatic or dramatic manner. To pray **in the Spirit** is to pray in the name of Christ, to pray consistent with His nature and will. To pray in the Spirit is to pray in concert with the Spirit, who "helps our weakness; for we do not know how to pray as we should, but the Spirit Himself intercedes for us with groanings too deep for words; and He who searches the hearts knows what the mind of the Spirit is, because He intercedes for the saints according to the will of God" (Rom. 8:26-27). As the "Spirit of grace and of supplication" (Zech. 12:10), the Holy Spirit continually prays for us; and for us to pray rightly is to pray as He prays, to join our petitions to His and our will to His. It is to line up our minds and desires with His mind and desires, which are consistent with the will of the Father and the Son.

To be "filled with the Spirit" (Eph. 5:18) and to walk in His leading and power is to be made able to pray **in the Spirit**, because our prayer will then be in harmony with His. As we submit to the Holy Spirit, obeying His Word and relying on His leading and strength, we will be drawn into close and deep fellowship with the Father and the Son.

THE MANNER OF PRAYER

Whenever he prays, the believer should **be on the alert with all perseverance and petition.** Jesus told His disciples to watch and pray (Matt. 26:41; Mark 13:33; cf. Luke 18:1). Paul counseled the Colossians to "devote [themselves] to prayer" (Col. 4:2). The Greek verb behind "devote" (*proskartereō*) means to be steadfast, constant, and persevering. It is used of Moses' faithful endurance when he led the children of Israel out of Egypt (Heb. 11:27). To be devoted to prayer is to earnestly, courageously, and persistently bring everything in our lives before God.

The parables of the persistent neighbor and the importunate widow were both told by Jesus to illustrate the manner in which His followers should pray. At the end of the first parable He said, "And I say to you, ask, and it shall be given to you; seek, and you shall find; knock, and it shall be opened" (Luke 11:9). At the end of the other parable He explained, "Now shall not God bring about justice for His elect, who cry to Him day and night, and will He delay long over them? I tell you that He will bring about justice for them speedily" (Luke 18:7-8).

To dispersed and persecuted Christians in the early church, Peter wrote, "Be of sound judgment and sober spirit for the purpose of prayer" (1 Pet. 4:7). To pray in the right manner is to pray sensibly, with our minds and our understanding as well as our hearts and spirits. "I shall pray with the spirit and I shall pray with the mind also" (1 Cor. 14:15), Paul said.

To pray in the right manner also involves praying specifically. "Whatever you ask in My name," Jesus promised, "that will I do, that the Father may be glorified in the Son. If you ask Me anything in My name, I will do it" (John 14:13). God answers prayer in order to put His power on display, and when we do not pray specifically, He cannot answer specifically and thereby clearly display His power and His love for His children. To pray, as young children often do, "God bless the whole world," is really not to pray at all. We must think about particular people, particular problems, particular needs, and then pray about those things specifically and earnestly, so that we can see God's answer and offer Him our thankful praise.

Most Christians never get serious about prayer until a problem arises in their own life or in the life of someone they love. Then they are inclined to pray intently, specifically, and persistently. Yet that is the way Christians should *always* pray. Sensitivity to the problems and needs of others, especially other believers who are facing trials or hardships, will lead us to pray for them "night and day" as Paul did for Timothy (2 Tim. 1:3).

Because the greatest problems are always spiritual, our greatest prayer concern and concentration—whether for ourselves or for others—should be for spiritual protection, strength, and healing. It is certainly appropriate to bring physical needs before our heavenly Father, but our greatest focus should be for spiritual needs—for victory over temptation, for forgiveness and cleansing of sins already committed, for unbelievers to trust in Christ for salvation, and for believers to have greater dependence on Him. The context of Paul's call to prayer is that of spiritual warfare, and the Christian's prayer should, above all, be about that warfare. Our greatest concern for ourselves and for other believers should be for victory in the battle against the enemy of our souls. Our deepest prayers for our spouse, our children, our brothers and sisters, our fellow church members, our pastor, our missionaries, and all others would be that they win the spiritual battle against Satan. Examining the prayers of Paul throughout his epistles yields the insight that he prayed for the spiritual well-being of the people of God (see, e. g., 1 Cor. 1:4-7; Phil. 1:9-11; Col. 1:9-11; 2 Thess. 1:11-12).

Many years ago a saint of God prayed:

> O Lord, in prayer I launch far out into the eternal world, and on that broad ocean my soul triumphs over all evils on the shores of mortality. Time, with its amusements and cruel disappointments, never appears so inconsiderate as then. In prayer, O God, I see myself as nothing. I find my heart going after Thee with intensity, and I long with vehement thirst to live with Thee. Blessed be the strong winds of the Spirit that speed me on my way to the new Jerusalem. In prayer all things here below vanish and nothing seems important but holiness of heart and the salvation of others. In prayer all my worldly cares and fears and anxieties disappear and are as little in significance as a puff of wind. In prayer my soul inwardly exalts with thoughts of what Thou art doing for Thy church, and I long that Thou shouldest get Thyself a great name from sinners returning to Thee. In prayer I am lifted above the frowns and flatteries of life to taste the heavenly joys. Entering into the eternal world I can give myself to Thee with all my heart forever. In prayer I can place all my concerns in Thy hands to be entirely at Thy disposal, having no will or interest of my own. In prayer I can intercede for my friends, ministers, sinners, the church, Thy kingdom, with greatest freedom and brightest hope as a son to his Father and as a lover to his beloved. And so, O God, help me to pray always and never to cease.

THE OBJECTS OF PRAYER

Elsewhere Paul commands us to pray for unbelievers, for government leaders, and for others, but here the focus is on **all the saints**. It is only **saints**, Christian believers, who are involved in the spiritual warfare for which God provides the armor Paul has just been describing and who are able to pray in the Spirit.

It is not inappropriate to pray for ourselves any more than it is inappropriate to pray for physical needs. But just as the Bible primarily calls us to pray about spiritual needs rather than physical, it primarily calls us to pray for others rather than ourselves. Even when he was concerned about his own needs, Paul does not mention that he prayed for himself but that he asked other believers to pray on his behalf, as he does in the next two verses (Eph. 6:19-20). The greatest thing we can do for another believer, or that he can do for us, is to pray. That is the way the Body of Christ grows spiritually as well as in love. When one member of the Body is weak, wounded, or cannot function, the other members compensate by supporting and helping strengthen it. Samuel said to the people of Israel, "Far be it from me that I should sin against the Lord by ceasing to pray for you" (1 Sam. 12:23). With God's own Holy Spirit to indwell us and help us even when we do not know how to pray (Rom. 8:26), how much more do we as Christians sin against God when we fail to pray for fellow **saints?**

The spiritually healthy person is devoted to the welfare of others, especially fellow believers. On the other hand, the root of both psychological and spiritual sickness is preoccupation with self. Ironically, the believer who is consumed with his own problems—even his own spiritual problems—to the exclusion of concern for other believers, suffers from a destructive self-centeredness that not only is the cause of, but is the supreme barrier to the solution of, his own problems. Usually such selfishness isolates him from the other believers, who if they were intimately involved in fellowship with him, would be regularly praying for his spiritual welfare.

Praying for others with sincerity and perseverance is, in God's immeasurable grace, a great blessing and strength to our own souls. D. Martyn Lloyd-Jones reported that before the outbreak of the Spanish civil war that country was experiencing such an epidemic of neuroses that psychiatrists could hardly handle them all. But the war, terrible and destructive as it was in most respects, had the unexpected effect of "curing" many of Spain's thousands of neurotics. When they became concerned about the welfare of their families, friends, and country instead of their own, their neuroses disappeared and hospitals and clinics were almost emptied of such cases. "These neurotic people were suddenly cured by a greater anxiety," an anxiety that reached beyond their own selfish welfare. (*The Christian Soldier* [Grand Rapids: Baker, 1977], pp. 357-58.)

THE SPECIFIC ILLUSTRATION

and pray on my behalf, that utterance may be given to me in the opening of my mouth, to make known with boldness the mystery of the gospel, for which I am an ambassador in chains; that in proclaiming it I may speak boldly, as I ought to speak. (6:19-20)

Paul did not plead, **pray on my behalf,** in order that his ankles, raw and sore from his shackles, might be healed, or that he might be freed from prison and suffering. His deep concern was that **utterance may be given to me in the opening**

383

of my mouth, to make known with boldness the mystery of the gospel. When Satan tempted him to keep quiet about Christ, he wanted God's help to be bold and faithful to proclaim the gospel. He wanted help in his own battle against Satan, and he pleaded with his brothers and sisters at Ephesus to pray toward that end.

That he was in chains was incidental. His great concerns were for the mystery [see on 3:3] of the gospel, for which he was an ambassador, and for those to whom he was sent to proclaim it. He wanted fellow believers to pray for his victory in the spiritual warfare that this ministry provoked from Satan. Paul confronted the enemy face to face and knew he was not able to win in his own resources.

Compared to most believers Paul was gifted, courageous, morally upright, and spiritually strong beyond measure. Yet he greatly needed God's help and the help of fellow Christians. He knew that the power and blessings he had were not of his own doing, and his spiritual maturity and effectiveness were grounded in that awareness. God cannot use the self-sufficient person, because such a person feels no need for God. It is the humble believer who knows his own need and is genuinely poor in spirit whom the Lord can use and bless.

Paul also needed the prayers of fellow believers because he was a leader. Our enemy knows that when he strikes the shepherd, the sheep will scatter (Matt. 26:31), and church leaders—even as the Lord Himself—are Satan's special targets. The more faithful and fruitful a pastor is, the more his people need to pray for his strength and protection. He is more subject to the devil's schemes to make him discouraged or self-satisfied, hopeless or superficially optimistic, cowardly or overconfident. Satan uses every situation—favorable or unfavorable, successful or unsuccessful—to try to weaken, distract, and discredit God's gifted men in their work of "equipping of the saints for the work of service" (Eph. 4:12).

In a letter written shortly after Ephesians, Paul testified, "My circumstances have turned out for the greater progress of the gospel, so that my imprisonment in the cause of Christ has become well known throughout the whole praetorian guard and to everyone else, and that most of the brethren, trusting in the Lord because of my imprisonment, have far more courage to speak the word of God without fear" (Phil. 1:12-14). Even in prison it was important to Paul that he would make known with boldness the mystery of the gospel, because it was his own boldness that attracted the praetorian guard to the gospel and that inspired boldness in other witnessing Christians. Even when he requested prayer for himself, Paul's purpose and motive were selfless—to further the gospel, to encourage other believers, and to glorify his Lord.

Realizing that the Ephesian Christians could not pray specifically or intelligently for him without more information, Paul added, But that you also may know about my circumstances, how I am doing, Tychicus, the beloved brother and faithful minister in the Lord, will make everything known to you. And I have sent him to you for this very purpose, so that you may know about us. Tychicus, an Asian, had been chosen to accompany Paul and the others in taking the relief offering to Jerusalem (Acts 20:4-6), was with Paul during his first Roman imprisonment, and was frequently sent on missions by the apostle (see 2 Tim. 4:12; Titus 3:12). He not only delivered this letter for Paul but the one to Colossae as well, in both cases being instructed to give the recipients additional information about the apostle's situation (Col. 4:7-9). In both of these texts he is called **the beloved brother,** because he was especially dear to Paul.

In addition to informing the Ephesian believers, **Tychicus,** who was commended as a **faithful minister in the Lord,** was to encourage them: **that he may comfort your hearts.** The letter itself would seem to have been encouragement enough, but Paul knew that a personal word from someone who had been with him recently would be an added **comfort** to their **hearts.** The man in chains sought to **comfort** others.

THE BENEDICTION

Peace be to the brethren, and love with faith, from God the Father and the Lord Jesus Christ. Grace be with all those who love our Lord Jesus Christ with a love incorruptible. (6:23-24)

In its beautiful clarity and simple dignity, the apostle's closing benediction resists being analyzed. It is not unlike others of Paul's benedictions, yet it seems uniquely to reflect the themes of this rich epistle. Certainly **peace** (cf. 1:2; 2:14-15, 17; 4:3; 6:15), **love** (cf. 1:15; 4:2, 15-16; 5:25, 28, 33), and **faith** (cf. 1:15; 2:8; 3:12, 17; 4:5, 13; 6:16) are recurring touchstones in the thought of this great letter. Little wonder Paul gathers all three together and prays that they would be the experience and commitment of all believers.

Grace, or divine favor, was the gift Paul desired for **all those who love our Lord Jesus Christ with a love incorruptible.** That is the love that belongs to true believers; so Paul is really identifying the ones who will receive grace as only those whose love is not temporary and thus untrue but permanent and thus genuine!

To apply obediently in the power of the Holy Spirit the principles of **peace, love,** and **faith** taught in this epistle will yield to every believer the blessing and favor of God.

Bibliography

Eadie, John. *Commentary on the Epistle to the Ephesians.* Minneapolis: James and Klock, 1977.

Foulkes, Francis. *The Epistle of Paul to the Ephesians: An Introduction and Commentary.* Grand Rapids: Eerdmans, 1963.

Harrison, Norman B. *His Very Own: Paul's Epistle to the Ephesians.* Chicago: Moody, 1930.

Hendriksen, William. *New Testament Commentary: Exposition of Ephesians.* Grand Rapids: Baker, 1967.

Keil, D. F., and Delitzsch,F. *Commentary on the Old Testament in Ten Volumes.* Grand Rapids: Zondervan, 1973.

Kent, Homer A., Jr. *Ephesians: The Glory of the Church.* Chicago: Moody, 1971.

Lightfoot, J. B. *Notes on the Epistles of St. Paul.* Grand Rapids: Zondervan, 1957.

Lloyd-Jones, D. Martyn. *The Christian Soldier: An Exposition of Ephesians 6:10-20.* Grand Rapids: Baker, 1977.

——————. *The Christian Warfare: An Exposition of Ephesians 6:10-13.* Grand Rapids: Baker, 1976.

MacDonald, William. *Ephesians: The Mystery of the Church.* Wheaton, Ill.: Harold Shaw, 1968.

Meyer, F. B. *Bible Commentary.* Wheaton, Ill.: Tyndale, 1979.

Moule, Handley C. G. *Ephesian Studies: Lessons in Faith and Walk*. London: Pickering and Inglis, n.d.

Packer, James I. *Evangelism and the Sovereignty of God*. Chicago: InterVarsity, 1961.

Simpson, E. K. *Commentary on the Epistles to the Ephesians and Colossians*. Grand Rapids: Eerdmans, 1970.

Vincent, Marvin B. *Word Studies in the New Testament, Vol. III: The Epistles of Paul*. New York: Scribner's, 1904.

Wiersbe, Warren. *Be Rich: An Expository Study of the Epistle to the Ephesians*. Wheaton, Ill.: Victor, 1977.

Indexes

Index of Greek Words

Index of Hebrew/Aramaic Words

Index of Scripture

Index of Subjects

Moody Press, a ministry of the Moody Bible Institute, is designed for education, evangelization, and edification. If we may assist you in knowing more about Christ and the Christian life, please write us without obligation: Moody Press, c/o MLM, Chicago, Illinois 60610